Innovation, Intellectual Property, and Economic Growth

Innovation, Intellectual Property, and Economic Growth

Christine Greenhalgh

Mark Rogers

Princeton University Press
Princeton and Oxford

Published by Princeton University Press,
41 William Street, Princeton, New Jersey 08540

In the United Kingdom: Princeton University Press,
6 Oxford Street, Woodstock, Oxfordshire OX20 1TW

Library of Congress Cataloging-in-Publication Data

Greenhalgh, Christine.
    Innovation, intellectual property, and economic growth / Christine
    Greenhalgh and Mark Rogers.
      p. cm.
    Includes bibliographical references and index.
    ISBN 978-0-691-13798-8 (cl.: alk. paper)
    ISBN 978-0-691-13799-5 (pb.: alk. paper)
    1. Diffusion of innovations. 2. Technological innovations–Economic
    aspects. 3. Economic development. 4. Intellectual property.
    I. Rogers, Mark, 1964– II. Title.
HC79.T4G687 2010
338.9–dc22   2009020082

British Library Cataloging-in-Publication Data is available

This book has been composed in LucidaBright using TEX
Typeset and copyedited by T&T Productions Ltd, London
Printed on acid-free paper. ∞

press.princeton.edu

Printed in the United States of America

10 9 8 7 6 5 4 3 2 1

To the memory of my parents, Vera and John Graham, who always supported me in my career, and to my husband, Peter, who is my rock.

Christine Greenhalgh

To my family—Shona, Callum, and Tegan—for all the love, support, and fun they surround me with.

Mark Rogers

Contents

Preface

What Is This Book About?

This book is about understanding the complex process of innovation and how this leads to economic growth. The term "intellectual property" is also in the title since its role is central to many issues surrounding the incentives to innovate. The sustained economic growth of what are now the leading economies is the most dominant and important feature of world economic history. This sustained economic growth has changed the lives of billions of people, both those in the successful countries and those in poor countries. Economic growth allows the provision of more goods and services per capita. These can be so-called merit goods, such as housing, education, and health care, or they can be cars, air travel, and military equipment. High rates of economic growth often underpin changes in political power, as well as creating social change and allowing governments to pursue social policies. In short, economic growth matters. This means that we are acutely interested in understanding when and how innovation creates economic growth and whether intellectual property rights help or hinder the process.

Who Is This Book For?

This book is aimed at a number of potential audiences. The key audience is undergraduate or graduate students taking courses on the economics of innovation, intellectual property, or economic growth. The style of the book is "textbook," in the sense that we strive to explain issues clearly, building from the basics upward, and each chapter has discussion questions on which to base student assignments. In some chapters we assume that readers have a basic knowledge of maths and microeconomics. Even so, there is a mathematical appendix to allow students to recap on core concepts. However, the book is different from some economics textbooks since it discusses in detail empirical analysis, historical aspects, and policy issues, as well as economic theory. This, we feel, is vital to an understanding of innovation, intellectual property, and growth. This also means that the book is useful to economists, researchers, and policy makers who want an accessible overview of economic aspects of innovation, intellectual property, and economic growth. It also means that specific chapters may be useful reading for a variety of courses, including those taught in law and management based degrees.

What Is Different about This Book?

There is a view held by many that innovation is the outcome of a free-market process. Capitalism, it is argued, creates firms, which then compete in price, quality, and in releasing new products. This "innovation machine" creates the "growth miracle of capitalism."[1] This book explores these ideas and, in summary, supports much of this argument. But if free markets alone achieved optimal innovation and growth, the economist's job would be simply to describe the system and warn of the dangers of interference. This book does not adhere to this view. Instead, we argue that the process of innovation is subject to many "market failures"—the idea that the market does not always achieve the best possible outcomes. It is these market failures that make understanding innovation and growth so important, so that public policy can be designed to improve upon these imperfect outcomes.

Manufacturing has historically been seen as the heartland of research and development and innovation, with inventions such as the internal combustion engine underpinning the development of the motor industry and the jet engine leading to high-speed aviation. In recent decades, intangible products, such as computer services and the Internet, have become equally important contributors to innovation and economic growth. Nowadays, we are as likely to think of innovation as the latest feature of interoperability between our mobile telephones and the Internet, which is driven by a combination of tangible silicon chips and intangible computer software. In all sections of this volume we place a high priority on covering all sectors of the economy, thus considering innovation in the services sector as well as in the production sector. Although much of our focus is on commercial (private-sector) innovations, many of the issues are relevant for innovations in the public sector.

It is fair to say that economists do not fully understand the mechanisms of economic growth. Leading researchers use titles such as *The Elusive Quest for Growth* (Easterly 2001) or *The Mystery of Economic Growth* (Helpman 2004), and there are thousands of books, research papers, and conferences devoted to the topic. This book differs from much of this literature in two ways. First, we consider both microeconomic and macroeconomic approaches. It is rare for economics textbooks to take such an approach, as specialization within economics is

---

[1] These phrases are taken from the title and subtitle of Baumol (2002).

now so strong that economists are generally forced into one or the other. Yet an understanding of the process of innovation and economic growth requires an understanding of both. Second, the book gives prominence to the role of intellectual property. Intellectual property rights (IPRs), as we shall see, have evolved as a solution to unfettered, free-market competition between firms; hence, from a microeconomic perspective, they are central to understanding the growth process. Equally, from a macroeconomic perspective, the debate between less developed and leading economies over when IPRs can and should be used is fundamental to understanding the challenges facing the poorest countries.

Innovation as the Driving Force of Economic Growth

It may seem self-evident that innovation is the driving force of economic growth, but there is still much confusion surrounding what drives growth. Some of this is due to the differences between the language and concepts used by microeconomists and macroeconomists. Ultimately, it is innovation by entrepreneurs and firms that creates change in an economy and some of this change is called economic growth. The literature on economic growth, however, often appears to stand distinct from this process, appearing to students and others as impenetrable mathematical models. When discussing these models we use a more formal, mathematics-based style than in much of this book (in order to allow readers insight into the actual economic models), but we also stress the intuition. Most importantly, we try to link the concepts and assumptions used in economic growth models to the microeconomics of innovation.

As in domestic markets, competition in international markets takes place via all three dimensions of quality, variety, and price. The stage on which this competition is played out has been expanding rapidly in the last few decades. Better communications and falling transport costs, as well as the development of significant new sources of supply from emerging markets, have driven this expansion. All of these factors have increased the size of the world market within which firms and countries compete. World trade has persistently grown faster than world gross domestic product. There is also a rapid increase in trade in similar products between countries with similar production characteristics, increasing the dimension of so-called intraindustry trade.

Just as innovation provides a competitive weapon for firms in a domestic market, it also provides firms with the ability to compete in international markets, where studies show that product variety and quality are as important as price in capturing market share overseas.[2] But if innovation is good for trade, the reverse is also true: international trade provides a source of information about the nature of other countries' inventions, both as these are embodied in goods and services and through contacts between firms.

An Outline of the Book

Our investigation of the economics of innovation and growth begins with analysis of the microeconomics of innovation. In parts I and II we investigate how the myriad of inventors, entrepreneurs, and firms in the economy deliver a continuing flow of innovations to the economy. Later in the book, in part III, we link this analysis to the explanation of growth in the macroeconomy and to the determination of patterns of trade between countries. Part IV looks at economic policy issues.

Chapter 1 starts by looking at the process of innovation and also the microeconomics of innovation. This chapter outlines a range of issues that are dealt with in more detail in later chapters. Chapter 2 looks at the role and nature of IPRs. In this chapter we analyze in more detail the incentives provided by IPRs, how each type of IPR operates, and how other types of incentives can be used. Chapter 3 focuses on the measurement of innovation, productivity, and growth. Even though these issues are vitally important, they are often omitted from textbooks. Chapter 4 looks at the "national system of innovation," which is how business, government, universities, and others interact to create innovation. Chapter 5 looks in more detail at how innovation affects firms and markets, including the empirical evidence we have on the rewards to innovation. Chapter 6 focuses on how firms use IPRs. There are various strategies and issues connected to the use of IPRs that are of critical importance. Chapter 7 looks at the diffusion of innovation. By this stage, previous chapters will have made clear that in order for society to benefit from innovations it is important that they are widely adopted.

In part III of the book we switch focus to the macroeconomics of innovation and growth. Chapter 8 discusses the standard economic growth models that are the basis of many economists' views of growth, providing a succinct review of economic growth models over the last fifty years. Chapter 9 widens the focus to look at globalization and innovation and chapter 10 looks at the issues and evidence on innovation, technology, and employment. These chapters together represent a concise summary of macroeconomic approaches to growth and innovation. Part IV focuses on policy issues, drawing together the implications

---

[2] For a review see Department of Trade and Industry (2003).

of the research surveyed in the earlier chapters. Chapter 11 takes up a microeconomic viewpoint, looking at the debates surrounding many policies to encourage innovation in firms, including IPRs. Chapter 12 focuses on two important international policy issues: trade-related intellectual property (TRIPS) and the globalization of research and development. Finally, there is also a mathematical appendix to explain some of the key mathematical concepts.

Acknowledgments

Both of us have been "working" on this book for many years. Having to teach both microeconomics and macroeconomics—as is the case at Oxford University—causes one to realize that "one hand often doesn't know what the other is doing." Too often microeconomic approaches to innovation fail to even acknowledge the macroeconomics of economic growth, and vice versa. Macroeconomic growth models assume perfect IPRs, while microeconomists argue about whether IPRs are useful at all. Microeconomists stress the role of innovation in growth, yet have no understanding of macroeconomic growth models or of measuring growth. While these divisions might appear justifiable from within the economics profession (where the idea of "gains from specialization" is a central concept), they often leave students, policy makers, and others confused. The solution, of course, was to write a book that combined microeconomic and macroeconomic perspectives, as well as including a section on policy.

To start and finish such a book required help from many institutions and individuals. Each of us must acknowledge the support of our colleges—Harris Manchester College (Mark Rogers) and St Peter's College (Christine Greenhalgh)—as well as the Economics Department at Oxford. The Oxford Intellectual Property Research Centre, with colleagues such as Derek Bosworth and Robert Pitkethly, also encouraged much of our research and thinking. Similarly, our association with the Intellectual Property Research Institute of Australia, and with Paul Jensen and Beth Webster in particular, was of great help. Christine Greenhalgh benefited from time spent as a Visiting Scholar at the Stanford Institute for Economic Policy Research in 2007, during which she also renewed contact with Bronwyn Hall at Berkeley, who has been immensely helpful and encouraging of this project. Various research projects supported by the Economic and Social Research Council, the U.K. Intellectual Property Office, the World Intellectual Property Office, and various U.K. government departments have all played their part in shaping our views and adding to our knowledge. Many conferences, workshops, and talks played a role both in informing us and allowing us to present our work, including those organized by European Policy for Intellectual Property, the European Patent Office, the Office of Harmonization for the Internal Market, the Intellectual Property Institute, and the regular interdisciplinary seminar at the Oxford Intellectual Property Research Centre. Joint work with various authors, including Ray Corrigan, Padraig Dixon, Christian Helmers, Mark Longland, and Yo'av Mazeh, was also important. All these factors got us to the starting line.

Richard Baggaley at Princeton University Press approached the project with enthusiasm and professionalism. After important guidance from three anonymous Princeton University Press reviewers, the process of completing the book was somewhat arduous. As ever, supportive families were important, and we also thank students and colleagues for their consideration and their motivational inquiries ("How is the book going?"). Once the book was nearly finished many colleagues made suggestions, small and large, to improve the book. The list included Esteban Burrone, Bob Cowley, Panos Desyllas, Padraig Dixon, Georg von Graevenitz, Bob Gomulkiewicz, Mary Gregory, Mary Hallett, Christian Helmers, Paul Jensen, Cédric Schneider, Teresa da Silva Lopes, Anthea Rogers, Beth Webster, along with more anonymous referees' reports from Princeton University Press. At the production stage we have been very greatly assisted by the professionalism in copy-editing of Sam Clark of T&T Productions Ltd. He has patiently corrected our grammar and spelling, and has ensured consistency and completeness in the cited references. This care and attention to detail have significantly improved the quality of the final text.

We hope the book fulfils its objective of explaining what insights economics can give into innovation and growth, together with providing an introduction into the workings of the intellectual property system and economic policy on innovation. Needless to say, in any areas where it falls short, the blame lies entirely with us.

References

Baumol, W. 2002. *The Free-Market Innovation Machine: Analyzing the Growth Miracle of Capitalism.* Princeton University Press.

Department of Trade and Industry. 2003. *Innovation Report. Competing in the Global Economy: The Innovation Challenge.* London: Her Majesty's Stationery Office. (See also the accompanying Economics Paper No. 7 with the same title.)

Easterly, W. 2001. *The Elusive Quest for Growth: Economists' Adventures and Misadventures in the Tropics.* Boston, MA: MIT Press.

Helpman, E. 2004. *The Mystery of Economic Growth.* Cambridge, MA: Harvard University Press.

Innovation, Intellectual Property, and Economic Growth

Part I

The Nature of Innovation

1

The Nature and Importance of Innovation

1.1 Introduction

This chapter begins by defining what economists mean by *innovation*. Economists have focused on two main types: *product* and *process*. A *product innovation* is the act of bringing something new to the market place that improves the range and quality of products on offer: for example, the Apple iPod is an innovation compared with the Sony Walkman, which was an earlier portable device for playing music. A *process innovation* is a new way of making or delivering goods or services: for example, going to visit the doctor and recording that you have arrived for your appointment by touching a screen instead of talking to a receptionist. We shall highlight the basis of such innovations in the discovery and development of many types of new knowledge. We begin by outlining the whole supply chain of innovation: from its basis in such activities as scientific invention, mathematical theorems, computing algorithms, and information gathering activity through to the widespread diffusion of this new knowledge embodied in new products and processes within the economy.

Section 1.3 looks at the microeconomic effects of innovation. Using the standard microeconomic concepts of costs, demand, and consumer surplus, the outcome of both process and product innovation are analyzed. Even at this stage we encounter differences depending on the availability of *intellectual property rights* (IPRs) and the type of market structure of the relevant industry. Section 1.4 looks at the interactive nature of innovation, whereby sectors of the economy can act as both producers and users of innovations. Section 1.5 considers the important question of whether or not the private market can deliver the optimal amount of innovation. If there is market failure, there will be less innovation than the amount society would ideally want. Here we stress two aspects of the process of innovation that suggest possibilities for market failure. The first is that new knowledge—which is created during the innovation process—is what economists term a *public good* and such goods tend to be underprovided by the private market. The second is that innovation can create *positive externalities* in the form of spillover benefits to customers and other firms and these cannot be captured as revenue by innovating firms, again leading to underprovision of innovation. Section 1.6 introduces the ways in which public policies, such as subsidies to research and development or the award of IPRs, can, to some degree, restore the efficiency of private firms and markets in the supply of innovation. Finally, section 1.7 briefly introduces an important process whereby firms compete through innovation, which will be discussed in more detail in subsequent chapters.

1.2   What Is Innovation?

Innovation can be defined as the application of new ideas to the products, processes, or other aspects of the activities of a firm that lead to increased "value." This "value" is defined in a broad way to include higher value added for the firm and also benefits to consumers or other firms. Two important definitions are:

- *Product innovation*: the introduction of a new product, or a significant qualitative change in an existing product.

- *Process innovation*: the introduction of a new process for making or delivering goods and services.

Some authors have emphasized a third category of innovation, that of organizational change within the firm, but we see this as being naturally included within the second category, as a type of process innovation.[1]

Product innovations may be tangible manufactured goods, intangible services, or a combination of the two. Examples of recent tangible product innovations that have had a very significant impact on the way people live and work are personal computers, mobile phones, and microwave ovens. Intangible products that complement these types of physical equipment include the various pieces of computer software needed to control flows of information through these devices, leading to the delivery of information, the supply of communication services, or the arrival of a correctly heated dinner. Equally, process innovations, which are new

---

[1] Joseph Schumpeter not only listed these three categories, but also defined as innovation the opening of a new market, or the development of new sources of supply for raw materials (OECD 1997, p. 28). We prefer to allocate these to entrepreneurial activity rather than to innovation.

ways of making and doing things, can arise from the use of new combinations of tangible and intangible inputs. A robotic machine to assemble cars can deliver welding services with even greater precision than a human welder, but is only as good as its computer control system.

Inherent in the above definitions of innovation is an element of novelty. The question then arises as to how much novelty is enough to identify any change as "innovation." A key issue here is to distinguish innovation, the bringing to market of a truly novel item, from imitation, the adoption of a new technique or design that is already in the market. A product or process can be *new to the firm, new to the domestic market,* or *new to the world market.* Clearly, the last of these, global novelty, is sufficient to qualify the product or process as an innovation. For those goods and services that are not internationally traded—whether due to the nature of the product, prohibitive transport costs, or restrictions on trade—the test of being "new to the domestic market" is sufficient to establish that there is an innovation within that economy. In our view, being "new to the firm" is an insufficient test for innovation, as the firm in question may simply be adopting a product design, or a production method, introduced by a competitor. In this book we call this the diffusion of innovation.[2] We define an innovation as *new to the firm and new to the relevant market.* Whether this relevant market is local or global is dependent on the product or process in question and the degree to which it is traded in a competitive global or local environment.[3]

Another feature of our two definitions of innovation is that the product or process must be introduced into the market place so that consumers or other firms can benefit. This distinguishes an innovation from an invention or discovery. An invention or discovery enhances the stock of knowledge, but it does not instantaneously arrive in the market place as a full-fledged novel product or process. Innovation occurs at the point of bringing to the commercial market new products and processes arising from applications of both existing and new knowledge. Thus we can see that innovation occurs at the kernel of a complex process, preceded by inventions and succeeded by the widespread adoption of the new

---

[2] *The Oslo Manual* (OECD 1997), which was the guide for undertaking survey work on innovation in the early phase of the Community Innovation Survey, had a baseline definition of innovation that includes "new to the firm," hence conceptually mixing up "diffusion" and "innovation" (although they do draw attention to this problem, see pp. 35–36). Hence, surveys of innovation by firms frequently enquire about products and processes that are new to the firm, but sometimes fail to identify which of these items are also new to the market. The U.K. government reports from the Community Innovation Survey have frequently quoted the larger measure as an indicator of British innovation.

[3] We will discuss in chapter 2 the fact that some IPRs, such as patents, which are geographically limited in coverage, have the effect of dividing up world markets into protected trade areas.

genre of products by customers, or the adoption of best-practice processes in the majority of firms. We call this final stage *diffusion*, and it is clear that the benefits of innovation to the economy and its citizens are not fully realized until this has taken place.

Defining Knowledge and Technology

Already we have begun to make continual reference to *knowledge* and *technology*. What do economists mean by these terms? Economically relevant *knowledge* is the whole body of scientific evidence and human expertise that is, or could be, useful in the production and supply of commodities and in the invention and design of new products and processes. Knowledge can be *codified*, as in a chemical formula or computing algorithm, or it can be *tacit*, as when a person knows how to do something that is not written down, like mixing and serving a perfect cocktail. When knowledge is embodied in individuals it is often referred to as *human capital*, to distinguish this valuable asset from physical capital, such as machinery or buildings. For an individual, the acquisition of new skills and knowledge through education and training increases his/her human capital.

Technology encompasses the current set of production techniques used to design, make, package, and deliver goods and services in the economy. So technology is the application of selected parts of the knowledge stock to production activity. Within the firm, the technology used determines its productive capability when combined with other inputs. Inventions and discoveries add to the stock of knowledge that can be applied to production. Some types of innovations, termed process innovations above, add to the available stock of technology for production, while product innovations add to the choice of products facing final customers.

The Stages of the Innovation Process

The innovation process has a number of stages that can be distinguished, as shown in figure 1.1.[4] At each stage of the process there are activities requiring inputs of knowledge, embodied in skilled personnel and specialized equipment, and investment of time in using these resources. Additionally, each stage, if successful, produces an output,

---

[4] In his book *The Economics of Production and Innovation*, Rosegger (1986) identified five stages in the process of technological change. This framework was largely directed to explaining the sources of manufacturing innovation. We have modified this picture to include a more modern view of knowledge production, including computing and services, but we acknowledge the inspiration of Rosegger for this diagram.

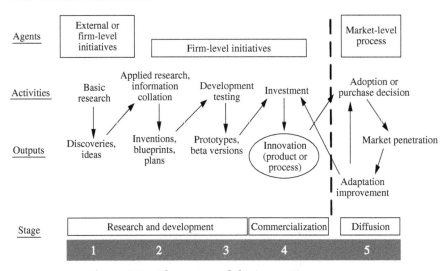

Figure 1.1. The stages of the innovation process.

initially intangible in the form of new knowledge but later tangible if applied to goods for sale—although sometimes remaining intangible if applied to some kinds of service activities.

The first stages (1–3) of the innovation process produce basic scientific knowledge, plans for new processes or blueprints, and initial prototypes of new products or processes. This is when we may talk of "inventions being made" and the hard work, or genius, of inventors. All of this activity is frequently lumped together as research and development (R&D), but it represents premarket activity by a variety of agents, including public scientific institutions, universities, lone inventors, and firms. It is only when stage 4 is reached, at the point where there is a marketable product or new process, that innovation is achieved. This phase of commercialization triggers the start of another chain of events, broadly characterized as diffusion (stage 5), which covers the widespread adoption of the new product or process by the market. It is also vital to understand that there is feedback between the various stages: innovation is rarely a linear progression through the stages shown. There is also feedback between the diffusion and innovation stages. As consumers, or other firms, start using the innovations, they often adapt or improve them, or relay information on how to do so back to the innovating firms.[5] This type of refinement, or incremental innovation, is often very important as the initial product or process is rarely perfect.

---

[5] This was discussed by von Hippel (2005) and earlier by Rosenberg (1982). We elaborate further on feedback effects later in this chapter.

Incremental innovation can be contrasted with *drastic* innovation. The first makes a small change to an existing process or product. Drastic or radical innovation introduces a completely new type of production process with a wide range of applications and gives rise to a whole new genre of innovative products.[6] Steam engines, the internal combustion engine, electricity, microprocessors, and the Internet can all be considered examples of drastic innovations. Their introduction dramatically changed the way the economy worked and a huge range of other innovations followed in their wake. Box 1.1 discusses the specific example of the laser, originally invented and patented in the late 1950s. The laser gave rise to a number of drastic product innovations, such as compact discs and laser printers, each of which then underwent a series of incremental innovations. In addition, the laser also led to a number of drastic process innovations, such as the use of lasers in welding and surveying.

For any single innovation, all of the stages 1–4 in this diagram are not always conducted in a single firm. In many sectors of the economy public research institutions and university departments will be contributors to the flow of new knowledge that can be translated by firms into innovations. We shall discuss this relationship between the so-called science base and private industry in chapter 4. Even where the relevant new knowledge is produced commercially there can be a separation of activity across firms. In fields such as biotechnology and pharmaceuticals, specialist firms exist to perform the R&D of stages 1 and 2, while other firms supply stage 3 testing services for potential new drugs. All of these activities can take place at arm's length from the final marketplace, under contract from the firms that will eventually bring successful new products to the market. This merely indicates that specialization and contracting-out can occur in any part of the innovation process, so long as suitable contracts can be written and enforced.

Box 1.1. The laser.

The laser provides an interesting case study in invention and innovation. Laser stands for "light amplification by stimulated emission of radiation." Some claim that the laser was invented in Bell Laboratories by Arthur L. Schawlow and Charles Hard Townes in 1957, although the science it was based on had been developed previously, and others were also working in the area. Bell Labs filed a patent application in 1958 and this was granted in 1960. A scientific paper by Schawlow and Townes was also published in 1959 describing the principle of making a laser. Gordon Gould at Columbia had also written down plans for a laser in

---

[6] A formal, theory-based definition of drastic process innovation is made in section 2.2.

1957, although he did not file for a patent until 1959. Since the U.S. patent system then worked on "first to invent," not "first to file" as in most other countries, this led to a series of legal disputes over the next thirty years surrounding who owned the intellectual property.

The scientific paper, and the initial patents, stimulated a race to build working lasers and improve their performance. Patents were, in turn, filed on many of the improvements. While the invention of the laser is an example of a radical invention, the huge numbers of subsequent improvements (called incremental innovations) in terms of wavelengths, power, size, and cost have dramatically influenced the laser's applicability. Over the last fifty years lasers have found applications in a wide range of scientific, industrial, and consumer applications. Industrial applications include surveying, weaponry, and medicine. They are also the basic technology that allows bar code scanners, compact discs, and laser printers to work. Lasers are also central to the use of fiber optic cables to carry huge volumes of data across the Internet and between computers.

1.3   The Microeconomic Effects of Innovation

We have already seen that there are two main types of innovation: *process innovation*, the introduction of new techniques for production, and *product innovation*, the offer for sale of a new type or design of a good or service product. Of course, these two are not always independent: often it is the introduction of a new process that permits the design and development of a range of new products, while the introduction of a new intermediate product permits a purchasing firm to change its production process. For the moment though, let us consider the different nature of the two kinds of innovation to examine how they impact on prices and costs. Their impact will, in turn, depend on the "market structure" in which the firm operates.[7] Market structure refers to the nature of competition between the firms in the market. The two polar cases are "perfect competition," where there are a larger number of firms, and monopoly, where one firm dominates the market.

The Effects of Process Innovation

The essential effect is one of cost reduction in production. In economics, total costs are divided into fixed and variable costs and, in turn, we can define average costs (ACs) and marginal costs (MCs). Figure 1.2 shows a simple case where, before the innovation, firms have costs AC_1 and MC_1,

---

[7] Innovation will also shape the market structure as the causality runs both ways.

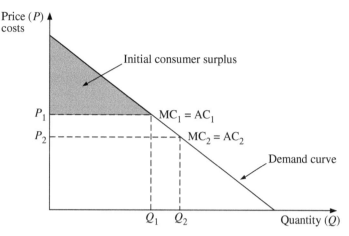

Figure 1.2. Process innovation in a perfectly competitive market.

which are equal (meaning there are no fixed costs). The demand curve for the industry is shown (and we will assume that this is unchanged in the case of a process innovation). If the industry is perfectly competitive, we assume that there are many firms, and each of these will set their price equal to MC_1, hence the output produced and sold is Q_1 (at price P_1).[8] Economists refer to the consumer surplus as a measure of benefit—it is the area between the demand curve and price—and this is the shaded area in figure 1.2. The process innovation is assumed to reduce the average or marginal cost of production. In our simple case, marginal and average costs are equal, so we can illustrate the impact of the process innovation by a fall to $AC_2 = MC_2$. This also means that the price to consumers has fallen (to P_2) and the consumer surplus has risen (it is now the area above P_2 and below the demand curve). It is important to note that there are no IPRs in this example. If the market is perfectly competitive, all knowledge about production is assumed to be known by all firms. Hence, as soon as the process innovation occurs we assume that all firms immediately start to use it (the problems with this assumption are discussed in chapter 7). In such a case there is no financial incentive to undertake R&D targeted toward creating the process innovation. Note that this occurs since prices are equal to marginal costs and average costs. This means that there are no economic profits to reward the innovator.[9]

---

[8] If a "perfectly competitive" market is unfamiliar, consult the mathematical appendix or a microeconomics textbook.

[9] Formally, the definition of average costs includes some return to the owners of capital and the managers of the firm; however, average costs do not include any additional return for innovation or entrepreneurship. The term economic profit signals when such returns are present.

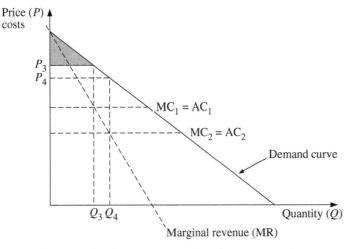

Figure 1.3. Process innovation for a monopoly.

The above case considered a perfectly competitive market with many firms selling an identical product. Given this situation, and the assumption of immediate knowledge diffusion, there is no financial incentive to develop a process innovation. Process innovations could occur if they originated by chance or were made by those unmotivated by financial incentives. Consider now a world where IPRs exist and where any process innovation could receive perfect protection. If one firm in the industry developed the process innovation discussed above, and secured a patent on it, it would be possible for that firm to undercut the price charged by any other firm. The innovator could produce and sell the good for a price $P_1 - \varepsilon$ (where ε is a small number). At this price it would sell almost Q_1, meaning that the profits it could make are approximately $(P_1 - \varepsilon - AC_2) \times Q_1$. Even if the innovator did not want to produce all of the market demand, in principle it could license its process innovation to all other firms and receive royalties equal to these profits. Introducing patents certainly increases the financial incentive to innovate.

Perfect competition is unlikely to occur in many industries so economists are interested in studying the other extreme form of market structure: monopoly. Assuming there is a permanent monopoly supplier with the demand and initial cost conditions specified above, would it have any incentive to make a process innovation? Figure 1.3 shows the same demand curve and initial costs as in figure 1.2 but in the case of a monopolist it will maximize profit by producing where marginal revenue (MR) is equal to MC_1. This means the price is P_3 and the output produced and sold is Q_3—less than when there is perfect competition—and the profits are $(P_3 - AC_1) \times Q_3$. If the monopolist develops a process innovation, it lowers marginal cost to MC_2. The new, lower marginal cost means that the monopolist will produce where $MR = MC_2$. This means a lower price (P_4), more output (Q_4), higher consumer surplus, and also higher profits for the monopolist. Thus, even with a monopolist, a process innovation will lower prices and benefit consumers. However, if the monopolist is not threatened with entry, there is no role for IPRs: the monopolist will receive additional profits since it is the only seller in the market.[10] This finding assumes that monopolists will always seek to maximize profits by cutting costs and making innovations, an assumption that many economists think is too strong.

The Effects of Product Innovation

The successful development of a new product results in a different configuration of changes in costs and rewards. In a perfectly competitive market, and in the absence of IPRs over the new product (i.e., we assume that any product innovation can be immediately copied), there is no gain to the innovator. This case of immediate imitation by all other firms in the market is very unlikely. More realistically, the innovator uses some form of IPR or, failing this, relies on secrecy or first-mover advantages to delay imitation (the same would be true in the process innovation case discussed above). Given this, we can represent the introduction of the new product with a new demand curve. Figure 1.4 shows the demand curve for a new consumer good. The position and elasticity of the demand curve depends on how much the new product is valued, which in turn depends on the availability of substitute products. If we assume that the firm has an IPR that prevents imitators, the firm acts like a monopolist and maximizes profits. Hence, figure 1.4 is the same as figure 1.3 except that it represents a new product. Note that the new product creates "consumer surplus": the triangular area above the price but below the demand curve. This is a measure of the surplus value to the consumers over and above the price they have to pay.[11]

However, because price (P_1) is greater than marginal cost (MC_1), consumer surplus is not maximized, since this would occur at Q^*. It is clear that rewarding innovations with profits (i.e., allowing P to be greater than MC) creates a further problem. Looking at figure 1.4, we can see

---

[10] If the monopolist is threatened with entry, this will alter the incentives. Further cases are discussed in chapter 5.

[11] More of the consumer surplus can be extracted by the firm if it can price discriminate. Equally, in some cases new products may be sold at low prices (i.e., less than P_1 shown) to achieve market share now with the view to increasing prices later. The possibility of such dynamic profit maximization is not considered by figures 1.1–1.3, which view the market as static.

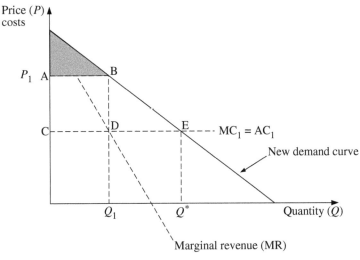

Figure 1.4. Product innovation for a monopoly.

that some of the lost consumer surplus is, in fact, profits to the innovator (i.e., area ABCD), but some of the lost consumer surplus is wasted (i.e., area BDE). For this reason, area BDE is called the "deadweight loss" associated with monopoly pricing. Consider as an example the situation where an important new drug, that can treat a serious disease, is developed. During the period of protection by a patent, it is sold at a higher price than its marginal cost of production. Some sufferers who could afford the drug if priced at marginal cost are not able to obtain it at this higher price; the number of people affected is proportional to the distance $Q^* - Q_1$.

If the product innovation creates a new variety or improves the quality of an existing product, then drawing a new demand curve is not the best way to conceptualize the change. Suppose the market is imperfectly competitive before this product innovation, hence the firm already faces a downward-sloping demand curve. By introducing a new product the firm aims to achieve an outward shift and steeper slope to the demand for its product (analogous to the effect of advertising, increasing product loyalty to the firm). Figure 1.5 shows such a demand shift. Note that even though consumers are charged a higher price, they buy more and have more consumer surplus. Of course, over time the market may become more competitive as more product innovation occurs and this may reduce prices. A general way of describing this situation is to say that consumers benefit from the increase in product variety and/or the rise in the quality of the products on offer. Even if a new product is more expensive than existing ones, if it has exactly the right set of

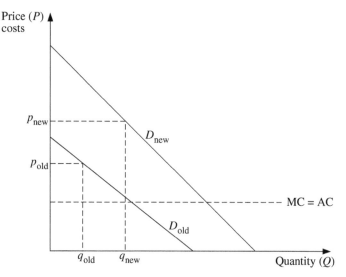

Figure 1.5. A product innovation represented
by a shift in the existing demand curve.

characteristics to match the customers' tastes, they may be happier to
buy this item. If the product has a broader and more favorable set of
characteristics than an earlier variety, then, even with a higher price,
it can still be seen as good value for money. (Further analysis of these
alternative situations is given below in chapters 3 and 5.)

Can Product and Process Innovations Be Distinguished?

Conceptually yes, but in practical measurement terms it is often difficult to make this distinction. The basic reason is that in many cases
of innovation, one firm's finished product can become part of another
firm's production process. Innovation measurement at the level of the
firm suggests that product innovations are in the majority (see Scherer
1984), while in the context of the economy they result in a large amount
of process innovation. Some examples are new fertilizers that improve
the productivity of agricultural production; new weaving machinery that
enables the textile industry to create superior fabrics; cash dispensers
that allow the banking industry to offer people access to their money at
any time of day or night; and new computer software that permits firms
in many sectors to organize information more efficiently.

A more detailed explanation of this issue is illustrated in box 1.2,
where we outline a simplified Leontief input–output model of an economy.[12] Although economic theory often analyzes supply as if there was

---

[12] For a fuller treatment of this type of model see Leontief (1986).

a single-stage production process, transforming raw materials directly into final goods and services sold to consumers, this is an extreme simplification. In reality, much economic activity is devoted to the production of intermediate goods and services, which are supplied to other firms as semifinished products. In fact, the gross output of each sector (denoted by X in box 1.2), reflecting economic activity before netting out the amount reabsorbed as inputs, is much bigger than its contribution to gross domestic product (GDP) (labeled F in box 1.2). For example, total gross output was around 1.7 times GDP in the United Kingdom in recent data. Even from so-called final goods F, the share of GDP items purchased by firms for investment (I) also returns into production as capital inputs to the production process in the next period.

Box 1.2. Leontief's input–output flow matrix.

The Leontief input–output matrix is a way of visualizing how an economy is integrated. As an example we will consider a two-sector economy, consisting of manufacturing, sector M, and services, sector S.

In current-period production, each sector buys some of the other's products to use as inputs (A_{MS} and A_{SM}). Each sector also uses part of their own sector's output as inputs (A_{MM} and A_{SS}). Gross output X (where total $X = X_M + X_S$) is therefore bigger than the net output for final demand F (where total $F = F_M + F_S$) due to the absorption of part of gross output as intermediate goods.

$$
\begin{array}{c}
\text{Flow to} \\
\overbrace{\hspace{4cm}} \qquad \text{Gross} \\
\begin{array}{cccc}
& \text{M} & \text{S} & \text{F} \qquad \text{output} \\
\text{Flow from} \left\{ \begin{array}{l} \text{M} \\ \text{S} \end{array} \right. & A_{MM} + A_{MS} + F_M & = & X_M \\
& A_{SM} + A_{SS} + F_S & = & X_S
\end{array}
\end{array}
$$

Further interrelationships occur in the next period arising from investment. Each sector's final demand F is divided between consumption, C, and investment, I.

Thus

$$F_M = C_M + I_M,$$
$$F_S = C_S + I_S,$$

but investment in each sector also involves the purchase of some of the other sector's output (B_{MS}, B_{SM}). Investment in each sector also involves use of part of own final output (B_{MM}, B_{SS}). These investment flows again produce a mixing of sectoral outputs.

$$
\text{Flow from} \begin{cases} \text{M} \\ \text{S} \end{cases} \quad \begin{matrix} \text{M} & \text{S} & \text{Investment} \\ B_{MM} + B_{MS} & = & I_M \\ B_{SM} + B_{SS} & = & I_S \end{matrix}
$$

with "Flow to" spanning M and S above.

The row sum is the total investment of goods and services produced by each sector. The column sum (not shown) is the total investment of goods and services within each sector.

Flows of Innovation Round the Economy

Every process innovation within a sector causes lower costs of inputs supplied to user firms. Every product innovation within a sector causes new product varieties of inputs for user firms. These can lead to new processes of production in the user industry, due either to new intermediate products A, to new investment products B, or to cost changes that make different techniques more profitable.

1.4   Interaction between Producers and Users of Innovation

The description in figure 1.1 characterizes R&D, innovation, and diffusion as a simple, sequential process, although you might have noticed one arrow drawn from right to left between stage 5 and stage 4. As discussed above, firms can be involved in some or all of the distinct stages but the sequence of activities appears to flow strongly from left to right: from basic R&D to subsequent commercial application in one innovating firm, and later spreading out via the diffusion process to many firms and customers. Not all authors see this linear model as an adequate depiction of the processes leading to innovation and diffusion. The Leontief input–output model (box 1.2) already raises the question of which sectors are supplying innovation to which other sectors, creating a relationship between the producers and the users of these innovations.[13] Once these innovation supply relationships are established, there can be many instances where users of innovations feed back information about the product's performance, making suggestions for improvements and in this way helping to create the next generation of products they will buy. This alternative viewpoint requires the linear model employed above to be modified, to allow for interaction between innovators and their

---

[13] For an application of the Leontief model in tracing the production and use of innovations, see Scherer (1984, chapters 3 and 15).

customers, including information feedbacks. Many companies encourage customer feedback, especially with respect to innovation. Proctor & Gamble, one of the world's leading consumer product firms, spends hundreds of millions each year on monitoring and understanding customers' demands (including monitoring blogs and Web sites). In the software industry, the release of "beta versions" are specifically designed to allow users to provide feedback. For example, a beta version of Microsoft's Windows Vista was released in January 2005, after which various changes were made before Vista was released in February 2006.

Pavitt (1984) was among the early exponents of the idea that innovation is a complex interactive process, exhibiting considerable variability across sectors as to whether innovations were mainly produced in-house by the firm or imported in the form of new equipment supplied by specialist producers. He created a taxonomy of sectoral patterns of technical change, examining each industry group to see what were the dominant patterns of production and use of process and product innovations. He initially identified four distinct groups of industries in terms of their technology acquisition and use: those that are *supplier dominated*, importing new elements of process technology but making little contribution via in-house R&D; *scale intensive producers*, who contribute quite a lot of their own innovations and work these into profit through the operation of large-scale continuous production processes; *specialized suppliers*, whose main focus is the generation of product innovations in intermediate goods or capital equipment for use in other sectors; and *science-based* sectors, where firms engage intensively in in-house R&D based on advances in universities and public research institutions to produce both new products and new processes. His categorization was later refined and extended to include a group of service industries termed *information intensive*, which includes firms in finance, retail, and publishing (see Tidd et al. 2001). A further change since Pavitt's work in the 1980s has been the rise of information technology companies, so Greenhalgh and Rogers (2006) included a sixth category of *software-related* companies in their examination of sectoral differences in innovation using Pavitt's taxonomy.

1.5 Innovations and Market Failure

We have already seen that an innovation can benefit more people and companies than just the innovating firm. If the firm cannot charge all the beneficiaries of its innovation, then there is a problem of matching incentives to the value of the activity, which may lead to an undersupply of innovations. The possibility that the market system, guided by the independent actions of private firms, will not lead to the optimal outcome is called "market failure." Microeconomists are particularly interested in instances of market failure and we will consider four cases now. First, that the new knowledge underlying the innovation is a *public good*. Second, that innovation is a *private good with positive externalities*. The third case concerns whether innovation is subject to uncertainty and large fixed costs, which, together with imperfect capital markets, can lead to underinvestment. The fourth example is whether competition to be the first to innovate creates duplication and excess costs.

Case 1: Is New Knowledge a Public Good?

The defining characteristic of a public good is that it is *nonrival*, which means that any single use of the public good does not affect its availability to other users. A nonrival good is one that can be used simultaneously by many people; its use by one person does not make it harder for other people to use the same nonrival good, nor does it reduce the value of the good to the first user when a second user is present. The typical textbook example is defense of the country, which provides a service for an entire population. An example of a nonrival knowledge good is a mathematical theorem.

   A public good may also be *nonexcludable*: its use by one party still implies access for all, which cannot easily be blocked. In this case we call it a pure public good. Thus in the case of defense, it is not possible to exclude some members of society from enjoying its value. For our knowledge example, the key issue is how easily it can be accessed, as it does not simultaneously appear in the ether. Even in the days of paper and print, reproduction of a mathematical theorem was easy; with the arrival of the Internet the transmission of the theorem across the world is hard to suppress. An important example of these issues is the human genome project (HGP). A consortium of countries led by the United States started the HGP in 1990 with the aim of mapping the chemical composition of DNA. This publicly funded project was officially completed in 2003 and the knowledge is available on the Internet. Interestingly, a private firm, Celera, was started in 1998 to compete with the publicly funded HGP and it made thousands of patent applications in an attempt to claim intellectual property over the knowledge (i.e., make the knowledge excludable). However, various rulings by the United States Patent and Trademark Office (USPTO) and judgements by the courts have meant that very few patents have been granted. Celera ultimately donated its knowledge to the public domain in 2005 (see Angrist and Cook-Deegan 2006).

Once the nonrival public good has been provided, or discovered in the case of knowledge, the marginal cost of an extra user of such a good is zero. Economic theory tells us that resources are allocated efficiently when prices are equated to marginal costs. If a positive price is charged, then the price of a nonrival good is above zero, so there is a loss of efficiency, as some potential users may be excluded. If a zero price is all that is possible, then private firms motivated by the desire for profit will not produce or develop it. This was pointed out by Arrow (1962, p. 616): when discussing R&D activity in firms, he concluded that

> Any information obtained... should, from a welfare point of view, be available free of charge.... This ensures optimal utilization of the information, but of course provides no incentive for investment in research.

Geroski (1995, p. 91) agreed with the notion of innovation as a nonexcludable good:

> The feature of inventive and innovative activity that most clearly sets it apart from other strategic investments made by firms is the problem of appropriability.

The problem of appropriability refers to the idea that the innovator cannot obtain the full value of its innovation from potential users. Perhaps we should consider whether there is a spectrum of types of new knowledge and innovation, not all of which conform to the "pure public good" definition.

Is every type of new knowledge nonrival? Consider the discovery of a new technology, based on biotechnology research, for designing drugs that have important curative properties. The use of the derived innovative process by one economic actor certainly does not preclude its use by another, but, unlike the pure mathematical theorem, the use by a second or third party will affect the market value of the discovery to the first producer. Even though the use by the imitator does not deplete the knowledge stock of the inventor, it certainly depletes his profits. So within the commercial world, the value of the new knowledge can be rival, even though the knowledge itself is intrinsically nonrival.

Is all knowledge nonexcludable? Clearly, in some cases its creator may be able to use IPRs to protect some of its value. But even without IPRs there is the possibility of using secrecy. If a food or drink supplier offers a new item for sale, he does not have to simultaneously reveal the recipe by which it was created. He can also write contracts with his employees to constrain them not to reveal the recipe. (This has been the approach taken by the producers of Coca Cola for many years.) Thus in many instances producers can prevent other producers from benefiting freely from the use of the new knowledge, when trade secrecy is a legitimate possibility as it is in many countries.

Case 2: Are There Externalities from Innovative Activity?

To continue our attempt to identify causes of market failure we can separate new knowledge from its application in a variety of innovations and then consider another useful economic model of commercial innovation: that of a private good with externalities.[14] Production externalities arise when the profit-seeking activities of one firm create positive or negative effects for other firms and where these side effects are not priced and cannot be sold through the market. Positive externalities occur when the unpriced effects arising from one producer's activity improve the profits of other firms, as seen in our examples of new intermediate goods, or when the innovation improves the welfare of consumers more than the extent of any charge for the product decreases consumers' welfare, as happens when a better-quality final product is supplied for the same price.[15]

It is useful to classify the different stages of R&D, innovation, and diffusion illustrated in figure 1.1 into a spectrum of types of public and private goods. Basic research has more the nature of a *public good* because its applications can be in different fields (and diverse applications are nonrival). For example, recent research into how a spider creates and spins its silk is leading to applications in medicine for building human tissue and in cosmetics for better hair shampoo (as reported on *The Material World*, BBC Radio 4, November 9, 2006). Also, once a scientific discovery is made it is hard to suppress it or keep it secret, so basic scientific knowledge is also more likely to be nonexcludable. In contrast, when we get to the point of a particular application of knowledge, a firm undertaking near-market applied R&D and introducing a specific innovation is closer to supplying a private good with externalities.

---

[14] Negative externalities, such as pollution, tend to dominate discussions in microeconomics textbooks, but positive externalities from knowledge generation are equally important.

[15] Some economists refer to these as "pecuniary externalities," since they occur in relation to prices. There is also a link to the microeconomic concept of consumer surplus, which is generated when some consumers do not pay their full reservation price for the product they are buying. Given the possible confusion, it is wise to explain clearly what is meant when using these terms.

Case 3: Indivisibilities, Uncertainty, and Capital Markets

Further insights concerning possible market failure come from other areas of economic theory, as much R&D has the characteristic of indivisibility of investment and uncertainty of returns. Indivisibility refers to the idea that the project cannot be broken down into smaller, more manageable units. This indivisibility means that projects have up-front costs, known as "fixed costs."[16] If these are very large, they can act as a barrier to undertaking the project. Where there are large fixed costs in creating knowledge, but small marginal costs in supplying it once a discovery is made, this makes competitive market pricing unlikely, as it will not cover all the costs. A good example is the creation of new software: there are very large fixed costs in writing and perfecting the software code, while the production and distribution costs can be negligible. The low production and distribution costs, or marginal costs as economists call them, suggest that the software should have a low price (equal to marginal cost ideally). But such a low price will generate very little revenue and will not therefore compensate the creator for the fixed costs incurred.

Uncertainty is inherent in the innovation process, as decisions to bear risk by doing R&D cannot be separated as an element of choice from decisions to wait for returns (investment), as noted by Arrow (1962). This is because insurance against the failure to discover something important and profitable by undertaking R&D is not on offer. This concentration of risk onto particular firms who decide to engage in R&D may lead to underinvestment, especially in smaller firms, which cannot use product diversity to spread their R&D risk within the firm.[17]

Both uncertainty and indivisibilities could be solved if capital markets worked perfectly. This refers to the idea that investors would correctly evaluate the expected value of any investment project (including R&D projects) and would allocate funds to the projects with the highest returns. Uncertainty can be dealt with by investors diversifying their portfolios. However, there are reasons to expect problems in financing innovation. Banks, venture capitalists, and other investors attempt to find the best projects, but there can be difficulties in understanding and

---

[16] If these costs are unrecoverable, in that what they purchase has no resale value, they are known as "sunk costs."

[17] This argument is, in fact, more complex than it may seem. It is based on the assumption that entrepreneurs and firms are risk averse. If they are, in fact, risk takers, then this "market failure" may not occur. In addition, larger firms may be able to reduce uncertainty by carrying out a range of R&D activities, again alleviating the market failure. Finally, one should be asking what is societal choice with regard to investment in uncertain projects and how does the market outcome compare to this.

evaluating the project if it is related to innovation. Put simply, the innovator may be the only one who fully understands the project; hence the investor must trust the judgement of the innovator. Venture capitalists have considerable experience in evaluating innovative projects, but they themselves have fixed costs. For example, a full evaluation of a project may cost \$40,000; hence if the innovator is only seeking investment of \$100,000 this may preclude the venture capitalist becoming involved.

Case 4: Patent Races and Duplication

The final possibility for the existence of market failure concerns the fact that firms may compete head-to-head in the innovation process. So far we have implicitly assumed that each firm produces a different product or process innovation. However, it is possible that firms compete to make exactly the same innovation (e.g., finding a cure for a specific type of illness). In such situations there may be duplication of R&D. However, since it is often not possible to foresee such cases, it is not easy to prevent such duplication. The economic literature has characterized this situation as a "patent race," with the implication being that the winner takes all of the returns. However, as we see in our later discussions, doing R&D in a common field is often necessary for firms that wish to engage in the exchange of information and technology and to benefit from others' advances. We return to these issues below in chapters 6 and 11.

Summing Up

This discussion highlights the likelihood of various market failures occurring in the process of generating innovations. The first key insight comes from the appropriability problem for firms that invest in new knowledge. If a new discovery can be easily replicated, depleting the profits of the inventor, this creates a serious possibility of market failure resulting in underinvestment of resources in innovation.

The second key insight comes from the fact that many innovations require considerable amounts of R&D expenditure. Such investment is often highly uncertain and there are no insurance markets with which to offset these risks, so this may discourage optimal levels of investment. In addition, some investment projects may require very large fixed costs, hence even the largest firms may be discouraged without government support (e.g., nuclear power, or the creation of a new passenger aircraft). If capital markets worked perfectly, these issues may not cause problems, but this is unlikely to be the case. These arguments also suggest that investment in some types of innovation may be too low or nonexistent.

The third key insight comes from thinking about the price of an innovation. Once an innovation has been made, its availability will be too low if there are private property rights over what should be a free public good, since the price will be set too high and this monopoly pricing inhibits diffusion. But if we always insist on immediate marginal cost pricing, there will be little incentive to invest. Thus Arrow (1962, pp. 616–17) states that "in a free enterprise economy the profitability of invention requires a suboptimal allocation of resources." Some reward system or a degree of private ownership is needed for what may really be a public good if there is to be an incentive to produce it.

1.6 Restoring Incentives to Invent and Innovate

We can now explore some standard solutions provided in the literature for correcting market failure to see if these offer solutions in the case of R&D and innovation. There are four main policy options for solving the problem of underprovision in the cases of public goods and private goods with positive externalities.

Solution 1: Public Provision of a Public Good

Government subsidy to basic research exists in many countries through the funding of university research and of special research agencies in fields such as defense and agriculture. This follows the idea that basic science is a public good. Funding is provided from general taxation and the results of the research are distributed freely without the need for the users of the knowledge to pay more than the marginal cost of its reproduction. This method of financing and provision is less suitable for near-market commercial research, where firms will have competing interests, but is more appropriate for the scientific end of basic research, where there are noncompeting uses in a variety of fields of application. Nevertheless, as we shall discuss below (chapter 4), many publicly funded institutions now engage in the privatization of ownership of their outputs through the use of IPRs and charging licensing fees above those of marginal reproduction costs.

Solution 2: Club Provision of a Local Public Good

A local, or impure, public good arises in the situation where a number of consumers value a service or facility that is nonrival up to a point, but congestion and rivalry then occurs. Provided that exclusion is possible, a club can be formed in which members all pay a fixed fee to join and there-after pay a low marginal cost price to use the facility. An example would be a golf club that requires members to pay a large initial fee on joining followed by modest green fees when playing a round. As the club has a well-defined territory from which nonmembers can be excluded, those who join can be confident that their initial investment in membership awards them rights of access that cannot be eroded by nonmembers.

What relevance has this to innovation? This type of solution can occur where there is a need for specialized R&D with the characteristics of high initial fixed costs together with low marginal costs in use. For the club to be feasible, there must be a possibility of exclusion, so that only those who contribute to the initial fixed costs are permitted to use the facility or information. This arrangement can come about where there are a limited number of players in a given product field, who can all benefit from investment in developing a new process or technique that could reduce their production costs and/or raise their product quality.

A research joint venture (RJV) represents an agreement to share the financing of R&D between several firms, or between government and one or more private firms, together with an agreement for joint use of the sci-entific output. Provided that all the major potential users of the research output engage in the collaboration, this works to achieve a social opti-mum, as there are few problems of exclusion from the use of the dis-coveries, which might cause market distortion.[18] These agreements are more likely to occur where the users of the invention do not compete too closely; an example is that Japanese firms are known to collaborate in basic research but not in near-market research, where the uses of innova-tion become more closely competitive (Goto 1997). In some cases where there are only two, or a small number of, firms, a merger between them will have the effect of removing the public good problem. This solution is also known as "internalizing the externality."

Our two remaining methods of solving the underprovision of innova-tion are derived from the economics of markets exhibiting externalities in production.

Solution 3: Pigovian Subsidies

The classic solution to externalities was proposed by Pigou (1932), who advocated the use of taxes or subsidies to correct negative or posi-tive externalities respectively. In the case of innovation arising from

---

[18] As noted above (p. 19), resources are allocated efficiently when price equals marginal cost. If some large potential users remain outside of the RJV, so do not share the patents, they may be excluded by licensing fees that are above marginal cost.

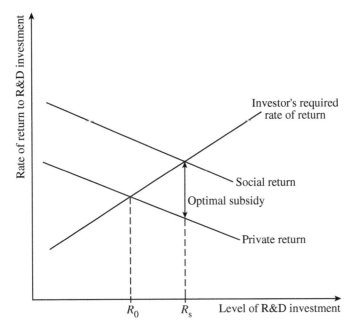

Figure 1.6. The role of R&D subsidies in correcting market failure.

Notes. Without any subsidy, private investors equate their expected private return to their required rate of return (the rate that covers the cost of investment funds) and the result is a level of investment of R_0. The socially optimal level of R&D investment is where the social return is equated to the opportunity cost of funds. The social return is higher due to the positive externalities of R&D. With a subsidy to R&D the government effectively raises the private return to equal the social return and so private investors now choose the socially preferred higher level of investment R_s.

production, this involves a subsidy to the activity that benefits other producers. In this way the innovator is rewarded at the social marginal cost and thus faces the correct incentive to produce innovative products and ideas. In the case of R&D, the role of the subsidy is to raise the private rate of return to equal the social rate of return (see figure 1.6). Governments often finance basic research in universities and research institutes; however, there is not always a government subsidy for near-market research. Among the G5 countries, the United States, Japan, and France offer tax concessions to companies engaging in R&D but Germany does not and the United Kingdom did not do so (except for small firms) until 2002.

Why might a government be unwilling to offer any subsidy to R&D? One difficulty is in identifying which of the firm's expenses should be classified as constituting R&D, which merit the tax concession or subsidy, as opposed to general production and marketing expenses, which do not. Another difficulty is that some R&D is very successful while other projects are not. If all R&D is subsidized at the same rate, regardless of how successful it is, then government is rewarding projects that are generating no positive externalities as well as those that are doing so. Just as problematic is the fact that much R&D would still be done in the absence of any R&D subsidy. In this case the government contribution represents a gift to those companies that are persistently active in R&D. We shall discuss these issues further in chapter 11, where we examine a number of policy instruments to promote innovation.

Solution 4: Definition of Property Rights

The insight of Coase (1960) was that, in dealing with externalities, any unpriced spillover (an externality) could be brought within the market system (or internalized) if a property right can be assigned over the externality (whether good or bad). Once property rights are assigned, contracts can be written and the market can then function. Those who create positive externalities can charge others for these benefits, while those who create negative externalities, such as pollution, can be charged by the recipients. In regard to innovation activity, the parallel is that, if intellectual property rights can be defined (and defended in law) and a system of private bargaining and contracting for the use of the invention or information can be established, then the market may be able to move closer to achieving the socially optimal level of innovation. The requirements for this to work are divisible, measurable externalities; small numbers of affected parties who can then engage in contracts; full information for those affected about the values of the intellectual property assets; and the rights to license the intellectual property.

Patents, copyright, trademarks, and design protection systems can be viewed as coming in this orbit (albeit they predate the Coase theorem). Two important caveats arise in interpreting IPRs in this way. The first concerns Coase's symmetry result for common externalities such as pollution: it makes no difference to the achievement of a socially efficient outcome whether the right to pollute is assigned to the polluter or the polluted. In this example the pollution occurs as a byproduct of another activity that is the main motivation of the producer. This result does not carry over to IPRs, where we are considering the right to ownership of the whole of the benefits flowing from an innovation that has yet to be discovered. The innovator requires future property rights to provide an incentive. If all the returns were preassigned to the future beneficiaries, they are unlikely to be willing or able to combine to offer him a fee to invent, particularly given the uncertainty of the R&D process and the users' difficulty in valuing something that does not yet exist. However, some stages of an ongoing R&D process can be subcontracted, with contracts being drawn up at the outset, detailing the ownership of future IPRs and the allocation of the rewards from licensing technology.

The second caveat regarding IPRs as Coasian property rights is the issue of how far knowledge is a nonrival public good rather than a rival private good, as we discussed above. Nonrival goods can sometimes be made excludable: a good is said to be excludable if it is possible to prevent its use by others. Acquiring an IPR for a particular creation of knowledge may be an example of making a nonrival good excludable.[19] Economists are particularly interested in this feature of IPRs. Economists and others have long argued that strong property rights applied to rival goods result in efficient outcomes. In contrast, strong property rights for nonrival goods involve a trade-off.

The Trade-off between Incentives and Monopoly Power

To give people an incentive to produce socially desirable new innovations, IPRs allow the creators of a nonrival good to appropriate the returns of their innovation for themselves. But since IPRs make a nonrival good excludable, this gives rise to inefficiency, since the price of the good will be above the marginal cost of producing it. In other words, granting an IPR to an entity is tantamount to conferring a monopoly. The knife-edge on which the intellectual property law tries to balance is that of defining enough private property rights to preserve adequate incentives for innovation while avoiding the gift of excessive monopoly power, which will lead to socially inefficient exploitation of that creation. Economists are then left to adjudicate as to the desirability of using IPRs, given that they act as a spur to innovation and also as an instigator of monopolistic inefficiency.

This trade-off between encouraging innovation and suffering the consequences of monopoly has been noted by many writers and was formally analyzed in a modern way by Nordhaus (1969). We shall explore these issues of monopoly gains and distortions more fully in chapter 2. In addition, understanding whether these monopoly costs of IPRs are less than the benefit to society emanating from the spur that IPRs give to innovation will provide a major theme for parts II and IV of this book.

---

[19] However, the boundaries of any IPR are "fuzzy" due to the difficulties of complete enforcement and the possibility that competitors learn from the documentation of the innovation.

1.7 Firms Competing through Innovation

Up to now our discussion has focused on the nature of innovation and the incentives faced by individual firms without much consideration of the interactions between firms in the marketplace. One of the first authors to discuss this interaction was Schumpeter (1942), who coined the now-famous term "creative destruction" to describe the outcome of the process of innovation by competing firms interacting in a given marketplace. This was a perceptive appreciation of the tension between the benefits from innovation and the costs to other firms that are standing still in terms of product design and technology. Thus the term "creative" refers to the profitable opportunities seized by innovators, which ultimately benefit not just them but the whole society. The word "destruction" refers to the process whereby the innovator is taking away customers, and therefore profit, from existing producers. In this situation of competition for market share through the introduction of novel products and processes, there is likely to be a continual churning of market leadership. Pervasive uncertainty about any firm's continued existence is the norm if it fails to innovate or to catch up quickly with the leaders through imitation.

This description of the interaction between firms points out a basic incompatibility between perfect competition (in the absence of IPRs) and modern entrepreneurial activity, because immediate imitation reduces the incentives to innovate to zero. Perfect competition may then be inferior to another more concentrated market structure that is more conducive to innovation, particularly in markets where IPRs cannot easily be assigned.[20] In his later writings Schumpeter championed oligopoly, seeing this as a market structure whose competitive practices of intensive competition between a few large firms, creating new products and lowering costs, achieved more for social welfare than either perfect competition or monopoly. However, the debate about the merits of large and small firms as innovators and the optimal degree of market concentration has continued in the literature to this day. We shall return to this topic in chapter 5.

It should be clear from the discussion above that IPRs are central to the process of innovation. The basic argument is that IPRs award temporary monopoly rights, something society does not want, in order to provide incentives to innovate, something society does want. However, in reality the IPR system creates a complex set of decisions for firms.

---

[20] In most mixed-market economies today, the antitrust or competition policy authorities are charged with taking innovation into account when enforcing antimonopoly laws.

Chapter 6 discusses in detail how firms can benefit from the IPR system, including a discussion on when the IPR system may be detrimental to certain firms. Following this, in chapter 7, we examine how innovations spread across the economy, so that ultimately the innovative product or process becomes the new standard for consumers or producers. At the point where the process of diffusion is complete, society is reaping the full benefit of the new knowledge.

1.8   Conclusion

This chapter has provided an introduction and overview of the nature of innovation. There should be little doubt that innovation is a complex process—even defining innovation is problematic! The genesis of innovation derives from a wide range of sources and its development involves various stages, often involving considerable investment. Although we can outline the stages of innovation (figure 1.1), progression through them is not linear and there are important feedbacks in the process. While entrepreneurs and private firms are central actors in the process, there is a critical role for government in providing a legal infrastructure and supplying basic scientific knowledge. Many aspects of the process are subject to market failures and the existence of the IPR system is one attempt to remedy some of these. All of these issues are returned to in part II of the book. In the rest of part I we continue with our microeconomic analysis by considering the role of IPRs in chapter 2 and the thorny issue of how we can observe and measure innovation and productivity in chapter 3.

Keywords

Invention, innovation, and diffusion.

Product and process innovation.

Intellectual property rights.

Market failure.

Public goods.

Externality.

Appropriability.

Coasian property rights.

Pigovian subsidies.

Creative destruction.

Questions for Discussion

(1) How would you distinguish between an invention and an innovation?

(2) What are the key characteristics of a public good? Is all new knowledge a public good?

(3) What is a positive externality? How does this differ from a public good?

(4) How does innovation create positive externalities? Why are they a problem?

(5) What are the key market failures surrounding investment in innovation?

(6) Does the creation of intellectual property rights help or hinder the markets for innovative goods and processes?

References

Angrist, M., and R. Cook-Deegan. 2006. Who owns the genome? *The New Atlantis: A Journal of Technology and Society* Winter:87–96.

Arrow, K. 1962. Economic welfare and the allocation of resources for invention. In *The Rate and Direction of Inventive Activity* (ed. R. Nelson). National Bureau of Economic Research/Princeton University Press.

Coase, R. 1960. The problem of social cost. *Journal of Law and Economics* 3: 1–44.

Geroski, P. 1995. Markets for technology: knowledge, innovation and appropriability. In *Handbook of the Economics of Innovation and Technical Change* (ed. P. Stoneman), chapter 4. Oxford: Basil Blackwell.

Goto, A. 1997. Co-operative research in Japanese manufacturing industries. In *Innovation in Japan* (ed. A. Goto and H. Odagiri). Oxford: Clarendon.

Greenhalgh, C. A., and M. Rogers. 2006. The value of innovation: the interaction of competition, R&D and IP. *Research Policy* 35:562–80.

Leontief, W. 1986. *Input–Output Economics*, 2nd edn. Oxford University Press.

Nordhaus, W. 1969. *Invention, Growth and Welfare: A Theoretical Treatment of Technological Change.* Cambridge, MA: MIT Press.

OECD. 1997. *The Oslo Manual: Proposed Guidelines for Collecting and Interpreting Technological Innovation Data.* Paris: Organisation for Economic Cooperation and Development.

Pavitt, K. 1984. Sectoral patterns of technical change. *Research Policy* 13:343–73.

Pigou, A. C. 1932. *The Economics of Welfare*, 4th edn. London: Macmillan.

Rosegger, G. 1986. *The Economics of Production and Innovation*, 2nd edn. Oxford: Pergamon Press.

Rosenberg, N. 1982. *Inside the Black Box.* Cambridge University Press.

Scherer, F. M. 1984. *Innovation and Growth: Schumpeterian Perspectives.* Cambridge, MA: MIT Press.

Schumpeter, J. A. 1942. *Capitalism, Socialism and Democracy,* reissued 1975. New York: Harper & Row.

Tidd, J., J. Bessant, and K. Pavitt. 2001. *Managing Innovation: Integrating Technological, Market and Organisational Change.* John Wiley.

von Hippel, E. 2005. *Democratizing Innovation.* Cambridge, MA: MIT Press.

2

The Nature and Role of Intellectual Property

2.1 Introduction

In our preface we stressed the fundamental role of innovation in driving economic growth. In chapter 1 we saw that IPRs can play a crucial role in offering incentives to innovate. In this chapter we explain much more about the nature and role of IPRs. We also outline some of the legal and practical issues that managers, entrepreneurs, and policy makers may encounter. To begin, section 2.2 returns to the issue of why IPRs are awarded and fills in more details. The main forms of IPR established and protected by law are patents, trademarks, designs, and copyright. While these forms of IPR dominate legal, management, and economic discussions of IPRs, there are further IPRs, including trade secrets, database rights, plant variety rights, and performers' rights. Sections 2.3–2.6 look at each of the main forms of IPR: *what* it covers, *how* to get this IPR, *how strong* is the IPR, its *geographical* coverage, whether there is a *market* for this IPR, and its use by different sectors. Section 2.7 deals with three additional questions that are important: is patenting always the best option, what is the optimal length of protection, and are there other ways of providing incentives to innovate?

2.2 Why Are Intellectual Property Rights Awarded?

As we saw in chapter 1, the basic justification for IPRs is that they give people an incentive to produce socially desirable new innovations. Without some guarantee of private ownership, innovators might not put resources into innovative activity, as their findings would rapidly be imitated, leaving them with little or no profit. This happens as knowledge has the characteristics of a public good: it is nonrival, meaning it can be used by many without being used up; and it is nonexcludable, as it cannot be easily defended from imitators. So IPRs assist the creators of

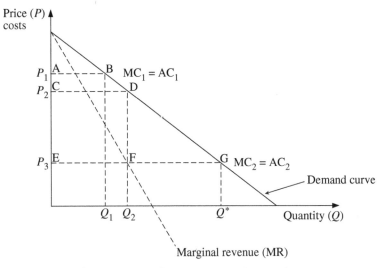

Figure 2.1. A drastic process innovation.

a nonrival good (the innovative knowledge or design) to appropriate the returns of their innovation for themselves alone. But since IPRs make a nonrival good excludable, they introduce inefficiency for the duration of the right. The IPR, in effect, gives the creator a monopoly right and this causes the price of the good to be above the marginal cost of its production. Consumers lose because a monopolist restricts output to raise prices: that is, they lose out because not enough of the innovative good is being sold.

In chapter 1 we illustrated the microeconomic effects of certain process and product innovations (see figures 1.2–1.4), but here we now develop this discussion. In particular, figure 1.2 showed the case of the process innovation where the fall in costs was relatively small. This is called a nondrastic process innovation. Figure 2.1 shows the case of a drastic process innovation. The key difference is that the process innovation has caused the new cost (MC_2) to be so much lower than the old cost (MC_1). This means that the innovator now acts like a monopolist. Let us describe the situation in figure 2.1 in more detail. Before the cost-reducing process innovation many firms produce and sell at price $P_1 = MC_1 = AC_1$ (i.e., the market is perfectly competitive). After the innovation, one firm acquires a patent for the innovative technique that allows production at cost MC_2. With the new cost at MC_2, the profit-maximizing price is P_2 (profit maximization occurs where $MR = MC_2$, hence quantity Q_2 is produced and sold at P_2). The patent holder can either supply all of the market at price P_2 or issue licenses to others for the use of the patented technology, charging them $P_2 - MC_2$. When the patent expires the product price falls to $P_3 = MC_2$.

Economists are particularly interested in the *welfare* implications of such cases and we now look at these in detail. The total *social welfare* gain from the innovation in the long run is given by the area ABGE, all of which accrues to consumers by increasing their *consumer surplus* (which measures the difference between the amount they actually pay and the maximum amount they would be willing to pay for this quantity of the product). During the patent period the innovator produces less than Q^* and receives profits of CDFE. These profits provide the incentive for innovation and are generated by the fact that $P_2 > MC_2$. However, this incentive to innovate is lower than the long-run welfare gain by the welfare loss of monopoly, triangle DGF, plus the short-run gains from price reduction accruing to customers of area ABDC.[1]

This means that even with IPRs—a patent in this case—there are suboptimal incentives to commit resources to innovation, since the temporary monopoly profits are less than the overall welfare improvement to society. This represents a possible market failure and is sometimes referred to as an *appropriability* problem. In this case the appropriability problem stems from analyzing consumer surplus in a market. The previous chapter also discussed the case of positive externalities occurring, whereby the knowledge related to the innovation has a beneficial impact on other firms. Some authors also use the term "appropriability problem" to refer to positive externalities, since the innovator is unable to appropriate the benefits accruing to other firms.

2.3 Patents

What Can Be Patented?

To obtain a patent the inventor has to satisfy the patent-granting authority that he has met three conditions. The invention has to have *novelty* (in the worldwide domain), it has to embody a significant *inventive step* (so must be nonobvious, even to experts in the field), and it must be capable of *industrial application*. Even if the invention meets these tough conditions, there are some areas of invention that are excluded by law from ever being patented, although these exclusions vary somewhat between countries. In Europe and the United Kingdom there is a

---

[1] There is a caveat if the innovator can "price discriminate"—meaning charging different prices to different customers. In the extreme case of perfect price discrimination, the innovator could extract all of the consumer surplus ABGE in profits. However, price discrimination in general is difficult and perfect price discrimination is an extreme case.

broad list of *exclusions* from patenting.[2] These are discoveries (of something that preexisted and was not created by the inventor), scientific theories/mathematical methods, aesthetic creations, methods of doing business, databases and computer programs, animal or plant varieties, and methods of treatment and diagnosis. In contrast, the United States allows patents for computer software and for business methods, which we shall discuss further below. Some of the excluded categories have other IPRs besides patents associated with them, such as copyright or design.

In his book *From Edison to iPod*, Mostert (2007) gives numerous examples of patents and of many other forms of intellectual property, together with advice on what to protect and how to do it. His title reflects the lengthy time span from the patenting of the electric lightbulb by Thomas Edison at the USPTO on February 15, 1881, to the ubiquitous product of the present day, the iPod, a brand of portable media player designed and marketed by Apple and launched on October 23, 2001. Even so, the Edison patent was by no means one of the first in the United States—Eli Witney's mechanical device of a cotton gin was patented nearly ninety years earlier in 1794. The protection of discovery and writing was in fact thought sufficiently important to be written into the U.S. Constitution, where article I, section 8 states:

> Congress shall have power to promote the progress of science and useful arts, by securing for limited times to authors and inventors the exclusive right to their respective writings and discoveries.

From this evolved the specific legislation relating to patents and other IPRs in the United States, but this was not the earliest legislation by a long way. The first formal European patent was thought to have been granted by the City of Florence in 1426 to Brunelleschi for a vessel to transport marble. The first patent law was in Venice in 1474 in order to reward inventors or protect certain products (for up to ten years) (Guellec and van Pottelsberghe 2007). In many cases the awarding of a patent was arbitrary, or driven by corruption. The English Parliament passed the Statute of Monopolies in 1623 as an attempt to ensure that patents were awarded to inventors. Even so, the patent system only gradually evolved into one that provided uniform, and relatively low-cost, incentives to inventors (MacLeod 1988).

As we will see, there are now hundreds of thousands of patents granted each year. Although most patents turn out to have little or no value (see

---

[2] The U.K. 1977 Patent Act is based on the European Patent Convention of 1973; hence U.K. and European patent law are similar.

chapter 6), let us consider three examples of important recent patents. In 1989, Nintendo was granted a U.S. patent (no. 4,799,635) for "A system for determining the authenticity of computer software when used with a main processor unit," which has been important in defending its market share. In 1987 Bruce Roth was granted a U.S. patent (no. 4,681,893) for a chemical compound that lowers blood cholesterol, which is one of the patents behind Pfizer's drug Lipitor. Lipitor, which is the trademarked product, is the world's top-selling drug (with sales of around $10 billion per year). James Dyson is a British inventor who in the late 1970s started work on a bagless vacuum cleaner that would have high suction. From the early 1980s Dyson filed for a succession of patents that underlie the Dual Cyclone (a trademark) vacuum cleaner. The company Dyson founded is now the largest vacuum cleaner maker in the world, with a share of around 30%, although he has faced a series of legal challenges to the validity of his patents.

How to Get a Patent?

A patent application requires full documentation of the invention for which protection is sought. This document is then scrutinized by a patent examiner to see if it meets the three conditions of novelty, nonobviousness, and suitability for industrial application. A patent is only granted if successful on all three conditions. The firm or the inventor has to pay fees at the start of the application and, to keep the patent alive to its full term, he or she needs to follow renewal procedures. There are fees for all stages of this procedure and, in many countries, the marginal costs rise with the duration of the patent.

Dimensions of Patents: Length, Breadth, and Geographical Coverage

How long does a patent last if it is granted? The monopoly right to exploit a patented invention is assigned to the creator for up to twenty years, after which the property right expires and the right to exploitation is open to all without fee or further restriction.[3] There is an exception to the twenty-year rule in respect of medicines, where the patent may be unworkable for several years while the new drug is being tested and approved by the regulatory authority, such as the Food and Drug Administration (FDA) in the United States or the European Medicines Agency in Europe. In such cases the patent holder can apply for a maximum of five

---

[3] The length of patent protection has varied through history. Most recently, the Trade Related Intellectual Property Agreement (TRIPS) requires all countries to have a minimum protection of twenty years. Prior to this the United States had a seventeen-year term. Note, however, that patent protection requires the holder to pay renewal fees periodically.

extra years of protection, with the justification for the extension being the short time it has been marketed and the need to recoup the development costs of the drug.[4] However, this extension only serves to restore parity between pharmaceuticals and other items, not to offer a longer term of protection.

The second important dimension of a patent is its breadth, which determines how near to the original invention another party can get without being judged to have infringed the right of the patent holder. This is partly determined by what claims of originality are accepted by the patent examiner in their scrutiny of the application. It is also affected by how far back in the chain of scientific discovery the patent arises. Clearly a patent on a very basic component, or an element of a process, that will be used in a wide range of applications will have a wider impact on a range of users and potential competitors than one for a very specialized product or process affecting a narrow set of users.

The patent property right is geographically limited to the area of the legal jurisdiction under which it is registered. For example, to gain protection in both the United States and Europe, the firm has to apply for and obtain patents in each area. Within the European Union the firm can either apply country by country or via the European Patent Office (EPO) for multicountry coverage; so to gain protection in the United Kingdom a firm could seek a patent via the U.K. Patent Office or the EPO.[5] Some smaller countries still do not offer the opportunity to apply for a patent. Moves to get worldwide coverage of IPR systems are being made by the World Trade Organization (WTO) through the TRIPS provision, which requires those seeking membership of the WTO to comply with minimum standards in respect of their IPR systems.[6]

A Market for Patent Rights?

Once a patent is granted, the documentation about the ownership, content, and coverage of the IPR means that the right is saleable (if the owner wishes to take an immediate full private profit). Alternatively, the use of the technique, or other inventive step, can be licensed to others at the discretion of the patent holder, providing returns to an inventor who

---

[4] This is denoted as a "patent term extension" in the United States, or as "supplementary protection" in Europe.

[5] It is also possible to make an international application for protection in more than one country under the Patent Cooperation Treaty administered by the World Intellectual Property Organization (WIPO) in Geneva. However, this does not lead to a worldwide patent being granted; rather it simplifies and reduces some costs in the process of applying to the different country authorities.

[6] Chapter 12 discusses TRIPS in more detail.

does not wish to pursue production.[7] Firms can also engage in patent pooling with one or more other firms, offering their IPRs in exchange for access to other firms' IPRs; they can even make advance contracts for the interfirm exchanges of technology where they see large advantages in reducing uncertainty and time lags in contracting. All these features of patents mean that a market for property rights in knowledge can be established; however, this description does not exhaust the impact of new patents.

A key feature of the patent system is that the process requires information about the invention to be disclosed. In most countries, but not in the United States, patent applications are "published" eighteen months after application and while the examination of their validity is still being conducted. This releases the new knowledge into the public domain and also allows others to challenge the application if they think it should not be awarded. In the United States, historically there was no "publication" requirement, which meant secrecy was maintained for longer (i.e., until the grant of the patent, which could take years) and there was no possibility to object. However, in 1999 U.S. patent law changed and required publication if the inventor intended to seek protection in other countries where the eighteen-month rule applied (Landes and Posner 2003, p. 362). Thus, even before the grant of a patent, and certainly during the period of private monopoly ownership, the novel technology underlying the patent is documented and publicly available. So the technology is in the public domain, which reduces the possibility of duplication of research effort.[8] The U.S. patent system also differs in that a patent is awarded to the first party to invent, not the first one to apply as in most other countries.[9] If one firm files but another firm can show evidence that they discovered it earlier, then the patent application would be refused. In Europe the patent is awarded to the first party to file the application, but a challenge can still arise if the patent is claimed for something already in the public domain (hence it would fail the novelty requirement).

This feature of patents means that the opportunity arises for learning and discovery to occur, which is a benefit to other researchers that is not being priced in a market transaction. Therefore positive externalities are being generated, as other firms and individuals can build upon the

---

[7] Arora et al. (2001) provide a full and important discussion of these ideas.

[8] In addition, in many countries there are statutory provisions for research exemptions to license fees in the use of patented materials to undertake research. For a review of these provisions and discussion of the variation in provisions across OECD countries see Dent et al. (2006).

[9] Although the United States Patent Reform Act 2009, which is currently under consideration, would change this to "first to apply."

technological or scientific advances of the patent holder.[10] There can be opportunities to make a breakthrough that has a large commercial value as a result of a rather modest further expenditure on R&D. This type of sequential discovery and patenting is characterized as "standing on the shoulders of giants." Hence there is by no means a complete and perfect market for the new knowledge created by inventors, even when they choose to protect this by patenting their inventions. So in trying to evaluate how effective patents are as an appropriation mechanism for firms, we are forced to conclude that they are imperfect. At best they compensate firms for a significant fraction of the social benefit of the innovation.

Who Uses Patents Most?

Across the economy the highest users of patents are the manufacturing and extractive industries. This high concentration is observed among firms with large R&D expenditures and/or complex products requiring many component parts or processes. Hence the biggest users are in the pharmaceutical industry, aerospace, motor vehicles, electrical/electronic goods, and the extraction of oil and gas. Although not every innovation in these sectors can or will be patented, it is likely that the propensity to patent varies less than the rate of innovation, so a rise in the number of patents in any sector will reflect a rise in innovative activity. Thus if we are judging patents as a potential measure of innovation (see chapter 3), then patent records can at least permit economists to assess changes in the rate of such activity in these sectors. Table 2.1 shows the top ten patentees, in terms of patents granted, at the USPTO and the EPO. We can see that Japanese firms are very active, especially in the United States. While ranking firms according to their number of patents provides some information, there is also a need to assess the "quality" or ultimate value of the patents, something we discuss in more detail later in this book.[11]

2.4 Trademarks

While the basic justification for IPRs is that they provide incentives for innovation, in the case of trademarks this is augmented by a new

---

[10] As discussed in chapter 1, an externality is defined as when the activity of one agent affects other agents' utility or productivity and there is no accompanying payment. These externalities cause markets to function inefficiently.

[11] The USPTO stopped highlighting its patent rankings in 2005, stating that "In ceasing publication of the top 10 list, the USPTO is emphasizing quality over quantity by discouraging any perception that we believe more is better" (www.uspto.gov/web/patents/notices/ceasingpatentslist.htm).

Table 2.1. Top patentees in the United States and Europe.

Company	Number of USPTO grants, 2006	Company	Number of EPO grants, 2006
IBM	3,621	Phillips	4,425
Samsung	2,451	Samsung	2,355
Canon	2,366	Siemens	2,319
Matsushita	2,229	Matsushita	1,529
Hewlett-Packard	2,099	BASF	1,459
Intel	1,959	LG Electronics	1,214
Sony	1,771	Robert Bosch	1,093
Hitachi	1,732	Sony	1,088
Toshiba	1,672	Nokia	882
Micron	1,610	General Electric	768

Sources. U.S. patents: part B of "Patenting By Organizations 2006" (available at www. uspto.gov/go/taf/topo_06.htm). EPO patents: "Facts and Statistics 2007" (available at www.epo.org/about-us/office/statistics/top-applicants-2006.html).

argument. Trademarks are used to signal to consumers that the product is of a certain, consistent quality. This means that a trademark can reduce the search costs of consumers, hence the firm can charge a higher price, and the firm's profits may increase. The need for a signal is due to the "information asymmetry" between seller and buyer.[12] The signaling argument for trademarks is linked to the basic justification for IPRs: firms would be reluctant to invest in new product innovation if the new product could not be distinguished from imitations.

Firms in many sectors compete continuously through horizontal and vertical product differentiation, launching new varieties and better qualities of existing products and entering into new fields of production. They may then apply for trademarks on their new product names, including the symbols used to distinguish these new brands of goods and services, which they use when making expenditures on advertising and market promotions. Hence new trademark applications can signal the launch of new products or new fields of activity for the firm. Their trademark stocks become part of the intangible assets of the firm alongside its patents, contributing part of the value of the firm in the event of mergers or hostile takeovers.

Examples of trademarked products are everywhere. We already mentioned two important trademarks above—Lipitor and Dual Cyclone—but

---

[12] Information asymmetry is a potential cause of market failure and is a major topic in microeconomics. A survey of the economics of trademarks can be found in Landes and Posner (1987, 2003) and Ramello (2006). Theoretical discussions of how trademarks and brands function are found in Tadelis (1999) and Choi (1998).

there are many others. Proctor & Gamble is a leading consumer products company, with brands such as Always, Bounty, Crest, Folgers, Gillette, Pampers, and Tide, which are all trademarked. Trademarks are also held on related marketing phrases and logos—such as Pampers Baby Dry and Crest Whitestrips Premium. The energy drink "Red Bull" was created in 1987 by Dietrich Mateschitz in Austria (although it was based on a similar Asian drink called Krating Daeng—Thai for Red Bull). The successful marketing of Red Bull as a worldwide brand means it now has around 70% of the market for energy drinks. Using trademarks to establish and defend its brands has been one element of this success. Again, it is not simply the name Red Bull that is trademarked but also related phrases and logos, such as "never underestimate what a Red Bull can do" (U.S. trademark 3315026, 2007).

What Can Be Registered as a Trademark?

A trademark can be any sign (word, logo, or picture) that distinguishes the goods and services of one trader from those of another.[13] Since 1993 in the United Kingdom, trademarks can also be distinctive shapes, colors, or sounds, although rather fewer such applications have been made. The conditions are that the mark must be distinctive, not a word in common usage, nor deceptive or contrary to law or morality, and not similar or identical to any earlier marks. Almost all common brand names fall into this category of IPRs, such as Heinz 57 Varieties, or Starbucks the coffee house chain, along with many instantly recognizable logos, like the Shell yellow and red emblem, the Nike Swoosh, and the design of some containers, such as the contoured bottle of Coca Cola.

How Is a Trademark Obtained?

The first route is parallel to the method of gaining a patent, through a process of application, examination, and grant. However, a firm can also have unregistered trademarks: these are established by the act of trading under a given sign and gaining a reputation for the products using that sign. Unlike filing for a patent, in seeking a registered trademark the applicant does not have to reveal much information about the product to acquire the right to trade under a given name or sign. Even so,

---

[13] Legally, you do not need to register a trademark at an intellectual property office; however, doing so is relatively cheap and will assist in any legal disputes. A registered trademark can use the ® symbol.

the application is made in one or more product classes, and the registered trademark cannot automatically be transferred later to areas of economic activity that are new to the firm.[14]

Length, Breadth, and Geographical Coverage

Unlike patents and most other forms of IPRs, trademark protection can be indefinite, provided that the producer continues to produce and trade in the product classes covered by its trademark. For a registered mark there is an initial period of ten years in Europe and the United Kingdom, at which point a renewal fee is due to continue the registration. As with patents, the legal territory of application limits the domain of protection that it affords, so for coverage in one country a firm can apply either directly to its local office, or in Europe (since 1996) it can seek a multicountry Community trademark. There is also a system to streamline simultaneous applications to many countries based at the World Intellectual Property Office and referred to as the Madrid Protocol.

A Market for Trademark Rights

As noted, the main role of a trademark is that of offering the buyer of the product a guarantee of the origin and quality of the brand being offered for sale. For this reason, maintaining a trademark requires the firm to be engaged in the production of the good or the supply of the service. Hence, the sale of a trademark is normally associated with a transfer of ownership of a firm or part of a firm. Put another way, unlike patents, you cannot in general simply think of a trademark, register it, and then subsequently sell it.

Who Uses Trademarks?

Trademarks can be registered by all sectors of industry, including firms in manufacturing, utilities, services, and even government organizations. Table 2.2 shows the top U.S. trademarking firms and top European Community trademarking firms in 2006. For the United States, consumer product firms dominate the table, but a telecommunication firm is second and an insurance company is fourth. The first and third Community trademarkers are pharmaceutical companies, with the second (L'Oreal)

---

[14] In the United Kingdom, the United States, Europe, Australia, and other countries there are forty-five trademark classes. In the United Kingdom, a new trademark application can be filed under three classes at no extra charge and additional classes can be paid for. Despite this, the average number of classes applied for is around two, as firms need to prove that the product is (or will be) used in each class specified.

Table 2.2. Top trademarkers in the United States and Europe.

Company	U.S. trademarks registered in 2006	Company	Community trademarks registered in 2006
Mattel	639	Glaxo	154
Deutsche Telekom	429	L'Oreal	138
Novartis	134	Novartis	135
American Int'l Group	126	El Corte Ingles	127
Disney Enterprises	120	Barilla	115
Proctor & Gamble	117	Bristol-Myers Squibb	106
Mars	101	Proctor & Gamble	105
IGT	96	Viacom International	104
Beautybank	93	Lidl Siftung	87
Nedboy, Robin	90	Sony	76

Sources. U.S. trademarks from the USPTO's "2007 Performance and Accountability Report" (p. 138). The data for the top Community trademarkers were obtained directly from the Office for the Harmonization of the Internal Market.

being a cosmetics and luxury goods firm and the fourth (El Cortes Ingles) being a Spanish-based retail company.

Table 2.3 shows the proportions of large U.K. firms in different sectors that made applications for trademarks and patents via the U.K. office and the European offices in the period 1996–2000. In nine out of twelve sectors (the exceptions being agriculture, construction, and real estate) more than half of the firms applied for a U.K. trademark and more than one quarter for a Community trademark between 1996–2000. Comparing the activity rates for trademarks and patents demonstrates the much more limited spread of patent activity, where high activity rates are confined to the manufacturing and utilities sectors. Looking across sectors at trademarks and taking manufacturing as a benchmark, the retail services sector has a higher incidence of firms active in U.K. marks while activity in the hotels and catering sector also runs close to the manufacturing level.[15]

2.5 Designs and Utility Models

What Is Protected?

Design rights protect the external, visible features of the appearance of a product. This can include some items in which the design is integral to

---

[15] Note, however, that in both cases their activity rates are lower in Community marks, as may be expected since they are selling their services mainly within the United Kingdom.

Table 2.3.   Proportion of firms applying for IPRs by sector.

Sector	Number of firms in sample	U.K. trademarks	Community trademarks	U.K. patents	EPO patents
1. Agriculture/ mining	67	0.19	0.12	0.21	0.12
2. Manufacturing	640	0.67	0.55	0.40	0.35
3. Utilities	26	0.85	0.62	0.50	0.42
4. Construction	89	0.39	0.22	0.22	0.09
5. Finance	191	0.52	0.26	0.05	0.06
6. Real estate	112	0.22	0.12	0.03	0.01
7. Wholesale	181	0.52	0.33	0.12	0.07
8. Retail	132	0.75	0.40	0.08	0.05
9. Hotel/catering	54	0.65	0.35	0.06	0.00
10. Transport/ communication	115	0.57	0.43	0.10	0.05
11. Business services	259	0.57	0.43	0.08	0.06
12. Other services	188	0.56	0.37	0.10	0.12

Source. Greenhalgh and Rogers (2008, table A2). These data relate to large U.K. firms observed over the period 1996–2000.

the product performance; for example, this right protects the design of semiconductor chips. To register a design the creator must provide drawings and/or photographs detailing all the dimensions and characteristics of the item.

In many countries—but not the United States, the United Kingdom, or Canada—there is also a "utility model" IPR. According to Suthersanen (2006) there are seventy-five countries that operate some form of "utility model," which is best described as a blend of a design and a patent, usually requiring a limited examination but valid only for a short period. For example, in 2001 Australia introduced an "innovation patent," which requires a lower inventive step than a full patent but can only be enforced for eight years. Australia's "innovation patent" is one form of a "utility model." It is normally awarded after one month if it passes a basic examination, however, it is only enforceable after certification (a more complete, and costly, process). Hence, utility models are sometimes referred to as a second-tier patent system, often intended to assist smaller firms and individual inventors.

How Is a Design Right Obtained?

Design rights can be registered, but they need not be, as the novelty of a design can be established by an act of original creation and the intellectual property right of the creator then arises automatically from having undertaken this creative action. Firms may still wish to register their designs if they see this as providing a better basis from which to issue a legal challenge to another firm producing an infringing copy.

How Long and What Geographical Coverage?

In the United States a "design patent" (as a design right is called there) has fourteen years' duration. In the United Kingdom design rights last for ten years after the first marketing of the product, subject to a limit of fifteen years from the creation of the design.[16] As with patents and trademarks, the protection is limited to the country in which the design is registered. A European design right was introduced in 2003. The utility models have varying periods of protection according to the country concerned.[17]

Who Uses Design Rights?

As with patents, the manufacturing sector dominates the statistics of design rights, but the pattern across manufacturing industry differs from that seen for patents, with less dominance by high R&D activities and a higher representation of firms producing textiles, toys, and furniture. Table 2.4 shows that the top ten U.K. patenting firms includes those noted for high-technology consumer goods; the leaders in design rights include firms in the fields of home goods and apparel. Nevertheless, trademarks show the greatest diversity of product lines across the top ten firms, with everything from pharmaceuticals and aerospace to cosmetics and the national lottery.

2.6 Copyright

What Can Be Protected?

This right covers literary and creative works including books, plays, their published editions and performances, dance performances, music, paintings, sculpture, sound recordings, films/videos, and broadcasts. Computer software can also be covered by copyright, which is especially

---

[16] However, there is a further complexity in that, for products other than semiconductor chips, licenses must be granted to other producers wishing to copy the design after the first five years of the ten-year term.

[17] Utility models are not something specified by the TRIPS rules, hence they represent an opportunity for countries to formulate one aspect of IPRs for their own circumstances (see Suthersanen 2006).

Table 2.4. The top ten U.K. IPRs scoreboard 2003.

	U.K. patents		U.K. trademarks		U.K. designs
NEC	209	Glaxo group	118	Oriental Weavers	90
Hewlett-Packard	196	Unilever	104	TY Inc.	90
Samsung	177	National Lottery	87	Mainetti	72
Schlumberger	172	British Telecom	82	Keel Toys	47
IBM	171	ICI	80	Nike	44
Baker Hughes Inc.	120	Westwood Consulting	59	Withit	38
Ericsson	115	Embraer Aeronautica	58	Mayfair Brassware	34
Motorola	113	Boots	46	Black & Decker	33
Visteon Corporation	112	GlaxoSmithKline	42	Nokia Corporation	33
Ford	100	Avon Products	40	Devonshire Statuary	30

Source. Patent Office (2003).

Notes. These figures relate to intellectual property rights for the U.K. territory obtained through the U.K. Patent Office. They do not include any further patent or trademark rights obtained by these firms via the EPO, some of which may include coverage in the U.K. territory.

important in Europe where patents are not generally allowed for software.[18] Copyright gives the creator exclusive right to copy, reproduce, distribute, adapt, perform, or display their work.

How Is Copyright Obtained?

Copyright is in general an *unregistered right*, meaning it is obtained automatically by the act of creating the work. Authors can use written statements for assertion of copyright, but this is not absolutely necessary as long as they have some evidence that they wrote the book. In the United States, however, prior to 1989 copyright did require registration (and renewal) and even after 1989 creators can and do register their copyright at the U.S. Copyright Office. There is no equivalent office in the United Kingdom, although the *Gowers Review* (HM Treasury 2006) did recommend that one be created.[19]

The requirement to register and renew copyright in the United States lapsed when the United States joined the Berne Convention in 1989 (the Convention prohibits mandatory registration). The Berne Convention was an agreement between countries that was started in 1886 at the instigation of Victor Hugo (a famous French poet and novelist, 1802–85). The Convention asserted the so-called moral rights of authors, rather than the Anglo-Saxon economic approach to copyright, and allowed protection for the author's life plus fifty years. In contrast, in the United States at the time copyright protection was twenty-eight years (renewable by fourteen years if the author was still alive). The Berne convention also applied "national treatment," meaning that the copyright laws for nationals had to be extended to foreigners. The fact that the United States did not respect national treatment was a contentious issue in the nineteenth century as foreign authors, such as Charles Dickens and Victor Hugo, had their work immediately copied and sold. Currently, around 163 countries are signatories to the Berne Convention.

Length, Breadth, and Coverage

Copyright of written and art works is now generally valid for the author's lifetime plus seventy years afterwards. This benefits the creator's heirs

---

[18] The situation regarding software patents is complex and evolving. In the United States software patents are much more common, with around 200,000 now having been granted (Bessen and Meurer 2008, p. 22) compared with around 30,000 by the EPO (European Commission Press Release, 2002, MEMO/02/32). Discussions of the legal and policy issues can be found in Bessen and Meurer (2008) and Guellec and van Pottelsberghe (2007).

[19] The fact that the United States has registration data means that economic analysis can be conducted (see Landes and Posner 2003, chapter 8). For example, for the period 1940–70 only around 5% of music recordings had their copyright renewed.

as well as the creator. Music and other recordings are copyright for fifty years, so a singer can find that his copyrights on recorded performances have expired before his death.[20] It is important to note here that copyright does not protect the ideas contained in a given work; rather it protects the particular way the idea is expressed in the document or artistic creation. However, it does cover a wide range of mediums for transmission, including the Internet. Thus it is a breach of copyright to post verbatim extracts from a work on the Web without the author's permission, but it may not be a breach of copyright to write up a parody of a serious article for the purpose of humor or satire.[21]

The geographical spread of copyright is worldwide in those countries in which copyright is recognized by the law (i.e., the countries that are signatories to the Berne Convention). So this right is very broad in geographical terms, but rather narrow in terms of what it protects. In addition there are the "fair use" (U.S. terminology) and "fair dealing" (U.K. terminology) exceptions. In short, these mean that most countries allow single-use exceptions to copyright for purposes of private study, research and education, archives, and reporting. These exceptions typically relate to reprographic copying and quotations and limit the amount of the work that can be copied or quoted within the law. An issue now facing copyright authorities is whether the fair use distinction can be preserved in the digital era.

A Market for Copyrights?

Because of the ease of copying with modern technologies, both legal markets and "gray" markets operate widely for copyright works. An example of a legal market would be the film rights paid to an author whose successful play or novel is being adapted for the screen. Other examples are music royalties paid by concert promoters, or by radio and television media, for performances of copyright works. Sometimes these royalties are paid to "collecting organizations" that gather up small amounts of payment not covered by bipartite contracts and pay these out to authors and songwriters.

---

[20] In the United Kingdom the singer Cliff Richard, who first started recording in the 1950s, has campaigned to increase the length of protection. The *Gowers Review* (HM Treasury 2006) rejected the arguments for such an extension but the European Commission proposed an extension from fifty to ninety-five years in July 2008.

[21] Parody is a complex area subject to a variety of judgements in the courts concerning whether a particular instance is a breach of copyright or an allowed "fair use." For example, in a 1994 case about a parody of a pop song, Campbell v. Acuff-Rose Music, Inc., the United States Supreme Court stated that a parody as a form of criticism or comment could be deemed to be fair use of a copyrighted work.

However, big problems exist in respect of "gray markets" circulating illegal or "pirated" copies. These arise from two sources. The first is that of private individuals when copying or passing on copies to a friend. In the famous case of Napster, a file-sharing service was used to copy music from peer to peer without payment of royalties during the late 1990s. This system was eventually challenged and ruled to be in breach of copyright. Subsequently, this very successful brand name was taken over by a public company, Roxio, who now supply music and other digital files using a pay service. The second type of infringement is the deliberate reproduction and supply of copies by countries that are not enforcing the law of copyright even if they notionally recognize it. China is one of the countries most often cited as a source of supply of such items, although its membership of the WTO since December 2001 has caused it to revisit the issue of control of such practices (see also section 12.5).

Who Uses Copyright?

Obviously this right is of importance to the media and publishing industries, but also successful individual authors and their families can gain large amounts of revenues from exercising this IPR. For economists trying to document the extent of use and value of copyright the problem is that, as this is an unregistered right, we have difficulty in tracing how much of it exists and the size of the revenue flows generated by this IPR (see Corrigan and Rogers (2005) for a full survey).

Indirect evidence of the value of copyright is provided by cases of infringement that are taken through the courts, but these are only a selection of copyrights that have been subject to serious challenge and where it is worthwhile to spend large amounts on lawyers' fees in their enforcement. Many of these cases are settled out of court before coming to a final judgement, so details of the payments made in settlement are not always known. Another small proportion of the value of copyright is documented by the flows of revenue into the accounts of the authors' collecting societies. Again this is sufficiently partial to be of limited use in assessing the true value of copyright as an IPR. Government reports on innovation are often reduced to citing the percentage of GDP generated in those sectors for which copyright is an important and relevant form of intellectual property, as an indicator of the importance of this IPR.

2.7 Further Questions about IPRs

Is Patenting Always the Best Route to Protection?

As noted above, a patent application requires the inventor to disclose whatever they wish to protect. In contrast, a firm may choose to keep its new knowledge as a *trade secret*, which is also protected in law. Thus a firm that chooses not to patent can obtain the backing of the law relating to trade secrets for exercising control of its private information. So even in an industry producing the types of innovations that might be patented, firms do not always go down this route if they consider that their best interests are served by keeping their inventions secret.

To qualify in law as a trade secret there must be *information* that generates some *economic advantage*, which is *not generally known* outside the firm, and which is the subject of *effort to maintain its secrecy* in the firm. The greatest benefit of taking this alternative route to patenting is that the knowledge can be protected indefinitely. Trade secrets or confidential information can be of a technical nature, but this category of intangible assets also covers much business or market information. Examples of technical information that could be candidates for IPRs include designs for specialized equipment, formulas and recipes for food products, novel methods of manufacture, and computer software. By contrast, business information such as future plans for prices and products, market predictions, input costs, and personnel contracts are significant elements of confidential information that could not easily be used to gain IPRs.

Trade secrecy law empowers firms to take reasonable steps to prevent acts of industrial espionage to steal its secrets by offering it the chance to seek redress if leakage occurs. The firm can require its employees to sign contracts that prohibit the disclosure of confidential information to competitors. Even workers leaving the firm's employment can be bound over not to disclose such information. The law also provides for the right to sell or purchase confidential "know-how" under contract without fear of loss. Thus contracts for technical services can include confidentiality clauses to prevent leakages. Clearly, keeping technical information secret is only a good strategy if reverse engineering or other analysis, such as chemical identification of the components of the product, is difficult to achieve. A famous example is the recipe for Coca Cola, which has never formally been disclosed, although clearly some substitute brands come close to mimicking this product.

If IPRs Are Offered, Should They Be of Uniform Length?

Or, if not, does economic theory offer a guide to varying the length of the right? The basic rationale of awarding an IPR is to provide an incentive to innovate or, more specifically, to undertake R&D. The longer the length of protection, the higher this incentive will be. However, once awarded,

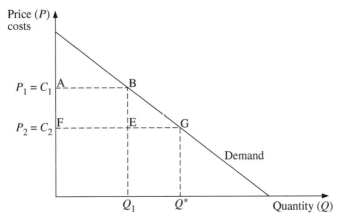

Figure 2.2. Process innovation in a competitive market.

an IPR will tend to raise the price paid by consumers and limit the output of the good. Hence, the longer the protection, the longer prices will stay high (assuming that prices fall when the IPR expires). The basic trade-off, between encouraging innovation and lowering prices as soon as possible, suggests a policy of only providing just enough incentive to ensure the innovation occurs. The problem with this is that different innovations have different costs (depending on the nature of R&D) and different profit potential (depending on demand) and no one knows these in advance. This means IPRs need to have some uniform length, at least across innovations with similar R&D cost structures and demand outcomes. Box 2.1 discusses how economists have investigated the optimal patent length, but in the main text we will simply state two general principles.

- The duration of protection should vary according to the nature of demand for the product, being short for items with price elastic demand and longer for inelastic demand. This means that the IPR system should reserve longer protection for items without close substitutes to minimize the welfare loss to society of the patent monopoly.

- The duration of protection should vary with the marginal cost of the R&D required to make a breakthrough, so that the reward to the inventor is proportional to the marginal resource investment, being longer for those that are most costly.

This said, there are some major practical problems with applying these principles, hence IPR policy in practice is largely one of "one size fits all."

Box 2.1. The optimal length of patent protection.

Figure 2.2 shows a fall in costs, from C_1 to C_2, associated with a new process innovation. A patent can protect the innovation for T years. Before the innovation we assume that the price in the market was $P_1 = C_1$ (i.e., the market was perfectly competitive). After the innovation we assume that the innovator licenses the innovation and receives royalties (profits) of ABFE. We know from the discussion in chapter 1, and in section 2.2, that society would prefer to have amount Q^* produced so that welfare is maximized. This will happen when the patent expires. During the patent, producing at Q_1 means that area BEG is lost consumer surplus; this area BEG is normally called the *deadweight loss*. (Formally, welfare is defined as consumer surplus plus producer surplus, but in this example with constant marginal and average costs there is no producer surplus.)

In order to understand the policy choice we must assume some relationship between R&D and cost reduction. The standard assumption made is that more R&D generates more process innovation, in our example represented by a lower C_2, but at a diminishing rate. Hence, if we increase T, firms will allocate more to R&D, resulting in more process innovations (although the marginal effect on cost reduction will become smaller and smaller). This suggests that increasing T is a good idea since there will be more process innovation. However, as T is increased, the deadweight loss is suffered for a longer period, which is not good for welfare. There is, therefore, a trade-off: longer T stimulates more R&D and more innovation, but it causes the deadweight loss to be suffered for longer.

As in much of economics, given this trade-off, we can find the optimal T if we know all of the parameters and functions involved. The intuition is that we find the specific T^* where the marginal benefit from increasing T (more innovation and profits) equals the marginal cost to welfare from prolonging the deadweight loss. To find T^* we need to known two important relationships. The first is the precise relationship, or functional form, between R&D and cost reduction. When invention is easy and big cost reductions can be achieved with small R&D, then T^* is short. The second is the nature of demand, and specifically the demand elasticity. To see this, note that the area of the triangle BEG—the deadweight loss—depends on the slope of the demand curve. More generally, highly elastic demand curves will create larger deadweight losses and, ceteris paribus, this will mean shorter T^*.

Nordhaus (1969) provides the first analysis of optimal patent life and Scherer (1972) extends this treatment as well as providing a graphical treatment. Others have extended the discussion into the optimal breadth of patents (Klemperer 1990) and also considered what is optimal when there is duplication in R&D due to a patent race (Wright 1983; Gilbert and Newbery 1983). Scotchmer (2004), Stoneman (1987), and Tirole (1988) give textbook treatments.

Are There Alternative Ways of Providing Incentives to Innovate?

The most frequently used alternative instrument is that of an R&D subsidy. Does the intellectual property policy agency need to offer incentives via both IPRs and R&D subsidy? We have already demonstrated in figure 2.1 that an IPR owner does not capture the full social reward of his invention even within the market for the product and we have also noted the existence of knowledge spillovers to other inventive firms. R&D also produces innovations that can be either genuinely novel innovation likely to attract an IPR, or incremental innovation, building on recent breakthroughs but not attracting any patents. In addition, R&D supports the firm's ability to keep up with the field in "best-practice" technology and "state-of-the-art" product design via adoption and learning from others (Cohen and Levinthal 1989; Griffith et al. 2004). So even if the firm never gets to the front as an innovator, it can benefit both itself and the wider economy if it undertakes R&D.

These arguments indicate that R&D subsidies and IPRs can be complementary incentive policies for innovation, as R&D covers a wider range of socially beneficial activity than that resulting in a patent or other IPR. Even this policy combination of IPRs with an R&D subsidy may not reach all the parts of the economy engaging in innovative activity. Service-sector firms report few patents and very little R&D, but have become increasingly innovative if judged by their applications for new trademarks (see Greenhalgh and Rogers 2008).

2.8 Conclusions

This chapter began with an analysis of the welfare effects of a patent. The analysis showed that a patent does create incentives to innovate but these incentives are lower than the full social benefit of the innovation. This situation is referred to as the appropriability problem and represents a residual market failure even in the presence of an instrument designed to eliminate market failure.

The main part of this chapter was devoted to a discussion of each of the major types of IPRs. We described in detail what can be protected under each IPR and how each IPR can be used.[22] It should be clear that there is a wide variety of complex IPRs that offer opportunities for profits to firms that invent and innovate. Each system of rights has its strengths and weaknesses, so these legal instruments are the subject of constant review by lawyers, economists, and business analysts to see if they are fit for purpose. Their fundamental purpose is to stimulate invention, innovation, creativity, and R&D and to achieve technology improvements that benefit a wide range of people and businesses in the long run.

In the last section we started the process of examining whether IPRs are "fit for purpose" by looking at whether patents are the best route to protection, what is the optimal patent length, and how R&D subsidies fit into the picture. The question of how IPRs function and whether they are effective policy instruments is examined in more depth in subsequent chapters.

Keywords

Incentive effects.

Appropriability.

Patents, trademarks, designs, copyright.

Welfare and consumer surplus.

Optimal length of protection.

Trade secrecy and other means of appropriation.

Questions for Discussion

(1) How does intellectual property differ from tangible property, such as a house or a car?

(2) Do patents provide socially optimal incentives?

(3) Why do firms use trademarks?

(4) Should copyright be made shorter or longer than at present?

(5) Why do different industries make use of different types of rights?

(6) What factors influence the optimal length of an intellectual property right?

---

[22] For further information on systems of IPRs, see the Web sites of the EPO (www.epo.org), the USPTO (www.uspto.gov), and the U.K. Intellectual Property Office (www.ipo.gov.uk).

References

Arora, A., A. Fosfuri, and A. Gambardella. 2001. *Markets for Technology: The Economics of Innovation and Corporate Strategy.* Cambridge, MA: MIT Press.

Bessen, J., and M. J. Meurer. 2008. *Patent Failure: How Judges, Bureaucrats, and Lawyers Put Innovators at Risk.* Princeton University Press.

Choi, J. 1998. Brand extension as informational leverage. *Review of Economic Studies* 65:655–69.

Cohen, W., and D. Levinthal. 1989. Innovation and learning: the two faces of R&D. *Economic Journal* 99:569–96.

Corrigan, R., and Rogers, M. 2005. The economics of copyright. *World Economics: The Journal of Current Economic Analysis and Policy* 6(3):53–174.

Dent, S., P. Jensen, S. Waller, and E. Webster. 2006. Research use of patented knowledge: a review. STI Working Paper 2006/2, OECD Directorate for Science, Technology and Industry.

Gilbert, R., and D. Newbery. 1982. Pre-emptive patenting and the persistence of monopoly. *American Economic Review* 72:514–26.

Greenhalgh, C. A., and M. Rogers. 2008. Intellectual property activity by service sector and manufacturing firms in the UK, 1996–2000. In *The Evolution of Business Knowledge* (ed. H. Scarbrough). Oxford University Press.

Griffith, R., S. Redding, and J. Van Reenen. 2004. Mapping the two faces of R&D: productivity growth in a panel of OECD countries. *Review of Economic Statistics* 86(4):883–95.

Guellec, D., and B. van Pottelsberghe. 2007. *The Economics of the European Patent System.* Oxford University Press.

HM Treasury. 2006. *Gowers Review of Intellectual Property.* London: Her Majesty's Stationery Office.

Klemperer, P. 1990. How broad should the scope of patents be? *Rand Journal of Economics* 21:113–30.

Landes, W. M., and R. A. Posner. 1987. Trademark law: an economic perspective. *Journal of Law and Economics* 30(2):265–309.

——. 2003. *The Economic Structure of Intellectual Property Law.* Boston, MA: Belknap/Harvard University Press.

MacLeod, C. 1988. *Inventing the Industrial Revolution: The English Patent System, 1660–1800.* Cambridge University Press.

Mostert, F. 2007. *From Edison to iPod: Protect your Ideas and Make Money.* London: Dorling Kindersley.

Nordhaus, W. D. 1969. *Invention, Growth and Welfare.* Cambridge, MA: MIT Press.

Patent Office. 2003. *Facts and Figures.* London: Her Majesty's Stationery Office.

Ramello, G. 2006. What's in a sign? Trademark law and economic theory. *Journal of Economic Surveys* 20(4):547–65.

Scherer, F. 1972. Nordhaus' theory of optimal patent life: a geometric reinterpretation. *American Economic Review* 62(3):422–27.

Scotchmer, S. 2004. *Innovation and Incentives.* Cambridge, MA: MIT Press.

Stoneman, P. 1987. *The Economic Analysis of Technology Policy.* Oxford University Press.

Suthersanen, U. 2006. Utility models and innovation in developing countries. Issue Paper Number 13, International Centre for Trade and Sustainable Development, Geneva.

Tadelis, S. 1999. What's in a name? Reputation as a tradeable asset. *American Economic Review* 89(3):548–63.

Tirole, J. 1988. *The Theory of Industrial Organization.* Cambridge, MA: MIT Press.

Wright, B. 1983. The economics of invention incentives: patents, prizes and research contracts. *American Economic Review* 73(4):691–707.

3

The Measurement of Innovation, Productivity, and Growth

3.1 Introduction

The first part of this chapter explores the difficult question of how to observe and measure the innovation that is taking place in firms and industries. Before we can assess empirically the impact of innovation on economic activity we have to define and measure it using appropriate quantitative indicators. As we saw in chapter 1 (see figure 1.1), the innovation process is lengthy and complex. Some of the measures we develop will be snapshots taken at one point in the complex process from scientific invention to commercial innovation and, finally, to widespread diffusion. Some of the indicators will be of inputs into the innovation process, which is subject to a large amount of uncertainty in its output. Other indicators may be closer to measures of achieved output from innovative effort, but there are a variety of such proxy measures and each of these proxies has a varying degree of coverage across different sectors and industries. To gain anything approaching a full picture we shall have to look at a wide range of measures of innovation. Even then some elements of innovative activity will remain beyond our observation.

The second part of this chapter looks at the measurement of productivity and economic growth. Measurement issues at the firm, industry, and economy level are considered. One of the aims is to define the concepts (and jargon) relating to productivity and growth, as these can create confusion. For example, we discuss the meaning of total factor productivity and how quality adjustment affects our view of growth. There is also a comparison of the growth rates in major and emerging markets. The objective is to provide readers with a solid background in the definitions, measurement issues, and recent trends in productivity and growth.

3.2   How Can Innovation Be Measured?

Innovation Surveys

One way of determining how much firms are innovating is to ask them about their activities. This has been done on a regular basis in recent years in Europe, where each country has conducted a Community Innovation Survey (CIS). Although this sounds like a straightforward way to generate data, there are a number of complexities in ensuring that the definition of innovation is the same in each country and that firms respond appropriately. When the CIS began in 1991, the questionnaire only asked firms what new products and processes they had introduced, without distinguishing whether or not these activities were new to the market rather than just new to the firm. This confuses what many economists consider to be genuine innovative activity (in being first to market) with the adoption of best practice introduced elsewhere, the latter being something economists call the diffusion of innovation (again see figure 1.1). Later CIS surveys have added further questions to distinguish which of the firms' innovations were new to the market or industry, but many government publications tend to quote the all-inclusive measure, which makes firms seem overly innovative.[1]

Another suggestion for using data generated by firms to measure their innovation activity is called "literature-based innovation output indicators." This type of data set can be built up by monitoring press releases about new products that are sent by firms to trade and technical journals.[2] The advantage claimed for this source of information is that small firms, which may be excluded by innovation surveys, will be represented in data gleaned from these searches.[3] Even though the proportion of very small firms that innovate is quite low, because there are so many such firms, this can still amount to a significant share of innovation in a given sector or an economy. The U.S. Small Business Innovation database looked at 8,072 innovations in 1982 and this gave rise to substantial research on causes and outcomes (e.g., Acs and Audretsch 1990). The U.K. Science Policy Research Unit (SPRU) database used a panel of industry experts to assess the most important innovations by any U.K.

---

[1] For definitions now in use see OECD/Eurostat (2005). This manual still uses "new to the firm" as the minimum definition of innovation, while acknowledging that this includes the diffusion of innovation as well as its creation.

[2] Gort and Klepper (1982) provide an early example using *Thomas' Register of American Manufactures*.

[3] In the Community Innovation Survey many countries exclude firms with less than ten employees.

firm over the period 1945–83. The SPRU database of 4,300 major innovations has subsequently been used for a variety of empirical research (e.g., Geroski 1990).

Assessing the "Inputs" to Innovation

Conceptually, we can think of innovation requiring one or more inputs. The most important input is often thought to be R&D. Firms conduct R&D by employing skilled personnel (in addition to those needed for production) and also by using specialized equipment. In some, but not all, firms, separate accounts are kept of these expenditures on R&D activity. Separate R&D accounting is more likely in larger firms and is also more likely in countries where the government has introduced tax incentives to encourage R&D.[4]

The recorded level of R&D expenditure by firms gives us our first proxy of innovative activity.[5] It is a "proxy" since R&D spending does not measure successful outputs from the effort to invent and design new products and processes. However, analysis shows that much of R&D expenditure is D (development) rather than R (research), as any novel technology has to be embedded in the firm's production activity and product range. So the effort expended in bringing new products and processes to market may be quite well measured by R&D expenditure in many sectors of the economy. Even so, the high uncertainty of outcomes means that not all R&D expenditure will lead to innovation. In addition, there may be a time lag between the expenditure of resources on R&D activity and the delivery of a commercially viable product, particularly in industries with stringent product safety testing such as those for new drugs.[6] Thus, even if R&D expenditure is useful as an indicator of broad differences between firms and industries in their rates of innovation, it is not able to identify the precise level and timing of innovation.

R&D activity within a firm can also help it to learn from its competitors and this contributes to the diffusion of new technology. Many authors have noted what can be termed "the two faces of R&D."[7] It can be argued that firms in rapidly developing technology fields need to do R&D—if they are not at the best-practice frontier—in order to understand what

---

[4] Such tax incentives are introduced to try to increase R&D expenditures (see chapters 1 and 11).

[5] See the discussion and survey in Griliches (1990). He discusses the origins of the idea that R&D is an input into a "production function for knowledge," something that theoretical growth models often use (see chapter 8). Pavitt (1985) challenged this interpretation of R&D expenditure as an input measure.

[6] Empirical studies show that R&D can have an impact on output or profits for up to ten years after expenditure (see Lev and Sougiannis 1996).

[7] Work by Cohen and Levinthal (1989) is often cited as the seminal article.

their competitors have invented and to be able to adopt best-practice technology and design. Griffith et al. (2004) used the "two faces" concept of R&D to explore relationships between R&D and industrial productivity in twelve OECD countries. They find that countries behind the frontier increase their productivity growth by doing R&D.[8] Using this approach R&D can be seen partly as a proxy measure of the flows of ideas between firms and countries. The innovative capability of a firm, and its absorptive capacity for new technology, is also signalled by the number of *highly skilled workers* employed, particularly scientists and engineers. This indicator is another input measure of innovation activity alongside R&D expenditure.

Measuring "Outputs" from Innovation

The generation of IPRs, which try to ensure that firms can profit from R&D before their inventions are copied, provides another measure of innovation. As we saw in chapter 2, there are several important types of IPRs and these are used with varying intensity by different sectors of the economy. In the economic analysis of innovation, patent statistics have been very widely analyzed as a proxy for innovation "output."[9] In contrast, trademarks and designs have not enjoyed broad coverage in the economic literature as innovation measures, even though they are registered in a wider range of sectors than are patents.

The positive benefits of patents as indicators of innovation are:

- patents indicate an invention that is often a precursor to an innovation;
- they represent inventions with an expected value above the cost of patenting;
- the invention has been subjected to a test for novelty and nonobviousness;
- patents are classified by technical fields providing information about changes in the directions of invention;
- data are available for many countries and for long time periods.

---

[8] Specifically, they use "total factor productivity (TFP)" (see discussion below) and model its growth as depending on R&D, and the interaction of R&D with the TFP gap to the frontier country. They also include trade and human capital to explain TFP growth via catch-up, finding that only human capital (proxied by education attainment data) is significant.

[9] For early studies of patents as indicators of innovation see Pavitt (1982, 1985); for more recent surveys see Archibugi (1992), Patel and Pavitt (1995), and Griliches (1990). A seminal work on patents was Schmookler (1966).

The disadvantages of using patents as innovation indicators are:

- patents indicate inventions and these may not become innovations;
- not all inventions are patented by firms due to the alternative of trade secrecy;
- some types of inventions cannot be patented;
- sectors vary in the intensity of use made of the patent system;
- some patents are used as a purely anticompetitive strategy;
- different countries have stricter or looser regimes relating to patent awards.

Given this list of problems it is surprising that there have been few attempts to generate other types of data relating to intellectual property. Specifically, the use of trademarks appears to have some potential and the following factors are relevant.

- Registration of trademarks requires a fee to be paid, hence their registration signals a net expected value.
- Trademarks are used extensively in every sector, whereas patents are dominated by the manufacturing sector.
- Trademarks will be sought for more minor innovations than patents, such as new varieties of existing products, as there is no novelty test.[10]
- New and small firms are much more likely to use trademarks.

In a study of the U.K. economy in the late 1990s, Greenhalgh and Rogers (2008) demonstrate that firms in service sectors such as retailing, and hotels and catering, matched or exceeded manufacturing firms in their propensity to register U.K. trademarks (see table 2.1), while firms in all sectors typically obtained vastly more trademarks than patents within a five-year period. These findings indicate that there is merit in looking at both trademark and patent data.

The Use of an Innovation Index

The large number of potential measures of innovation, as well as their complex and overlapping nature, has led to the development of methods for combining these into an innovation index. Such an index can be calculated at the firm, industry, and country level. In short, an innovation index seeks to combine a number of other measures into a single

---

[10] The downside of this is that trademarks may be associated with some elements that would be better described as diffusion rather than innovation, if the products are close imitations of existing ones.

figure. A major problem in constructing any such index is how to combine the measures. One solution to this problem is to form a weighted sum according to the importance of each measure on some performance measure. For example, Feeny and Rogers (2003) combine information on R&D, patents, and trademarks to construct an innovation index for Australian firms. The weights they use are based on regression analysis of the impact of the components on the firm's market value.[11] Box 3.1 discusses the various measures used in constructing the country-level European Innovation Scoreboard. Many other indices have been constructed but they all follow similar principles.

Box 3.1. Components of the European Innovation Scoreboard in 2006.

Many different innovation scoreboards have been created comparing firms, countries, and even cities. The basic method is to collate various different variables and then combine these into an index. Below we set out the components of the European Innovation Scoreboard.

1. Input: Innovation Drivers.

   (i) Science and engineering graduates per 1,000 population aged 20–29 Eurostat.

   (ii) Population with tertiary education per 100 population aged 25–64 Eurostat, OECD.

   (iii) Broadband penetration rate (number of broadband lines per 100 population) Eurostat.

   (iv) Participation in lifelong learning per 100 population aged 25–64 Eurostat.

   (v) Youth education attainment level (percentage of population aged 20–24 having completed at least upper secondary education) Eurostat.

2. Input: Knowledge Creation.

   (i) Public R&D expenditures (percentage of GDP) Eurostat, OECD.

   (ii) Business R&D expenditures (percentage of GDP) Eurostat, OECD.

   (iii) Share of medium–high-tech and high-tech R&D (percentage of manufacturing R&D expenditures) Eurostat, OECD.

   (iv) Share of enterprises receiving public funding for innovation Eurostat (CIS4).

---

[11] In fact, they also analyze the association of design applications with market value but, finding no significant association, design applications are dropped from the innovation index (i.e., they are given a weight of zero).

3. Input: Innovation and Entrepreneurship.

(i) Small and medium-sized enterprises (SMEs) innovating in-house (percentage of all SMEs) Eurostat (CIS3).

(ii) Innovative SMEs cooperating with others (percentage of all SMEs) Eurostat (CIS4).

(iii) Innovation expenditures (percentage of total turnover) Eurostat (CIS4).

(iv) Early-stage venture capital (percentage of GDP) Eurostat.

(v) Information and communication technology (ICT) expenditures (percentage of GDP) Eurostat.

(vi) SMEs using organizational innovation (percentage of all SMEs) Eurostat (CIS4).

4. Output: Applications.

(i) Employment in high-tech services (percentage of total workforce) Eurostat.

(ii) Exports of high-technology products as a share of total exports Eurostat.

(iii) Sales of new-to-market products (percentage of total turnover) Eurostat (CIS4).

(iv) Sales of new-to-firm products (percentage of total turnover) Eurostat (CIS4).

(v) Employment in medium–high and high-tech manufacturing (percentage of total workforce) Eurostat.

5. Output: Intellectual Property.

(i) EPO patents per million population Eurostat.

(ii) USPTO patents per million population Eurostat, OECD.

(iii) Triadic patent families per million population Eurostat, OECD.

(iv) New community trademarks per million population OHIM8.

(v) New community designs per million population OHIM7.

The source of the data for the variables is shown at the end of each line (e.g., Eurostat, OECD, the CIS, and the Office for Harmonization in the Internal Market (OHIM)). It is clear that R&D data make a substantial contribution, with component 2 having three different measures (public, business, and medium–high-tech). Also, IPRs are important with variables for patents and trademarks. "Triadic patent families" (5(iii)) refers to a patent that has been granted in the EPO, the Japanese Patent Office (JPO), and the USPTO. In addition, looking through the list we can see that education, communications, SME activity, and venture capital are also represented. Chapter 4 discusses the fact that innovation needs to be supported by a wide range of activities in an economy.

3.3 Illustrations of Innovation Statistics

Innovation Survey Data

As discussed above, innovation surveys are used to gather data direct from firms. Many small surveys are conducted by government departments, but the most ambitious in recent years are the Community Innovation Surveys. Table 3.1 shows data on innovative activities from CIS3, which was conducted in 2001 and asked about the period 1998–2000. The first column in the table shows the percentage of firms that reported any innovation activity based on a question about whether they had introduced any product or process innovation that was new to the firm. Note that this is the broadest measure and it potentially includes imitation and adoption. As can be seen, these percentages are quite high and also vary substantially across countries.

The subsequent columns of table 3.1 look at different aspects that are closer to the economic definition of innovation. It is clear, for example, that "new-to-market product innovations" are much less common: for example, only 6% of U.K. firms reported such an innovation over the period 1998–2000, although most of the other EU countries reported figures twice as high. These statistics can be useful in assessing country performance, but it is important to stress that there may not be consistency across countries. For example, the response rate to the survey varied from 21% to 63% of firms.

R&D in the EU, the United States, and Japan

To illustrate the levels of R&D taking place in different countries it is common to look at the share of GDP devoted to this activity. However, the absolute amount or "scale" of activity also matters for R&D since, as discussed in chapter 1, the knowledge created by R&D can be regarded as a "public good." Alternatively, we can say that R&D produces spillovers (or positive externalities). Spillovers from R&D are more likely to spread within countries due to direct contacts between inventors, and most often a common language, than they are to spread across country

Table 3.1. Percentage of firms involved in innovative
activities over the period 1998–2000.

	Innovative activities	Product innovation	New-to-market product innovation	Process innovation
Belgium	50	40	14	31
Denmark	44	37	19	26
France	41	29	10	21
Germany	61	42	13	34
Italy	36	25	14	26
Sweden	47	32	12	20
U.K.	36	21	6	17

Source. Community Innovation Survey 3 data, reported in Lucking (2004).

Notes. The table shows the percentage of firms (>10 employees) that reported innovations over the period 1998–2000. The percentages are based on survey data of a subsample of firms within each country. Note that the response rate for the survey varied dramatically across countries, from 21% in Germany to 63% in France, which implies difficulties in comparing data across countries.

Table 3.2. R&D in Europe, Japan, and the United States.

Country	R&D/GDP (%)	Value of R&D (millions of euros)	Annual growth of R&D (%)
EU15	1.99*	149,231	4.31*
EU25	1.93*	154,941	3.98*
Germany	2.50	43,507	2.70
France	2.19	27,727	2.36
U.K.	1.87*	23,314	3.52*
Japan	3.12*	87,968	2.18*
U.S.	2.76	227,030	2.69

Source. Frank (2005).

Notes. Ratios of R&D to GDP are for 2003 (or 2002 when asterisked). The values of R&D quoted are all for 2002 in constant 1995 prices, converted to euros using purchasing power standards of comparable goods and services. Growth of R&D is annual average growth in real value from 1998 to 2003 (or from 1998 to 2002 when asterisked).

boundaries.[12] Table 3.2 shows the GDP share, the absolute value, and the recent annual growth rates of R&D in Europe, Japan, and the United States.

---

[12] The Griffith et al. (2004) study discussed above is one empirical study of R&D spillovers between countries. Other important studies include Coe and Helpman (1995) and Keller (2002). These types of studies tend to find that while international R&D spillovers are important there is still a domestic economy bias. The wider issue of international knowledge spillovers is discussed in Rogers (2003).

The share of GDP devoted to R&D is highest in Japan at more than 3%, followed by the United States with 2.75%, while the average for the EU15 countries is close to 2%.[13] These differences have existed for many years and, feeling the need to catch up, the EU has adopted a target of reaching an R&D intensity of 3% by 2010.[14] At present, few countries within Europe are within sight of this target; Sweden and Finland are two small countries with ratios of 4.27% and 3.51%, respectively, but in absolute spending terms Germany, France, and the United Kingdom are the three largest R&D spenders in Europe (accounting for around 60% of total R&D in the EU). Thus the EU average share of GDP devoted to R&D is driven by these three big spenders. Historically, most reported R&D has taken place in manufacturing rather than services, so the amount of spending will vary depending on the balance of the economy.[15]

The absolute level of R&D spending in the United States has historically been more than twice that in any other individual country, with Japan taking second place in the country rankings and Germany coming third. In the period since the mid 1990s, the United States has drawn further ahead as its annual rate of real R&D spending grew by 38% from 1994 to 2000 (see Frank 2005, graph 3). Even when compared with the combined forces of the EU15, its spending is now 50% higher than Europe and it has drawn away from Japan to reach a level of 2.5 times Japanese R&D. Within Europe, Germany remains the "strong man" in R&D terms, spending nearly 60% more than France and 87% more than the United Kingdom.

These different amounts of spending are driven by both the size of these economies and by the currently higher shares of GDP devoted to R&D by the top three players in the world. Even so, the rates of growth in absolute spending varied inversely with the R&D share during 1998–2003, suggesting that serious efforts to catch up (at least in R&D/GDP shares) are being made by the United Kingdom and the lower-spending EU countries.

Workers in R&D

The share of the labor force classified as R&D personnel is generally lower than the share of GDP devoted to R&D expenditure in advanced

---

[13] These data relate to the gross expenditure on R&D, which includes spending by both private business and government. In chapter 4 we examine this breakdown between public and private spending.

[14] This is part of the Lisbon Agenda set out by the EU in March 2000.

[15] For example, in 2005 manufacturing accounted for around 70% of total R&D in the United States and around 73% of R&D in the United Kingdom (National Science Foundation 2007; Office of National Statistics 2006).

Table 3.3. R&D personnel in Europe and Japan in 2004.

Country	R&D personnel/ labor force (%)	R&D personnel (FTEs)	Share working in BES (%)	Share working in GOV (%)	Share working in HES (%)
EU25	1.49	2,040,667	53.7	14.3	31.0
EU15	1.59	1,867,505	56.2	13.2	29.5
Germany	1.85	469,100	63.5	15.3	21.1
France	1.71*	346,078*	55.8*	14.8*	27.5*
Japan	1.66*	882,414	65.8	7.0	25.4

Sources. Column 1 is from figure 3.2 of Eurostat (2007); this ratio is based on head count figures; FTE ("full time equivalent") reflects figures adjusted for part-time working. Column 2 is extracted, and columns 3–5 are calculated, from table 3.1 of Eurostat (2007).

Notes. "BES" is the business enterprise sector, "GOV" is the public sector, and "HES" is the university sector. Asterisked figures are for 2003. Figures are not available on these definitions for the United States or the United Kingdom.

countries, as shown by comparing table 3.3 with table 3.2. We would expect this since the average wage of an R&D worker exceeds that in the labor force as a whole, so their cost share of the wage bill, and hence of GDP, will be higher than their share of a head count of workers. Also, it seems likely that some employees, who are in fact working to test and market new products and processes, are not recorded by firms as being part of their skilled R&D workforce, which it sees as limited to those engaged in inventing and designing novel items.[16] It is also possible that R&D is more capital intensive than is typical production activity across the nation. What is more surprising is that the rank order of the shares of R&D personnel across nations differs from that of expenditure shares, with Japan now ranking lower than Germany and France. Even so, the ratios of R&D personnel/labor force were 2.51% in Sweden (2003)

---

[16] Obtaining information on hidden R&D workers is, by definition, not easy. Historically, significant growth in formal R&D departments is associated with U.S. firms in the early twentieth century and this continued after World War II (Nelson and Wright 1992). Firms such as General Electric, Du Pont, and Kodak set up formal R&D laboratories before World War I. After World War II there was a surge in U.S. companies setting up R&D departments (Nelson and Wright 1992, p. 1951). The formalization of R&D may also raise reported R&D expenditures, even if overall "research and development" expenditures remain constant; hence comparing data across time periods, and across countries, can be problematic. Jones (1995, p. 760), for example, notes that the number of reported scientists and engineers working in R&D increased fivefold between 1950 and 1987, and uses this as evidence that Romer-type R&D models (see chapter 8) are not realistic. However, it is difficult to assess accurately changes in R&D effort in a period when formal R&D departments are being created. Nevertheless, Nelson and Wright and others argue that the United States developed a world-beating research infrastructure in the twentieth century (see also Rosenberg 1994).

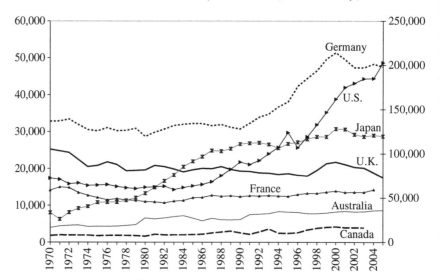

Figure 3.1. Patent applications by domestic residents in leading economies (note that the scale for the United States and Japan is on the right-hand axis).

Source. World Intellectual Property Organization (www.wipo.int/ipstats/en).

and 3.24% in Finland (2004) according to Eurostat (2007), showing these two countries as the most innovation intensive, as seen above for R&D expenditure.

Trends in Intellectual Property Rights by Country

Figures 3.1 and 3.2 show the trends in patent and trademark applications by domestic residents in seven major countries since 1970. As the numbers of U.S. and Japanese applications are much larger, being in the order of three to four times the levels in other high-activity countries, their values are shown on the right-hand axis in each figure. In addition, the Japanese patent applications have been scaled down by a factor of three, since each Japanese patent is commonly thought to represent around one third of a U.S. patent (i.e., the Japanese system breaks down an invention into more discrete stages).[17]

---

[17] Dividing Japanese patent applications by three in an attempt to allow international comparisons is clearly crude. The background is that all patent applications consist of a number of "claims," which define the subject matter of the invention. Before 1988 most Japanese patents contained only one claim, whereas other countries allowed multiple claims. This system was known as "sashimi"—or "thinly sliced"—after a Japanese fish delicacy. A change to the Japanese patent system in 1988 allowed multiple, dependent claims, which aligned Japan with other major countries. This implies that it is difficult to compare pre- and post-1988 data on patent applications. Sakakibara and Branstetter (1999) are the source of the above information. They also analyze whether the 1988 reforms had a significant positive impact on patenting activity in Japan. They find little evidence that it did.

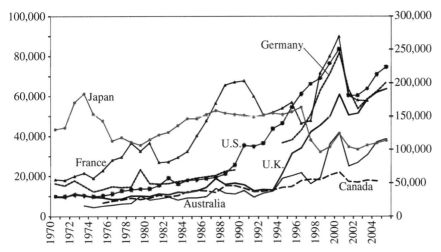

Figure 3.2. Trademark applications by domestic residents in leading economies (note that the scale for the United States and Japan is on the right-hand axis).

Source. World Intellectual Property Organization (www.wipo.int/ipstats/en).

Figure 3.1 shows that patent applications started to rise in Japan and the United States in the 1980s, but this growth was not seen in other countries. Whereas Japan's patenting levels flattened out in the 1990s, U.S. patenting activity accelerated in the 1990s. The rapid rise in U.S. patenting has led to a debate over whether the U.S. patent system is functioning properly (see Jaffe and Lerner (2004), Hall (2005), and the discussion in chapter 11 for analysis). However, comparing these patent figures with national trends in absolute R&D spending shows that the United States significantly increased its innovative activity on both the R&D measure and the patent measure during the 1990s. Germany is the only other country to show significant growth in patents in the 1990s, while in the United Kingdom there is, if anything, a slight downward trend in the rate of patenting since 1970.

Figure 3.2 shows trademark applications by domestic residents. Overall, these series are more volatile than those for patents. This volatility reflects, in part, the fact that trademarks are an indicator of new product innovation and marketing activity, which tend to react to economic conditions, and not of inventive effort, which is more continuous.[18] Most of the countries show strong growth in the 1990s, with a sudden correction in 2000, which was a point of retrenchment after what was termed the "dot-com" boom of the late 1990s.

---

[18] We discuss the question of whether new product introductions tend to be procyclical in chapter 6.

3.4 Productivity at the Firm, Industry, and Economy Level

Our interest throughout this book is to link together the microeconomics of innovation with the macroeconomics of economic growth. Having explored the complexities involved in measuring microinnovation, we now consider some indicators of firm, industry, and macroeconomic growth related to technological change. This section outlines some of the key issues encountered when trying to measure and compare productivity levels and growth rates across firms, industries, and economies.

Partial and Total Factor Productivity

While the term productivity is used widely, there is often confusion as to its precise meaning. In the most basic sense, productivity means "output per unit of input." The definitions of output and input can vary widely, hence the possibility of confusion. As an example, a car factory could measure the number of cars produced per worker in a year (or per week, etc.). This is a very crude measure of labor productivity, as it does not adjust for any of the complementary factors used in production.[19] Clearly, workers with good equipment and top-quality inputs will produce more than those without good tools and raw materials. Alternatively, the factory could measure cars per million dollars of capital—a crude measure of capital productivity. Again we can easily imagine that a firm that employs more workers with higher skills will utilize its capital more efficiently and produce more cars.

For the market sector, output is normally defined in monetary terms and, specifically, as value added. Value added is defined as sales minus raw materials used, as this indicates what the firm has truly produced when transforming the raw materials into the final product. It is, therefore, analogous to GDP at the economy level. In nonmarket sectors, such as education and law enforcement, output cannot be measured in monetary units. This makes measuring productivity more difficult and leads to the use of measures such as "exams passed" or "arrests made," which can only partially capture the output of such services.

The most common inputs considered are labor and capital. Hence we can define a measure of labor productivity (value added per unit of labor) and capital productivity (value added per unit of capital). These measures are called partial measures of productivity since they only tell

---

[19] For example, in 2006, Nissan was estimated to use 20.5 labor hours to assemble a car, followed by Honda (21.1), Toyota (22.1), General Motors (22.2), and Ford (23.2). As might be expected, different car models, and different assembly plants, have different labor productivities (see Harbour Consulting 2007).

part of the story. For example, high labor productivity is often largely explained by high levels of capital per worker (e.g., in mining and the steel industry). Similarly, high capital productivity will be present when labor is used intensively.

Economists encapsulate their thinking about the relationship between inputs and outputs by using a production function. A common production function is the Cobb–Douglas, which has the form

$$Y = AK^\alpha L^\beta, \quad 0 < \alpha < 1, \, 0 < \beta < 1. \tag{3.1}$$

In equation (3.1), Y represents value added, K represents physical capital, L represents labor, and A represents "technology." The term "technology" in this context is a catchall that includes any impact on Y that is not accounted for by K or L. This could include process or product innovations that raise value added (note that process innovation can include new organizational methods). This function is discussed in more detail in the mathematical appendix and is also used in chapter 8. Equation (3.1) makes clear that output is created by using both capital and labor inputs, which again indicates the drawback of partial measures of productivity. It also indicates that the level of technology (A) will influence the output from a given level of capital and labor.

While in theoretical discussions of macroeconomic growth it is common to refer to A as the stock of technology, in productivity studies A is most often called total factor productivity (TFP), or sometimes multifactor productivity (MFP).[20] The most common use of TFP is when studying the growth of output (value added) through time. TFP growth is the increase in the output over time that is not accounted for by increases in labor and capital inputs. This is calculated from (3.1) as follows (where g_X represents the growth rate of element X):

$$g_A = g_Y - \alpha g_K - \beta g_L. \tag{3.2}$$

This says that the growth in TFP is equal to the growth in value added less α times the growth in capital input and β times the growth in labor input. The derivation of equation (3.2) and some of the difficulties in calculating TFP are explained in the mathematical appendix. In short, the measurement of TFP is derived under a number of simplifying assumptions, meaning that TFP should be used with some caution.[21]

---

[20] The fact that A can have different interpretations is confusing, and this has attracted discussion over what are the fundamental issues (Lipsey and Carlaw 2004), but for our purposes we simply highlight the two interpretations.

[21] An introduction to the issues is in Hulten (2000).

Measurement Difficulties

While the definitions of labor and capital productivity appear straight-forward, it is important to note that there are a number of measurement difficulties. The measurement of value added requires data on sales and raw materials (including energy). Financial accounts for larger firms will normally report sales data and will also report a "cost of goods sold," which is an accounting term for raw materials and labor costs. Provided they separately report labor costs, it is then possible to obtain a measure of value added from public company account data. Government statistical agencies will also collect data that allow the calculation of value added.

A more difficult problem is encountered if the researcher wants to assess the growth of value added through time. There is a need to deflate the value added data so as to obtain the real growth in value added excluding inflation. National statistical agencies report GDP deflators, and often sector and industry deflators as well, and these can be used to deflate value added. However, some argue that unless firm-level—or at least detailed industry-specific-level—deflators can be obtained, there is the possibility of bias in calculating productivity growth. For example, if there is a firm or industry that has been able to raise its prices through time due, say, to less intense competition, this will register as rapid value added growth, and ultimately high productivity growth, even though its real "output per unit of input" growth may be low. The deflation issue is also related to index numbers and "hedonic prices." The difficulties surrounding these issues mean that there can be a real concern over our ability to measure the real productivity growth over time. Box 3.2 discusses these issues in more detail.

Box 3.2. Quality adjustments and difficulties in measuring output growth.

A good way to understand the issues is to consider how the price, and output, of light has varied since 1800. Nordhaus (1998) discusses this issue and others in a paper entitled "Quality change in price indexes." As technology has changed—from candles, to oil lamps, to electric lightbulbs—the "output" of light has grown dramatically. The true output can be measured in lumens per hour; hence it is possible to calculate how much one lumen-hour cost over time. On the other hand, statistical agencies have also recorded the prices of candles, lamps, and electric lightbulbs. These prices are used to calculate the official price index for light over time. Nordhaus finds that there is a massive difference between the official and true series, with the official price series hugely overestimating the price of light. This is because the official, or conventional, series does not take account of the substantial technological changes that have raised the number of lumens per dollar spent on lighting. How much is the difference between the conventional and true indices? Nordhaus (1998, p. 63) states that "The conventional price of light has risen by a factor of about 1,000 relative to the true price" over the 1800–1992 period.

Another good example of the problems faced in tracking the true increase in output through time comes from the ICT sector and, in particular, measuring the output of computers. Over the last twenty years or so new computers have increased in speed, memory size, portability, and quality at a rapid pace. At the same time the price paid for a computer has fallen. Hence, just using the total sales of computers will underestimate the true value of computers. It would be better to adjust the price of a computer to reflect the true value that it represents compared with previous models. This adjustment process is made in a number of countries, such as the United States, France, and Denmark, but not in all OECD countries. Specifically, the method often used is a so-called hedonic price index. This is a method that evaluates the value associated with each aspect of a computer's performance, such as processor speed and memory.

The method involves running a regression of the log of price (P) on the log of speed (S) and memory (M) plus other characteristics—call these X:

$$\ln(P) = a_0 + a_1 \ln(S) + a_2 \ln(M) + a_3 \ln(X) + e.$$

The coefficients a_1, a_2, and a_3 then give a method of assessing the true price of a new computer with new levels of speed and memory. This, in turn, can be used in a variety of ways to produce a price index that produces a more accurate picture of technological, or quality, changes across time (see Triplett 2004). The fact that different countries use different techniques implies that cross-country comparisons of ICT sectors should be treated with caution (Wyckoff 1995).

There is a range of difficulties in accurately measuring the capital and labor input of firms. Published accounts of larger firms normally contain details on balance sheet items, such as tangible fixed assets and current assets. There may also be information on intangible assets, such as intellectual property (although generally accountants do not value assets unless they have a clear market value, i.e., purchased intellectual property is included but internally generated intellectual property may not be). Many firms also lease capital equipment; hence to get the true capital input it may be necessary to impute a capital services value. Similarly, some studies try to control for capital utilization, as this is likely to vary over the business cycle. The best measure of labor input is likely to be hours worked, but this is often not available at the firm level. Hence, there are issues of imputing a value of hours worked for a firm based on estimates of part time and overtime work (Rogers (1998) provides an overview of these issues).

There are no simple solutions to many of the difficulties discussed above. Students, researchers, and policy makers need to be aware that economic research into productivity is far from an exact science. For example, even though there has been substantial effort devoted to the econometric estimation of production functions (see Ackerberg and Caves 2004), there are still concerns that the basic accounting data used create problems (see Felipe et al. 2008).

3.5   Comparing Productivity and Growth across Countries

In this section we provide a short summary of some of the techniques, issues, and data on cross-country comparisons of productivity and growth. By economic growth we mean the growth in the amount of gross domestic product (GDP) per head of population.[22] An initial task is to show how GDP per capita can be decomposed into separate components:

$$\text{GDP per capita} = \frac{\text{GDP}}{\text{population}} = \left[\frac{\text{GDP}}{\text{hours}} \times \frac{\text{hours}}{\text{workers}} \right] \times \frac{\text{workers}}{\text{population}}. \quad (3.3)$$

This shows how GDP per capita depends on three components. The first, GDP per hour, is a measure similar to the labor productivity measures discussed above (i.e., it is a partial productivity measure, although now it is defined at the economy level and reflects output per hour worked). The second, hours per worker, simply informs us how much, on average, workers are at work rather than at leisure. For example, in the United States the average worker puts in 1,809 hours per year and in Japan workers do 1,784, whereas in the United Kingdom the figure is 1,648, and it is lower still in France (1,468) and Germany (1,355). The ratio of workers to population—the activity ratio or employment participation

---

[22] GDP measures the aggregate output or "value added" produced in an economy in a given year. The "domestic" refers to the fact that any person or firm within the geographical boundaries of the country is included. The "gross" refers to the fact that GDP does not make an allowance for depreciation. Gross national product (GNP) is similar, except only nationals of the country are included (e.g., the profits of foreign companies are excluded). See any macroeconomics textbook for a full discussion.

ratio—reflects the fact that in any society there are those too young or too old to work; there are also those in tertiary education or physically unable to work; there are also unemployed workers. The U.S. and U.K. worker to population ratio is around 0.72, with Germany at 0.67, France at 0.62, and Japan at 0.70.[23] Differences in hours of work per worker and activity ratios will influence the level of GDP per capita across countries, but as these ratios change fairly slowly the main influence on the growth of output per capita will be changes in productivity.

How do levels of GDP per capita compare across countries? The first thing to say is that there are massive differences between the poorest and richest countries in the world. In 2000 the poorest country was estimated to be the Democratic Republic of Congo with a GDP per capita of $359. The United States had a GDP per capita of $34,364—a multiple of ninety-six times Congo's GDP per capita.[24] Such enormous differences are driven by the huge differences in GDP per hour worked—or labor productivity. Labor productivity is, in turn, determined by capital per worker and technology levels. Chapters 8 and 9, which discuss models of economic growth and globalization, provide background into why such immense differences occur. A second important issue concerns the methodology of comparing GDP across countries. Clearly, comparisons require conversion of GDP into a common currency, normally the U.S. dollar. This could be done at market exchange rates, but market exchange rates can fluctuate widely and are driven by specific factors. Hence the standard solution is to use "purchasing power parity" (PPP) exchange rates. PPP rates are calculated by comparing a broad range of prices in each country—including tradable and nontradable goods—and using the ratio of average prices as the exchange rate. The process of calculating PPP has many difficulties and they can result in misleading comparisons, yet they are the most common method of converting GDP into U.S. dollars.[25] A further issue in comparing GDP per capita across time is to express the figures in so-called constant prices, which means to remove the impact of inflation.

---

[23] All these statistics come from the Statistical Annex of *OECD Employment Outlook 2007.*

[24] These data are taken from Heston et al. (2006), which is a database called the Penn World Table especially designed to allow such comparisons. The country with the highest GDP per capita is, in fact, Luxembourg ($48,217).

[25] GDP comparisons are very sensitive to PPP calculations. For example, in 2007 the International Comparison Program (www.worldbank.org/data/icp) revised downward the PPP rates for some emerging markets, including China and India. These revisions meant that China's share of world GDP fell from 15.8% to 10.9% (India's declined from 6.4% to 4.6%). The Penn World Table database contains an extensive discussion on the PPPs that it uses. Dowrick and Quiggin (1997) discuss an alternative to PPP for comparing the GDP per capita of countries.

Looking at differences in GDP per capita within OECD countries in 2005, most countries have 70–85% of the GDP per capita of the United States. There are a few countries—France, Belgium, the Netherlands, Ireland, and Norway—that just exceed the U.S. level of GDP per hour worked, but because of lower average hours worked and lower employment participation rates these countries still have lower GDP per capita (OECD 2006). Should OECD countries be concerned by the difference in GDP per capita with the United States? Some would point out that working fewer hours could be a rational choice and, since the value of leisure time is not measured in GDP, lower GDP per capita is not an issue. However, differences in GDP per hour, and low labor participation rates, are often of concern.

In 2000 the European Union launched the Lisbon Agenda, which aimed to raise Europe's productivity growth by increasing innovation. The Lisbon Agenda seeks to make the EU "the most dynamic and competitive knowledge-based economy in the world." A specific target was to raise the R&D/GDP ratio to 3% by 2010—a target that looks unlikely to be met. As mentioned above, the Lisbon Agenda was also concerned with increasing competition, reducing regulation, improving intellectual property, and reversing "brain drain." This policy stance reflected the fact that while between 1945 and 1995 the main EU countries had been closing the gap with the United States, since 1995 the United States has reversed this trend. We can see these trends by comparing growth rates across countries.

Table 3.4 compares the growth rate of GDP per hour worked across eight countries over the period 1970–2006. Of these countries, Australia, Canada, and the United States have the lowest growth over this period. The lower average growth of the United States over the period reflects the closing of the gap discussed above, although we can also see the reversal of this process since 1995, especially since 2000. The annual growth rate in the United States is relatively stable at between 1% and 2% in the different subperiods, whereas in many other countries growth varies more than this. For example, average growth rates in France, Germany, Italy, and Japan were all close to 4% in the 1970s—a decade when world oil shocks and inflation are generally thought to have been detrimental to productivity growth. The table also shows that Japan's growth in GDP per hour worked was above 2% in the 1990s, yet the Japanese economy as a whole stagnated in that decade.[26] How is it possible for

---

[26] Japan's annual average GDP growth was 0.5% in the 1990s; the comparable figure for the United States is 2.6%. Possible reasons for Japan's slow growth include poor fiscal policy, a liquidity trap, low investment in response to a boom in the 1980s, banking sector inefficiencies, and low TFP growth; see Hayashi and Prescott (2002) for a discussion.

Table 3.4. Annual average growth in GDP per hour worked (1970–2006).

	Australia	Canada	France	Germany	Italy	Japan	U.K.	U.S.
1970–80	1.5	1.8	4.0	3.7	4.0	4.2	2.7	1.6
1980–85	2.2	1.6	3.1	2.1	1.2	2.5	2.5	1.6
1985–90	0.2	0.4	2.7	2.5	2.3	4.2	1.4	1.3
1990–95	2.0	1.4	1.9	2.9	2.1	2.3	2.8	1.1
1995–2000	2.5	2.3	2.1	2.0	0.9	2.1	2.3	2.2
2000–2006	1.5	1.0	1.4	1.4	0.2	2.1	2.0	2.1
1970–2006	1.6	1.5	2.7	2.6	2.0	3.0	2.3	1.7

Source. OECD statistics database 2008.

labor productivity growth and aggregate GDP growth to diverge? Some of the reasons can be seen by studying equation (3.3), which shows that GDP per hour is only one component of GDP per capita. For example, Japan's population growth rate in the 1990s was low, at around 0.3% per annum (the United States's was 1.2%).

Table 3.4 also shows that the U.S. GDP per hour worked grew at 1.1% per annum between 1990 and 1995, and then grew by 2.2% between 1995 and 2000. This doubling of labor productivity growth has attracted much attention, in part since it has been associated with the high investment in information technology (IT). In the years before 1995 there was widespread surprise that the IT revolution of the 1980s and 1990s had had little impact on U.S. labor productivity growth.[27] The acceleration of productivity growth in the late 1990s was hailed as the long-expected productivity increase. Jorgenson et al. (2007) provide a review of U.S. labor productivity growth in the private sector over the 1990s and 2000s. They find that IT investment did increase labor productivity in the late 1990s, but that since 2000 non-IT investment and labor quality have become more important factors. This reminds us that what we have been considering in looking at GDP per hour is a partial productivity measure that is affected by investment in complementary factor inputs, especially capital.

Total Factor Productivity and Growth Accounting

As discussed above and set out in equation (3.2), TFP growth is a measure of the growth of output that is not attributable to labor or capital but is

---

[27] The lack of evidence of IT investment in productivity outcomes was known as the "computer productivity paradox." Robert Solow, writing in the *New York Review of Books* in 1987 (July 12), famously said "You can see the computer age everywhere but in the productivity statistics."

deemed to be linked to innovation and technological change. For example, U.S. TFP growth was estimated as 1.2% per annum in the 2000–2005 period by Jorgenson et al. (2007). This was calculated after allowing for the growth in capital (with IT and non-IT capital entered separately) and the growth in labor (with an adjustment for labor quality). Researchers often control for a variety of inputs, not just the basic labor and capital shown in equation (3.2). These types of calculations are also known as growth accounting.

Let us consider in more detail the figures estimated by Jorgenson et al. (2007). The authors state that labor productivity growth in 2000–2005 was 3.1% per annum.[28] This is "accounted" for by growth in IT capital (0.63%), non-IT capital (0.94%), labor quality (0.36%), and TFP (1.17%). These figures seem precise, but it is important to remember that the various measurement issues of capital, labor, and labor quality (also called human capital) mean that the estimates are sensitive to mismeasurements in the data. In addition, the TFP figure is really a "residual" that is unexplained. It is the growth in productivity left over after accounting for the changes in other inputs. The natural interpretation is that TFP growth comes from increases in efficiency or technology—defined in the broadest sense, since the country's output potential draws on its own past investment in innovation and on the adoption of new technology designed elsewhere—but it still remains a "residual" from a calculation rather than a direct measure of efficiency or technology.

A famous historical study on TFP was by Solow (1957), although there had been previous attempts (see Griliches 1996). Solow found that TFP growth—or technical change as he called it—accounted for 88% of increases in GDP per capita in the United States over the period 1909–49. This high figure was challenged by various subsequent studies, many of which found a reduced contribution of TFP growth (e.g., Denison 1967; Jorgenson and Griliches 1967), sometimes to virtually zero. These subsequent studies, on the United States and European countries, used different measures of labor and capital, and also adjusted for a variety of other "measurement" issues.[29] For example, rather than just including the number of workers as labor, one can attempt to measure the skill and

---

[28] Note that the 3.1% labor productivity refers to the U.S. private sector, whereas Table 3.4 refers to economy-wide labor productivity.

[29] Young (1992) presents an influential study on Hong Kong and Singapore, finding that only 4% of Singapore's rapid growth in 1970–90 could be attributed to TFP growth (the equivalent figure is 35% for Hong Kong). Once again these figures caused a debate (see, for example, the comments on Young's paper in the *NBER Macroeconomic Annual*). Overall, as stressed in the main text, it is important that these studies are "accounting" for growth and not "explaining" it.

education level of workers. The result is to include a new factor of production called "human capital." Growth accounting can provide insight into the growth process, but it should be stressed that it is accounting for growth and not trying to explain the fundamental driving forces. For example, one might find that human capital is important, but it does not explain whether this is driven by government policy or firm-level investments. Equally, it is likely that new technology and innovation generate new opportunities for capital investment. This is not something that growth accounting tries to uncover: it simply allocates some of growth to capital without attempting to explain why capital growth occurred. Uncovering why growth occurs requires growth models and empirical analysis (see chapters 8 and 9).

Emerging Markets

China's rapid economic growth in recent decades has had dramatic impacts on the world economy. Thirty years ago few would have predicted that the reforms led by Deng Xiaoping would have resulted in China now accounting for around 11% of world GDP. Has China's economic growth been unique in recent history?

Table 3.5 shows a selection of other, mainly successful, emerging markets to allow some insight into this question. The table shows average GDP per capita growth rates by decade.[30] A first comment to make is that Japan, which is now a high-income economy, is also included in the table. However, in the early 1950s Japan was a relatively poor country. Japan's growth rate from the 1950s and 1960s was very high—averaging 9.74% in the 1960s. Brazil, South Korea, Taiwan, and Thailand also grew rapidly in the 1960s, although note that China and India did not enjoy such success. Since 1981 China's growth rate has accelerated. Taking the 1980s and 1990s together, China's average growth rate exceeds Japan's in the 1950s and 1960s, but not by much. Hence, China's rapid growth is exceptional but not unique. The table also shows that countries experiencing growth rates above 6–7% subsequently tend to slow down.

While there are many reasons for rapid growth, a useful starting point is to think of poorer countries catching up with richer countries. Rapid growth is helped by the ability to learn and imitate the techniques of production used in more advanced countries, denoted as "technology

---

[30] Note that in newspapers, and in general discussion, it is often only GDP growth that is discussed (i.e., commentators do not adjust for population growth). Chapter 8 discusses growth models that make clear this distinction. As an example, a country could have a GDP growth rate of 5% but, if its population growth is also 5%, it is clear that the average GDP per person is static. Hence, only reporting GDP growth can be misleading if one is interested in assessing standard of living.

Table 3.5. Average growth of GDP per capita in emerging markets.

	Brazil	China	India	Japan	Korea	Taiwan	Thailand
1951–60	3.93	4.11	1.57	7.54	1.03	4.44	−0.15
1961–70	4.34	1.45	2.69	9.74	5.82	7.04	5.07
1971–80	5.38	4.18	1.61	3.18	5.93	7.75	4.62
1981–90	0.21	8.43	3.48	3.43	7.90	6.59	6.08
1991–2000	0.53	9.15	3.41	1.01	5.19	5.49	3.03
2001–4	0.09	7.44	4.19	0.72	4.09	2.16	3.97

Source. Penn World Table Version 6.2.

Note. Calculated using GDP per capita in constant-price (year 2000) dollars.

transfer." This combined with the availability of low wages can generate increased trade, investment, and growth. As countries catch up, the opportunities to grow as fast start to dwindle, causing the growth rate to fall. The catch-up model, together with a discussion of the potential benefits of globalization, is discussed in chapter 9.

3.6 Conclusion

This chapter has discussed a wide range of issues relating to the measurement of innovation and productivity. Without an understanding of these issues there is a danger of being misinformed by the many statistics available. Designing good innovation policy requires a correct assessment of the existing situation, as well as subsequent evaluation of the impact of the policies, for which measures of innovation and productivity growth are required.

The chapter investigated a range of measures of innovative activity, each of which has strengths and weaknesses in terms of its coverage of the innovation activities of different sectors of the economy. The use of innovation survey data comes with a statistical health warning due to the inherent difficulty of distinguishing innovation from diffusion in surveys of firms. Looking at the innovation production process, there are a greater number of "output" measures than of "input" measures, but this does not automatically ensure a higher quality of data. There is a considerable contrast between the quality and coverage of data sources arising through compulsory registration activity to obtain the IPR (patents) and those arising where registration is optional (trademarks, copyright, and designs). Furthermore, counting IPRs as if each one was of equal value and significance is problematic—a point we shall explore further in chapter 5 when we consider the variability of the value of patents and trademarks. Overall, it is clear that there is no single, or best, measure of innovation. Instead, in any situation, a range of possibilities is likely to exist and the researcher or policy maker needs to choose appropriately.

At the macroeconomic level we expect to observe the benefits of domestic innovation spreading across the economy through the process of diffusion of new technology. There are also gains from technology transfer from other countries and the imitation of foreign innovations. All these increments to domestic knowledge and technology raise the productivity of existing resources, leading to increased GDP per capita. It is important to understand that there are a range of measurement and conceptual issues in productivity and growth studies. The second part of this chapter gave a primer in these. Lastly, the chapter also looked at some of the economic growth experiences of different countries since World War II.

Keywords

Innovation inputs.

Innovation outputs.

Production function.

Partial productivity of labor or capital.

Total factor productivity.

Quality adjustment.

Growth accounting.

Questions for Discussion

(1) List the input, and output, measures of innovation. How should one deal with so many possible measures?

(2) "R&D is the only important measure of innovation." Discuss.

(3) Choose a selection of firms, or countries, and attempt to produce a ranking or innovation scoreboard.

(4) What is meant by partial productivity measures? Should only total factor productivity be used?

(5) What measurement issues should be considered when comparing GDP per capita across countries? What about when comparing GDP per capita through time?

(6) What is the use of growth accounting studies?

References

Ackerberg, D., and K. Caves. 2004. Structural identification of production functions. Mimeo, University of California, Los Angeles.

Acs, Z., and D. B. Audretsch. 1990. *Innovation and Small Firms.* Cambridge, MA: Harvard/MIT Press.

Archibugi, D. 1992. Patenting as an indicator of technological innovation: a review. *Science and Public Policy* 19(6):357–68.

Coe, D., and E. Helpman. 1995. International R&D spillovers. *European Economic Review* 39:859–87.

Cohen, W., and D. Levinthal. 1989. Innovation and learning: the two faces of R&D. *Economic Journal* 99:569–96.

Denison, E. 1967. *Why Growth Rates Differ.* Washington, DC: Brookings Institute.

Dowrick, S., and J. Quiggin. 1997. True measures of GDP and convergence. *American Economic Review* 87(1):41–64.

Eurostat. 2007. *Science, Technology and Innovation in Europe.* Luxembourg: The European Commission.

Feeny, S., and M. Rogers. 2003. Innovation and performance: benchmarking Australian firms. *Australian Economic Review* 36(3):253–64.

Felipe, J., R. Hasan, and J. McCombie. 2008. Correcting for biases when estimating production functions: an illusion of the laws of algebra? *Cambridge Journal of Economics* 32:441–59.

Frank, S. 2005. R&D expenditure in the European Union. in *Statistics in Focus: Science and Technology*, Volume 2. Brussels: The Statistical Office of the European Communities/Eurostat.

Geroski, P. 1990. Innovation, technological opportunity and market structure. *Oxford Economic Papers* 42:586–602.

Gort, M., and S. Klepper. 1982. Time paths in the diffusion of product innovations. *Economic Journal* 92:630–53.

Greenhalgh, C. A., and Rogers, M. 2008. Intellectual property activity by service sector and manufacturing firms in the UK, 1996–2000. In *The Evolution of Business Knowledge* (ed. H. Scarbrough). Oxford University Press.

Griffith, R., S. Redding, and J. Van Reenen. 2004. Mapping the two faces of R&D: productivity growth in a panel of OECD industries. *Review of Economics and Statistics* 86(4):883–95.

Griliches, Z. 1990. Patent statistics as economic indicators: a survey. *Journal of Economic Literature* 28(December):1,661–707.

———. 1996. The discovery of the residual: a historical note. *Journal of Economic Literature* 34(3):1,324–30.

Hall, B. 2005. Exploring the patent explosion. *Journal of Technology Transfer* 30(1/2):35–48.

Harbour Consulting. 2007. "The Harbour Report" (available at www.harbourinc.com/resources/files/media/2007PressRelease.pdf).

Hayashi, F., and E. Prescott. 2002. The 1990s in Japan: a lost decade. *Review of Economic Dynamics* 5:206–35.

Heston, A., R. Summers, and B. Aten. 2006. Penn World Table Version 6.2. Center for International Comparisons of Production, Income and Prices at the University of Pennsylvania.

Hulten, C. 2000. Total factor productivity: a short biography. NBER Working Paper 7471.

Jaffe, A., and Lerner, J. 2004. *Innovation and Its Discontents: How Our Broken Patent System is Endangering Innovation and Progress, and What to Do About It.* Princeton University Press.

Jones, C. 1995. R&D-based models of economic growth. *Journal of Political Economy* 103(4):759–84.

Jorgenson, D., and Z. Griliches. 1967. The explanation of productivity change. *Review of Economic Studies* 34(3):249–83.

Jorgenson, D., M. Ho, and K. Storoh. 2007. A retrospective look at the US productivity growth resurgence. Staff Report 277, Federal Reserve Bank of New York.

Keller, W. 2002. Geographical localization of international technology diffusion. *American Economic Review* 92(1):120–42.

Lev, B., and T. Sougiannis. 1996. The capitalization, amortization, and value-relevance of R&D. *Journal of Accounting and Economics* 21:107–38.

Lipsey, R. G., and K. I. Carlaw. 2004. Total factor productivity and the measurement of technological change. *Canadian Journal of Economics* 37(4): 1,118–50.

Lucking, B. 2004. *International Comparisons of the Third Community Innovation Survey (CIS3)* (available at www.berr.gov.uk/files/file9657.pdf). London: U.K. Department of Trade and Industry: Technology, Economics, Statistics and Evaluation (TESE).

National Science Foundation. 2007. Expenditures for US industrial R&D. Info-Brief 07-335 (September).

Nelson, R. R., and G. Wright. 1992. The rise and fall of American technological leadership: the postwar era in historical perspective. *Journal of Economic Literature* 30(4):1,931–64.

Nordhaus, W. D. 1998. Quality change in price indexes. *Journal of Economic Perspectives* 12(1):59–68.

OECD. 2006. *OECD Compendium of Productivity Statistics.* Paris: OECD Publishing.

OECD/Eurostat. 2005. *Oslo Manual: Guidelines for Collecting and Interpreting Innovation Data*, 3rd edn. Paris: OECD Publishing.

Office of National Statistics. 2006. *Business Enterprise Research and Development 2005.* London: Office of National Statistics (www.statistics.gov.uk).

Patel, P., and K. Pavitt. 1995. Patterns of technological activity: their measurement and interpretation. In *Handbook of the Economics of Innovation and Technical Change* (ed. P. Stoneman), chapter 2. Oxford: Basil Blackwell.

Pavitt, K. 1982. R&D, patenting and innovative activities: a statistical exploration. *Research Policy* 11(1):33–51.

——. 1985. Patent statistics as indicators of innovative activities: possibilities and problems. *Scientometrics* 7(1–2):77–89.

Rogers, M. 1998. The definition and measurement of productivity. Working Paper, Melbourne Institute for Applied Economics and Social Research.

——. 2003. *Knowledge, Technological Catch-up and Economic Growth.* Cheltenham, U.K.: Edward Elgar.

Rosenberg, N. 1994. *Exploring the Black Box: Technology, Economics and History.* Cambridge University Press.

Sakakibara, M., and L. Branstetter. 1999. Do stronger patents induce more innovation? Evidence from the 1988 patent law reforms. NBER Working Paper 7066.

Schmookler, J. 1966. *Invention and Economic Growth*. Cambridge, MA: Harvard University Press.

Solow, R. 1957. Technical progress and the aggregate production function. *Review of Economics and Statistics* 39:312–20.

Triplett, J. 2004. Handbook on hedonic indexes and quality adjustments in price indexes: special application to information technology products. STI Working Paper 2004/9, OECD.

Wyckoff, A. 1995. The impact of computer prices on international comparisons of labour productivity. *Economics of Innovation and New Technology* 3(3–4): 277–93.

Young, A. 1992. A tale of two cities: factor accumulation and technical change in Hong Kong and Singapore. *NBER Macroeconomics Annual* 7:13–54.

Part II

The National Innovation System

4

The National Innovation System

4.1 Introduction

This chapter documents and discusses the way that universities and government provide the science base necessary to fuel the process of innovation. The role of business enterprises is still central to innovation, but their effectiveness relies on support from universities and government. When consumers buy a new product, or benefit from process innovation that lowers prices, it might appear that the innovating firm has acted alone. In fact, the origins of the innovation may come from research done at a university and this could have been financed by government. As we saw in chapter 3, intellectual property has taken on an increasingly important role in recent decades, and this chapter discusses the increasing use of intellectual property by universities. Understanding the entire innovation system is vital to avoid misguided policies and, more generally, to maximize innovation and productivity growth. The complex, interrelated system that is behind innovation is often called the *national innovation system*.

4.2 The National Innovation System

> The national innovation system essentially consists of three sectors: industry, universities, and the government, with each sector interacting with the others, while at the same time playing its own role.
>
> Goto (2000, p. 104)

This quotation neatly summarizes the three-way interaction underlying any economy's ability to produce commercial innovations.[1] Clearly, innovation by private business does not take place independently of other important actors and institutions. The three main groups of players and their principal roles are as follows.

---

[1] Leydesdorff and Meyer (2006) analyze this set of trilateral relations in what they term a "triple helix" model. The term "national system of innovation" is often thought to have originated from an edited book by Lundvall (1992), although it has antecedents dating back many centuries. Broad-ranging discussions are in Nelson (1993) and Freeman (1995).

Universities. These institutions undertake basic science and technology research to discover new knowledge and expand the knowledge base. In turn this generates new possibilities that can be exploited by business. Universities educate the scientists and technicians needed by business and government, as well as the next generation of university scientists. In many countries, scientific research and training is also done by public research laboratories.

Government. The government designs innovation policy and sets the parameters of the IPR system. Government departments may commission research related to public goods, such as defense and health. They also use tax revenues to finance universities and public research institutions and they may also offer subsidies to business R&D.

Business. Firms conduct R&D to develop new commercial products using the science knowledge base, acting within the constraints and opportunities of the IPR system and the R&D policy framework. When successful, they launch product and process innovations in response to the perceived needs of their customers and markets. Entrepreneurs start up new firms in response to market opportunities and, if successful, these provide the basis for the large firms of the future.

There are overlaps in the objectives and activities of these three types of actors. In the modern era universities can sometimes produce commercially viable products, while some parts of private business will be conducting elements of basic research and are not just focused on the near-market applications of university science. The government has a strong interest in the commercial viability of domestic industries, which depends in part on their innovation record, as viable industries create jobs, earn profits, and also contribute tax revenues. Government also has an interest in supporting the quality of domestic universities, thus acting as the custodian of the part of tax revenues used to fund public science, and guaranteeing the quality of manpower for the science base and industrial R&D of the future.

4.3 The Central Role of R&D

The extent and nature of R&D expenditures are thought of as major indicators of the national system of innovation. Chapter 3 has already presented some information on R&D, but here we disaggregate the economy-level figures. The first issue is to investigate the sources of funding for R&D.

Who Funds R&D?

Historically, the funding of R&D was shared between two domestic purses: those of the government and private business. In recent years a third source of finance has assumed importance in several countries: overseas finance for R&D conducted in the domestic economy. A further source of funding is the set of "nonprofit institutions," including charitable trusts, some of these having been set up by wealthy individuals following success in industry. A recent example is The Bill & Melinda Gates Foundation, while others rely on the collection of personal donations for particular fields of research, such as Cancer Research UK.

Across the group of countries that are major investors in R&D, the government share of funding of gross R&D spending varies quite widely, from a low of below a quarter in Japan to a high of 40%+ in France (see table 4.1). However, government funding of R&D expressed as a share of GDP in Japan is, in fact, fairly close to the European average, so there is no strong indication of a lack of government effort in Japan. Rather, Japan's business expenditure on R&D is relatively high, thus the total share of GDP devoted to R&D in Japan is higher than in other countries. For G5 countries, the new phenomenon of cross-country R&D investment has been most significant in the United Kingdom and France, which are the two lowest spenders among the G5 countries. Possible reasons for high externally funded R&D include the unexploited potential of the science base and a relatively low cost of undertaking R&D in these countries.[2]

Where Is R&D Being Conducted?

When examining where countries are doing their R&D, we can look at its distribution across the three main institutions of private business, government research institutes, and the higher education sector (see table 4.2). Business conducts about two thirds of national R&D on average, but this share is higher in the United States and Japan and lower in

---

[2] The share of total R&D funded from overseas is 19.2% in the United Kingdom, 7.3% in France, 3.7% in Germany, and 0.3% in Japan (see OECD (2005); no information on the United States is available). Comparing the relative cost of undertaking R&D in OECD countries has been done, most recently, by Dougherty et al. (2007). They find that compared with the United States (100%), the United Kingdom's relative R&D cost in 1997 was 89%, while the figure for France was 96%. In particular, the relative cost of scientists, engineers, and other R&D employees is low in the United Kingdom and France. Since labor costs account for around 50% of total R&D costs, low labor costs have a large effect (the cost of materials, capital, and overheads are, in fact, more expensive in the United Kingdom and France than in the United States). The differences in relative costs of R&D also mean that comparing nominal R&D/GDP ratios across countries, as in tables 4.1 and 4.2, can be slightly misleading (i.e., according to Dougherty et al. one should "scale up" the United Kingdom's ratio by 1.12 (1/0.89)).

Table 4.1. Funding of R&D by government and business.

Country	R&D/GDP in 2004	R&D/GDP funded by GOV in 2005	GOV R&D/ total R&D ×100%	Percentage of R&D funded by BES in 2003
EU25	1.86	0.74	39.8	54.3
EU15	1.92	0.76	39.6	54.6
Germany	2.49	0.76	30.5	67.1
France	2.16	0.94	43.5	50.8
U.K.	1.79	0.73	40.8	43.9
Japan	3.20	0.71	22.2	74.5
U.S.	2.66	1.06	39.8	61.4

Source. Eurostat (2007).

Notes. "GOV" is the government sector and "BES" is the business enterprise sector. Columns 1 and 4 are drawn from table 2.1, column 2 comes from figure 1.2 of Eurostat (2007), while column 3 is our own calculation. Although these data compare figures from different years, these intensities and ratios to GDP are rather stable from year to year.

the United Kingdom and France. The comparison with sources of funding thus shows net transfers from government to industry in most countries. The exception here is Japan, where business funding matches the business R&D activity share. For the one third of R&D that is not done by business, countries vary in the proportions of this conducted by government, with the lowest share of government R&D activity occurring in the United Kingdom and Japan. Japan is notable both for the low share of total R&D funded by government finance and the low share of R&D conducted directly by government, although it still has the highest percentage of GDP for R&D conducted within higher education.

An analysis of trends between 1980 and 2000 conducted by Bloom and Griffith (2001) shows that the United Kingdom was unique among the G5 countries in showing a persistently falling proportion of R&D to GDP over the whole of this period. Why was this the case? Closer examination shows that business effort was broadly constant, but the falling total was due to cuts in government R&D expenditures begun during the 1980s.[3] Reduced support for defense-related industries in that period was not replaced by equivalent government support for other sectors with a civil orientation, so it seems that the "peace dividend" went into tax cuts. Although it was the first to reduce its R&D spending for defense purposes, the U.K. government was not unique. From the mid 1980s onward both the United States and France also reduced their

---

[3] The 1980s in the United Kingdom was the period known as the "Thatcher era," when the prime minister, Margaret Thatcher, initiated many changes in British public policy.

Table 4.2. The conduct of R&D by business, government, and universities in 2003.

Country	R&D/GDP conducted by BES	R&D/GDP conducted by GOV	R&D/GDP conducted by HES	Sum of columns 1–3	Total R&D/GDP
EU25	1.22	0.25	0.41	1.88	1.90
EU15	1.26	0.25	0.42	1.93	1.95
Germany	1.76	0.34	0.43	2.53	2.52
France	1.37	0.36	0.42	2.15	2.18
U.K.	1.24	0.18	0.40	1.82	1.88
Japan	2.40	0.30	0.44	3.14	3.20
U.S.	1.86	0.33	0.37	2.56	2.67

Source. Table 2.8 of Eurostat (2007).

Notes. "BES" is the business enterprise sector; "GOV" is the government sector; "HES" is the higher education sector. Figures are for 2003. The United Kingdom, Japan, and the United States have significant "other institutions" conducting R&D (e.g., private nonprofit), hence the sum of BES, GOV, and HES can be less than total R&D/GDP.

defense-related R&D, so that government funding of R&D as a percentage of GDP fell in both these countries in the 1990s and their total R&D/GDP shares stabilized or fell.

The pattern of R&D spending by governments varies significantly across countries as shown by table 4.3. In Europe and Japan about one third of government research spending is routed through general funding of universities, a classification that does not attract any allocation in U.S. data, although federal agencies in the United States certainly support individual research projects by university personnel.[4]

U.S. government funding of R&D is highly concentrated on three categories: defense, health, and space research, with defense attracting more than half of U.S. government R&D spending. Outside of the health sector, the U.S. industry and energy sectors receive negligible allocations of government R&D expenditure. In Europe, the R&D spending share to defense varies across the major countries, being high in the United Kingdom and France and much lower in Germany. It is similarly low in Japan—a historical legacy of the treaties restricting the defense activity of Germany and Japan after World War II. Higher shares of R&D spending are directed into industry and universities in Germany and into the energy sector in Japan.

---

[4] According to the Council on Governmental Relations (1999), in 1997 federal agencies provided almost 60% of total support for research performed at U.S. universities. The main agencies disbursing funds are the National Institutes of Health, the National Science Foundation, and the Office of Naval Research.

Table 4.3. Percentage allocation of government
R&D support by objective in 2005.

Country	Land	Health	Energy	Industry	University	Defense	All other
EU25	9.6	7.3	2.8	10.9	32.0	13.6	24.0
EU15	9.3	7.3	2.7	10.9	32.4	13.8	23.8
Germany	8.9	4.4	2.9	12.4	40.3	5.8	26.0
France	6.5	6.1	4.5	6.2	24.8	22.3	29.5
U.K.	8.5	14.7	0.4	1.7	21.7	31.0	22.0
Japan	10.3	3.9	17.1	7.1	33.5	5.1	23.0
U.S.	4.5	22.8	1.1	0.4	—	56.6	14.6

Source. Table 1.4 of Eurostat (2007). Figures for Japan relate to 2004.

Notes. A list of the socioeconomic objectives and their grouping for this table follows (the classifications follow the Nomenclature for the Analysis and Comparison of Scientific Programmes and Budgets (NABS)). "Land": exploration and exploitation of the earth; infrastructure and general planning of land use; control and care of the environment; agricultural production and technology. "Health": protection and improvement of human health. "Energy": production, distribution, and rational utilization of energy. "Industry": industrial production and technology. "University": research financed from general university funds. "Defense": defense. "All other": social structure and relationships; exploration and exploitation of space; nonoriented research; other civil research. (For all except the United States, the largest component of "All other" is nonoriented research. For the United States the largest component of "All other" is exploration and exploitation of space.)

4.4 The Government–University Axis

Chapter 1 considered whether new knowledge was best characterized as a public good (nonexcludable and nonrival in use) or as a private good having some positive externalities. We indicated that any discovery arising from basic scientific research was closer to the economic concept of a public good, as it had the possibility of being used in a variety of noncompeting applications (so was nonrival). Publishing scientific research in academic journals implies that the research is nonexcludable (as long as access to journals is not restricted). This would suggest that the provision of basic scientific research could and should follow the model of public provision of public goods, with funding coming from the taxpayer followed by virtually free distribution of findings (for example, via journals in public libraries).[5] With no restrictions on the possible

---

[5] There is recent concern over how accessible publicly funded research actually is, since many academic journals have (increasingly) high access costs. Recent estimates for the United Kingdom suggested that subscription costs to academic journals increased by 50% between 1998 and 2003 (House of Commons 2004, p. 5) and there is concern that high costs will damage the United Kingdom's research and education capabilities. This has led to a debate about the market structure of academic publishing and also whether "open access" business models can succeed (McCabe and Synder 2005).

application of science to commercial applications, this would lead to the widest possible social benefit from the public R&D expenditure.

The Historical Traditions of Science

In the eighteenth and nineteenth centuries most universities shunned the commercial world.[6] In the last century, universities became important centers of scientific enquiry, the nature of which was, in some respects, closer to commercial innovation. However, the general subject of enquiry and the particular choice of topic were often decisions made by individual scientists and their academic departments. The view that science, and its development into new technology, was fundamentally important to society slowly became clear, especially after the experiences of World War II. After 1945, governments became much more active in influencing and directing science.[7] Nowadays, in the United States, individual professors apply to government-supported funding agencies and their applications are subject to "peer review" by other scientists, who judge the likely "scientific importance" of the research, not its potential commercial applicability. In the United Kingdom and Europe a considerable amount of basic government funding is allocated to universities to distribute as they choose, with further funds coming via peer-reviewed systems of allocation like those in the United States so that, at least at the margin, extra funds are allocated to the highest-quality bidder.

When the research is completed and documented, the results of these publicly funded studies are presented at seminars and published as articles in specialist science journals, leading to the full and immediate disclosure of findings. In this environment, negative findings or falsification of others' work are also seen as contributions to knowledge. Before 1980

---

[6] There are exceptions to this statement. Scottish universities in the eighteenth century were commercially aware: for example, James Watt was an instrument maker at Glasgow University. In the nineteenth century, a few German universities had links with chemical and mining industries, such as the University of Giessen which, according to Cardwell (1994, p. 253), had a school in organic chemistry that was "the first of the modern international research schools." However, the medieval universities of England, France, and Germany took little interest in commerce. In the United States the "land grant" universities, established from the mid-nineteenth century by the federal government granting land to the states, were specifically aimed at advancement in agriculture, mechanics, and home economics (see Mowery and Nelson (2004) for an analysis of U.S. universities and innovation). Individuals, and the networks between them, played an important part in scientific advance and its application to industry in the industrial revolution in the United Kingdom. See, for example, Jenny Uglow's 2002 book on *The Lunar Society*, whose members included Arkwright, Erasmus Darwin, Priestley, Watt, and Wedgwood.

[7] The Vannevar Bush report to the U.S. president in 1945 stressed the need for trained scientists to "strengthen the centers of basic research which are principally the colleges, universities, and research institutes" (from the executive summary).

there were rather few instances of universities taking out patents to protect their inventions and derive revenues from licensing their technology.
Although the publication of books and journals is of course subject to
copyright, the ideas in such creative works are not themselves protected,
but only the particular form of their expression. Thus the approach was
essentially one of public finance for advances in knowledge that were
put back into the public domain for all to access and use in commercial
developments and applications, excluding direct plagiarism. This practical arrangement mimics the theoretical model of the public provision
of a public good, in this case scientific knowledge, with the public purse
bearing the costs of knowledge production, which is then made available
to all at a zero marginal cost, reflecting its nonrival nature in use.[8]

Thus a significant proportion of scientific research conducted in industrialized economies has historically been done without any expectation
that the scientists concerned will earn private returns on any innovations they help to develop. Given the typically small monetary rewards
available for pure research, what motivated these researchers? Science
researchers may be motivated by a love of knowledge or by the satisfaction gained from puzzle solving (Hull 1988), but economists have come
to recognize that the most plausible explanation for such behavior is that
scientists are interested in establishing *priority* and the (high) status and
(modest) monetary rewards that flow from attaining priority. The notion
of priority is due to the work of Merton (1957, 1988), who argued that
scientists are concerned with being the first to communicate a significant new development in their field. The reward or gain from establishing priority has been described by Stephan (1996) as "the recognition
awarded by the scientific community for being first." The importance of
priority gives this type of scientific research some of the character of
a race where the winner takes all. Financial remuneration for this type
of scientist is an additional motivating force as, although the academic
earning profile is rather flat in science, Stephan notes how a variety of
extra-institutional awards await the successful scientist through prize
money and consulting fees.

In the United Kingdom this old model of public provision of science
began to change in the early 1990s, commencing with the Technology

---

[8] Adams (1990) investigates whether the publication of scientific articles has any association with subsequent productivity growth. Using counts of worldwide scientific articles (from 1868 onward) he calculates a relevant stock of knowledge for twenty-seven
U.S. industries over the period 1953–80. He finds that knowledge is a "major contributor
to productivity growth," although the lag time is around twenty years. Importantly, the
link between scientific knowledge stock and productivity is conditioned on the number
of scientists and engineers working in the industry. In other words, industries must have
the "absorptive capability" to benefit from scientific knowledge.

Foresight Programme. The aim of this was to concentrate government funding into "hot spots" of technological research, where it was felt that the returns to social investment would be higher (i.e., where there were many possible applications that would be commercially viable). Beginning in 1993, tripartite committees of government, academic, and industry representatives were asked to identify strategic areas for science research funding in which funding would be concentrated. The likely outcome of such a policy is to reduce funding for basic science projects where the commercial applications are unclear.

In the United States similar concerns about more recent changes in funding allocation have been expressed by leading scientists such as Kornberg (2007). In his view, a system whereby government funding to individual scientists is awarded on a peer review basis for research projects, as historically occurred in the United States, is superior to a system that awards funds to universities or research institutes, as occurs in Europe. This is based on the belief that peer review encourages the funding of the most exciting and original scientific ideas. Historically, under the U.S. system those awarded funds could often pursue further ideas not listed in their original proposal, leading to unexpected breakthroughs. With the present ceiling on funds being made available through such bodies as the U.S. National Institutes of Health, which fund medical science research, the competition for funding is intensifying. This will have the effect of reducing risk taking in the exploration of novel scientific ideas—both in the proposals for new grants and in the conduct of existing grants—which could have drastic effects on the rate of innovation. In Kornberg's view, every major new medical treatment has arisen from a basic scientific discovery by research that was *not* directed to commercial products.

4.5 The University–Business Axis

Changes in the Institutional Environment for Science Research

During the last quarter century there has been considerable change in the relationship between scientific research institutions and private business, leading to a substantial rise in the commercialization of university-based technologies. The forces acting for change have included both the technology policies of governments, aiming to increase the number of commercial applications of publicly funded science, and the increasing complexity and expense of scientific research, driving firms to seek partnerships with the public science sector. In addition, the university sector in many countries has been under pressure to take more students, often without matched funding from governments, leading university administrators to seek other sources of funding. This sea change in the science-industry collaborative process has been achieved in four main ways.

University intellectual property. By universities patenting their scientific inventions and then licensing their use to industry.

Research joint ventures (RJVs). By universities and firms engaging in jointly funded research and agreeing how to share the findings via contracts about future patents and licenses.

Spin-outs. By the scientists from academic institutions actively forming new companies to develop and manufacture products that apply their scientific findings.

Personnel pooling. By exchanging and sharing science and engineering personnel between commercial firms and academic departments.

There have been two accompanying institutional changes: the development of technology transfer offices within universities and the growth of science parks, both of which are discussed below.

The Growth of University Intellectual Property

U.S. universities have a long history of developing scientific inventions and working closely with business.[9] The role of intellectual property in these collaborations varied across universities and, in particular, there was an issue about who owned the IPR arising from federally funded research (in 1970, 70% of university research was funded federally while only 2.6% was funded by industry (Mowery et al. 2001, p. 102)). Some universities negotiated agreements with specific federal departments in order to keep the intellectual property, but many did not. By 1980 this led to an estimated patent stock of some 28,000 patents owned by federal government, but of these fewer than 5% were licensed to industry (Council on Governmental Relations 1999, p. 2). A major inhibiting factor to technology transfer from the laboratory to industrial commercialization was that the government made these publicly owned inventions available through nonexclusive licenses. As companies could not gain

---

[9] Mowery et al. (2001, p. 101) contains the statement:

> Throughout the 1900–1940 period, U.S. universities, especially public universities, pursued extensive research collaboration with industry. Indeed, the academic discipline of chemical engineering was largely developed through collaboration between U.S. petroleum and chemicals firms and MIT and the University of Illinois.

exclusive rights, they were reluctant to invest in and develop new products. This indicates a possible problem with the basic "public good" view of knowledge, which suggests that new knowledge can simply be made freely available. The problem is caused by the difference between knowledge and innovation in situations where there are competing uses of the knowledge. Innovation builds on new knowledge but generally requires considerable investment in development before it is commercially useful, hence the preference for exclusive licensing. Without the certainty associated with a license the firm may not be willing to invest.

After the passing of the U.S. Patent and Trademark Law Amendment Act (the Bayh–Dole Act) in 1980, the relationship between U.S. universities and industry was dramatically reformed. The act provided for all universities and individual scientists to retain ownership of inventions arising from federally funded research. In return, universities are expected both to file for patent protection and to ensure commercialization through licensing. Exclusive licenses are now permitted, with an emphasis where possible on the manufacture of products within the United States. The motivation for the act was to speed up technology transfer from the laboratory to the marketplace. U.S. universities were thus presented with a new potential source of revenue from licensing, but to generate that revenue required them to target resources toward the process of filing patents and licensing technologies by creating *technology transfer offices* (TTOs). These offices are staffed by skilled administrators and university technology managers, who assist with patent filing and licensing. The offices also develop research partnerships with industry, increasing the flow of funds into the science base for research commissioned by business. These trends have been mirrored in the United Kingdom and Europe by similar policy developments that aim to increase the commercial orientation of university research and raise the share of funding of this research coming from private business (see box 4.1). This said, there are a number of concerns about such policies.

Collaboration in Research

University–business links have increased in importance and popularity in many industrialized countries, not just in the United States. Joint collaboration may take many forms, as discussed by Poyago-Theotoky et al. (2002). Enterprises may approach academic units within universities to conduct R&D on the firm's behalf, or alternatively a university researcher may approach a firm with a view to commercializing a particular innovation or idea. Another increasingly common intermediate type of partnership investigated by Hall et al. (2002) is where universities and firms join forces to work on a new product or technology together. In this case, neither party can produce or commercialize the idea by relying solely on its own resources.

One implication of university–business links is that they expose the party with more knowledge (usually the university scientist) to the party with less knowledge, hence making the knowledge more widely known. This may be described as a beneficial research spillover. Another positive effect of industry collaborations is more exploitation of fundamental knowledge since, as Poyago-Theotoky et al. (2002) point out, knowledge is usually only appropriable if the creator of knowledge can communicate his ideas to someone who is in a position to commercialize the idea. Negative effects of university–business linkages may include adverse effects on the quantity and quality of fundamental research, on the time allocated to teaching by academics, and on the culture of "open science."

The result of changes in U.K. and U.S. government policy toward university science funding has been the establishment of TTOs in many universities (see box 4.1). As stated above, their primary aim is to manage patenting and licensing of technology to industry. Their impact is evident in the growth of patents and income from licensing and also in the number of new companies set up with links to universities. Even so, the amount of license income remains small in relation to the overall level of research funding. In fact, Thursby and Thursby (2007) estimate that "a very large" number of U.S. TTOs are a net drain on university finances (i.e., the royalties do not even cover their own costs).[10] On average in U.K. universities in 2004, according to survey data in Unico (2005), annual rates of license income (royalties) were around 1% of research funding. They are nearer to 3% of research funding in the United States. In addition, in directly funded U.K. public-sector research establishments, recently surveyed by Technopolis (2007), large rises in the number of licensing agreements were found, alongside rising incomes from intellectual property licensing and from business consultancy.

Box 4.1. Sources of research funds for Oxford and Stanford universities.

To give an indication of the research activities and business links of universities we take a look at two world-leading universities. Each university has a track record that has, in many different ways, led to substantial innovation and growth in their economies. Oxford's famous spin-off

---

[10] They have income data on around 140 U.S. TTOs but not all of these report costs, hence the need to estimate.

companies include Oxford Instruments and PowderJect. Oxford's technology transfer is managed by ISIS Innovation, which has helped forty spin-outs since 1997 and manages over two hundred license agreements. Stanford's record is even more impressive, with spin-outs including Hewlett-Packard, Sun Microsystems, Cisco, and Silicon Graphics. Stanford's Office of Technology Licensing oversees technology transfer. It concluded seventy-seven licenses in fiscal year 2006–7 and brings in $50 million in royalties each year.

The figures below show how each university classifies its research income.

Oxford University (2006–7)	Pounds, million
Total research income	346
Research grants and external sponsors	248
Block grants from HEFCE	98

Stanford University (2004–5)	Dollars, million
U.S. government sponsored research	578
Non-U.S. government sponsored research	105

Sources. 2006/7 Stanford University Budget Book, appendix schedule 14 (p. 97); University of Oxford Annual Review Web site.

Note that Oxford receives a considerable block research grant from the Higher Education Funding Council for England (HEFCE) that is distributed by the University of Oxford. Oxford University also receives funding from competitive (government) research grants and external funding from "private nonprofit" foundations, such as the Wellcome Trust.

Spin-outs, Start-ups, and the Growth of Science Parks

When universities commercialize their science by starting new companies these are often termed *spin-outs* in the United Kingdom or *start-ups* in the United States (see box 4.1 for some examples). The comparative survey evidence of Unico shows that the United Kingdom was relatively more active in creating spin-outs per unit of research resource: in 2004 one such firm was created for every £11 million of research expenditure in the United Kingdom compared with one per £50 million in the United States. Many start-ups initially locate near to universities. In fact, a common feature of the developing relationship between university and industry is the establishment of university *science parks*, often called *research parks* in the United States or *technology parks* in Asia. These are areas where clusters of new and existing firms locate near to university science departments. Thus science parks are a form of infrastructure that can smooth the transfer of technology from universities to firms. Are science parks cost effective? A comparative study of U.K. firms located on and off university science parks by Siegel et al. (2003) used a database of "matched pairs" of firms to explore what benefit, if any, was derived from the science park location. They found that science park firms performed better than non-science park firms, both in terms of generating new products and also in terms of number of patents.

In the United States, research parks are not as often clustered around universities as they are in the United Kingdom. Here it is possible to study the value of formal links between universities and research parks, as well as the effects of the distances between the two (see Link and Scott 2003). The rate of growth of U.S. research parks is positively linked with proximity to a university. Formal links between a university and a science park generate more scholarly publications and patents within the university, and proximity to a science park increases the likelihood of a shift in curriculum from basic science to applied research.

Personnel Linkages

Another aspect of the developing relationship between universities and private firms is the increase in the direct employment of university personnel in companies. Scientists help the company in a number of ways, including facilitating knowledge transfer from university laboratories, signaling the quality of the firm's research to financial markets, and in forming the strategy of the company. Audretsch and Stephan (1996) present interesting statistics on the U.S. biotechnology industry, analyzing forty-five biotechnology firms with links to 445 university scientists during 1990–92. Their sample indicates that scientists fill formal roles in companies as follows: 9% are founders, 82% sit on scientific advisory boards, 5% act as advisory board chairmen, and 9% are major stockholders. (The same individuals may of course hold more than one of these positions.) They also find that 70% of the research links between university scientists and enterprises in the U.S. biotechnology industry are outside the region where the firm is located. Geographical proximity is important when the nature of the knowledge transmission is informal, but proximity is much less important for formal knowledge transfers, since such transfers of knowledge will be carefully planned in advance. However, it is still the case that geographical proximity matters, and Audretsch and Stephan find that it matters more for founders than for scientific advisors.

Two related studies for Europe by Mason and coauthors (Mason and Wagner 1999; Mason et al. 2001) are interesting in this regard. Universities and related research institutes are considered part of a "knowledge infrastructure" in Mason et al. (2001) and differences in this national knowledge infrastructure are used to compare samples of electronic establishments in the United Kingdom and France. The electronics sectors in both of these countries have quite extensive formal links with university-based researchers. About half of the sampled French enterprises had some link with universities, compared with 80% of British enterprises. This difference is due in part to the longstanding relationships of French firms with public research laboratories. The relationships in France between universities and enterprises were found to be more stable than those in the United Kingdom. The authors argue that the faster rate of new relationship building in the United Kingdom is due to the need of British universities to mitigate financial problems, caused partly by cutbacks in central government funding. Thus the authors find that British universities have tended to be more proactive in finding funding for their electronics research and were more disposed to conduct market-driven research.

Consequences of the New University–Business Relationship

The changing nature of university–business relations raises a number of important questions.

- Does increased commercialization shift research away from fundamental research toward applied, developmental research? If so, is such a shift detrimental to economic growth in the long run?

- Does exclusive patenting and licensing of university research reduce the diversity of commercialization attempts?

- Do the transaction costs associated with patenting and licensing dissuade some firms, especially smaller ones, from attempting commercialization?[11]

- Do some universities fail to account for the true cost of TTOs and finding licensees?

---

[11] For a smaller firm the cost of a license may discourage it from pursuing a commercialization project. Even for larger firms high transactions costs can occur if there are multiple licenses needed to conduct commercialization. Such transactions costs are linked to the idea of the "tragedy of the anticommons," which refers to the idea that, in an environment of many patents, the cost of ensuring all the aspects of one's research are correctly licensed is prohibitive. Heller and Eisenberg (1998) argue that this was the case in biomedical research. Heller (1997) introduces the term "anticommons" in a discussion of shop rental in Moscow.

- What are the implications for science education of turning many professors into company advisors or managers?

Has the growth in university patenting and associated licensing biased effort away from fundamental research?[12] Thursby and Thursby (2002, 2007) discuss the somewhat limited evidence on this question for the United States and, overall, they find little evidence of a shift in research orientation.[13] Instead, the rises in patenting and licensing tend to reflect increased awareness, willingness, and expertise of faculty members and TTOs.

Jensen and Thursby (2001) have analyzed the issue of university licensing in the United States in the wake of the Bayh–Dole Act. They ask whether the commercial use of federally funded research would be increased or reduced without university patent licensing. The issue at stake was whether incentives for research, such as university patent licensing, constituted an unnecessary extra step to commercialize invention, or whether such an incentive helped take useful inventions out of the research lab and into the marketplace. Jensen and Thursby's results show that most licenses are very embryonic, and commercialization would be impossible without further collaboration and assistance from the inventor, implying that university patent licensing is often necessary for commercial exposure and commercial success. Indeed, 71% of cases reported that cooperation between inventor and licensee was required for successful development.

David (2005) cautions against the adoption of the Bayh–Dole model in Europe, as recommended by the European Commission (2003).[14] In his view, the movement toward the university harnessing the "output" of university professors (i.e., the advancement of knowledge) often neglects a proper evaluation of the costs to their universities and overstates the potential revenue gains. He cites evidence of several studies in Europe

---

[12] Mowery and Shane (2002) assert that the number of U.S. universities that are involved in licensing rose by 800% over the period 1980-2000; at the same time, the number of university patents increased by 400%.

[13] They use publications in "fundamental" science journals as a method of tracking research orientation. Their data indicate that the percentage of faculty members (in Ph.D.-granting departments) who register a possible discovery with university TTOs was around 10% in the mid 1990s, leaving 90% of faculty—in any specific year—not having a direct interest (Thursby and Thursby 2007, p. 634). Mowery and Shane (2002, p. vi) also quote evidence that only around 7% of knowledge transferred from MIT's departments of mechanical and electrical engineering to industry involves patents.

[14] Mowery et al. (2001) consider the impact of the Bayh-Dole Act on three U.S. universities: California, Columbia, and Stanford. Their conclusion is that, although patenting activity increased in the 1980s, the main reasons for this were the increase in biotechnology-related research (which started in the 1970s) together with changes in federal patent policies that made biomedical patents easier to obtain, and patent enforcement stronger.

that show a high rate of patenting by academics in Italy, France, and Germany during the 1980s and 1990s, but with the ownership of these patents belonging to the individuals concerned, not to their universities. David suggests that insisting on university ownership would complicate the licensing to private firms, without necessarily increasing the rate of invention. He also argues that large R&D-intensive firms in the United States are generally no longer very enthusiastic about the Bayh–Dole regime. In an earlier paper, David (2001) also points out the difficulties that the strengthening of copyright and database protection has introduced for researchers' ability to continue to share scientific data freely. He recommends that ownership rights of scientific databases should include provisions for the compulsory licensing of the contents of the database at marginal cost to interested research bodies. Despite these warnings, there is considerable enthusiasm within top research universities for the patenting and commercialization of university-based technology.[15]

Interestingly, a study by Zucker and Darby (1996) found that prominent researchers in biotechnology appeared to have outstanding research records even after involvement in patenting and other forms of commercialization. Siegel et al. (2003) found that researchers with commercial interests tended to reinvest some of the funds gained from commercial sources in new equipment and student support. On the other hand, not all examples of researcher involvement in commercial concerns appear to have positive educational outcomes. Stephan (2001) suggests that industry links will reduce the time available for the more traditional responsibilities of academics, including teaching, administration, and supervision. Work by Louis et al. (2001) found that university and research institute scientists with commercial links tended to reject requests for research results from other academics more than academics with no such commercial links; a very similar result was also found by Blumenthal et al. (1997).

4.6 The Government–Business Axis

A government's involvement in stimulating and regulating the other two players on the national innovation stage takes many forms. The key areas of government policy related to innovation are as follows.

(1) IPRs policy (the enforcement of IPRs can be influenced by national policy, as is legislation to some extent).

---

[15] Some of this is due to the fact that licensing revenues can be large. U.S. universities received $1.4 billion in revenues in 2005 (Siegel et al. 2007, p. 640).

(2) Tax policy (corporate tax policy can affect innovation in various ways, but key areas include R&D tax concessions, rules surrounding intellectual property, and venture capital).

(3) Competition policy (the stance of competition policy, especially when decisions involve innovation, e.g., when a firm has a dominant market position but also leads the industry in terms of innovation).

(4) Government–business targeted funding of specific research, technology, and small business.

(5) Standard setting (the government is involved in setting various standards for measurement, performance, safety, testing, and interoperability).

(6) Procurement policies (as a large purchaser of goods and services, the government can influence business activity, e.g., its decisions about purchasing computers).

These areas of policy cover a huge range of issues and most of them are covered in future chapters of this book. A discussion of points (1) and (2) are left until chapter 11. Point (3) is discussed further in chapter 5, but there is also some discussion in chapter 11. Points (5) and (6) are also discussed in chapter 11. Below we briefly discuss point (4).

Audretsch et al. (2001) studied one such program, the Small Business Innovation Research (SBIR) program in the United States. This program began in 1977 at the National Science Foundation (NSF) to encourage those activities of small businesses that were judged to be of commercial merit. A 1982 act required government departments with external research programs greater than $100 billion to set aside funds worth 0.2% of their research budget to SBIR initiatives; the level of funding was increased to 1.25% in 1987 and to 2.5% in 1996. Audretsch et al. find that the social rate of return of many of the SBIR programs was much higher than the private return. This suggests that the SBIR was useful in correcting market failures arising from underinvestment in "socially valuable research in emerging technologies." They also computed a social rate of return and compared it with the opportunity cost of the funds committed to the SBIR by government departments and found that the projects were of high economic value when measured on this basis. The authors conclude that:

> There is ample evidence that the SBIR program is stimulating R&D; as well as efforts to commercialize that would not otherwise have taken place.
>
> Audretsch et al. (2001, p. 1)

Another U.S. policy is discussed in box 4.2.

Box 4.2. The U.S. partnership for a new generation of vehicles.

An American public–private initiative that has attracted interest is the 1993 "Partnership for a New Generation of Vehicles" (PNGV). This program was introduced with the goal of furthering research on energy-efficient vehicles (Sperling 2001). The question he then addresses is whether the provision of public funds for R&D to the three private-sector participants (Ford, General Motors, and Chrysler) significantly affected their behavior for the better. Sperling's review of the motor industry finds that smaller, non-PNGV motor firms were much more efficient and quick at introducing commercially viable energy-efficient technologies. PNGV did bring benefits in terms of focusing the federal government's transport R&D budget, and it helped stimulate technological advances in fuel cell technology. These benefits are extremely difficult to measure, and Sperling suggests that the greatest benefit of the program may have been what he refers to as the "boomerang effect." The boomerang effect emanates from the increased motivation given to European and Japanese carmakers by the PNGV, which spurred them on to greater efforts in their own research, which had the effect of further accelerating the American efforts. Another interesting conclusion concerning the effectiveness of public R&D funding for such projects is that such funding should occur when the targeted technology is far away from commercialization since manufacturers have powerful incentives to provide their own funding when a potentially lucrative project is close to being marketed. Sperling's analysis suggests that a more fruitful use of the R&D funds would have been to award such funds on a competitive basis outside of the PNGV as grants to small companies, universities, and other research centers.

Research consortia may arise spontaneously between private firms, or the government may choose to directly subsidize such a consortium. Potential benefits to firms and society of research consortia include internalizing and maximizing research spillovers; the elimination of wasteful duplication of effort, leading to reductions in costs; and the pooling of risk. Agreements to share research results can also improve the diffusion of inventions into a range of alternative applications. Consortia may also allow economies of scale in research. Lastly, research joint ventures can obviate the need for full-scale mergers (which may apply to the current trend in the pharmaceutical industry toward huge and ever-larger mergers).

Branstetter and Sakakibara (2002) examine data on every research joint venture in Japan between companies where the joint venture involved the government (from 1980 to 1992). The results indicate that consortia enjoy greater benefits when they do basic rather than applied research. They also find that the design of a consortium is more important than the level of resources dedicated to it, suggesting the importance of strategic factors. Three key characteristics of a consortium for research efficiency are complementary research assets; high potential for spillovers within the consortium; and the lack of rivalry between member enterprises in their final product markets. These results, as the authors note, may be expected to apply to research consortia in any country. However, government support for such programs may diminish somewhat in Japan, where there is a growing realization that the activist public–private technology partnerships that had characterized postwar Japan may be of little relevance in fast-changing high-technology industries (Goto 2000).

4.7 National Innovation Systems in Emerging Markets

This chapter has focused on the national innovation system (NIS) in leading economies. The NIS approach is also relevant to emerging markets. In order to illustrate the issues we will consider two economies that have experienced rapid growth since the 1960s: South Korea and Taiwan. Then we will consider more recent developments in China and India.

South Korea and Taiwan

In the early 1960s South Korea was one of the poorest economies in the world with a GDP per capita less than that of Sudan and less than a third of Mexico's. In the 1960s, Korean firms accounted for only 2–3% of the total R&D in the economy. Korean universities also did little research (Kim and Kim 2005). Hence, in the 1960s the government took the lead by setting up research institutes. These were focused on understanding overseas technology, including reverse engineering, in order to aid technology transfer, as well as training researchers for the private sector. As Korea's economy grew in the 1970s (see table 3.5), private firms became increasingly important and they were encouraged to do R&D, often with the help of government tax incentives and cheap finance. Korea's large family-owned firms (called "chaebols") came to dominate R&D.[16] The government developed the university sector by establishing the Korea Advanced Institute of Science and Technology in 1971, with the aim of conducting high-quality research and training high-caliber

---

[16] Korean firms such as Samsung, Hyundai, and Lucky Goldstar (LG) were among twenty firms that accounted for around 70% of total private R&D. See also box 9.2, which discusses Samsung.

scientists. Throughout the 1970s and 1980s the government strengthened and broadened its research institutes and the universities. These
policies, along with direct tax and financial support, acted to stimulate
private-sector R&D. Overall, Korean R&D expenditure rose from 10 billion won in 1970 to 9,440 billion won in 1995, representing an increase
in R&D/GNP from 0.4% to 2.7% (Kim and Yi 1997, table 2).

Taiwan was also a poor country in the 1960s, although better off than
South Korea in terms of GDP per capita and with a better education system. Like Korea, its rapid growth in subsequent decades was based on
Taiwanese firms using new technology and production methods. The
government played an important part in this process, for example by
setting up the Industrial Technology Research Institute (ITRI) in 1973.
By 2003 the ITRI had more that 6,000 patents in force worldwide and
had helped more than 30,000 firms in Taiwan. The ITRI was vital to the
establishment of Taiwan Semiconductor Manufacturing Company and
United Microelectronics Corporation (two of the largest computer chip
manufacturers in the world) (Peng et al. 2006).[17] In addition, many Taiwanese firms acted as subcontractors to foreign firms in developed countries, and these firms supplied technical details on production methods. A difference with Korea is that Taiwan's industry was dominated
by small and medium-sized enterprises (SMEs), not large chaebols as in
Korea. In general, the SMEs could not afford to undertake substantial
R&D projects, hence government support for R&D was high.[18] In addition, the SMEs often formed "clusters" of firms around an industry, which
encouraged knowledge sharing.[19] Hence in both Korea and Taiwan the
process involved building up the capacity of domestic firms to produce
higher-value products using more sophisticated processes. Doing this
is difficult and required the support of both government and universities. R&D was at the center of the process. Initially, the R&D built up
firms' capability to understand technology, but in latter decades these
firms became innovators. It should be stressed that in both Taiwan and

---

[17] The ITRI was instrumental in establishing many other spin-out companies. Importantly, the ITRI would provide finance and technology, lend out employees, and allow
the spin-outs to use ITRI's research laboratories.

[18] Even by the mid 1980s, the government share of R&D in Taiwan was around 60%,
compared with 20% in Korea (Mowery and Oxley 1995).

[19] For example, in 1963 the U.S.-owned Singer company made a small investment in
Taiwan. An agreement had been made with Singer that 80% of components were to
be sourced locally, which led to the establishment of many SMEs. In the 1970s four
large, domestic companies emerged and Taiwan's exports of sewing machines grew from
$0.2 million in 1964 to $70 million in 1979 (Hobday 1995, p. 127). The initial impetus
in this case came from foreign direct investment (FDI), something that occurred in other
industries as well.

Korea the initial steps often involved technology from abroad, by allowing FDI, engaging in joint ventures with U.S. and Japanese firms, and also through licensing agreements.[20] In addition, economic growth was closely linked to exporting, which provided both demand for output and access to new technology, as well as information on customer needs (see also chapter 9).

China and India

China and India are two countries with large populations that have achieved high rates of growth in recent years (see table 3.5). What can be said about the NIS in these economies? For China there are similarities with the South Korean and Taiwanese experiences. China has often kick-started growth by using technology from abroad, including FDI and joint ventures. Many large multinationals have sourced production in China, thereby transferring knowledge and technology into Chinese factories. Exporting to overseas markets, often the United States, enabled very rapid growth plus the associated benefits mentioned above.[21] Investment in R&D also increased substantially: the ratio of R&D to GDP increasing from 0.6% in 1995 to 1.3% in 2005. Since China's GDP more than doubled in this period, absolute R&D expenditure increased by more than four times.[22] As in Korea, this increase has been driven by firms, with their share of R&D increasing from 27% in 1990 to 68% in 2005. A notable feature of China's R&D is the amount carried out by multinationals. Lundin and Serger (2007) estimate that around 29% of China's manufacturing R&D is carried out by foreign firms (see box 12.1 for some examples).

India followed a strategy characterized by import substitution and socialist policies in the three decades after its independence in 1947. Economic growth was relatively low until 1980, but then picked up in the 1980s and 1990s (see table 3.5), and then increased further in the five years to 2006 (to around 6% per annum according to International Monetary Fund data). There are many factors involved in these changes in growth, perhaps most importantly the shift in policies to encourage

---

[20] Both countries were greatly helped by good political, trade, and educational links with the United States. Both countries were allowed access to U.S. markets and many students studied at U.S. universities.

[21] China's export to GDP ratio was 40% in 2006, South Korea's 43%, and India's 23% (World Bank country indicator Web site; note that the World Bank does not report separate data for Taiwan and includes this in China's data).

[22] The statistics in this paragraph come from Lundin and Serger (2007) and Schaaper (2004). Increasing R&D by this amount requires qualified scientists and engineers and Schaaper describes the improvements in university education and research.

private enterprise, but our focus here is on the NIS.[23] India's R&D to GDP ratio increased from 0.17% in 1958 to 1% in 1987 (it has since declined to around 0.7% (Kumar 2001, p. 26)). Since independence, the Indian government has focused on science and technology, including expanding university education. By 1999, Indian universities had seven million students enrolled, with two million of these in technical subjects. These developments, together with other policies to encourage R&D, were vital to two of India's most important sectors: pharmaceuticals and computer software.

India's software industry has experienced rapid growth, much of this based on outsourcing from U.S. and EU companies, hence exports of software have grown from $131 million in 1990 to $7.8 billion in 2002, which was 16% of total exports (D'Costa 2003). India's pharmaceutical industry grew rapidly after 1970, when a new Patent Act was introduced. The new act removed patent protection on pharmaceuticals, chemicals, and food, as well as reducing the length of protection on other product and process inventions. In the 1970s and 1980s India developed a major industry in producing generic pharmaceuticals, including for export, and through time some companies developed their own innovative compounds (Kumar 2003). Exports of pharmaceuticals increased from 0.5% of total exports in 1970 to around 4% in 2000. While the developments in software and pharmaceuticals have been impressive, there is a concern that India's growth potential is limited to these and a few other sectors (Lall 1999).

Patenting, National Innovation Systems, and Performance

The above sections have covered a vast number of issues. It should be stressed that understanding the reasons for high rates of economic growth in emerging markets requires much more than knowledge of their national innovation systems (see, for example, chapters 8 and 9). However, it is important to realize that the growth of firms does rely on such a system, whether in an advanced economy or in an emerging market. It is also clear that there are many different aspects to the national innovation system. Table 4.4 shows a frequently used summary measure of comparative performance in knowledge and invention: the number of patents granted by the USPTO. The table shows the rapid increase in patenting by South Korea and Taiwan, reaching over 7,000 in 2007.

---

[23] Rodrik and Subramanian (2004) discuss the reasons for the changes in India's economic growth rate. Many commentators highlight the onset of liberalization after the balance of payments crisis in 1991; however, it is clear that economic growth had improved during the 1980s.

Table 4.4.   U.S. patents granted to firms from emerging markets.

Country	1987	1990	1995	2000	2005	2006	2007
Brazil	35	45	70	113	98	148	118
China	23	48	63	162	565	970	1,235
India	12	23	38	131	403	506	578
Korea	105	290	1,240	3,472	4,591	6,509	7,264
Mexico	54	34	45	100	95	88	88
Russia	0	0	99	185	154	176	193
Taiwan	411	861	2,087	5,806	5,993	7,920	7,491

Source. The USPTO's "Patent Technology Monitoring Team Report," available online.

In contrast, China had 1,235 and India 578 in 2007. The rapid growth in China's patenting is noteworthy (and since grants lag applications, we also know that this figure is set to rise further still). In comparison, Brazil, Mexico, and Russia all have low levels of patents and no clear upward trend, suggesting that growth in these countries will have to be based on raw materials and agribusiness rather than the technological transformation of industry.

4.8   Conclusions

The national innovation system, which is the system within which knowledge, invention, and innovation interact, is central to economic performance. This chapter has shown how the interplay between business, university, and government has many, often complex, aspects. Central to the system is the role of R&D, which can be undertaken by universities, governments, and businesses. Choosing the right mix between the three partners to achieve maximum efficiency of R&D is of fundamental importance, although there are no simple rules to follow in order to do this. This is illustrated by the experience of several emerging markets where R&D, although often kick-started by government, was then steadily decentralized to the private sector.

The main part of the chapter focused on developed economies. A major issue here is the new environment for R&D. While it is unlikely that the new trends in the collaborations between government, universities, and firms will be reversed, it is not clear that the changes that have occurred are uniformly beneficial. The effect on the overall rate of innovation is still largely unknown, as is their influence on the composition of R&D in universities (ie., between R&D spent on the commercial aspects of known science, as compared with fundamental scientific discovery). Implicit in the shift of policy from the free distribution of science to the patenting of scientific findings by universities is a view that the commercialization of science will be enhanced by establishing an orderly market for licensing. This *license-based model* has replaced the previous public-good model, or some would say "free-for-all," in the distribution of public scientific knowledge.

What are the arguments supporting the license-based model? First, it could simply be that firms only value what they pay for. Second, if most university research output still requires additional development costs, firms are unwilling to commit to these unless exclusive licenses are on offer. Third, licenses have aided in the general promotion of the links between universities and business, which may then direct more resources into collaborative and commercial research. However, the license-based model—and indeed the stress on university–business partnerships in general—may reduce research in basic science. Will this diminish the future rate of innovation? Some eminent scientists think so: Kornberg (2007) believes that in his field of research—the way in which genes function to control infectious disease, or fail to control diseases such as cancer—many of the exploratory projects that led to fundamental breakthroughs during the last thirty years would not be funded today. In contrast, Thursby and Thursby (2007) report data from an analysis of eleven major U.S. universities that indicate little, if any, change to the nature of research (see section 4.5). Hence there is an ongoing debate about the effects of universities seeking intellectual property.

Keywords

National innovation system.
Start-ups and spin-outs.
Science parks.
Technology transfer offices.
License-based model.

Questions for Discussion

(1) Identify the three main partners within the NIS. Should they play complementary or competing roles in generating innovation?

(2) What are the main ways in which universities and private businesses interact?

(3) Is it a good idea for university science departments or individual academics to patent their scientific research findings?

(4) If universities do patent, should they offer licenses to one or more firms? How much should the licenses cost? Should government regulate these activities?

(5) In public–private partnerships, is the presence of government a "dead hand" or a necessary catalyst for innovation?

(6) Discuss the role of government in supporting the NIS in emerging markets.

(7) Do national statistics on the number of patents tell us anything important?

References

Adams, J. 1990. Fundamental stocks of knowledge and productivity growth. *Journal of Political Economy* 98(4):673–702.

Audretsch, D., and P. Stephan. 1996. Company-scientist locational links: the case of biotechnology. *American Economic Review* 86(3):641–52.

Audretsch, D., A. Link, and J. Scott. 2001. Public/private technology partnerships: evaluating SBIR-supported research. Dartmouth College Working Paper 01-01 (January).

Bloom, N., and R. Griffith. 2001. The internationalisation of UK R&D. *Fiscal Studies* 22(3):337–55.

Blumenthal, D., E. G. Campbell, M. S. Anderson, N. Causino, and K. S. Louis. 1997. Withholding of research results in academic life science: evidence from a national survey of faculty. *Journal of the American Medical Association* 277(15):1,224–28.

Branstetter, L., and M. Sakakibara. 2002. When do research consortia work well and why? Evidence from Japanese panel data. *American Economic Review* 92(1):143–59.

Cardwell, D. 1994. *The Fontana History of Technology*. London: Fontana.

Council on Governmental Relations. 1999. *The Bayh-Dole Act: A Guide to the Law and Implementing Regulations*. Washington, DC: Council on Governmental Relations.

David, P. 2001. Will building good fences really make good neighbors in science? In "Intellectual property protection and internet collaborations." A report of the EC-DG Research Strata Working Party (April).

———. 2005. Innovation and universities' role in commercializing research results: second thoughts about the Bayh–Dole experiment. Stanford Institute for Economic Policy Research Discussion Paper 04-27 (May).

D'Costa, A. P. 2003. Uneven and combined development: understanding India's software exports. *World Development* 31(1):211–26.

Dougherty, S., R. Inklaar, R. McGuckin, and B. van Ark. 2007. International comparisons of R&D expenditure: does an R&D PPP make a difference? NBER Working Paper 12,829.

European Commission. 2003. *Communication on the Role of the Universities in the Europe of Knowledge*. Brussels: Commission of the European Communities.

Eurostat. 2007. *Science, Technology and Innovation in Europe*. Brussels: Commission of the European Communities.

Freeman, C. 1995. The national system of innovation in historical perspective. *Cambridge Journal of Economics* 19:5-24.

Goto, A. 2000. Japan's national innovation system: current status and problems. *Oxford Review of Economic Policy* 16(2):103-13.

Hall, B., A. Link, and J. Scott. 2002. Universities as research partners. *Review of Economics and Statistics* 85(2):485-91.

Heller, M. A. 1997. The tragedy of the anticommons: property in the transition from Marx to Markets. William Davidson Institute Working Papers Series no. 40.

Heller, M. A., and R. Eisenberg. 1998. Can patents deter innovation? The anticommons in biomedical research. *Science* 280:698-701.

Hobday, M. 1995. *Innovation in East Asia*. Cheltenham, U.K.: Edward Elgar.

House of Commons. 2004. Scientific publications: free for all?. House of Commons Scientific Committee HC399-I.

Hull, D. 1988. *Science as a Process*. University of Chicago Press.

Jensen, R., and M. Thursby. 2001. Proofs and prototypes for sale: the tale of university licensing. *American Economic Review* 91(2):240-59.

Kim, D. S., and D. K. Kim. 2005. The evolutionary responses of Korean government research institutes in a changing national innovation system. *Science, Technology and Society* 10:31-55.

Kim, L., and G. Yi. 1997. The dynamics of R&D in industrial development: lessons from the Korean experience. *Industry and Innovation* 4(2):167-82.

Kornberg, R. 2007. Talk given at the seminar "Innovation policy for the next presidency" at Stanford University, June 1, 2007. See also R. Kornberg's statement to the Subcommittee on Science, Technology and Innovation, Senate Committee on Commerce, Science and Transportation, May 2, 2007 (supplied by the author).

Kumar, N. 2001. National innovation systems and the Indian software industry development. Background paper for World Industrial Development Report 2001, UNIDO.

———. 2003. Intellectual property rights, technology and economic development experiences of Asian countries. *Economic and Political Weekly* 18:209-26.

Lall, S. 1999. India's manufactured exports: comparative structure and prospects. *World Development* 27(10):1,769-86.

Leydesdorff, L., and M. Meyer. 2006. Triple helix indicators of knowledge-based innovation systems: introduction to the special issue. *Research Policy* 35(10): 1,441-49.

Link, S., and J. Scott. 2003. U.S. science parks: the diffusion of an innovation and its effects on the academic missions of universities. *International Journal of Industrial Organization* 21(9):1,323-56.

Louis, K. S., M. S. Anderson, L. Jones, D. Blumenthal, and E. Campbell. 2001. Entrepreneurship, secrecy, and productivity: a comparison of clinical and non-clinical life sciences faculty. *Journal of Technology Transfer* 26(3):233-45.

Lundin, N., and S. Serger. 2007. Globalization of R&D and China. IFN Working Paper 710, Research Institute of Industrial Economics, Sweden.

Lundvall, B. 1992. *National Systems of Innovation*. London: Pinter.

Mason, G., and K. Wagner. 1999. Knowledge transfer and innovation in Britain and Germany: intermediate institution models of knowledge transfer under strain? *Industry and Innovation* 6(1):85–110.

Mason, G., J. P. Beltramo, and J.-J. Paul. 2001. Knowledge infrastructure, technical problem solving and industrial performance: electronics in Britain and France. Discussion Paper 189 (November), National Institute of Economic and Social Research.

McCabe, M., and C. Synder. 2005. Open access and academic journal quality. *American Economic Review* 95(2):453–58.

Merton, R. 1957. Priorities in scientific discovery: a chapter in the sociology of science. *American Sociological Review* 22(6):635–59.

———. 1988. The Matthew effect in science. II. Cumulative advantage and the symbolism of intellectual property. *Isis* 79(299):606–23.

Mowery, D., and R. Nelson. 2004. *Ivory Tower and Industrial Innovation: University-Industry Technology Transfer Before and After the Bayh-Dole Act in the United States*. Stanford University Press.

Mowery, D., and J. Oxley. 1995. Inward technology transfer and competitiveness: the role of national innovation systems. *Cambridge Journal of Economics* 19: 67–93.

Mowery, D., and S. Shane. 2002. Introduction to the special issue on university entrepreneurship and technology transfer. *Management Science* 48(1):v–ix.

Mowery, D., R. R. Nelson, B. Sampat, and A. Ziedonis. 2001. The growth of patenting and licensing by U.S. universities: an assessment of the effects of the Bayh-Dole act of 1980. *Research Policy* 30:99–119.

Nelson, R. (ed.). 1993. *National Innovation Systems: A Comparative Analysis*. Oxford University Press.

OECD. 2005. *Science and Technology Statistics*. Paris: OECD.

Peng, B.-W., H.-G. Chen, and B.-W. Lin. 2006. A Taiwan research institute as a technology business incubator: ITRI and its spin-offs. *Comparative Technology Transfer and Society* 4(1):1–21.

Poyago-Theotoky, J., J. Beath, and D. Siegel. 2002. Universities and fundamental research: policy implications of the growth of university-industry partnerships. *Oxford Review of Economic Policy* 18(1):10–21.

Rodrik, D., and A. Subramanian. 2004. From Hindu growth to productivity surge: the mystery of the Indian growth transition. IMF Working Paper 77.

Schaaper, M. 2004. An emerging knowledge-based economy in China? STI Working Paper 2004/4, OECD.

Siegel, D., D. Waldman, and A. Link. 2003. Assessing the impact of organizational practices on the productivity of university technology transfer offices: an exploratory study. *Research Policy* 32(1):27–48.

Siegel, D., R. Veugelers, and M. Wright. 2007. Technology transfer offices and commercialization of university intellectual property: performance and policy implications. *Oxford Review of Economic Policy* 23(4):640–60.

Siegel, D., P. Westhead, and M. Wright. 2003. Assessing the impact of university science parks on research productivity: exploratory firm-level evidence from the United Kingdom. *International Journal of Industrial Organisation* 21(9): 1,357–69.

Sperling, D. 2001. Public–private technology R&D partnerships: lessons from U.S. partnership for a new generation of vehicles. *Transport Policy* 8:247–56.

Stephan, P. 1996. The economics of science. *Journal of Economic Literature* 34(September):1,199–235.

———. 2001. Educational implications of university–industry technology transfer. *Journal of Technology Transfer* 26(3):199–205.

Technopolis. 2007. Third annual survey of knowledge transfer activities in public sector research establishments. Report to the Department for Innovation, Universities and Skills (July).

Thursby, J., and M. Thursby. 2002. Who is selling the ivory tower? Sources of growth in university licensing. *Management Science* 48(1):90–104.

———. 2007. University licensing. *Oxford Review of Economic Policy* 23(4):620–39.

Uglow, J. 2002. *The Lunar Society*. London: Faber.

Unico. 2005. UK university commercialisation survey: financial year 2004. Report, Unico (available at www.unico.org.uk).

Zucker, L., and M. Darby. 1996. Star scientists and institutional transformation: patterns of invention and innovation in the formation of the biotechnology industry. *Proceedings of the National Academy of Sciences* 93(23):12,709–16.

5

Innovative Firms and Markets

5.1 Introduction

The last chapter discussed how the process of innovation relied on the interaction between three main actors: business, universities, and government. This chapter focuses on the business sector as this is generally regarded as the most critical. It is the business sector that often conducts the majority of R&D; it also supplies new capital goods to consumers and producers. We also take a much more detailed look at the way competition in markets interacts with the process of innovation. The overall aim is to provide a framework for understanding whether the market system produces the optimal level of innovation. In order to do this the chapter discusses various aspects of the market system and asks questions such as: What role do entrepreneurs play in the process of innovation? What problems do innovative new firms face? How do market conditions impact on rates of innovation?

In answering these questions we take a predominantly economic approach by focusing on the incentive structures facing firms and the competitive interaction between firms. However, we also cover some of the management and legal issues surrounding innovation. The later part of the chapter reviews how empirical work can assess the private value of innovation and evaluates how market structure affects the propensity to innovate. We also draw attention to how such empirical work can inform our understanding of markets and contribute to innovation policy debates.

5.2 Entrepreneurship and New Firms

We have already mentioned *inventors* and *entrepreneurs* in previous chapters and it is now time to be explicit about their role in innovation within firms. An inventor is defined as someone who generates the new ideas on which innovations are based. For a firm to be innovative it can either employ inventors, or it can have good access to external idea sources (e.g., universities), or both. An entrepreneur can be defined in different ways, but our preferred definition is "someone who searches for new ideas and exploits them commercially."[1] Thus the basic nature of entrepreneurship is that of finding opportunities that have not yet been exploited. This can be achieved by "gap-filling," discovering niche markets that are not yet supplied, or it can be done by gaining a share of mainstream supply to core markets. The exploitation of an idea involves innovation (as defined in chapter 1). Many entrepreneurs start a business to exploit their idea; hence entrepreneurs are closely linked with the process of firm creation. It is possible that the inventor becomes an entrepreneur by setting up a business, although the skills needed to be a successful entrepreneur are different from the skills needed by an inventor. Entrepreneurial activity is, therefore, the major force behind the creation of new firms that introduce new products or processes to the market. The markets in which these firms operate become the testing ground for a new generation of ideas; successful ideas will enable firms to become part of the next generation of larger firms, either through growth or via takeover by larger firms, while firms with unsuccessful ideas fail.[2] Does this process of ideas generation, firm formation, and market selection work optimally? In general, economists and policy makers are concerned that it does not for three reasons:

(1) Not enough entrepreneurs are being "created."

(2) Entrepreneurs select nonproductive activities.

(3) Entrepreneurs, with good ideas, fail to succeed.

These failures could be due to lack of access to critical resources, lack of training and expertise, or because there are barriers to entry in existing markets. The third reason requires some more background on markets and will be left to section 5.4 below. In this section we consider reasons (1) and (2).

---

[1] Joseph Schumpeter (1883–1950) was an early economist to stress the role of entrepreneurship. Entrepreneurship is often defined as the pursuit of opportunity without regard to resources currently controlled. This conveys the important idea that entrepreneurs are not constrained by their present circumstances, or even the present market conditions, hence their actions can lead to major changes in the economy. This also indicates how entrepreneurship differs from management (which is about directing resources already under your control). Drucker (1985) and Shalman (1999) provide good introductions to entrepreneurship.

[2] This idea is related to the product life cycle of industries, where there may be an initial growth of new entrants with competing new products. Over time there is a shakeout of products and firms, with the most innovative firms tending to survive and a fall in the total number of firms in the industry (see Gort and Klepper (1982) for some case studies and Klepper (1996) for a theoretical model).

Do societies encourage a sufficient number of entrepreneurs and which activities do they select? Baumol (1990) makes the bold claim that, to a rough approximation, all societies throughout history have had similar entrepreneurial capacity—from the Romans to medieval China to the Renaissance in Europe—but that they differ greatly in how this is used. He uses the idea of nonproductive activities, such as crime or profiteering (also known as rent seeking) within government jobs, and asserts that low-growth societies divert too many "entrepreneurs" into these activities. The extent of such diversion depends on the cultural, regulatory, and legal characteristics of the society. Baumol discusses historic societies in an attempt to prove his hypothesis. In a modern context, the United States is often regarded as a country where the culture and education system strongly encourage entrepreneurship, and where the regulatory and legal system allows this to be channeled into creating new firms that contribute to GDP (i.e., to productive activities).[3] In contrast, in many developing countries it is often argued that onerous regulation and corruption channel entrepreneurs into criminal or rent-seeking activities.[4] There is, therefore, agreement with Baumol's main hypothesis that entrepreneurial capacity can be diverted into different activities, but is latent entrepreneurial capacity the same across countries? One study on how many people would like to be self-employed indicated vast differences across countries, suggesting latent capacity does vary.[5] Furthermore, policy makers are often keen on ensuring that the education system alerts pupils to the possibility of entrepreneurship, indicating that it may be possible to influence latent capacity.

Can larger firms also be entrepreneurial? One response to this is "yes, if the firm allows its employees to act in an entrepreneurial way." It is, however, often difficult to allow employees to act in such a way, since this clashes with the standard planning and budgetary controls imposed in large organizations. Some organizations try to balance the situation

---

[3] There are some studies that attempt to test these ideas using recent cross-country survey data on entrepreneurship. For example, Ardagna and Lusardi (2008) use World Bank Global Entrepreneurship Monitor (GEM) data on thirty-seven countries to analyze the factors influencing entrepreneurship, including the impact of regulation (they find that greater regulation reduces entrepreneurship).

[4] An important book related to these ideas is by Hernando de Soto (2000). He argues that the poor legal systems, and specifically the lack of land ownership registries, mean that poor people cannot borrow capital to invest in small businesses.

[5] Blanchflower et al. (2001, p. 683) find that around 80% of workers in Poland would like to be self-employed, compared with 71% in the United States, 45% in the United Kingdom, and around 41% in France and Japan. (The data are from surveys done in 1997–98.) "Self-employment" is not the same as "entrepreneurship," but they are likely to be positively correlated.

by having schemes whereby employees with a new idea can bid for funds, which they can then use in any way they see fit (as an independent entrepreneur would be able to). However, it is clear that large firms can be innovative. So what is the difference between entrepreneurship and innovation? As indicated above, a distinction is that entrepreneurship is not a managed, planned process; there is an element of so-called bootstrapping, where the entrepreneur seeks resources as and when needed. Larger firms do sometimes do this, but they normally pay more attention to planning the process. Drucker (1985) argues that large firms do not need to rely on being entrepreneurial, as they can systematically pursue innovation in a way that small firms cannot. Thus Drucker argues that, to remain successful, large firms must innovate and they can do this in a systematic, organized, and rational way.

This implies that there are two routes to innovation. One relies on the insight and determination of individual entrepreneurs; the other is for existing firms to search systematically for opportunities by using formal R&D or other team-based activities. In any successful economy both individual entrepreneurs and innovative firms are important.[6]

5.3 Innovation and Firms

Why Do Firms Innovate?

For a microeconomist, the dominant reason for a firm to innovate is assumed to be to maximize the stream of current and future profits.[7] A firm innovates in order to raise sales or reduce production costs, hence increasing profits. The increase in profits is the return on investing in innovation, for example by spending on R&D in previous years. Since

---

[6] Audretsch and Thurik (2001) argue that small, entrepreneurial firms are playing an increasingly important role in modern—or knowledge-based—economies. They contrast this with the 1950s and 1960s when large firms were dominant (the managed capitalism of J. K. Galbraith's 1956 classic *American Capitalism: The New Industrial State*). One indicator of the importance of smaller firms in an economy is the share of R&D accounted for by SMEs (small and medium-sized enterprises: those with less than 250 employees). OECD (2003) states that SMEs account for around 15% of total R&D in the United States, compared with 25% in the EU. In Italy, 65% of R&D is done by SMEs, while in Japan it is only 7%.

[7] Justifications for this include (a) that the shareholders of the firm will always want as much profit as possible and (b) that if a firm does not maximize profits it will be competitively forced out of the market by those that do. Both of these justifications are subject to debate. Shareholders may not always be able to control managers sufficiently to ensure they maximize profits. This is known as the principal–agent problem. See Hodgson (1993) for a discussion of whether the profit-maximization argument is realistic in an evolving market.

the outcome of investing in R&D is uncertain, firms invest when the expected returns are positive.[8] This profit-maximizing view of innovation has advantages, but it also implies that all firms can be viewed as identical profit-seeking mechanisms. There is no allowance for differences in history, culture, organizational structure, management style, or personnel, which in the case of innovation may be important.[9]

In the management literature the reasons for innovating are far more diverse, including to survive, to increase market share, and to meet the needs of customers. Each of these can be linked back to the idea of maximizing profits, but they do give greater insight into the actual pressures and opportunities facing firms and managers. For example, von Hippel (1988) discusses how the feedback and ideas that firms get from their customers can lead to innovation. This discussion also suggests that, although profits may be the ultimate objective, there may be many firm-level factors that can prevent, or alter the effectiveness of, innovation. This book is not intended as a management guide to making firms innovative, but we will mention a number of aspects: the right of employees to challenge authority, tolerance of failure, open communications to customers and external knowledge sources, teamwork, and flexibility.[10]

Innovation Strategies

For any incumbent firm already supplying a particular market, a key choice concerns whether to be a *leader* or a *follower*. A leader pursues innovations by investing in R&D and attempts to protect these innovations using IPRs. A follower relies on adopting, imitating, or inventing around new innovations developed by others, which can involve obtaining a license and making royalty payments to the innovator.

For most product markets the option of just standing still in technology terms, whether in product design or production techniques, does not exist. So firms are continually making choices about the following aspects of their innovation activity: how much should be invested in R&D, which inventions are to be protected by formally registered IPRs, when to launch new products, when to install new production methods, and

---

[8] Sometimes authors distinguish between two types of uncertainty: technological and market. Technological uncertainty occurs since the process of innovating can involve creating new scientific and engineering knowledge. Market uncertainty comes from the fact that until the product is launched the actual demand for the product is unknown.

[9] Nelson (1991) provides a discussion of why firms differ.

[10] There are a large number of management books on this topic. Some recent contributions are Carlson and Wilmot (2006) and Skarzynski and Gibson (2008).

when to license their technology to other firms.[11] Each of these activities offers benefits and costs, and these are in turn determined by the internal characteristics of firms, such as their preexisting portfolio of IPRs and their product range, and the external characteristics of the markets in which they are operating.

Another set of decisions concerns whether to work with other firms, universities, or public institutions. As discussed in chapter 4, certain innovations may naturally develop from university research or public research. Firms may also be faced with a strategic choice of whether to enter into joint R&D with other firms, some of which may be competitors. Cooperation with other firms has a number of advantages, including the sharing of fixed costs, the pooling of risk, the avoidance of duplication of R&D, the sharing of knowledge, and the cross-fertilization of ideas. Smaller firms may be especially interested in some of these advantages. It is important to state that cooperating with competitors is normally illegal under competition (antitrust) laws, but there are exemptions for R&D cooperation. In particular, exemptions for R&D insist on various conditions that ensure the results of the R&D do not create market power or a reduction of competition.[12]

5.4 Markets and Innovation

Creative Destruction and Dynamic Competition

In his groundbreaking work on the nature of capitalist economies, Schumpeter (1942, chapter 7) describes what he famously termed "the process of creative destruction." Entrepreneurs and firms introduce new products or processes into the market, thus enjoying a temporary monopoly and high profits. However, in general, any successful new product or process calls forth imitation and ultimately the innovator's profit is eroded. The term "creative destruction" thus represents an appreciation of the tension between the gainers and losers from innovation: "creative" refers to profitable opportunities for inventors and innovators, and for their customers, while "destruction" refers to the taking

---

[11] There are other innovation-related choices to be made, such as whether to focus on their historic core business or to diversify, and when to take over other firms that have complementary market share and IPRs.

[12] Hemphill (2003) discusses U.S. and EU policies. In 2000 the United States issued "antitrust guidelines for collaborations among competitors" and the European Union introduced new R&D "block exemption" rules on January 1, 2001. In short, these stipulate that the results of the cooperative R&D must be available to all participants. There is also a market share condition: an R&D block exemption is not available if the parties involved are competitors with joint market share of 25% or above (the equivalent figure for the United States is 20%).

away of market share and profits from existing producers and the loss of jobs for their workers. In this dynamic situation the continuous churning of market share and of firms in production is the norm.

As an example, consider the idea mentioned above that the market is a testing ground for new ideas. In the United Kingdom one estimate suggests that only 35% of new firms survive their first five years; estimates of the two-year survival rate for the United States are around 80%.[13] Should we be concerned about such high exit rates? On the one hand they could be the result of the market place selecting the better products and the most efficient firms. This process of destruction is often thought to be a major strength of capitalist economies, hence we should be unconcerned with high exit rates.[14] On the other hand it could be that some of the exiting firms do, in fact, have good products, or have the potential to be efficient, but lack the critical complementary assets to capitalize on opportunities.[15] The importance of complementary assets for successful innovation was first mooted by Teece (1986, 2006). Examples of complementary resources include skilled labor, finance, information, access to IPRs, legal advice, and accountancy services. There is also the possibility that new firms are being forced out of the market by incumbent firms, or, more problematically, perhaps new firms do not enter a market due to barriers to entry erected by incumbent firms.

A growing economy is therefore characterized by both new firm entry and incumbent firms innovating, with competition between all firms. This competition leads to creative destruction, which encourages the best products and processes to survive. Economists are interested in the nature and outcomes of this competitive process and, in particular, whether it is optimal. Note that here "competition" refers to the rivalry between different products and processes in the market. This type of competition occurs over time, as new firms and products enter and old firms and products exit, hence it is often called *dynamic* competition. In contrast, many microeconomics textbooks only focus on competition between a fixed number of firms on the basis of price, which can be called price competition or *static* competition. Why might dynamic competition be nonoptimal? There are a number of possible reasons:

---

[13] Comparable data on survival rates are being compiled by the OECD Entrepreneurship Indicators Programme, which is where the U.S. estimate comes from. They estimate the comparable U.K. figure to be 83%. The five-year survival rate of 35% comes from Disney et al. (2003, p. 92).

[14] Economists sometimes make an analogy with Darwinian evolution—the idea of survival of the fittest and natural selection. See Hodgson (1993) for a full discussion of the strengths and weaknesses of such an analogy.

[15] This relates to point (3) above in section 5.2.

(1) Insufficient entrepreneurial capacity, or such capacity is being diverted, hence too few new firms are being started in the market sector (as discussed in section 5.2 above).

(2) New firms are entering but their failure rate is too high due to their inability to access critical resources.

(3) New firms are prevented from entering a market due to barriers to entry, either strategically erected by incumbents or arising from regulatory restrictions.

(4) Dynamic competition between incumbent firms is low, with few new products being released or new processes developed. This results from a lack of incentive to innovate, regulatory constraints, or insufficient funds being available to finance R&D. The latter could be caused by high levels of price competition between incumbents, which reduces profits and the ability to invest.

We look in more detail at reasons (2)–(4) in section 5.4. Before this we note two important issues. The first is that it is possible for there to be too much dynamic competition, with too many firms or products being launched, which wastes resources. The intuition behind this is that each new firm pursues its own profitability rather than acting according to society's best interests. Since new firms use resources (e.g., labor and capital) it is possible that too many new firms are started, and too many resources are used, in comparison with what society would want. Box 5.1 reviews some models that focus on the optimal number of products. This said, most economists and policy makers are concerned that there is too little dynamic competition, and associated new products, in most sectors of the economy.

A final point is that the idea of dynamic competition allows us some insight into the apparent tension between antitrust, or competition, policy and IPRs. In simple terms, antitrust policy is intended to heighten competition between firms, and specifically to prevent monopolization.[16] Yet IPRs give firms a monopoly right to exploit a product or process. This apparent contradiction can be resolved by pointing out that

---

[16] How antitrust can achieve such an outcome is much debated. Hart (2001) provides a history of U.S. antitrust policies between 1890 and 2000. He indicates that the antitrust policies with respect to technology and innovation have varied through time. For example, in the 1970s, 1980s, and 1990s, the so-called Chicago school successfully advocated a low-intervention, or "hands-off," stance. It was assumed that innovation would naturally occur, creating competitors and new products to challenge any monopolies. They also stressed how failing firms could use antitrust laws in attempts to alter their fate. From 2000, Hart argues, there was a swing back to the need to intervene. Network externalities and "lock-in" could create situations where a dominant firm maintains its position even though its products were not the best.

both antitrust law and intellectual property law are designed to optimize dynamic competition and thereby innovation and growth in the economy. Hence, awarding a monopoly right for a patent is part of the process of encouraging innovation, which also means that the monopoly power will be short lived.

Box 5.1. Does competition generate the optimal number of products?.

Initially we need to be clear about what *optimal* means. As in standard microeconomics textbooks we define optimal as when social welfare is maximized (i.e., when the welfare, or benefit, to all members of society is at its highest level). Welfare, in turn, can be defined as the sum of consumer and producer surplus. Let us assume that each firm has only one product. This means we can talk about products or firms interchangeably. We can also think about how many firms enter a new market as a well-defined example of new product creation.

We should also be clear that each product is differentiated from every other in some way. This is often referred to in terms of product characteristics (e.g., a car has many characteristics such as CO_2 emissions, safety, number of seats, color, etc.). In the economics literature there is a distinction between horizontal and vertical differentiation. Horizontal differentiation refers to a situation where there is no universal consumer ranking of all the products available in the market: which one is preferred by any buyer is simply a matter of individual preference. Vertically differentiated products have a common ranking by all consumers—from best to worst—and the only reason why consumers do not all buy the best product is differences in price.

When considering whether new firm entry is optimal there are three main aspects, or forces, at work. The first is the *business-stealing effect.* This suggests that competition between firms for profits will cause too many new firms to enter. Each firm only considers the profits it could make and not the impact on others. The second arises because private firms do not consider the consumer surplus generated by their new products. This is often called the *appropriability effect,* since it is normally not possible for a firm to appropriate the entire consumer surplus for its product. The appropriability effect suggests that there is too little entry and too few products. Finally, a new product may also generate a *knowledge spillover effect* by demonstrating new knowledge or technology to competitors. Again, private firms do not consider such knowledge spillovers in their decision making, indicating that there may be too little entry. In general, therefore, we cannot be sure whether markets contain the optimal number of products as it depends on the relative weight of each effect.

Effect	Description	Outcome
Business-stealing effect	New firms ignore loss of profits by incumbents	Too many products
Appropriability effect	Firms cannot appropriate all consumer surplus	Too few products
Spillover effect	New products demonstrate knowledge to other firms	Too few products

Different theoretical models provide different answers to the optimal product range question. Salop (1979) put forward a model called the *circular city model*. This model considers a new city where shops could locate on a perfect circle. Each shop sells the same product but is differentiated due to its distance from customers. Customers have to pay transport costs, hence the closest shop is preferred if its price is lower than or equal to others. Such a model can represent products with different characteristics. In this case the circle represents consumers' preferences, hence they choose the product that is closest to their preferences, as long as the price is not too high. This is a case of horizontal product differentiation. Assuming that each product (shop) has a fixed cost of entry and that the products (shops) are equally spaced around the circular preference domain, Salop shows that there is too much entry. The specific assumptions used by Salop mean that the business-stealing effect dominates.

Vertical product differentiation presents some additional issues. If all people agree that there is one best product in a market, it suggests that the optimal number of products is simply one. However, if lower-quality products are available at lower prices, and people's incomes vary, this result depends on the price per quality, as well as the income distribution. Modeling this situation is complex and it is not clear how many products competitive entry will create (Shaked and Sutton 1983). Some researchers have asked a slightly different question: Given a market structure (either monopoly or competitive), which one will generate the most new (vertically differentiated) products? The answer to this question is again complex, depending on whether the existing monopoly is threatened by new entrants or not, and on whether new products completely displace old products (Gilbert and Newbery 1982; Greenstein and Ramey 1998). Thus there are cases when a threatened monopolist has greater incentives to introduce new products than do producers in a competitive market (something at odds with Arrow's 1962 result, discussed below in section 5.4).

Lack of Resources for New Firms

As already noted, there are a number of possible resources that new firms may have difficulty in accessing. These include skilled labor (also called human capital); finance from banks, stock markets, and venture capital firms; and information on standards, technology, foreign markets, IPRs, legal issues, management practices, and accountancy. In fact, some argue that many start-ups fail due to poor cash flow management. It may be that some cash flow problems are caused by the firm having poor products; hence we could argue that the cash flow problems just reflect the firm's viability. On the other hand, some basic knowledge of cash flow forecasting and management might be all that is needed to ensure innovative firms survive in the market. There are similar dilemmas with evaluating other possible resource constraints. For example, a new firm may claim that banks are unwilling to lend money to innovative firms, but the bank's reluctance may reflect its evaluation that the firm is likely to fail. However, this evaluation is normally based on a business plan prepared by the firm, hence there may be a role for education and training in how to prepare business plans.

In response to these difficulties the generic policy response is to provide a range of support programs aimed at new firms and entrepreneurs. These can include free advice on setting up and running small businesses, subsidized training for owners or staff, and subsidized rent (possibly at business parks or centers especially for small firms). Governments also regularly review and attempt to streamline the administrative and regulatory burden placed on new and small firms. For high-technology firms there are often a range of grants, research cooperation possibilities, and prizes to encourage and support R&D. A further major area of policy concern is finance, especially venture capital. Governments often work hard to establish, fund, and support a venture capital industry that pays attention to smaller firms. The subject of policy to support smaller firms is further discussed in section 11.4.

Barriers to Entry

Incumbent firms—meaning those firms currently operating in the market—can attempt to erect barriers to entry. Such barriers can restrict or prevent new entry and therefore limit competition, hence raising the profitability of incumbents. The first notable study on profitability, and its association with concentration and barriers to entry, was done by Bain (1956) on U.S. manufacturing industries.[17] He used the eight-firm

---

[17] Concentration refers to the market share held by the largest firms in the market. For example, the four-firm concentration ratio might be 0.6, meaning the largest four firms account for 60% of the market's sales.

concentration ratio and various measures of barriers to entry, including existence of product differentiation, existence of scale economies, and absolute capital requirements. Bain found that barriers to entry were the most important influence on profitability, with higher concentration only exerting a slight boost to profits if barriers to entry were present. Moreover, only when concentration rose above 0.7 did profits receive a boost. Bain's study set the path for a raft of subsequent empirical work, although in recent years these types of empirical studies have been regarded as crude attempts to study complex behavior. One reason was an argument put forward by Demsetz (1973), often called the "efficiency view." This held that high concentration was the *result* of successful, innovative, and efficient firms coming to dominate the market. These firms also had higher profitability; hence any association between concentration and profitability was simply reflecting the evolution of the industry and not "barriers to entry." Another reason is that a barrier to entry needs to be a credible deterrent. For example, an incumbent firm may invest in surplus capacity as a possible barrier to entry. This signals to potential entrants that it could increase production, and lower price, if entry occurs. The threat of such a price war might be thought of as a barrier to entry. However, is this threat credible? If entry does occur, a rational incumbent would reevaluate its decision to have a price war, since this would hurt both the entrant's profits and its own. Hence, unless the barrier to entry is credible—or time consistent—then it cannot act as a deterrent (see Tirole 1988). These complexities mean that it is difficult to undertake empirical analysis on barriers to entry.

For our purposes we are especially interested in potential barriers to entry that can adversely affect dynamic competition and the innovation process. There are two important possibilities: R&D expenditures and use of the IPR system. A number of authors have argued that high R&D expenditures by incumbents can act as a barrier to entry. The argument is that it may be difficult for entrants to start successfully the extensive R&D programs necessary to keep pace with incumbents' rates of innovation. While there may be some truth in this, it is not clear whether dynamic competition suffers. The high rates of R&D spending by incumbents may lead to rapid innovation whether or not new entry occurs. This said, there is often a belief that smaller firms that come up with "radical" or "disruptive" innovations may face substantial barriers to entry, even if these are not overt. The large size of incumbent firms implies that if a small firm is to capture market share it needs to acquire substantial assets and distribution capability, in addition to developing its innovation. Encouraging the entry of such firms is difficult, but IPRs aim to provide some protection. At the same time it may be possible for incumbent firms to use the IPR system as a barrier to entry, for example, by extensively trademarking or threatening to use patent litigation. These issues are discussed in the next chapter.

Market Structure and the Innovating Firm

Let us consider how market structure affects the potential of firms to innovate. We focus on whether or not they have a monopoly, or face intense competition, in production and/or in R&D. Schumpeter (1942) asserted that large firms operating in concentrated industries constitute the engine of technological progress.[18] He argued that monopoly and oligopoly firms are more able of conducting meaningful R&D because they can use funds earned from profits to finance R&D. Schumpeter argued that oligopolistic market structures, with their perceived intensity of product and factor cost competition, will achieve more innovation and thus make a greater contribution to social welfare than the severe price competition exhibited by perfectly competitive market structures.

Many reasons have been advanced since Schumpeter's (1942) work as to why large firms may be the engines of technological and innovative progress, and these have subsequently been formulated as two hypotheses (Symeonidis 1996). The first hypothesis postulates a positive relationship between the incentive to innovate and market share or power. Large market share implies greater certainty that a new product will also achieve higher market share and generate profits. Higher profit margins, due to market power, also provide finance for R&D, which is important since capital markets may be reluctant to fund innovative projects. The second hypothesis states that large firm size and innovation are correlated. This hypothesis was based in part on Schumpeter's belief that a large diversified firm would be better able to reap the benefits of innovation, regardless of where in the industry's product range innovation happened to occur. Furthermore, the large fixed costs of some research projects mean that only large firms have the necessary resources. Finally, large firms may also be better able to manage the risk associated with innovation (i.e., they can have a diversified portfolio of research projects).

Nevertheless, Arrow's (1962) analysis countered the Schumpeterian view of the relative returns to innovation for a competitive firm as

---

[18] In early work, Schumpeter (1934) stressed the role of entrepreneurs, and the small firms they start, as the driving force of innovation. There does appear to have been an evolution in Schumpeter's thinking over time, although Hagerdoorn (1996) argues that Schumpeter's early work did mention large firms (and his later work still discussed entrepreneurs).

opposed to a monopoly. Arrow argues that, when effective IPRs exist, competitive producers have a higher incentive to innovate than a monopoly (see figures 1.2 and 1.3 and related discussion). The monopolist already enjoys excess profits due to existing barriers to entry and thus the returns to innovation offer only a small extra profit.[19] Nevertheless, in Arrow's competitive industry, IPRs offer the opportunity for a competitor to become a temporary monopolist. However, Arrow's analysis ignores two possible points. First, there may be financial constraints on R&D investment by smaller competitive firms, as borrowing to undertake R&D with its uncertain outcomes will command a high risk premium. Second, it also assumes that IPRs are perfectly effective in protecting firms from imitation, something that is not always the case.

Continuing from these early analyses there has been a plethora of papers analyzing the relationship between market structure and innovation; a few of the models relating to process innovation are summarized in table 5.1. As this shows, whether we expect to see more rapid innovation with a more competitive market structure, or with greater concentration of production, depends on the IPR regime in use and on the dynamics of the R&D process.

These opposing views lead to the idea that there is potentially a nonmonotonic relationship between competition and innovation performance (see figure 5.1), which has quite a long history in economics (see Scherer 1992). Schmidt (1997) argues that the desire of managers to avoid bankruptcy is important in promoting innovation, even as market share falls. Although greater competition in the market lowers the return to innovation by reducing the output of each firm, it also increases the risk of bankruptcy. The fear of this encourages managers to innovate to ensure the survival of the firm and hence of the manager's job. When competition is intense the output effect dominates, but before this happens the incentive to innovate will peak at some intermediate level of market concentration. Aghion and Griffith (2005) also argue that there are contrasting forces in the relationship between innovation and competition that create an inverted U shape (see figure 5.1). With rising competition, innovation provides the opportunity to enhance profit in sectors with low variation in costs and profits; against this is the Schumpeterian effect whereby higher competition reduces the differential rents of innovation in sectors with some degree of technology and profit variation.

---

[19] This is sometimes called a "replacement effect" of one monopoly profit stream by another.

Table 5.1. Competition and innovation: models and predictions.

Author (date)	Market structure in production and in R&D	IPR regime	Model prediction	Competition policy implications
Static models of process innovation with certainty of R&D outcome				
Arrow (1962)	*Either* both production and R&D are pure monopoly; *or* both are perfectly competitive	IP rights are exclusive and awarded to first inventor (although redundant for pure monopoly)	Incentive to invest in R&D is higher with pure competition than with monopoly	Promote competition to increase the rate of innovation
Gilbert and Newbery (1982)	Monopoly in production pre-innovation, but competition in R&D from a potential entrant	Intellectual property rights are exclusive and awarded to the highest "bidder" (who invests most in R&D)	Monopoly has most to gain by becoming the inventor	Duopoly is not preferable to monopoly
Dasgupta and Stiglitz (1980)	A number (N) of identical firms compete in R&D	Intellectual property rights are nonexclusive (e.g., innovation is a trade secret, and if another inventor finds the same process they can use it)	Increasing the number of firms reduces the industry R&D intensity	*Prefer* an oligopoly to perfect competition; *but* this oligopoly is wasteful as it duplicates R&D

Table 5.1. Continued.

Author (date)	Market structure in production and in R&D	IPR regime	Model prediction	Competition policy implications
Dynamic models of process innovation with uncertainty in R&D outcome				
Reinganum (1981)	N firms compete in R&D to innovate; probability of invention is an exponential function of R&D expenditure	Intellectual property rights are exclusive and awarded to the first firm to invent	As N rises the probability of invention rises so the time to invention is shortened	Prefer to have more firms to increase rate of innovation, even though each unsuccessful firm gains nothing from its R&D expenditure
Reinganum (1983)	Monopoly in production pre-innovation, but competition in R&D from a potential entrant; probability of invention is an exponential function of R&D expenditure	Intellectual property rights are exclusive and awarded to the first firm to invent	For a drastic process innovation the potential entrant will invest more than the incumbent; for a nondrastic innovation the reverse can occur	Market dominance can change hands over a succession of patent races
Doraszelski (2003)	Competition in R&D between a leader and a follower firm; probability of innovation success depends on both current R&D and cumulative past R&D within each firm	Intellectual property rights are exclusive and awarded to the first firm to invent	Dominance by one firm may or may not occur depending on how the R&D success probability relates to cumulative R&D	With increasing returns to R&D experience, can expect to see continued market dominance by incumbent; with decreasing returns, the follower will invest more than the leader to catch up

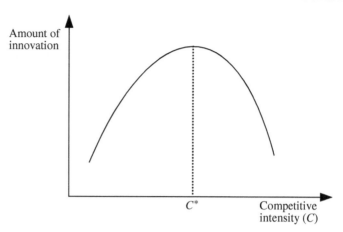

Figure 5.1. An inverted U shape between innovation and competition.

5.5 Empirical Evidence on the Returns to Innovation

This section looks at evidence on the impact of innovation on the performance of firms. Many of the empirical studies use R&D as a proxy for innovation and we use such studies here as a starting point. This allows us to discuss some of the evidence on the private rate of return to R&D investment. IPRs are also commonly used to assess innovation, for example, the stock of patents of a firm. Some of these results on IPRs are mentioned here, but a full discussion is left until chapter 6. There are many different ways of assessing firm-level performance, including:

- Market value studies. These can only be conducted for firms that are listed on a stock exchange. These studies look at the changes in the firm's share price or in its total market value to assess the impact of innovation.

- Productivity studies. In many cases measures of productivity can be calculated (see chapter 3) allowing an assessment of its association with innovation.

- Profitability studies. Data on firm-level profitability is often available, which allows an assessment of how past innovation is related to subsequent profitability.

- Survival studies. For microfirms and SMEs in particular, an analysis of survival rates can give some insight into the characteristics of successful firms.

- Growth studies. Data on growth rates of sales, assets, employment, and exports can all be used as performance measures. Especially for microfirms and SMEs these measures are often the only ones available. There is also a strong policy interest in studying "high-growth" small firms, as some of these will provide the next generation of large firms.

Initially we focus on market value and productivity studies. These studies dominate the economics literature and tend to use data on large firms. Large firms often account for the majority of GDP in an economy; hence there is some justification for such a focus. However, since our specific interest is innovation it is important not to ignore smaller firms. The most innovative of these will grow into large firms in future years. Data on microfirms and SMEs is often sparse, so undertaking market value or productivity studies may not be possible. Instead, studies on survival and growth rates of small firms are more common.

Market Value Studies of Innovation

The share price of a quoted company reflects the market's best valuation of the expected future dividends (or share repurchase payments) to be made by the company. The maintained assumption in the literature is that investors have *rational expectations*, which means they are forward looking, take account of all available information, and do not make systematic mistakes, so that financial markets are assumed to price shares correctly on average with some degree of random error (Hall et al. 2005). Investors' estimates of future dividend payments will be a function of the stock of tangible and intangible assets owned by the company. R&D and IPRs can be used as proxies for a firm's intangible assets (Hall et al. 2005). An advantage of this approach is that it is inherently forward looking, which distinguishes it from the productivity approach described below. The empirical specification of these studies is discussed in box 5.2.

Hall (1993b) uses a market value approach to assess the returns to R&D in U.S. manufacturing firms over the period 1973–91. For the full sample, R&D spending is strongly and positively associated with share market value. In fact, current R&D spending has a stronger association than the R&D stock (calculated by depreciating past R&D at 15%), which indicates that the share market considers current R&D a better indicator of future performance. The magnitude of the association suggests that the returns to R&D are two to three times those on normal investment. However, Hall then estimates the market value regression for each year between 1973 and 1991 separately. This shows that the return to R&D increased up until 1980 but then fell dramatically in the

1980s, suggesting that investment in R&D provided only one quarter of normal investment returns by the end of the 1980s. Hall discusses some possible explanations, including one that R&D depreciated much quicker in the 1980s and another that the stock market became more myopic. In another paper, Hall (1993a) shows that much of the decline in returns occurred in the computing/electronics sector and could be ascribed to the start of the personal computer revolution.

Hall and Oriani (2006) build on these results by analyzing manufacturing firms in France, Germany, Italy, the United Kingdom, and the United States over the period 1989–98. For the United States, their results still indicate relatively low returns to R&D (compared with 1980). There is also some evidence that Italy has a much lower return to R&D, compared with France, Germany, and the United States, which have similar returns. In contrast, the United Kingdom exhibits much higher returns to R&D (or, more accurately, the U.K. stock market expects future returns to be much higher). Why might there be such differences across countries? There are some data issues concerning reporting of R&D that could introduce differences, but it could also be due to variations in corporate governance, capital markets, and R&D funding. For example, in Italy there is a higher share of publicly funded R&D, which would tend to increase R&D expenditure and lower the private rate of return.[20]

There are many other papers that consider the market value of R&D. These studies give an indication of how market value analysis can inform debate on the incentive to invest in R&D and the wider process of innovation. Furthermore, there are many studies that extend the approach to looking at the value of patents and a few that look at trademarks. Studies related to IPRs will be reviewed in chapter 6, where we solely discuss firms and IPRs.

Box 5.2. The specification of an empirical model of market value.

The starting point for many empirical studies on innovation and market value is Griliches (1981). This assumes that the market value (V) of the firm (total equity plus debt) is determined by tangible and intangible assets, so that

$$V = q(K_{\text{tan}} + \gamma K_{\text{int}})^{\sigma}, \tag{5.1}$$

---

[20] The rationale for public support for private R&D is the presence of spillovers, or positive externalities, which mean that the social return to R&D is high (as discussed in chapter 1). At the same time the expansion of private R&D due to public subsidy would be expected to lower the private rate of return. For Italy, Hall and Oriani (2006) also discuss whether weaker rights for minority shareholders in Italy could be a contributing factor, i.e., such shareholders may fear that any return to R&D will be appropriated by major shareholders and this weakens the share price of R&D-active firms.

where K_{tan} is the book value of total tangible assets of the firm, K_{int} is the stock of intangible assets not included in the balance sheet, q is the "current market valuation coefficient" of the firm's assets, σ allows for the possibility of nonconstant returns to scale, and y is the ratio of shadow values of intangible assets to tangible assets (i.e., $(\partial V/\partial K_{int})/(\partial V/\partial K_{tan})$). In order to estimate equation (5.1) with simple linear regression techniques, one can take natural logarithms of (5.1) and, using the approximation $\ln(1 + K_{int}/K_{tan}) \approx K_{int}/K_{tan}$, it can be rearranged to

$$\ln V = \ln q + \sigma \ln K_{tan} + \sigma y \frac{K_{int}}{K_{tan}}. \tag{5.2}$$

Note that the approximation becomes poorer the larger the value of K_{int}/K_{tan}. An alternative approach is to estimate (5.1) using nonlinear regression techniques.

A problem for empirical studies is how to proxy K_{int}, the stock of intangible assets accumulated by the firm. Interpreted broadly, "intangibles" can be related to brand names, process or product innovations, advertising, managerial skill, human capital in the workforce, and other aspects of the firm. Although balance sheet data do, at times, contain a book (accounting) value for intangible assets, there is widespread agreement that this vastly underestimates the true stock of the intangible assets of the firm. R&D and IPRs (mainly patents) have been used as proxies for K_{int}. When R&D is used as a proxy it is feasible to use either (a) a recent year for R&D or (b) a stock of R&D (where this is calculated using an assumed rate of depreciation, e.g., 15%). Using a recent year often gives good results as it can be a better proxy of the stock market's expectation of returns to past and future R&D. Patent applications, publications, or grants have also been used extensively as proxies for K_{int} (either recent-year flows or stocks). Hall (2000) contains a review of methodology and recent studies.

Productivity Studies of Innovation

The advantage of the analysis in the previous section is that market value is a forward-looking measure of performance. The disadvantage is that it relies on the assumption of efficient markets and can only be conducted on firms that are quoted on stock markets. Another approach to assessing the value of R&D and IPRs, and implicitly the innovation they embody, is to assess their contribution to productivity. Box 5.3 provides a short introduction to the methodology of such empirical work.

Griliches (1984) contains various papers that pioneer the productivity approach. In general, almost all empirical studies find a positive association between doing R&D and subsequent increases in the firm's output from given amounts of inputs (implying a rise in "productivity"). What is more difficult to establish is the magnitude of the implied effect, as it is to be expected that rates of return will vary over time due to changing interest rates, depreciation rates, and risks. Some of the studies express their results in terms of a private rate of return to R&D.[21] Griliches and Mairesse (1990) found that U.S. manufacturing firms' rates of return to private R&D were around 20–40%; their study also included an analysis of Japanese firms, finding rates of return in the range 30–40%. Hall and Mairesse (1995) found returns to French firms in the 1980s between 22% and 34%, while Harhoff (1998) found a rate of return of around 20% for German firms from 1979 to 1989.[22]

Is a rate of private return to R&D of 20% or 30% high? If so, should policy makers be concerned, or is this simply a matter for private firms? The rates of return to R&D can be compared with the standard rate of return that firms use to make capital investment decisions, which is often called the *hurdle rate*. For many companies the hurdle rate is around 12%, suggesting that the returns to R&D are rather excessive.[23] Even so, high rates of return may be appropriate as they reflect high risk, such as the need to cover unexpected depreciation of R&D assets. Yet if the excess returns are higher than an appropriate risk premium, this suggests that there is not free entry into conducting R&D, since, if there was, the rate of return would be reduced to equality with other forms of investment. The potential causes of lack of free entry into R&D investment are of interest to policy makers.

Two possibilities are the inability of firms to raise finance for R&D projects and barriers to entry created by IPRs. Clearly, in the case of IPRs this is what we would expect if the intellectual property system were working to reward innovators. There is also the possibility that R&D requires complementary assets, which have been built up over time, hence making returns to R&D a function of past history of other investments, not just current R&D activity. Lastly, it may be that there

---

[21] Empirical studies also estimate the elasticity of R&D or patent stocks with respect to value added (see box 5.2). It is possible to calculate the rate of return of R&D using an estimated elasticity and knowing the R&D intensity. A drawback of estimating a constant elasticity across a sample of firms is that it implies that the rate of return varies inversely with R&D intensity.

[22] Part of the reason for the wide bounds on these reported rates of return concerns the econometrics. All estimates are subject to statistical uncertainty, which gives rise to confidence intervals. In addition, researchers tend to report the results from a number of different empirical specifications, as a check on the robustness of results.

[23] Poterba and Summers (1995) surveyed chief executive officers of Fortune 1000 companies and found that the average hurdle rate was 12.2%.

are constraints in the supply of scientists and engineers.[24] We return to these policy issues in chapter 11. It is also worth noting that high rates of return to R&D are incompatible with some R&D-based models of economic growth. Such models assume free entry into R&D, which implies that the rate of return to R&D should fall to competitive levels (see section 8.3).

The R&D and productivity approach can be extended in various ways to consider other topics of interest. For example, Lokshin et al. (2008), in a study of Dutch manufacturing firms (from 1996 to 2001), examine whether contracting out R&D enhances a firm's productivity. They find that it does only when the firm conducts internal R&D as well. The implication is that the firm needs to develop internal absorptive capacity in order to benefit from external R&D and it does this by conducting its own R&D.[25] Other studies analyze issues such as (a) differences in productivity effects from basic versus applied R&D, (b) the role of firm size, (c) variations in R&D returns across industries, and (d) whether government-funded R&D is as productive as privately financed R&D.[26]

This literature has shown empirical evidence consistent with positive private returns to R&D in enhancing productivity both for individual firms and for industry-wide aggregates. Most of these studies focus solely on manufacturing firms, as this is the sector that traditionally reports the most R&D. There are also studies that investigate the role of IPRs in increasing productivity and we shall examine these in chapter 6.

It is important to stress that the empirics refer to the private returns to R&D, not the *social* returns. Many empirical studies show that the social returns are higher than the private returns. This is consistent with the view that R&D has a "public good" aspect, or that R&D has positive externalities (see chapter 1). For example, Bernstein and Nadiri (1988) find social rates of return between 10% and 160% in U.S. high-tech industries; Wolff and Nadiri (1993) find social rates of return to R&D in U.S. industries between 27% and 42%. Box 5.3 discusses how social rates of return can be estimated and chapter 11 discusses policies to encourage R&D.

---

[24] A further discussion of this is in Rogers (2006).

[25] See chapter 2 above, where we discuss the two faces of R&D; see also Cohen and Levinthal (1989).

[26] Examples of these types of studies are as follows. Lichtenberg and Siegel (1991) find that basic R&D has a stronger association with productivity than applied R&D. Rogers (2006, forthcoming) finds that rates of return to R&D in the United Kingdom are higher for SMEs than for large firms. Tsai and Wang (2004) find that the rate of return to R&D in Taiwanese firms is higher in high-tech industries. Hall and Mairesse (1995) consider a number of different issues for French manufacturing firms in the 1980s, including the effect of government-funded research in private firms.

Box 5.3. Relating inputs to output using a production function.

The production function is a relation between production capacity defined by inputs and output (see the mathematical appendix). It can be specified as

$$Y = AL^{\alpha_1} K^{\alpha_2}, \tag{5.3}$$

where Y is value added (or output measure used), L is labor (total employment), K is the stock of tangible capital, and A is a scalar representing technology. All these variables are at the firm level. Many factors affect the level of technology in the firm. The most commonly used proxies in empirical analysis are expenditures on R&D, patenting activity, spending on training or human capital measures, and information technology investment. Note that the productivity literature uses "technology" as the key variable of interest, whereas the market value approach used intangible assets. The latter reflects an accounting background, while the term technology reflects an economic approach (see chapter 8).

A typical empirical approach would be to take natural logs of equation (5.3) and specify an equation for estimation such as

$$\ln Y = \beta_1 \ln(\text{R\&D}) + \beta_2 \ln(\text{Patents}) + \alpha_1 \ln L + \alpha_2 \ln K, \tag{5.4}$$

where both R&D and patents are used to proxy the level of technology A. The "stocks" of R&D and patents are often used in estimating (5.4), rather than the value in a specific year. This is because the aim is to proxy A (technology), which is built up over time. Calculating a stock normally involves assuming that R&D or patents depreciate at a rate of around 15% per year (see Hall (2007) for a critique of this). Estimating (5.4) requires a data set of firm-level variables and will yield estimates of the coefficients β_1 and β_2, which are the elasticities of output with respect to R&D and patents. (An elasticity indicates the percentage change in value added for a percentage change in R&D stock or patent stock.) Note there are a number of problems with estimating (5.4): see Griliches and Mairesse (1995) and sections A.1 and A.8 in the mathematical appendix.

For R&D, many researchers are also interested in the marginal rate of return to R&D (i.e., how much additional value added does a dollar of R&D provide). As the mathematical appendix shows, we can rewrite equation (5.4) with growth of value added as the dependent variable and this allows us to estimate the rate of return to R&D directly. This means we estimate the following first difference in logarithms, or growth, equation:

$$\Delta \ln Y = \alpha_3 \frac{\text{R\&D}}{Y} + \alpha_1 \Delta \ln L + \alpha_2 \Delta \ln K. \tag{5.5}$$

Estimating (5.5) has a number of other advantages to (5.4), including the fact that α_3 is an estimate of the marginal returns to R&D. However, this transformation relies on the rate of depreciation of R&D assets being small and this is not always the case at the level of the firm due to erosion of returns by competitors (Hall 2007).

When equations (5.4) and (5.5) are estimated with firm-level data the results refer to private elasticities and rates of return. Kafouros (2004) provides an overview of productivity and R&D analysis. If the researcher is interested in the social returns, there are two basic options. One is to enter an additional variable in the regression to represent the R&D done by other firms. If the coefficient on this variable is positive and significant, this indicates R&D spillovers from other firms. A second method is to use industry-level or sectoral data instead of firm-level data. This means that any spillovers between firms will be subsumed in the coefficients.

Other Studies

Empirical studies on the relationship between profitability and R&D are less common. Lev and Sougiannis (1996) consider the impact of R&D on subsequent profits for a sample of U.S. public companies (1975–91). They find a positive relationship, with the "impact" of R&D lasting around seven years. In a study of major innovations by U.K. companies, Geroski et al. (1993) also found that there was a profit increase (again for around seven years after the innovation was introduced). Since profits are one component of value added, these results should be expected. There is, perhaps, greater interest in understanding the performance of innovative smaller firms. The major problem here is that data sets on smaller firms are much less common. In particular, in many cases small firms need not report R&D data or the data necessary to construct productivity measures. Some data sets, such as the Community Innovation Survey (CIS), do allow firm-level analysis on innovation and some measures of performance. A recent example is Griffith et al. (2006), who look at R&D, innovation, and productivity using the CIS across four European countries. As expected, innovation is linked with productivity, although it does appear that the link is stronger in some countries than in others. Studies of firm survival also indicate a strong association between innovative activity and improved chances of survival. Webster et al. (forthcoming) show this for Australian firms and Helmers and Rogers (2008) for U.K. firms.

5.6 Evidence on Interactions between Competition and Innovation

Schumpeter's provocative claims about the beneficial role of large firms operating in concentrated markets have provoked a huge empirical literature. If his claims are true, then the traditional preoccupation of the competition authorities with opposing mergers that increase concentration, as well as preserving opportunities for entry of smaller new firms, might have negative trade-offs for the rate of innovation.

Most of the literature concerned with testing the second Schumpeterian hypothesis—that innovation increases with firm size—has regressed some measure of innovative output or input on a measure of size, usually using cross-sectional data on firms from one or many industries (see Symeonidis 1996). Studies in this tradition, starting with the work of Scherer (1965), have been criticized as failing to recognize or deal with numerous methodological problems.[27] As mentioned above, perhaps the most serious fault of much empirical work in this area is the implicit assumption that causality runs from firm size (and market structure) to innovation. In fact, it is now widely recognized that variables such as firm size, market structure, and innovation are endogenous variables within systems in which the most important factors determining overall economic outcomes are technology, institutions, demand, strategic considerations, and randomness (Sutton 1996; Symeonidis 1996).

Cohen (1995) provides a summary of the older empirical evidence: "The consensus is that…size has little effect on innovation and that larger firms have no advantage in the conduct of R&D and perhaps a disadvantage." This statement is only partly borne out in the analysis of firm size as a determinant of patenting and trademark activity for a large sample of U.K. firms by Greenhalgh and Rogers (2007). In their analysis of both manufacturing and services firms, larger firms were

---

[27] For example, there is a serious sample selection problem arising from the nonrandom nature of samples, since the sample of firms studied typically only included those firms that reported R&D. A further issue is whether studies manage successfully to control for firm characteristics other than size. This creates problems for empirical work since the intensity of R&D varies across firms. A related problem is the need to control for industry effects. Since firm size and innovation are likely to be affected by attributes of the overall industry, such as the level of technological opportunity and regulatory considerations, studies that use interindustry and intraindustry data need to control for the industry-level effects in order to obtain unbiased estimates of the effect of the specific influence of firm size on innovation. Moreover, as Cohen (1995) notes, controlling for industry effects in firm-level data can be extremely difficult given that many large firms are often composed of smaller units that operate in separate industries.

significantly more likely to be intellectual-property active in any given year than smaller firms, but across the active firms the number of IPRs per employee was negatively associated with firm size.

This takes us on to the literature concerned with testing the first of Schumpeter's two hypotheses, which postulated the existence of a positive correlation between innovation and market share. Again, interpreting the empirical literature in this area gives rise to several difficulties. Most work has regressed a measure of innovative activity on a measure of industry concentration. This assumes that concentration unidirectionally causes innovative activity, whereas in practice it is almost certainly the case that there is two-way causality. Two early reviews of this literature (Scherer 1992; Geroski 1994) agreed that Schumpeter was wrong to believe that large monopolistic corporations are the driving forces of technological innovation (see also Gilbert 2006). Scherer (1992, p. 1,430) concludes:

> Whether it would be desirable to reallocate U.S. innovative activity away from venture firms … to the well-established giants lauded in [Schumpeter (1942)] remains questionable.

Instead, industry characteristics such as technological opportunity and appropriability conditions may be more important in determining innovation.

Even so, explorations of the role of market structure have continued. In a study of U.S. firms in the late 1980s, Hall and Vopel (1996) demonstrate that high market share helps with exploiting the results of past R&D, but the stock market's valuation of current R&D spending is also clearly linked to the size of the firm. Blundell et al. (1999), using a data set of U.K. manufacturing firms responsible for major innovations between 1972 and 1982, found that higher market share raised the stock market valuation of an innovation.[28] In a more recent study of U.K. production firms from 1989 to 2002, Greenhalgh and Rogers (2006) use a novel dynamic measure of market structure, which associates lack of market competitiveness with the persistence of excess profits. They find that the sectors that are the least competitive have the highest returns to R&D, when assessed via stock market valuation. Furthermore, within the most dynamically competitive sector (which was found to be the science-based manufacturing industries), firms with larger market shares also

---

[28] They also noted that the impact of market share does appear to vary across industries, although they only reported separate results for the pharmaceuticals industry.

have higher R&D valuations.[29] These studies thus give some support to Schumpeter's claims that oligopoly may outperform competition as a market structure to promote innovation. Even so, there may be limits to how far lowering competition will improve innovation. Aghion and Griffith (2005) have offered empirical evidence to support their hypothesis of an inverted U-shaped relationship between the degree of competition and the rate of innovation (see figure 5.1). In their study, using large, quoted U.K. companies that obtained patents in the United States between 1968 and 1997, there is first a rising rate of patented innovation as the index of product market competition rises and then a falling off of patent rates as competition rises further.

Several papers have focused on one specific industry, which can reveal details of the innovation process, in the manner suggested by Teece (1986, 2006), where complementary factors play a role in the distribution of returns. For example, Gambardella's (1995) study of the biotechnology industry showed that small firms often come up with radical new innovations and discoveries but are unable to take the commercialization of the product much further. He notes that the "result has been a new division of labor, with smaller firms specializing in early research and larger firms conducting clinical development and distribution." This conclusion suggests a much more subtle process of technological innovation than the one postulated by Schumpeter. As another example, Gruber's (1992, 1995) studies reveal the importance of "first-mover advantage" in determining market share and innovative output in the semiconductor memory chip industry. Firm-specific learning is important in this industry; in the face of rapid overall industry quality improvement, an early innovator is more capable of learning how to improve product quality than a late entrant to the industry, who will have less time to learn how to improve quality. These examples of detailed work on particular industries reveal just some of the subtlety of the mechanisms relating innovation, firm size, and market share.

5.7 Conclusions

In this chapter we have explored the complex issues of why firms innovate and what constraints affect their ability to do so. The initial task was

---

[29] These authors also explore the interaction between market share and the value of intellectual property, again seen through variations in the stock market value of the firm. They find that the stock market assigns higher values to both patents and trademarks when these are obtained by firms with higher market shares, although there is considerable variability in the size and significance of this interaction across different technology groups.

to consider the role of entrepreneurship and new firms in bringing innovative products and processes into the market. For an economist, there
are three important questions relating to this. First, are there enough
entrepreneurs in society? Second, do these entrepreneurs select "productive" activities, where productive is defined as activities that raise GDP?
In all countries, some entrepreneurs choose illegal activities, such as
illicit drugs, corruption, or rent-seeking activities, and there is a need to
minimize this. Third, if entrepreneurs enter the market with innovative
products, do they gain access to the resources they need? In discussing
this last issue we need to consider the dynamic process of competition
(see section 5.4). New firms may be unable to gain access to finance,
skilled labor, technology, or information and this may force innovative
products out of the market. This, in turn, leads us to the general case
of barriers to entry: incumbent firms may attempt to prevent new firms
entering.

Section 5.5 considers the empirical evidence on the returns to innovation. In this chapter, the focus is on R&D, with a discussion of the empirical returns to IPRs left until chapter 6. This evidence is interesting in its
own right but it also provides background as to how empirical work can
contribute to policy debates. The private rates of return to R&D can be
investigated using either market value or productivity approaches (see
boxes 5.2 and 5.3). Both approaches suggest that private rates of return
to R&D are higher than for standard, tangible investment projects. Some
of these excess returns could be a reward for higher risk, but high rates
of return also suggest that there is not free entry into R&D. This could
be due to barriers—for example, raising finance, lack of skilled labor or
IPRs—but there is also the possibility that R&D requires complementary
assets that have been built up over time (e.g., tacit knowledge and skilled
labor). The productivity approach can also be used to estimate the social
returns to R&D. Many studies have suggested that the social returns are
higher than private returns, implying that there are positive externalities
to R&D.

The chapter also discusses the extensive debate over market structure and innovation, reviewing both theoretical aspects (section 5.4)
and empirical evidence (section 5.6). Schumpeter's first hypothesis was
that firms with larger market shares should innovate more. Large market share gives more certainty about recouping ex post returns; it
also implies more current profits to finance R&D. Schumpeter's second
hypothesis was that larger firms should innovate more, since large size
implies diversification of R&D risks and ability to finance. Empirical evidence on the second hypothesis is mixed. Large firms are more likely to
do R&D or be intellectual-property active, but those smaller firms that are

R&D or intellectual-property active generally have higher intensities (e.g., R&D/sales, or patents per employee). Investigating Schumpeter's first hypothesis has led to substantial theoretical work that tries to understand the relationship between market structure, competition, and innovation. Some basic cases of the differences between monopoly and perfect competition were already considered in chapter 1. As theoretical papers add realism to these basic cases, we find that the implications become dependent on yet further assumptions (e.g., assumptions about the IPR regime in place). Empirical work that tries to understand the relationship between competitive intensity and innovation reinforces these aspects. Innovation, market structure, and competition are all likely to be part of an endogenous process and other, more fundamental factors may drive outcomes. Nevertheless, there is interest in looking for associations between competitive intensity and innovation intensity. A possibility throughout various different studies is that there may be an inverted U-shaped relationship (see figure 5.1), although economists are a long way from being able to identify the optimal degree of competition (C^* in figure 5.1). In the next chapter we examine how firms use IPRs in the process of innovation and we explore the extent of private returns to innovation further, by examining empirical studies of the returns to particular types of IPRs.

Keywords

Entrepreneurship.

Creative destruction.

Dynamic competition.

Market structure: monopoly, oligopoly, and perfect competition.

Barriers to innovation.

Private and social returns to R&D.

Market value and productivity studies.

Questions for Discussion

(1) Should policy makers attempt to encourage entrepreneurship?

(2) Are entrepreneurship and innovation different?

(3) Why do firms innovate?

(4) What costs and benefits accrue to firms from innovation?

(5) What are Schumpeter's two main hypotheses concerning innovation? How would you test them?

(6) What have we learned from empirical studies about the returns to R&D?

(7) What sectors of the economy are omitted in these studies and why?

(8) How does competition affect innovation in theory and in practice?

References

Aghion, P., and Griffith, R. 2005. *Competition and Growth: Reconciling Theory and Evidence.* Cambridge, MA: MIT Press.

Ardagna, S., and A. Lusardi. 2008. Explaining international differences in entrepreneurship: the role of individual characteristics and regulatory constraints. NBER Working Paper 14012.

Arrow, K. 1962. The economic implications of learning by doing. *Review of Economic Studies* 29(1):155–73.

Audretsch, D. B., and A. R. Thurik. 2001. What's new about the New Economy? Sources of growth in the managed and entrepreneurial economies. *Industrial and Corporate Change* 10(1):267–315.

Bain, J. 1956. *Barriers to New Competition.* Cambridge, MA: Harvard University Press.

Baumol, W. 1990. Entrepreneurship: productive, unproductive, and destructive. *Journal of Political Economy* 98(5):893–921.

Bernstein, J. I., and M. I. Nadiri. 1988. Interindustry R&D spillovers, rates of return, and production in high-tech industries. *American Economic Review* 78:429–34.

Blanchflower, D. G., A. Oswald, and A. Stutzer. 2001. Latent entrepreneurship across nations. *European Economic Review* 45(4–6):680–91.

Blundell, R., R. Griffith, and J. Van Reenen. 1999. Market share, market value and innovation in a panel of British manufacturing firms. *Review of Economic Studies* 66:529–54.

Carlson, C., and W. Wilmot. 2006. *Innovation: The Five Disciplines for Creating What Customers Want.* New York: Random House.

Cohen, W. 1995. Empirical studies of innovative activity. In *Handbook of the Economics of Innovation and Technological Change* (ed. P. Stoneman). Oxford: Basil Blackwell.

Cohen, W., and D. Levinthal. 1989. Innovation and learning: the two faces of R&D. *Economic Journal* 99:569–96.

de Soto, H. 2000. *The Mystery of Capital: Why Capitalism Triumphs in the West but Fails Everywhere Else.* Oxford University Press.

Dasgupta, P., and J. Stiglitz. 1980. Industrial structure and the nature of innovative activity. *Economic Journal* 90:266–93.

Demsetz, H. 1973. Industry structure, market rivalry, and public policy. *Journal of Law and Economics* 16:1–10.

Disney, R., J. Haskel, and Y. Heden. 2003. Entry, exit and establishment survival in UK manufacturing. *Journal of Industrial Economics* 51(1):91–112.

Doraszelski, U. 2003. An R&D race with knowledge accumulation. *RAND Journal of Economics* 34(1):20–42.

Drucker, P. 1985. *Innovation and Entrepreneurship: Practice and Principles.* Elsevier.

Galbraith, J. K. 1956. *American Capitalism: The New Industrial State.* Boston, MA: Houghton Mifflin.

Gambardella, A. 1995. *Science and Innovation: The U.S. Pharmaceutical Industry During the 1980s.* Cambridge University Press.

Geroski, P. 1994. *Market Structure, Corporate Performance and Innovative Activity.* Oxford: Clarendon Press.

Geroski, P., S. Machin, and J. Van Reenen. 1993. The profitability of innovating firms. *Rand Journal of Economics* 24(2):198–211.

Gilbert, R. 2006. Competition and innovation. *Journal of Industrial Organization Education* 1(1):Article 8.

Gilbert, R., and D. Newbery. 1982. Preemptive patenting and the persistence of monopoly. *American Economic Review* 72:514–26.

Gort, M., and S. Klepper. 1982. Time paths in the diffusion of product innovations. *Economic Journal* 92:630–53.

Greenhalgh, C. A., and Rogers, M. 2006. The value of innovation: the interaction of competition, R&D and IP. *Research Policy* 35(4):562–80.

———. 2007. Intellectual property activity by service sector and manufacturing firms in the UK, 1996–2000. In *The Evolution of Business Knowledge* (ed. H. Scarbrough). Oxford University Press.

Greenstein, S., and G. Ramey. 1998. Market structure, innovation and vertical product differentiation. *International Journal of Industrial Organization* 16: 285–311.

Griffith, R., E. Huergo, J. Mairesse, and B. Peters. 2006. Innovation and productivity across four European countries. NBER Working Paper 12722.

Griliches, Z. 1981. Market value, R&D, and patents. *Economic Letters* 7:183–87.

Griliches, Z. (ed.). 1984. *R&D, Patents and Productivity.* University of Chicago Press.

Griliches, Z., and J. Mairesse. 1990. R&D and productivity growth: comparing Japanese and US manufacturing firms. In *Productivity Growth in Japan and United States*(ed. C. R. Hulten). University of Chicago Press.

———. 1995. Production functions: the search for identification. NBER Working Paper 5067.

Gruber, H. 1992. Persistence of leadership in product innovation. *Journal of Industrial Economics* 40(4):359–75.

———. 1995. Market structure, learning and product innovation: the EPROM market. *International Journal of the Economics of Business* 2(1):87–101.

Hagerdoorn, J. 1996. Innovation and entrepreneurship: Schumpeter revisited. *Industrial and Corporate Change* 5(3):883–95.

Hall, B. 1993a. Industrial research during the 1980s: did the rate of return fall? *Brookings Papers on Economic Activity* Microeconomics (2):289–344.

———. 1993b. The stock market valuation of R&D investment during the 1980s. *American Economic Review* 83(2):259–64.

———. 2000. Innovation and market value. In *Productivity, Innovation and Economic Performance* (ed. R. Barrell, G. Mason and M. O'Mahoney). Cambridge University Press.

Hall, B. 2007. Measuring the returns to R&D: the depreciation problem. NBER Working Paper 13473.

Hall, B., and J. Mairesse. 1995. Exploring the relationship between R&D and productivity in French manufacturing firms. *Journal of Econometrics* 65: 263–93.

Hall, B., and R. Oriani. 2006. Does the market value R&D investment by European firms? Evidence from a panel of manufacturing firms in France, Germany and Italy. *International Journal of Industrial Organization* 24:971–93.

Hall, B., and K. Vopel. 1996. Innovation, market share and market value. Working Paper, UC Berkeley (available at http://elsa.berkeley.edu/~bhhall/ bhpapers.html#value).

Hall, B., A. Jaffe, and M. Trajtenberg. 2005. Market value and patent citations. *Rand Journal of Economics* 36:16–38.

Harhoff, D. 1998. R&D and productivity in German manufacturing firms. *Economics of Innovation and New Technology* 6:22–49.

Hart, D. M. 2001. Antitrust and technological innovation in the US: ideas, institutions, decisions, and impacts, 1890–2000. *Research Policy* 30(6):923–36.

Helmers, C., and M. Rogers. 2008. Innovation and the survival of new firms across British regions. Working Paper, Oxford University Economics Department.

Hemphill, T. 2003. Cooperative strategy, technology innovation and competition policy in the United States and the European Union. *Technology Analysis and Strategic Management* 15(1):93–101.

Hodgson, G. M. 1993. *Economics and Evolution.* Cambridge: Polity Press.

Kafouros, M. 2004. R&D and productivity growth at the firm level: a survey of the literature. Working Paper 57, Kent Business School.

Klepper, S. 1996. Entry, exit, growth, and innovation over the product life cycle. *American Economic Review* 86:562–83.

Lev, B., and T. Sougiannis. 1996. The capitalization, amortization, and value-relevance of R&D. *Journal of Accounting and Economics* 21:107–38.

Lichtenberg, F., and D. Siegel. 1991. The impact of R&D investment on productivity—new evidence using linked R&D-LRD data. *Economic Inquiry* 29: 203–28.

Lokshin, B., R. Belderbos, and M. Carree. 2008. The productivity effects of internal and external R&D: evidence from a dynamic panel data model. *Oxford Bulletin of Economics & Statistics* 70(3):399–413.

Nelson, R. R. 1991. Why do firms differ, and how does it matter? *Strategic Management Journal* 12:61–74.

OECD. 2003. *Technology and Industry Scoreboard.* Paris: OECD.

Poterba, J., and L. Summers. 1995. A CEO survey of US companies' time horizons and hurdle rates. *Sloan Management Review* 37(1):43–53.

Reinganum, J. 1981. Dynamic games of innovation. *Journal of Economic Theory* 25:21–41.

———. 1983. Uncertain innovation and the persistence of monopoly. *American Economic Review* 73:741–48.

Rogers, M. 2006. Estimating the impact of R&D on productivity using the BERD-ARD data. Report, Department for Business Enterprise and Regulatory Reform (available at www.dti.gov.uk/economics/RandDProductivityBERD_Final.pdf).

Rogers, M. Forthcoming. R&D and productivity: using UK firm-level data to inform policy. *Empirica*, in press.

Salop, S. 1979. Monopolistic competition with outside goods. *Bell Journal of Economics* 10:141–56.

Scherer, F. M. 1965. Firm size, market structure, opportunity and the output of patented inventions. *American Economic Review* 55:1,097–125.

———. 1992. Schumpeter and plausible capitalism. *Journal of Economic Literature* 30:1,416–33.

Schmidt, K. M. 1997. Managerial incentives and product market competition. *Review of Economic Studies* 64(2):191–213.

Schumpeter, J. 1934. *The Theory of Economic Development*. Cambridge, MA: Harvard University Press.

———. 1942. *Capitalism, Socialism and Democracy*. Harper and Row. (Reprinted version issued in 1992 by Routledge, London.)

Shaked, A., and J. Sutton. 1983. Natural oligopolies. *Econometrica* 51(5):1,469–83.

Shalman, W. 1999. *The Entrepreneurial Venture*. Cambridge, MA: Harvard University Press.

Skarzynski, P., and R. Gibson. 2008. *Innovation to the Core: A Blueprint for Transforming the Way Your Company Innovates*. Cambridge, MA: Harvard Business School.

Sutton, J. 1996. Technology and market structure. *European Economic Review* 40:511–30.

Symeonidis, G. 1996. Innovation, firm size and market structure: Schumpeterian hypotheses and some new themes. Working Paper 161, OECD Economics Department.

Teece, D. J. 1986. Profiting from technological innovation. *Research Policy* 15(6): 285–305.

———. 2006. Reflections on profiting from innovation. *Research Policy* 35(8): 1,131–46.

Tirole, J. 1988. *The Theory of Industrial Organization*. Boston, MA: MIT Press.

Tsai, K. H., and J. C. Wang. 2004. R&D productivity and the spillover effects of high-tech industry on the traditional manufacturing sector: the case of Taiwan. *World Economy* 27(10):1,555–70.

Von Hippel, E. 1988. *The Sources of Innovation*. Oxford University Press.

Webster, E., H. Buddelmeyer, and P. Jensen. Forthcoming. Innovation and the determinants of company survival. *Oxford Economic Papers*, in press.

Wolff, E., and M. Nadiri. 1993. Spillover effects, linkage structure and R&D. *Structural Change and Economic Dynamics* 2:315–31.

6

Intellectual Property Rights and Firms

6.1 Introduction

Chapter 5 discussed the gains to firms from innovation, mainly relating this discussion to their investment in R&D. This chapter explores how firms use IPRs in more detail and surveys the empirical studies on the value of IPRs. As we saw in chapter 2, firms hold some monopoly power during the period of their IPR (in the geographical territory within which the right is protected). Hence, on average, we expect to be able to demonstrate that acquiring IPRs is of value to firms. However, further investigation suggests that the gains from IPRs can arrive via different routes, depending on the type of innovation, the characteristics of the firm, and the use made of the IPR. It is also important to stress that there may be circumstances in which firms prefer to take alternative routes, such as maintaining secrecy, or contributing to "open source" development of knowledge. These are all possibilities for enhancing the value added of the firm. Also, in some cases, certain types of IPRs were not always an option: the finance industry, for example, has been innovating for decades, but it was only in 1998 with the State Street Bank court decision in the United States that patenting business methods became a possibility.[1] During this discussion it is natural to consider some aspects of whether the current system of IPRs is optimal for promoting innovation; something we return to in chapter 11.

The structure of the chapter is as follows. The next section reviews the basic ideas of how firms benefit from IPRs. Section 6.3 explores the returns to IPRs, starting with the question of whether IPRs are critical to firms gaining value from innovation. It then looks at the skewness in returns from IPRs. The stylized fact is that a low percentage of IPRs generates the bulk of the returns. Section 6.4 looks at markets for IPRs. Many argue that a substantial benefit of the patent system is that it allows a

---

[1] For example, Tufano (1989) considers innovation in investment banks, while Lerner (2002) reviews the developments in financial innovation prior to and following the State Street Bank decision.

market for technology to develop. However, there are also concerns that patents can create adverse outcomes through so-called *patent trolls* and *patent thickets*. Section 6.5 looks at the cost of obtaining and enforcing IPRs, and section 6.6 reviews IPR strategies with respect to patents and trademarks. The final section discusses the methodology and insights from empirical studies on IPRs.

6.2 How Can Firms Benefit from IPRs?

With *process innovation* the firm gains profits via lower costs of production if they continue to sell the output at the same price. Alternatively, the firm can sell at a lower price and increase its market share by driving out competitors, possibly leading to later returns from increased market power. With *product innovation* the firm aims to raise profitability by increasing its market share and its sales. Also, a higher price can be charged for a higher-quality product. In both cases, the firm will effectively steal some profits from rival firms (the "business-stealing effect" discussed in box 5.1). Both process and product innovations can be protected by patents. In addition, trademarks and designs can help protect product innovations. In fact, in many circumstances firms use multiple IPRs to protect innovations. By way of shorthand, we can refer to the above as "market power" benefits.

Licensing is another route to obtaining value from IPRs, as this brings in revenues without having to engage in production.[2] For example, Baumol (2002) argues that competition and the pursuit of profits drive many firms to disseminate their technology, using both single patent license deals and broader technology exchange agreements between large firms, also known as *patent pools*. He argues that such technology-sharing agreements between incumbent firms save wasteful costs of reverse engineering by would-be imitators, or effort in inventing around a rival's patent. Patent pools also provide a degree of protection against firms outside the technology agreement, hence the existence of patent pools and extensive cross-licensing may act as a barrier to entry, so it is not clear whether such practices help or hinder innovation.

A further explanation for how firms benefit from IPRs is given by *signaling theory* (e.g., Long 2002). This assumes that there is an informational asymmetry between firms and outsiders (such as private investors,

---

[2] Much of our discussion here focuses on the market for patents to illustrate points of principle, but licensing is equally important for copyright, trademarks, and even trade secrets.

banks which may lend the firm money, and potential employees). This information asymmetry arises because the outsiders do not have knowledge of the full nature of current innovation activity and the future prospects of the company. Given this, firms need to signal their expertise and they can use the IPR system to do this. Patents, in particular, are costly to acquire and undergo an external quality check, hence they act as good signals, allowing firms to raise finance or attract talented employees.[3] It can be argued that this signaling view is especially relevant for new, smaller firms. For these firms, having a patent and/or a trademark can signal to banks or other investors that they have a potentially valuable innovation.[4]

Market power, licensing, and signaling are the basic ways in which firms can benefit from IPRs. In section 6.6 below we add some more detail of the specific strategies that firms use with respect to IPRs. However, let us consider here one case in which patents may create net losses for firms and society. This is caused by so-called *patent races*. The basic idea is that if several firms are racing to file a patent, which represents a "winner takes all" outcome, then they may spend more on R&D than is optimal.[5] Gilbert and Newbery (1982) and Wright (1983) formalize this argument. Patent races can also increase the duplication of R&D, although this can occur in any situation (see Chatterjee and Evans (2004) for a theoretical model). In practice, the overall extent to which firms pursue similar innovations is not clear so it is difficult to know how much weight to give to the patent race idea.[6]

---

[3] From this perspective, the signal value of an IPR is related to its "quality," and any deterioration in standards within the IPR system could affect this value.

[4] This feature of patents acting as positive information signals to venture capitalists, investing in start-ups in the software industry, has been surveyed by Mann (2005).

[5] To be precise, the argument is that inventing something over, say, four years costs x, whereas rushing to invent in two years costs $(x + \delta)$, where $\delta > 0$. Exactly, how δ varies with time is not clear, but the idea is that employing twice as many researchers, or making researchers work twice as hard, gives rise to greater costs.

[6] The duplication of R&D, separate from patent races, is thought to be a major issue inhibiting efficiency; the EPO (2007) states that up to 30% of R&D expenditure is wasted in redeveloping existing inventions. Calculating an exact figure for duplication is, clearly, difficult since firms—by definition—are not aware of it, but even if there appears to be duplication some of this may be due to firms investing in their absorptive capacity. Duplication can relate to patented inventions, hence patent offices stress the value of searching patent databases like www.espace.net. If a patent is in force, the efficiency issue concerns the availability of licenses and whether the market for technology is functioning well (see the discussion in section 6.4).

There are certainly specific examples of patent races: Chatterjee and Evans (2004) refer to the race between Texas Instruments and Casio to invent the first handheld calculator; there are also examples in pharmaceuticals where two or more companies pursue a drug for a specific illness.

6.3 Exploring the Returns to IPRs

Are IPRs Critical to Innovation?

At the outset, it is important to understand the difference between the formal IPRs that chapter 2 discussed (i.e., patents, trademarks, designs, and copyright) and *trade secrets* and *confidential information*. To a lawyer, trade secrets and confidential information are also considered part of intellectual property law. These are defined as technological know-how, formulas, computer codes, recipes, customer information, and similar. Companies can sue if they feel that trade secrets or confidential information have been stolen. Proving this can be difficult, hence firms are advised to consider formal registration of IPRs where possible so that ownership can be more easily proved and enforced.

If trade secrets and confidential information are included as part of the definition of intellectual property, then any "new to the market" innovation will, by definition, contain intellectual property. However, in general, asking whether IPRs are important for innovation seeks to understand whether *formal* IPRs are essential to achieving gains from innovation. The basic answer to this is no. Firms can and do use trade secrecy, and also first-mover advantages or lead time, as alternative strategies. Also, firms may not want to choose a patent since this involves revealing information about the invention. Even though the patent is supposed to protect against imitation, in practice it may do so imperfectly, hence secrecy may be preferred.

What is the evidence on whether patents are important? In the early 1980s a survey of U.S. manufacturing firms found that patents were a relatively *unimportant* way to exploit innovations, at least in the majority of industries (Levin et al. 1987). Similar results were found in a follow-up study in 1994 (Cohen et al. 2000). Further analysis of these data suggests that the "patent premium" was highest in pharmaceuticals, biotech, and medical equipment, followed by machines, computers, and chemicals.[7] For Europe, questions about the effectiveness of different methods of appropriating the returns from innovation are also asked in the Community Innovation Survey (CIS). Figure 6.1 shows the results from the 1990–92 CIS as reported in Arundel (2001). The bars show the percentage of R&D-active firms that gave their highest rating to the method

---

[7] Arora et al. (2008) study the patenting decisions of 1,478 U.S. R&D laboratories for 1991–93 and find that the returns to patents were most important in the optical instruments industry.

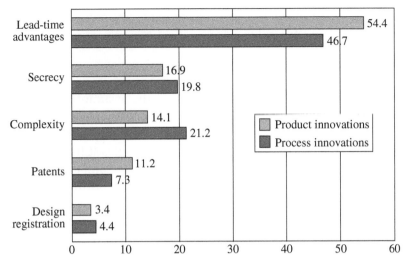

Figure 6.1. The effectiveness of different methods of appropriability.

Notes. The survey question asked respondents to "evaluate the effectiveness of the following methods for maintaining and increasing the competitiveness of product or process innovations introduced during 1990–1992." Five choices were given, from "insignificant" to "crucial."

specified (note that neither trademarks nor copyright were included in the survey question).

Does this evidence mean that a focus on patents is misguided? There are a number of responses to this. First, the dominance of lead time is, perhaps, to be expected since firms need to get their products to market in order to make profits. Hence, a better comparison is between secrecy and patents. Although secrecy still comes out on top (see figure 6.1), there are substantial numbers of firms that rate patents more highly than secrecy (around 18–30% in Arundel (2001)) and many rate patents and secrecy as equally important (around 25–40%).[8] Second, the surveys cannot tell whether patents were used more frequently by firms with higher-value innovations, of which one would expect fewer to exist (see the next section), or vice versa. Third, as reviewed in section 6.7, empirical studies show strong links between firm-level intellectual property activity and performance. Finally, as figure 3.1 indicates, in many countries patent use has risen since the early 1990s, which does indicate that firms have chosen to use more patents. Nevertheless, there is still widespread agreement that secrecy, first-mover advantages, and

---

[8] The figures are from Arundel (2001, table 1). Smaller R&D-active firms tend to rate patents as less important, suggesting that they have more difficulty in benefiting from the patent system.

complementary assets (see below) are generally more important than patents, even in R&D industries.[9]

Open Innovation, Open Source, and IPRs

The *open innovation* paradigm is built on the assumption that individual firms do not have the financial and personnel resources to carry out certain complex innovation projects; hence they must share knowledge, ideas, and inventions with other companies (Chesbrough 2006). This contrasts with a traditional view that large companies could both supply the finance and conduct the research behind the entire innovation project. Companies like IBM were assumed to be large enough to do this, but now even IBM uses open innovation in some cases.[10] The open innovation paradigm is, therefore, similar to a flexible and large-scale joint research project, which can include universities (hence it relates to the ideas in chapter 4 on national systems of innovation). Are IPRs conducive to open innovation or adverse to it? An original assumption was that the open innovation paradigm relies on payments between the members and in many cases these may be based around licenses and patents (West 2006). From this point of view, patents can provide the framework for the cross-payments within the research group, hence facilitating the formation and success of such projects. On the other hand, patents can introduce the possibility of *holdup*, where one patentee holds a project to ransom. Given this, it is not clear whether IPRs help or hinder open innovation, although there are some who take the view that the general increase in the use of IPRs is severely detrimental.[11]

What about innovation in areas such as computer software? Computer software code has always been covered by copyright; but, traditionally, software was considered to be close to "abstract ideas," which are excluded from being patented. In the United States, starting in the 1980s but accelerating in the 1990s, this view was increasingly relaxed and now software patents may account for up to 15% of all patents (Bessen and

---

[9] The issue of trade secrecy is not relevant to trademarks or copyright and, of course, firms do not need to formally register these IPRs. However, intellectual property lawyers recommend that firms formalize their intellectual property as much as they can since this makes it more likely that they will win in legal disputes and, in the United States, copyright registration is required before litigation. Section 6.7 discusses empirical research into the value of trademarks and copyright.

[10] The Eclipse project seeks to develop universal software platforms and had 162 members in September 2007, including IBM, Borland, SAP, Intel, and Nokia.

[11] Some have called the increasing use of IPRs the "second enclosure movement," whereby ideas and knowledge—the basic components of innovation—are being made into private property (see Boyle 2003; Lessig 2002).

Hunt 2007).[12] However, Hall and MacGarvie (2006) develop a range of measures to determine which patents should be classified as software patents and these suggest that Bessen and Hunt may have included too many patents that are hardware related.

Does growth in software patents suggest that IPRs, and patents in particular, have helped promote innovation in software? As always, the first issue is to understand the data. The estimates by Bessen and Hunt suggest that a large share of software patents was issued to manufacturing firms, principally in electronics, machinery, and instruments, with only a small share being issued to software publishers. These authors go on to suggest that the rise in software patenting may well have been due to strategic behavior by manufacturing firms as they attempted to build patent portfolios. They find little evidence of increases in R&D, software investment, or employment of programmers, which might suggest increases in innovation activity. Hall and MacGarvie are more cautious about the trend rise in software patenting, but also more positive about the real value of these patents. Using the market value approach described below they also find that software patents were valued similarly to other patents before permissive changes in legislation in the mid 1990s and were valued more highly afterwards (by a factor of two relative to other patents).

A related issue concerns the *open source* movement. With respect to software development, open source means not only do people have access to the source (fundamental) software code, but that developers can use this code to modify, sell, or give away new products without paying license fees. New products, however, must also make their source code available and extend the same license agreement to others. In effect, open source is covered by a specific, open form of IPR, which is often called a "public license" (e.g., Netscape released its browser source code under the Netscape Public License, which in turn was developed into Firefox). There are some good examples of where the open source innovation method has developed excellent and important products (e.g., Linux, Apache HTTP Server, Internet Protocol).[13] As argued by Gomulkiewicz (1999), far from being an unregulated "free for all," this system in fact relies on existing IPRs and legal contracts, as copyright exists in the source code, and the contract to ensure a free license is itself a legal tool. There are concerns that the open source approach is being threatened

---

[12] Bessen and Hunt (2007) also point out that some software-related patents were, in fact, issued in the 1970s.

[13] The open source movement has some parallels with academic research, where the traditional model was open and free dissemination of results to allow replication and advancement. Also, media, music, and arts communities often have an open source ethic.

by large firms increasingly using IPRs to "fence off" areas of knowledge (see footnote 11 on page 154).

Skewness in Returns

A key feature of the returns to IPRs is the skewness in returns. Let us consider patents initially. We noted in chapter 3 that one way of weighting patents according to their value is to use patent citations, which tend to be higher for more important patents. Even so, many empirical studies show that most patents have little or no value. One method of detecting this is to use data on patent renewals. In some countries, annual patent renewal fees must be paid, but this will only be done when the value of the patent exceeds this (relatively small) fee. For example, Schankerman and Pakes (1986) found that more than 50% of patents were not renewed past ten years in France, Germany, and the United Kingdom (see section 6.7 below for more details). An alternative method is to use survey data. The PatVal–EU survey found that 7.2% of patents were worth more than ten million euros, while 68% were worth less than one million, and 8% were worth less than thirty thousand euros.[14] The returns to trademarks and copyright appear to follow a similar skewness, although these have been less studied. Extremely valuable trademarks are often called brands. Coca-Cola regularly tops the world's most valuable brands (estimated at $65 billion), with Disney ($29 billion), Marlboro ($21 billion), and Google ($18 billion) all being in the top twenty as assessed by Interbrand–Business Week (2007). For copyright, the existence of blockbuster films and best-selling authors indicates the skewness. A survey of 25,000 authors in the United Kingdom and Germany found that in the United Kingdom the top 10% of authors earned 60% of total income, with the bottom 50% earning only 8% of total income (the distribution is slightly more equal in Germany (see Kretschmer and Hardwick 2007)).

The implications of such skewness can be subtle. For example, surveys of the value placed on IPRs may reveal that most firms have not received any value from using IPRs, but this does not imply that the *aggregate* value of IPRs is low. Another example is when empirical studies report the mean value of patents, because mean values are not a good indicator of central tendency in skewed samples. This also means that answering the question, "Is the IPR system working?" requires great care, since, for example, finding that 99% of firms do not use, or gain little value from, patents misses the fact that the other 1% may generate massive benefits for society.

---

[14] The survey covered inventors in France, Germany, Italy, the Netherlands, Spain, and the United Kingdom. The response rate to the survey was 35% (see Giuri et al. 2006). Gambardella et al. (2008) also discuss values of EPO patents using PatVal.

What Is the Role of Complementary Assets in Deriving Value from IPRs?

Obviously, obtaining IPRs is only the first step, as there are many factors enabling firms to profit from innovation. In an early paper, Teece (1986) had put forward the view that the ability to capture the returns from innovation was related to the complementary assets held by the innovator, to crucially important timing decisions on when to enter a market, and to the contractual structures employed by managers to access any complementary assets that were missing within the firm.[15] So what are the relevant sets of complementary assets and how might a firm's management strategy determine its ability to retain rewards from innovation? The list of major complementary assets includes the capacity to manufacture using related technology, product distribution facilities, after-sales service, marketing, advertising, as well as factors specific to the industry.

In this framework, intellectual property is just one of a set of opportunities within which firms have to construct their strategy for appropriation of returns, albeit still an important one. Gans and Stern (2003) explored the interaction between intellectual property and complementary assets. In their view, strategic choices of competition or cooperation between technology start-ups and incumbent firms depend strongly on these two factors. With a strong IPR regime, and where incumbent firms hold important specialized complementary assets that act as a barrier to entry, the start-up firm will gain higher profit from cooperation (either by licensing its innovation or by allowing itself to be taken over) than from competition in production. The authors conclude that, by enhancing the creation of "markets for ideas," IPRs may benefit both established firms and entrepreneurs by increasing the contracting options and thus decreasing the waste of resources involved in a high turnover of firms. Here we see support for the idea that it is not necessary for a firm to own all the complementary assets, as the key is whether access to these assets can be achieved via market contracts, such as the trading of IPRs for access to distribution networks.

6.4 Markets for IPRs

As noted above in section 6.2, firms have options about how to exploit their intellectual property. Exploitation solely within one company will

---

[15] Twenty years after Teeces's article appeared, a 2006 edition of *Research Policy* was entirely devoted to articles considering the impact of his shift of focus from IPRs to relevant complementary factors (see, inter alia, Nelson 2006; Teece 2006; Winter 2006).

not necessarily be the best way to obtain returns from what is a time-limited monopoly right, particularly when the firm may have a limited geographical distribution of its products. Thus firms may look for ways to gain higher revenues by marketing their IPR assets to others whose production is not in direct competition with their own. At the same time, some firms may specialize in trying to augment the returns to IPRs by buying and selling contracts related to these assets. These are normal activities in markets for tangible assets and we expect to see the same range of profit-seeking activity developing in markets for intangible assets.

The Decision to License Patents

There are many factors determining whether a firm decides to license. The following is a list of key factors that increase the likelihood of licensing taking place:[16]

- The strength of the particular patent in terms of its novelty (making it hard to invent around) and whether it is a general technology with a wide spectrum of applications.
- The greater the ratio of codified scientific knowledge to tacit knowledge, as accompanying tacit knowledge is more difficult to transfer under contract.
- The higher the value of the patent as denoted by breadth of coverage across geographical territory and by the number of claims in the patent.
- The smaller the size of the firm, as this means it is likely to lack some important complementary assets for the successful development of products.
- The patent is not in the core technology area of the firm.
- The firm faces considerable competition in its product market (in contrast, the more market power it has, the more easily it can extract adequate profits without licensing).

While all the above factors were found to have some significant impact, the largest difference between firms was that arising from firm size. In the smallest firms (employing less than 100 workers), 25% of patents were licensed, compared with 9% in large firms (employing more than 250 workers). These rates were inversely proportional to the share of

---

[16] For a recent summary of this theory and detailed empirical analysis for France, Germany, Italy, the Netherlands, Spain, and the United Kingdom, which gives rise to the list, see Gambardella et al. (2007).

patents held by these two types of firms: large firms held 76% of the sampled patents but the group of smallest firms held only 14% (Gambardella et al. 2007). This demonstrates the extent to which small firms are less likely to have the width of product range and the geographical distribution to gain all the returns from exploiting their IPRs.

Compulsory Licenses

Patent laws also allow the possibility of compulsory licenses. For patents, one rationale for compulsory licenses arises when there is a national emergency: for example, the need to produce vaccines to prevent infection. Compulsory licenses can also be requested if the patentee is failing to meet demand. More controversially, compulsory licenses can be imposed in cases relating to competition. If certain patents are viewed as preventing the process of competition, especially with respect to innovation, it is possible for courts to impose a compulsory license. One example, from 2002, was that the U.S. Department of Justice required Microsoft to provide uniform licenses to original equipment manufacturers (with royalty rates published on a Web site). The licenses covered protocols needed to create products that could work with Windows. Another example, from 2007, is the case of the U.S. chip maker, Rambus, which was ordered by the Federal Trade Commission (FTC) to license patented technology on its memory-related products with royalties at a specified level.[17] The use of compulsory licenses in cases such as these is, to some, a direct weakening of the patent system and has the potential to undermine the incentives to innovate. To others, compulsory licenses are a sensible method of reducing market power and encouraging competition. Court decisions in both the United States and Europe have reflected both sides of the debate, creating some confusion for policy (Delrahim 2004).[18]

Patent Trolls and Patent Thickets

Recently, the issue of patent licensing has become more controversial, especially in the United States. The most extreme case of this is specialist firms dealing only in IPRs, particularly patents. Such firms have been termed, pejoratively, *patent trolls*, as they search for and acquire

---

[17] See Love (2007) for these examples and a wide range of others from around the world. However, Rambus has appealed the FTC ruling and is awaiting a court date for this appeal (see http://en.wikipedia.org/wiki/Rambus).

[18] Compulsory copyright licensing is another aspect of the intellectual property system. For example, songs can often be recorded as long as copyright owners are informed and a standard royalty is paid.

patents in order to enforce them against potential or actual infringers, and to pursue opportunities for licensing. Importantly, these firms have not been involved in the relevant R&D, nor do they produce any products relating to the patent. This activity is quite legal and might be seen as improving the liquidity of the market in intellectual property, but the level of license fees is not subject to any restraint in the United States, leading to allegations of excessive profiteering. A severe problem of holdup can arise where a patent relates only to a small portion of the product, but the patent holder can obtain a preliminary injunction in the courts suspending all production while the dispute is adjudicated. This can lead to settlements out of court that are greatly in excess of the true value of the patent (see Henkel and Reitzig 2007).

Even within firms that are actively using their IPRs and not restraining any activity, there can be allegations that they acquire extra, related IPR in order to create a *patent thicket*, giving them the power to deny access to potential rivals for necessary technology (a barrier to entry). However, in the United Kingdom, patent law contains provisions that require a patent holder to grant a license on reasonable terms and, in the event that this is denied, the U.K. Intellectual Property Office may grant a compulsory license. This limits the incentive to act aggressively via either patent thickets or trolls. Even with such limits, the transaction costs associated with negotiating a raft of license agreements may act as a barrier to new firm entry.[19]

6.5 Costs of Obtaining and Enforcing IPRs

Acquiring and defending formal IPRs costs both managerial time and fees, and these costs need to be weighed against the benefits. The main costs are those of acquiring the IPRs and then defending them in law if infringed, or defending the company from others' claims of infringement. While the cost of IPR acquisition is a known amount of fees, the cost of litigation is subject to uncertainty as this involves a small probability of incurring large costs. Thus, firm size is again relevant to the ability to pay for IPRs, both for the initial fees to register IPRs and for the legal costs arising if it is necessary to litigate. For large firms these costs can appear modest in relation to their budgets, whereas for small firms these costs can be the difference between survival and bankruptcy. Even for larger firms, the damages awarded can be materially significant

---

[19] For example, some argue that biomedical research has been adversely affected: see Heller and Eisenberg (1998).

Table 6.1. Estimates of patent costs.

	England and Wales	Germany	France	U.S.
Application and renewal (£)	3,500	9,000	4,000	5,500
Litigation costs (£ thousands)	200–1,000	37–74	44–74	1,000–2,000

Source. Data are from IPAC (2003) and from the *Gowers Review* (HM Treasury 2006) and are estimates only.

if they are found to be infringing and the penalties are proportionate to their sales.[20]

Some evidence on these costs of filing and defense for patents within one country is presented in table 6.1 for some European countries and the United States, and this shows considerable variation in filing costs by country. The cost of an international patent is correspondingly higher: the *Gowers Review* (HM Treasury 2006) estimates that the cost of achieving triadic protection (i.e., a patent covering the United States/Europe/Japan) ranges from £39,000 to £69,000. The estimates in table 6.1 also indicate a wide variation in the costs of litigation across countries. There is also variation within countries according to which legal route is taken and how far up the hierarchy of the courts it is pursued (for example, from County Court to the High Court in the United Kingdom).

The costs of obtaining trademarks are lower than for patents. For example, in the United Kingdom a trademark application costs around $300 while a Community trademark costs around $2,000 (the renewal fees every ten years are similar amounts). Use of a trademark attorney may increase these costs substantially but, as with patents, the high costs are only encountered if legal disputes occur. Copyright does not need to be registered, but the U.S. Copyright Office currently charges $35 for an online registration.

Evidence on Outcomes of IPR Legal Disputes

Lanjouw and Schankerman (2001) study the determinants and outcomes of patent infringement and declaratory judgment suits using a sample of all patent suits reported by U.S. federal courts over the period 1978–99. They find that the threat of court action is very important: most

---

[20] The problem of risk from the high cost of litigation is modified where law firms are willing to take patent infringement cases on a contingent fee basis, typically on behalf of small inventor plaintiffs. Also the balance of power between large and small firms can be in favor of the smaller enterprise where a case of holdup is possible, as described above in section 6.4.

settlement occurs soon after a suit is filed, and sometimes before pre-trial hearings take place. Lanjouw and Schankerman conclude that this aspect of the enforcement process is desirable, since it implies that the use of judicial resources is minimized. However, individuals and smaller companies are much more likely to be engaged in a suit, conditional on the characteristics of their patents. Interestingly and importantly, what is significant for settlements is that firms have a portfolio of intellectual property to trade, or that firms have some other means of encouraging cooperative behavior. Again, this puts small firms and individuals, with their small intellectual property portfolios, at a disadvantage. Nevertheless, the authors do suggest that patent litigation insurance might be a plausible proposition.

In earlier related work, Lanjouw and Lerner (1996) study the use of preliminary injunctive relief in U.S. patent litigation. Preliminary injunctive grants prevent alleged infringers from using the infringed patent during the period of the trial. They investigate whether small firms, who are weaker financially than larger firms, would be unable to compensate the patentee for damage occurring during a trial if found guilty, or might not even be able to sustain an injunction. In other words, they test whether the possibility of increasing legal costs and the possibility of going out of business may lead defendants to settle on unfavorable terms. They find a positive relationship between plaintiff size and the likelihood that they will request an injunction. Interestingly, the difference between plaintiff and defendant size is also important, which Lanjouw and Lerner argue may be due to strong firms preying upon smaller and weaker firms in an effort to drive up the costs of their smaller competitors. They also cite unpublished work by Lerner that shows that patent cases involving smaller firms display a disproportionate concern with trade secrets, which Lerner concludes is due to the high costs, both direct and indirect, of patenting for these firms.[21]

6.6 IPR Strategies

Patenting Strategies

The basic, economic rationale for patenting is to obtain some monopoly power and increase the firm's profits. Patents can also be used as a signal

---

[21] Lerner (1995) studies the patenting behavior of forty-nine new American biotechnology firms. He finds that the firms with the highest litigation costs are more likely to patent in patent subclasses with no rival awards. He also finds that firms with high litigation costs face a lower likelihood of patenting in areas where there are firms who have a lower cost of litigation. It is possible that new firms do not make this decision purely on the basis of legal costs, but instead are driven to patent in areas where there are few older established competitors.

Table 6.2. Strategies for benefiting from patents.

Strategy	Description
Obtain market, or monopoly, power	Standard economic argument to increase profits. Lipitor, which is Pfizer's patented cholesterol-lowering drug, was estimated to have sales of $12 billion in 2007. The patent is due to expire in 2010.
To act as a signal	A patent may signal to financiers, granting agencies, customers, suppliers, universities, or others that the firm is innovative. Hsu and Ziedonis (2007) find some evidence for this in 370 U.S. start-up semiconductor firms.
To restrain power of suppliers	For example, Nokia has patents relating to loudspeakers and other components, even though these are manufactured by suppliers.
To build negotiating power	This relates to the idea of patent pools. Firms may need their own patents to enter cross-licensing.
To avoid being invented around	This is the idea of patent thickets. Having a number of patents covering similar areas makes it more difficult to invent around.
To prevent others from patenting ("blocking"), or developing certain technologies ("fencing"), or raise costs of entrants or rivals ("flooding" or "blanketing")	These strategies are self-explanatory. They result in patent thickets and/or act to change rivals' costs or strategies.

Sources. This table is a shortened version of a discussion in Guellec and van Pottelsberghe (2007). See also Granstrand (1999). Examples are from Web searches.

to banks, suppliers, or customers that the firm has valuable innovations. Previous sections have also mentioned patent trolls and patent thickets. In table 6.2 we summarize these and add a number of other more specific strategies for gaining value from patenting.

To illustrate the relevance of the last three strategies listed in table 6.2, it is interesting to consider Hall and Ziedonis (2001). They conducted a survey of 100 firms in the U.S. semiconductor industry. This industry is characterized by technological sophistication and extremely short product life cycles. The authors note that firms in the semiconductor industry tend to rely more on measures such as lead time, secrecy, and design capability than on patents. It is then surprising to see widespread and increasing use of patents in this industry. One interpretation is that the intense innovative competition in high-tech sectors rapidly erodes profits even with IPRs. However, Hall and Ziedonis conclude that many patents are registered so as to allow individual firms to quickly negotiate access to important external technologies. Thus, firms use large patent portfolios as "bargaining chips" to get around the problem of investment being delayed due to certain patents being held by external economic units. Such behavior leads to *patent portfolio races* on the part of firms trying to amass, for strategic reasons, large numbers of patents. Hall and Ziedonis observe that such behavior would not be observed if patent rights were awarded on a strictly "novel" basis, so that it would become very difficult to get a patent when a substantial body of "prior art" exists. This work highlights the need to take strategic factors into consideration when studying patent behavior, as proposed by Teece (1986, 2006).

Trademarking Strategies

The economic basis of the value of trademarks is that they help to solve the information asymmetry between seller and buyer; hence they act as a signal that the product is of a certain, consistent quality. In this way the search costs of customers are reduced, the firm can charge a higher price, and the firm's profits increase. Given this, trademarks are also important for innovation since, without them, imitation becomes more likely and less easy to defend against. In practice, these basic ideas give rise to a variety of strategies in the use of trademarks, and these are outlined in table 6.3.

6.7 Empirical Studies on the Value of IPRs

This section reviews some recent studies that investigate the value of IPRs. As with R&D studies, there are two main methodologies: stock market value studies and productivity studies. Either of these can be used to explore the value of patents and trademarks. There is also a third type of study that exploits the decision by the firm to renew a patent. As mentioned above, there are fees to renew a patent and firms will not pay these if they believe the patent has no further commercial value. These decisions lead to variations in patent length and this can be used as a source of information about patent values. In all empirical studies there are genuine difficulties in obtaining precise values for IPRs. As Hall (2000) notes, intellectual property assets are usually embedded within a particular product, and evaluating the separate contribution made by IPRs is difficult.

Table 6.3. Strategies for benefiting from trademarks.

Strategy	Description/examples
Signal origin and quality of product	Such a signal allows marketing and advertising to build this into a brand (e.g., Coca-Cola is the world's leading brand; the Intel Inside strategy was an example of signaling the origin of processors within a PC).
Families of trademarks	"McCafe," "McChicken," and "McFeast" use a common element to link products.
Multiple trademarks	The Intel Inside strategy includes words, logos, and a musical jingle. For reference, Intel currently has over 9,000 trademarks.
Umbrella or corporate trademarking	This is the idea of including a single name in many different trademarks. For example, Virgin Megastore, Virgin Atlantic, Virgin Brides.
Strategic opposition	Trademark owners monitor and object to new trademarks, or alter the new trademarks' content, so as to prevent potential competition.

Sources. Information is from Web sites and personal conversations with trademark lawyers.

Market Value Studies

One important recent contribution to this literature is the work of Hall et al. (2005). These authors construct citation-weighted stocks of patents (i.e., patents weighted by how many times they are cited in later patents) as a proxy for the firm's stock of intangible assets. The sample consists of over six thousand publicly traded U.S. manufacturing firms with data from 1965 to 1995, although data are only available for patent citations from 1976. Their specification of the firm's market value function is the standard one outlined in box 5.2. This empirical analysis includes R&D and finds a strong link between R&D and market value; in fact, the R&D stock is more closely correlated with market value than either patents or citations (see, for example, the early work of Cockburn and Griliches (1988)). Even so, Hall et al. (2005) show that citation-weighted patent stocks are more highly correlated with the firm's value than unweighted patent stocks. Even after controlling for firms' R&D, the citation variable is associated with increased market value. Firms with very heavily cited patents exhibit what the authors describe as "almost implausibly large" market value differences, predicted to be 50% higher than a firm with the same R&D and patent stocks but with only the median citation intensity. However, the benefit of hindsight, as to which have been the most cited patents, was not available to the stock market at the time of share valuation. This suggests that the patent citations are a proxy for innovation quality that is already known to the stock market.[22]

The work of Bloom and Van Reenen (2002) examines the role that patents play in determining the market value of large U.K. firms. Their sample is 236 firms that had taken out at least one patent in the United States between 1968 and 1996. They examine the impact of the patents on the firms' stock market value. They report three different specifications for the patent variable: patent stocks estimated using a fixed 30% depreciation rate; and two variants of citation-weighted patent stocks, using an imputation of future citations for one measure and a five-year cut-off for the other. They find that any one of these three measures of patents positively affects market value (in fact, the three measures are highly correlated (above 0.9) in their sample). Patents also affect market value much more quickly than they affect productivity measures, which are also analyzed (see below)—a result that is likely to be due to the time it takes to embody new innovations in work processes and to adjust physical capital to the new innovation.

Productivity Studies

The vast majority of analyses on productivity are conducted on firms in the production sector and, within this, the focus is on manufacturing firms. Bloom and Van Reenen (2002) estimate a production function of the kind outlined in box 5.3. However, the dependent variable in their regressions is based on firm sales, which the authors take as a measure of output, rather than the more appropriate value added.[23] The empirical results point to a significant and positive effect of the patent measures on sales. Patent stocks, when used as the sole measure of knowledge in a firm, are highly significant and have an estimated elasticity of 0.03, implying that total factor productivity will rise by 3% if total patent stocks are doubled.

Greenhalgh and Longland (2005) use a larger panel database for 1986–94 and they relate firms' output (this time measured by value added) to

---

[22] Another novel result in Hall et al. (2005) is that firms with a higher share of self-citations enjoy a higher market value, other things being equal. A self-citation is simply a citation made by a company to a patent already owned by that same company. Although self-citations may be strategic, Hall et al. note that such citations may mean the firm is successfully protecting positive downstream impacts and appropriating benefits for itself.

[23] Bloom and Van Reenen estimate a gross output production function using real sales as their dependent variable but do not include as regressors any variables related to the use of intermediate inputs; however, this use of a proxy for value added may be mitigated by their inclusion of firm fixed effects, which may partly capture the impact of omitted variables.

the contribution made by knowledge assets, as well as to the contribution made by capital and labor services. They examine the value of new patent publications in three geographical domains: the United Kingdom, the EU and the United States (arguing that these proxy more efficient production processes or improved product variety and quality). In addition, they widen the range of measures of IPR by using firms' trademark applications in the United Kingdom. They also examine both the size and duration of benefits to IPR protection for the firms in their sample. This question is of interest since it would be useful to know if the economic gains to IPR protection correspond to the length of protection enshrined in statute. This empirical analysis reveals that U.K. firms that apply for trademarks and patents and undertake R&D are more productive. Interestingly, the immediate productivity benefits revealed by panel data analysis appear to be fairly short-lived. Dividing their sample between firms that are located in high- and low-technology sectors shows that the dynamic returns for acquiring new IPR are nonsignificant for high-technology firms but significant for firms in low-tech sectors.[24]

Patent Renewal Studies

The above studies mainly focus on assessing the impact on the market value or productivity of the firm of an additional patent in the firm's stock of patents (or current patents as a proxy for the stock). Schankerman and Pakes (1986) argued that simple patent counts are unlikely to be good measures of the amount of innovative output, since the value distribution of patents themselves is so skewed. Therefore, adding up the number of patents issued to a particular entity is an uninformative measure of innovative output. Moreover, the marginal value of these patents is not a very accurate reflection of the skewed distribution of their economic value. Schankerman and Pakes (1986) demonstrated the existence of a skewed value distribution for the United Kingdom, France, and Germany by analyzing patent renewal data.[25] They use the renewal data to reveal information on the distribution of the value of patent

---

[24] These results are based on panel estimators that control for persistent, time-invariant differences in productivity between firms. Further analysis of these firm-level persistent differences show they are associated with the presence of R&D and IPR activity for both high- and low-tech firms. Firms that are never R&D or IPR active have persistently lower productivity. Hence Greenhalgh and Longland (2005) suggest that firms need to continually renew their stocks of intangible assets to improve both their production technology and their product offering.

[25] Their study covers all patents applied for in the United Kingdom, France, and Germany for the period from 1950 to 1979, but with no breakdown for industrial sectors in any of the countries. Schankerman (1998) presents estimates of the private value of patent protection among different technology fields.

rights. Forming this empirical distribution also facilitates estimation of the economic value of patents, albeit as a lower bound estimate, given that renewal only occurs if the anticipated value of the patent exceeds the renewal fees.

Between 1950 and 1979 France and the United Kingdom shared similar patterns of (institutionally imposed) slowly rising costs and falling rates of patent renewal with patent age. In Germany at this time, renewal costs rose rapidly after the patent had been in force for six years and initially high renewal rates fell more sharply after this point. The distribution of renewals by countries appears consistent with the hypothesis that renewal fees influence the decision to renew. In each country the distribution of patents by duration (and thus by imputed value) is extremely skewed. In the United Kingdom and France roughly 60% of patents survived five years but only a quarter survived past age thirteen, showing that the available legal maximum patent life is not relevant for the majority of patents because the value of the intellectual property falls to zero (either because of technological redundancy or due to commercial nonviability). The small proportion of patents that are renewed to the limit are, of course, those with highest value. Given the fact that the life of individual patents can vary so much, Schankerman and Pakes looked at the value of patents that survived to at least five years of age. Measures reveal similar values in France and the United Kingdom, but much higher values in Germany. This difference is probably reflective of the higher initial rejection rates in Germany.[26]

Harhoff et al. (1997, 1999) studied another refinement of the patent renewal approach. Their work was inspired by the observation that work on application and renewal data was silent on those patents that were renewed for the maximum possible duration. Since patents that are renewed for the maximum possible statutory term are presumably the most valuable, Harhoff et al. point out that the renewal studies will only uncover information on a small amount of the total value of a national patent portfolio. Harhoff et al. (1997) confirm the skewed value distribution found in many other studies, but present this result for the tail of the most valuable patent applications made in 1977 (when the maximum patent duration in Germany was eighteen years) and expiring at full term in 1995. The value estimates were obtained directly from patent holders through the use of a survey conducted in 1996, a year after the

---

[26] The ratio of patent grants to applications was only 33% in Germany, compared with 83% in the United Kingdom and 93% in France (Schankerman and Pakes 1986, table 1). This suggests that patents accepted in Germany are likely to be of a higher value than those in the other two countries.

final year's fees.[27] The survey asked the patent holders how much they would have sold the patent for soon after it was granted, assuming they had perfect knowledge at this time of the patent's contribution to future profitability. This method results in much higher extreme values; the estimated value levels are hundreds of times higher than those in other studies that use renewal and application data. The results also exhibit a high degree of skewness: the most valuable 5% of all German patent renewals accounted for over 50% of total sample patent value, and in the United States the most valuable 8.5% of patents account for around 80% of total patent value.

Returns to Trademarks

Analyzing the value of trademarks using empirical analysis is a recent area of research, but there appears to be a positive association between trademark activity and firm-level performance. Seethamraju (2003) analyzes the value of trademarks in 237 U.S. firms from selected industries in 1993–97, finding a positive role for trademarking on sales and also on market values. A more recent study of 300 Australian firms observed from 1989 to 2002 by Griffiths et al. (2005) found that the stock of trademarks was a significant determinant of profits, but with a smaller impact than either patents or registered designs; even so, the value of a trademark was rising over their data period.

Greenhalgh and Rogers (2007) analyze a large sample of publicly quoted U.K. manufacturing and services firms between 1996 and 2000. They explore the impact of undertaking any trademark activity and also the effects of increasing trademark intensity. The results indicate that a firm's stock market value is positively associated with trademark activity (as well as R&D and patents). They find larger differences between firms with and without trademarks in the service sector than for manufacturing. They also find bigger differences in Tobin's q when a services firm is applying for European Community trademarks, rather than just applying for U.K. marks. Increasing the intensity of Community trademarks appears to raise market value for both manufacturing and services, but this relationship weakened over their data period.[28] Since there was an

---

[27] German data were used because, as noted above, the German patent system is particularly rigorous in rejecting applications of low inventive output and because of its highly progressive renewal fee schedule.

[28] In the same paper, the authors investigate the relationship between trademarks and productivity levels and growth rates for both quoted and unquoted firms, using a value added production function. The results indicate that firms that trademark have significantly higher value added than those that do not (by between 10% and 30% across all firms).

increase in trademarks during the late 1990s (see figure 3.2), a fall in the estimated value of such activity might be expected. Greenhalgh and Rogers's interpretation of their findings is that, in general, trademark activity proxies a range of other, unobservable, firm-level characteristics, including innovation, that raise productivity and product prices.

These authors also analyze whether greater trademark intensity raises productivity growth. Higher trademark intensity has some positive association with productivity growth in services, but the results are relatively weak for manufacturing firms. These results for the relationship between productivity and trademarks were broadly consistent with those derived for their quoted firm sample using the market value approach, suggesting that stock markets are efficient in estimating the likely benefits of new intangible assets, and that managers are not just seeking trademarks to follow a "management fad." Even so, the marginal returns to extra trademarks per firm diminished quite rapidly over the period, as indicated by exploration of the interaction of time trends with trademark intensity, suggesting decreasing returns to further proliferation of product variety.

Are Patents and Trademarks Cyclical?

If firms compare the costs and benefits of IPRs one might expect activity to vary over the business cycle. Axarloglou (2003) finds that the introduction of new products tends to be pro-cyclical, and there is evidence that trademarking and new products are positively correlated (Axarloglou and Tsapralis 2004). There is also a debate over whether patenting is pro- or counter-cyclical (see Griliches 1990; Geroski and Walters 1995; Giedeman et al. 2006). Since most firms finance innovation out of cash flow, this implies that more funds may be available in boom periods, suggesting that patenting might be pro-cyclical. Alternatively, some argue that in boom periods the "opportunity cost" of R&D is high, since resources are needed for production, implying counter-cyclical patenting. The evidence suggests that pro-cyclical activity is more likely. This literature is related to an older one on whether patents are driven by demand conditions. Schmookler (1996) provided the seminal study, suggesting that invention and patenting were led by demand. Scherer (1982) provides empirical analysis that largely supports this demand-pull view.

Returns to Copyright

Empirical analysis of the value of copyright is hampered by the fact that there is (currently) no legal requirement to register creative work. Nevertheless, there are a few studies that generate some information on the economic role of copyright. A study for the United States in a period when copyright did require registering and renewal concluded that around 80% of copyright had little economic value (see Landes and Posner (2003), who looked at the 1910–91 period). Png and Wang (2006) look at the impact of copyright extensions on the production of movies in OECD countries, finding that an extension from fifty to seventy years after the end of an author's life did increase production by around 10%. This is a surprising result, since the net present value of such a twenty-year increase is very low (if a standard discount rate is used), but the result appears robust to a range of checks. Another approach is to use data on court actions. Baker and Cunningham (2006) look at the effect of U.S. federal court decisions that broadened copyright on the market value of firms. They find that a new copyright statute can raise return on equity by between 0.4% and 2.1%, while a high court decision can raise returns by 0.1% to 1.1%. In a similar type of study, Mazeh and Rogers (2006) find that plaintiffs in copyright disputes have higher market values than a peer group of similar firms. Overall, however, the empirical evidence on the value of copyright is sparse.

6.8 Conclusions

This chapter has analyzed the link between IPRs and firm performance. It is clear that the basic economic view that IPRs generate market power and therefore higher profits needs to be augmented. A straightforward extension is the role of licensing, whereby firms can license the use of their IPRs to others, providing a flow of income (royalties). Licensing enables firms to specialize in invention and innovation activities and, from this point of view, licensing and the associated markets for technology are potentially beneficial for society. This said, the increase in licensing has created some firms that specialize in buying patents in order to seek out licensing opportunities (so-called patent trolls). Such firms could be viewed as increasing the efficiency of the market, as, for example, specialist traders in antiques or art may do. However, there is an argument that such firms seek to exploit the patent system and the threat of legal action to extract unfair license payments. These issues relate to the functioning of the patent system more generally, something we return to in chapter 11. Another issue concerning the functioning of the patent system is the use of compulsory licenses. They represent societal decisions to alter patentee rights ex post and their use is much debated. This chapter also discusses the idea of patent races, which can dissipate the rewards to innovation.

There is also a need to analyze the more practical aspects of using IPRs. An important point concerns the cost of IPRs. In many cases the initial application fees are relatively low (although combining these with patent or trademark attorney fees can certainly cause problems for smaller firms). However, the legal costs on engaging in a dispute over IPRs can be much more substantial. Such disputes may be relatively rare but, even so, many firms think about whether they can pay for the cost of obtaining *and defending* IPRs. This may be one of the reasons why surveys of firms suggest that patents are a less important means of appropriation than "lead time" and secrecy. Evidence of legal disputes suggests that smaller and newer firms may be especially affected by the costs of legal disputes.

In advanced market economies, with large and sophisticated firms, it is probably not surprising that IPRs are used in a variety of different ways to derive benefits. Some of the strategies behind patenting include restraining supplier power and blocking rivals researching in certain areas (see table 6.2). Trademark strategies include umbrella trademarking and strategic opposition behavior. Understanding and using such strategies is important for managers and entrepreneurs. They also have implications for policy since they can affect the intensity of competition in the market.

Keywords

Licensing.

Patent races.

Patent thickets and trolls.

Skewness in returns.

Complementary assets.

Enforcement and legal costs.

IPR strategies.

Questions for Discussion

(1) Why are the returns to IPRs so skewed?

(2) Does the existence of patent trolls imply that the patent system is working well?

(3) When, if ever, should compulsory licenses be used?

(4) How can one empirically assess the value of IPRs to firms?

(5) Are small or large firms more likely to use the patent system? Does the patent system help or hinder new firms?

(6) Find some examples of (a) patenting strategies and (b) trademarking strategies.

References

Arora, A., M. Ceccagnoli, and W. M. Cohen. 2008. R&D and the patent premium. *International Journal of Industrial Organization* 26:1,153–79.

Arundel, A. 2001. The relative effectiveness of patents and secrecy for appropriation. *Research Policy* 30:611–24.

Axarloglou, K. 2003. The cyclicality of new product introductions. *Journal of Business* 76(1):29–48.

Axarloglou, K., and D. Tsapralis. 2004. New product introductions and price mark-ups. *Eastern Economic Journal* 30(2):223.

Baker, M., and B. Cunningham. 2006. Court decisions and equity markets: estimating the value of copyright protection. *Journal of Law and Economics* 49(2): 567–96.

Baumol, W. 2002. *The Free-Market Innovation Machine.* Princeton University Press.

Bessen, J., and R. Hunt. 2007. An empirical look at software patents. *Journal of Economics & Management Strategy* 16(1):157–89.

Bloom, N., and J. Van Reenen. 2002. Patents, real options and firm performance. *Economic Journal* 112:97–116.

Boyle, J. 2003. The second enclosure movement and the construction of the public domain. *Law and Contemporary Problems* 66:33–74.

Chatterjee, K., and R. Evans. 2004. Rivals' search for buried treasure: competition and duplication in R&D. *Rand Journal of Economics* 35(1):160–83.

Chesbrough, H. 2006. Open innovation: a new paradigm for understanding industrial innovation. In *Open Innovation: Researching a New Paradigm* (ed. H. Chesbrough, W. Vanhaverbeke, and J. West). Oxford University Press.

Cockburn, I., and Z. Griliches. 1988. Industry effects and appropriability measures in the stock market's valuation of R&D and patents. *American Economic Review* 78(2):419–23.

Cohen, W. M., R. R. Nelson, and J. Walsh. 2000. Protecting their intellectual assets: appropriability conditions and why U.S. manufacturing firms patent (or not). NBER Working Paper 7552.

Delrahim, M. 2004. US and EU approaches to the antitrust analysis of intellectual property licensing: observations from the enforcement perspective. US Department of Justice (available at www.usdoj.gov/atr/public/speeches/ 203228.pdf).

European Patent Office. 2007. Why researchers should care about patents. EPO online.

Gambardella, A., P. Giuri, and A. Luzzi. 2007. The market for patents in Europe. *Research Policy* 36:1,163–83.

Gambardella, A., D. Harhoff, and B. Verspagen. 2008. The value of European patents. CEPR Discussion Paper 6848.

Gans, J. S., and S. Stern. 2003. The product market and the market for "ideas": commercialization strategies for technology entrepreneurs. *Research Policy* 32:333–50.

Geroski, P. A., and C. F. Walters. 1995. Innovative activity over the business cycle. *Economic Journal* 105:916–28.

Giedeman, D. C., P. N. Isely, and G. Simons. 2006. Innovation and the business cycle: a comparison of the U.S. semiconductor and automobile industries. *International Advances in Economic Research* 12:277–86.

Gilbert, R., and D. Newbery. 1982. Pre-emptive patenting and the persistence of monopoly. *American Economic Review* 72:514–26.

Giuri, P., M. Mariani, S. Brusoni, G. Crespi, D. Francoz, A. Gambardella, W. Garcia-Fontes, A. Geuna, R. Gonzales, D. Harhoff, K. Hoisl, C. Lebas, A. Luzzi, L. Magazzini, L. Nesta, O. Nomaler, N. Palomeras, P. Patel, M. Romanelli, and B. Verspagen. 2006. Everything you always wanted to know about inventors (but never asked): evidence from the Patval-EU Survey. Discussion Paper 11, Munich School Of Management, University of Munich.

Gomulkiewicz, R. W. 1999. How Copyleft uses license rights to succeed in the open source software revolution and the implications for Article 28. *Houston Law Review* 36(1):170–94.

Granstrand, O. 1999. *The Economics and Management of Intellectual Property.* Cheltenham, U.K.: Edward Elgar.

Greenhalgh, C. A., and M. Longland. 2005. Running to stand still? The value of R&D, patents and trade marks in innovating manufacturing firms. *International Journal of the Economics of Business* 12(3):307–28.

Greenhalgh, C. A., and M. Rogers. 2007. Trade marks and performance in UK firms: evidence of Schumpeterian competition through innovation. Working Paper 300, University of Oxford, Department of Economics.

Griffiths, W., P. Jensen, and E. Webster. 2005. The effects on firm profits of the stock of intellectual property rights. Working Paper 4/05, Intellectual Property Research Institute of Australia, Melbourne.

Griliches, Z. 1990. Patent statistics as economic indicators: a survey. *Journal of Economic Literature* 28:1,661–707.

Guellec, D., and B. van Pottelsberghe. 2007. *The Economics of the European Patent System.* Oxford University Press.

Hall, B. 2000. Innovation and market value. In *Productivity, Innovation and Economic Performance* (ed. R. Barrell, G. Mason, and M. O'Mahoney). Cambridge University Press.

Hall, B., and M. MacGarvie. 2006. The private value of software patents. NBER Working Paper 12195.

Hall, B., and R. Ziedonis. 2001. The effects of strengthening patent rights on firms engaged in cumulative innovation: insights from the semiconductor industry. In *Entrepreneurial Inputs and Outcomes: New Studies of Entrepreneurship in the United States* (ed. G. Libecap). Advances in the Study of Entrepreneurship, Innovation, and Economic Growth, volume 13. Amsterdam: Elsevier.

Hall, B., A. Jaffe, and M. Trajtenberg. 2005. Market value and patent citations. *Rand Journal of Economics* 36:16–38.

Harhoff, D., F. M. Scherer, and K. Vopel. 1997. Exploring the tail of the patent value distribution. Working Paper 92-27, Wissenschaftszentrum, Berlin.

Harhoff, D., F. Narin, F. M. Scherer, and K. Vopel. 1999. Citation frequency and the value of patented innovation. *Review of Economics and Statistics* 81(3): 511-15.

Heller, M. A., and R. Eisenberg. 1998. Can patents deter innovation? The anticommons in biomedical research. *Science* 280:698-701.

Henkel, J., and M. Reitzig. 2007. Patent sharks and the sustainability of value destruction strategies. Working Paper (available at http://ssrn.com/abstract= 985602).

HM Treasury. 2006. *Gowers Review of Intellectual Property*. London: Her Majesty's Stationery Office.

Hsu, D., and A. Ziedonis. 2007. Patents as quality signals for entrepreneurial ventures. Mimeo (available at www.rotman.utoronto.ca/strategy/file/file/Hsu-Ziedonis-Signaling.pdf).

Interbrand–Business Week. 2007. All brands are not created equal: best global brands 2007. Report (available at www.interbrand.com/best_global_brands. aspx).

IPAC. 2003. *The Enforcement of Patent Rights*. Intellectual Property Advisory Committee of the UK Patent Office (available at www.intellectual-property. gov.uk/ipac/pdf/enforce.pdf).

Kretschmer, M., and P. Hardwick. 2007. Authors' earnings from copyright and non-copyright sources: a survey of 25,000 British and German writers. A study for the Authors' Licensing and Collecting Society, Bournemouth University Centre for IP Policy and Management (www.cippm.org.uk).

Landes, W., and R. Posner. 2003. *The Economic Structure of Intellectual Property Law*. Boston, MA: Belknap/Harvard.

Lanjouw, J., and J. Lerner. 1996. Preliminary injunctive relief: theory and evidence from patent litigation. NBER Working Paper 5689.

Lanjouw, J., and M. Schankerman. 2001. Enforcing intellectual property rights. NBER Working Paper 8656.

Lerner, J. 1995. Patenting in the shadow of competitors. *Journal of Law and Economics* 38(3):563-95.

———. 2002. Where does State Street lead? A first look at finance patents, 1971 to 2000. *Journal of Finance* 57(2):901-30.

Lessig, L. 2002. *The Future of Ideas: The Fate of the Commons in a Connected World*. New York: Random House.

Levin, R., A. Klevorick, R. Nelson, and S. Winter. 1987. Appropriating the returns from industrial research and development. *Brookings Papers on Economic Activity* 3:783-831.

Long, C. 2002. Patent signals. *University of Chicago Law Review* 69(2):625-79.

Love, J. 2007. Recent examples of the use of compulsory licenses on patents. Research Note 2, Knowledge Ecology International.

Mann, R. J. 2005. Do patents facilitate finance in the software industry? *Texas Law Review* 83(4):961-1,032.

Mazeh, Y., and M. Rogers. 2006. The economic significance and extent of copyright cases: an analysis of large UK firms. *Intellectual Property Quarterly* 4: 404-20.

Nelson, R. 2006. Reflections of David Teece's "Profiting from technological innovation." *Research Policy* 35(8):1,107-9.

Png, I., and Q. Wang. 2006. Copyright duration and the supply of creative work. Mimeo, National University of Singapore.

Schankerman, M. 1998. How valuable is patent protection? Estimates by technology field using patent renewal data. *Rand Journal of Economics* 29(1): 77–107.

Schankerman, M., and A. Pakes. 1986. Estimates of the value of patent rights in European countries during the post-1950 period. *Economic Journal* 96(384): 1,052–77.

Scherer, F. 1982. Demand-pull and technological invention: Schmookler revisited. *Journal of Industrial Economics* 30(3):225–37.

Schmookler, J. 1966. *Invention and Economic Growth.* Cambridge, MA: Harvard University Press.

Seethamraju, C. 2003. The value relevance of trademarks. In *Intangible Assets: Values, Measures and Risks* (ed. J. Hand and B. Lev). Oxford University Press.

Teece, D. J. 1986. Profiting from technological innovation. *Research Policy* 15(6): 285–305.

——. 2006. Reflections on "Profiting from innovation." *Research Policy* 35(8): 1,131–46.

Tufano, P. 1989. Three essays on financial innovation. Doctoral thesis, Harvard University.

West, J. 2006. Does appropriability enable or hinder open innovation? In *Open Innovation: Researching a New Paradigm* (ed. H. Chesbrough, W. Vanhaverbeke, and J. West). Oxford University Press.

Winter, S. G. 2006. The logic of appropriability: from Schumpeter to Arrow to Teece. *Research Policy* 35(8):1,100–1,106.

Wright, B. 1983. The economics of invention incentives: patents, prizes and research contracts. *American Economic Review* 73(4):691–707.

7

Diffusion and Social Returns

7.1 Introduction

To realize the full benefits of an innovation requires its widespread adoption across the economy. A new technical process needs to be adopted by other producers in the industry to achieve increased productivity everywhere. Equally, new products have to be supplied to other firms if these are intermediate goods and services, or to a wider range of consumers if the innovations are novel final products. As noted in chapters 1 and 2, even where a market price is paid for the good, or a license fee is paid for technology, there will be positive externalities for the buyers and users of innovations. It is these externalities that underpin the economic justification for policy intervention, such as allowing IPRs and/or subsidizing R&D to correct for the market's underinvestment in innovation. The first part of this chapter explores how the diffusion of innovation takes place and examines evidence concerning the speed of diffusion. Then it reviews evidence concerning the sectoral origins of innovation, and the destinations of its use, to identify the sectors and firms that generate social benefits from their innovations. We also explore the econometric evidence for the existence of beneficial spillovers between firms and industries.

Regardless of the sector of production in which the innovation occurs, the stages in the diffusion process will include:

Transfer of information to potential customers.

Decisions to adopt the innovation.

Eventual saturation of the market.

The first of these, which is an information flow about the availability of the new process or product, is hard to monitor across a wide range of innovations. For any particular innovation, potential customers can be surveyed to explore whether or not they have any knowledge of the new product or process, but this involves expensive market research. Still, this can be very useful information: if a product is widely known about but not selling strongly, then the innovator can conclude that it has not filled a niche; whereas if his product is selling slowly but is not in the public eye, the firm can decide to invest in more promotional activities. The rate of adoption of innovation is also costly to monitor at the aggregate level. The decision to adopt is made either by individual producers, in the case of new techniques and novel intermediate goods and services, or by individual customers, in the case of final consumer products. By following records of product sales we can observe adoption rates through time to get a descriptive picture of diffusion and perhaps also gain some evidence of the eventual saturation of the market.

Explaining why some firms or consumers adopt early and others later, and predicting their rates of take up in advance, is a complex task as many factors are involved in these decisions. Such information would be very useful to the sellers of the new products or processes, as it could help them to focus their marketing efforts more accurately. The adoption of new process technology among firms imposes costs: in the purchase of new machinery or the cost of retraining workers to use the new process, for example.[1] It can provide benefits for firms that would otherwise be noninnovators, helping them with the retention of their market share and improving their profitability. However, both the costs and benefits of innovation adoption are quite difficult to record, as they cannot easily be isolated from changes in general production costs.

Market saturation occurs when there is complete displacement of older production methods by a new technique or the displacement of earlier product varieties by the new types of goods and services. At this point the Schumpeterian notion of creative destruction is fully realized, as the innovative items have fully displaced the old, destroying the market for the obsolete techniques and products. What we observe in practice is usually incomplete saturation, as some firms will face financial constraints on their investment, or there may be a shortage of workers with the required skills. Equally, some consumers may never wish to adopt a new type of home product if they are not convinced that the extra benefits merit the costs. In explaining decisions to adopt new products and processes there are important contributions from sociological and organizational approaches (Rogers 1995). These stress the role of social norms, how decisions are made, and interconnectedness between firms and consumers. In this chapter we shall focus primarily on the economic approaches; these are exemplified in Stoneman (2002) and Hall (2004).

---

[1] Early adopters of new consumer products may also experience greater costs as certain features of the product may not be fully tested or optimized (e.g., new versions of software).

7.2 Modeling the Rate of Adoption of an Innovation

In this section we focus on two models of diffusion that have been explored in the economics literature: the *epidemic* model and the *rank* model. We then discuss a set of related issues concerning network and lock-in effects. A more extensive formal treatment of the modeling of diffusion can be found in the wide-ranging book by Stoneman (2002).

The Epidemic Model of Diffusion

To gain insights into the diffusion process, economists first borrowed some tools from the discipline of biology. There, the models were developed to explain such phenomena as the spread of disease across human or animal species, creating epidemics that can affect a large proportion of the population. In adapting such models for the explanation of the spread of an innovation, the negative aspect of the biological model, namely catching a disease, is reversed into the positive effect of obtaining information about a new, superior product or process and choosing to purchase it.[2]

This model posits that there is a random encounter between two individuals, the first of whom has already adopted the innovation. This results in the transfer of information about the innovation, which in turn can lead to its adoption by the second party. The basic assumptions of the model are:

(1) There is a fixed population of potential adopters, N, and all members of this population are identical in all characteristics except that at any point in time some finite number have already adopted the innovation while the remainder have not. (Think of an analogy with the beginning of an epidemic of influenza, when a few people already have the disease.)

(2) When a meeting occurs between an adopter and a nonadopter, there is a fixed probability, B, that the current nonadopter will become an adopter. (Formally, B reflects both the probability of a meeting taking place and an adoption occurring.)

(3) The chance of such a meeting occurring depends on the proportion of the population that have already adopted the innovation, D, which varies throughout the diffusion process.

(4) Such meetings are random encounters, so the probability that an adopter meets a nonadopter is proportional to $D(1 - D)$.

---

[2] The epidemic model is also called the contagion model for this reason.

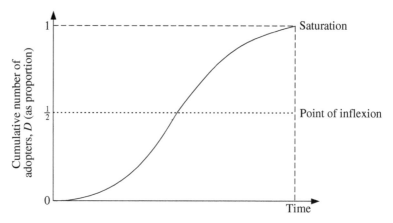

Figure 7.1. The cumulative path of adoption for an epidemic model.

Given this, we can express the rate of adoption (dD/dt) by

$$\frac{dD}{dt} = BD(1 - D). \tag{7.1}$$

Figure 7.1 shows the path of adoption associated with equation (7.1). This is often referred to as an S-shaped diffusion path and it shows the cumulative proportion of the population that have adopted the innovation.

The predictions of the epidemic model are that:

(a) The rate of adoption, dD/dt, follows a bell-shaped curve. Initially, there are a few leaders, followed by a gradual speeding up as adoption occurs; then there is a falling off as D rises further, since by now the uninfected rate $(1 - D)$ is falling. (As the influenza epidemic proceeds, more people are infected but eventually there are few people left to be infected, so the rate of infection falls.)

(b) The proportion of adopters (or cumulative density function of D) follows a Logistic curve, which has a flattened S-shape.

(c) The market for this innovative product will eventually become saturated when all have adopted, and the speed with which this happens depends on B, the probability that a transfer of information leads to an adoption.

An Economic (Rank) Model of Diffusion

The previous model provides a description of the rate of adoption without any economic underpinnings, as there is no role for prices and/or costs to influence the decision process. In particular, assuming identical individuals (for consumer goods) or firms (for intermediate inputs or processes) is a rather unrealistic assumption. A more sophisticated model allows for differences between the members of the population, N, to influence their likelihood of adoption of the innovation. The assumptions of this economic model are that tastes for adoption (or inertia) vary between firms/consumers. Possible reasons for this variety include that:

(i) Information search costs vary, as there are some smaller and more remote firms or customers.

(ii) The existing equipment of the firm or household (capital stock or consumer durables) varies by volume, age or vintage, and productivity, affecting the gains from purchases of new types of equipment.

(iii) Firms have different qualities of labor and these skills can affect their adjustment costs.

(iv) The levels and growth rates of sales vary across firms, and the costs of adjustment to a new process technology may be easier for those in growing markets.

The assumptions of the model are as follows:

(1) The differences across firms or consumers are represented by a single index (denoted by z), which ranks firms or consumers from those that are least likely to adopt the innovation to those that are most likely to.[3]

(2) The distribution of these z values across the population follows a Normal, or bell-shaped, curve.

Box 7.1 formally discusses the results of the model. Here we discuss it intuitively. When the initial cost of adopting the innovation is high only a small proportion of consumers or firms will adopt (those with z above a high threshold). Let us assume that the cost of adoption falls over time, which means more agents will adopt. As this process occurs, the rate of adoption increases due to the assumed bell-shaped distribution (i.e., the innovation is adopted by the large numbers in the middle part of the distribution). The rate of adoption reaches its maximum at the peak of the bell shape and then slowly declines.

Why would the cost of adoption fall over time? One reason is that adopters may learn from others about how to implement the innovation. The second concerns the price of the innovation. A common feature of new producer equipment and new consumer goods and services is that

---

[3] Hence Stoneman (2002) calls this the "Rank model" to highlight this assumption about preferences.

they are supplied at a falling price through time. As the market grows and supply expands, firms benefit from economies of scale in production of their innovative products. Also, depending on the IPR situation and whether or not licensing occurs, the entry of new producers may cause greater competitive pressure to arise, leading to profit reduction.

The predictions of this economic model are as follows:

(a) The frequency of adoption follows a bell-shaped curve, as long as the distribution of benefits for the product among the population follows a bell-shaped curve (see figure 7.2).

(b) The proportion of adopters follows a Probit function, which has a shape very similar to the flattened S-shape (see figure 7.1).

(c) Again, once this product or process becomes dominant, the market will become saturated, but this now depends on the rate at which the price of the product falls through time and the underlying distribution of tastes for adoption.

Box 7.1. Formal model of diffusion of innovation with heterogeneous purchasers.

The main text has already stated the first two assumptions:

(1) that there is an index, z, that ranks firms or consumers from least likely to most likely to adopt; and

(2) that z follows a Normal density function, $f(z) \sim N(\mu, \sigma^2)$.

The further required assumptions are:

(3) that $h(z)$ is the net flow of extra profit or consumer utility from adopting the innovation;

(4) that r is the firm's or customer's interest rate for this future stream of extra profit or utility that they will acquire if they adopt; and

(5) that p is the cost of purchasing and installing the innovative product or process, either in production if an intermediate good or in the home if a final good.

The decision to adopt then rests on whether or not the net gain is positive: that is, if

$$h(z)/r \geqslant p.$$

The left-hand side of this inequality is the present discounted value of $h(z)$ assuming that this continues for an infinite time and r is constant through time (see section A.2 in the mathematical appendix).

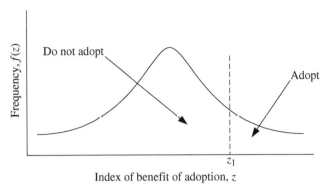

Figure 7.2. How characteristics determine rates of adoption.

The marginal adopter has, for example, the characteristic z_1, hence

$$h(z_1) = rp.$$

This means that as the cost of adoption (p) falls, the marginal adopter will shift to the left on figure 7.2, and the proportion adopting will be given by $D = 1 - F(z_1)$, where $F(\cdot)$ is the cumulative Normal distribution. If the cost of adoption falls steadily, then this will map out an S-shaped path for the proportion of firms or consumers adopting. Formally, the proportion of adopters (or the cumulative density function of D) follows a Probit function, which has a shape very similar to the Logistic S-shaped curve, namely a flattened S-shape.

Although this economic diffusion model places less emphasis on the process of random meeting and learning that determined the rate of adoption in the first model, it would be possible to incorporate such assumptions here too, so that tastes for adoption also became time-varying. It seems highly probable that some evolution of tastes through learning from others will occur alongside economic decisions to adopt based on current tastes and product price. Hence these two models should be seen as complementary approaches to predicting rates of adoption of innovations.[4]

These models suggest that there will be many factors affecting the propensity of any enterprise or final consumer to adopt an innovative

[4] Karshenas and Stoneman (1992) present and estimate a model of adoption of color televisions incorporating economic factors within an epidemic framework. Zettelmeyer and Stoneman (1993) extend this approach to analyze the diffusion of camcorders and CD players in the United Kingdom and cars in West Germany. More recently, Young (2007) has modeled five families of diffusion models including both the epidemic model and the moving equilibrium model and has shown that it is theoretically possible to distinguish between these models using patterns of initial acceleration in the adoption rates.

technique or product. These will be of two main types: those affecting the likelihood that information reaches the agent and those affecting his ability to learn from the information and act on it. There is some propensity for industries to cluster by geographical area (e.g., high-technology firms around universities and public research establishments). This suggests that physical proximity has a continuing role to play in the transfer of technical knowledge and the shared understanding of innovative products, even if this is diminishing in the era of modern communications systems. We also expect to see a role for financial constraints, which can inhibit the adoption of new products and processes. The ability to learn is affected both by the skills, or human capital, of those receiving new information and by the R&D history of the enterprise. This is the "second face" of R&D, or absorptive capacity, discussed in chapter 3, which reflects the need to be actively involved in R&D in order to learn from others in the field. A further issue is the fact that the value of adopting any innovation can be dependent on how many others have done so.

Network and Lock-in Effects

The diffusion of innovation will frequently be subject to *network* and *lock-in* effects. In network situations the ability of one adopter to benefit from a new product depends on what others have adopted. This can lead to the perverse effect that the system eventually saturating the market may not be the one that has the best qualities. Rather, it may be the one that was first to achieve a critical threshold of adoption, leading to it becoming the preferred system for later adopters despite its inferiority. It is to these issues we now turn.[5]

The presence of lock-in can be modeled by assuming that consumers face a cost of switching between products. This provides firms with an incentive to price the product low initially and then raise prices for existing customers. This is often seen in low prices for new customers (e.g., for mobile/cell phones). Another related example is the price of inkjet printers, which are set very low since firms intend to make money on selling replacement ink cartridges. Klemperer (1995) finds that switching costs can allow firms to reduce entry and raise average prices, causing a welfare loss for consumers, although this may not always be the case.

A famous example of networks and lock-in effects concerns the layout of a keyboard. Two original formats were QWERTY (reflecting the arrangement of letters along the top left) and a now little-known layout

---

[5] Katz and Shapiro (1994) and Varian et al. (2004) also provide overviews of these issues.

called Dvorak. David (1985) suggested that by the 1890s the QWERTY for-mat had a strong advantage since, once trained, a typist would not want to switch. In addition, the training of typists was subject to economies of scale and it was good for interoperability to have a single keyboard layout (or standard). The key argument is therefore one of lock-in (i.e., typists did not want to retrain, current typing schools had low costs) and network effects (i.e., the same keyboard meant typists could switch machines). These forces meant that once QWERTY had gained an advan-tage this led to widespread adoption and market dominance. David also suggests that QWERTY is an inferior layout since a Dvorak keyboard allows faster typing (although there is dispute over this: see Liebowitz and Margolis (1990)).

Another famous example is the choice between VHS and Betamax video format in the 1970s and 1980s. A different video cassette recorder (VCR) was required for each format; the VHS was originally developed by Mat-sushita and the Betamax by Sony. There are various aspects to the fight between VHS and Betamax. Some of these relate to standard aspects, such as the cost of the VCR, its recording time, and marketing efforts, but there are also network effects. The main network effect came from the fact that consumers valued access to a wide range of prerecorded movies on video. As soon as video rental stores started to favor VHS in the early 1980s, leading to more movies being supplied on VHS, this encouraged more consumers to buy VHS VCRs (see Park 2004). Other examples of where network effects occur include the choice between alternating cur-rent (AC) and direct current (DC) power, computer operating systems (e.g., Windows, Mac OS, Linux) and Internet browsers (e.g., Netscape, Internet Explorer, Firefox). In general, examples of lock-in and network effects can be found in a range of telecommunications, technology, and software products.

From an economic policy perspective, interest in lock-in and network effects comes from the possibility of market failure. We can illustrate the possibility of one type of market failure by considering the example of the fax machine. Its value comes from the ability to send faxes to others, but this means that the initial sales of fax machines have little value (i.e., there are few people to send faxes to). This gives rise to the possibility that no one buys a fax machine (or too few buy them). When the market fails to generate enough users, we say that the market outcome is not the socially optimal one.[6] A second possible market failure is that a less efficient product becomes universally used due to network effects (e.g.,

---

[6] Historically, the market for fax machines expanded dramatically from the mid 1980s, when the price of fax machines fell sharply, which might suggest this example is irrelevant. However, the issue is also whether the path of adoption was socially efficient.

the QWERTY keyboard). Again, this is not socially optimal since it would be better to have everyone using the more efficient product. Analysis of these situations is made more difficult since firms will compete with each other to dominate the market. As indicated above, Sony and Matsushita competed to dominate the VCR market knowing of the network and lock-in effects. This competition can keep prices low and speed up diffusion (a positive for consumer welfare) but it may lock consumers into an inferior product.

7.3   Statistical Evidence on Rates of Adoption

We now turn to the evidence about diffusion to see how far empirical studies reflect the theory. In a study of some of the earliest modern technological innovations in steel manufacturing and coal mining, Gold et al. (1970) found considerable variations in the rates of adoption of new process technologies (see figure 7.3). Their first key finding was that the speed of adoption was quite slow in most of the process innovations they studied: although two out of fourteen had diffused to the extent of supplying 70% of production after ten years, a larger number (six) had only diffused to supplying 20% after fifteen years. In addition, there was considerable variety in the eventual adoption rates compared with early adoption rates, so that several technologies that were initially slow to take off eventually dominated as the standard technology. Thus the likely importance of a new technology appears to be hard to predict from simple extrapolation of the adoption rate in its early years.

In a more recent study of the use of computers in manufacturing, Canepa and Stoneman (2003) studied a variety of dimensions of computer use in design and manufacturing activities. For these new technologies, as for earlier ones, there are slow rates of penetration of the potential markets (see table 7.1). Although the United States is often quoted as the world technology leader for invention and innovation, it did not have the fastest rates of diffusion in every technology explored here.[7] Considerable differences arise across advanced industrialized countries in the rates of adoption of these technologies (for example, compare diffusion rates by 1993 in neighbors Canada and the United States). Canepa and Stoneman support both the epidemic and the economic models of diffusion, stating that:

---

[7] The United Kingdom scores highly in diffusion for the three types of process reported. An explanation may be that U.K. manufacturing had closed a very large share of its capacity during the first half of the 1980s as a result of soaring sterling exchange rates from 1979 to 1985. The surviving firms would have been firms with high value added products and lower costs that were more able to withstand the lack of price competitiveness.

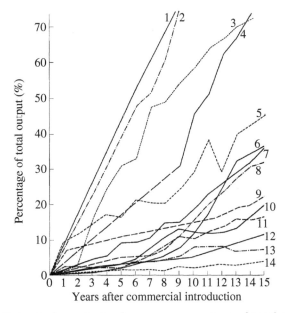

Figure 7.3. Output of new technology as a percentage of total output during the first fifteen years after the indicated year of initial commercial use.

Notes. 1, Bessemer furnace (1865); 2, continuous cold rolling, sheets (1927); 3, electrolytic tinplating (1940); 4, continuous hot strip mill (1926); 5, continuous cold rolling, strip (1930); 6, basic oxygen furnace (1954); 7, pelletizing (1956); 8, continuous miner (1948); 9, washing coking coal (1889); 10, machine loading, coal (1923); 11, byproduct coking (1895); 12, machine cutting, coal (1882); 13, open hearth (1870); 14, strip mining, coal (1914).

Source. Gold, B., W. S. Peirce, and G. Rosegger (1970). Diffusion of major technological innovations in U.S. iron and steel manufacturing. *Journal of Industrial Economics* 18(3):218–41, chart 1. Copyright © 1970 *Journal of Industrial Economics.* Reproduced with permission of Blackwell Publishing Ltd.

> [T]here are two main effects at work generating realised diffusion patterns. The first relates to information generation, spread and usage, labeled here an epidemic effect. The second is based upon a view that, given appropriate information, plants or firms adopt new technologies when it is (most) profitable to do so, they thus take account of the cost of acquiring new technologies.[8]

The above examples have indicated considerable differences in rates of diffusion of new process technology across both industries and countries. When we observe the adoption of new products by consumers, large variety in speed of adoption is equally apparent. Hall (2004) illustrates this variation for the United States, contrasting the slow rate of

---

[8] This conclusion follows a summary of many empirical studies; see Canepa and Stoneman (2003, p. 29).

Table 7.1. Cross-country diffusion of computer-related
process technology (percentage uptake).

	1989				1993			
	U.S.	Canada	U.K.	Switzerland	U.S.	Canada	U.K.	Switzerland
CAD/CAE	42	34	49	37	64	56	74	51
CAD/CAM	18	12	49	23	28	27	74	34
NC/CNC	45	27	88	41	51	34	95	48
LAN Tec	21	15	n.a.	16	32	17	n.a.	26
LAN Fac	18	11	n.a.	14	24	11	n.a.	22

Source. Figures are extracted from table 7 of Canepa and Stoneman (2003).

Notes. The column headed 1989 contains figures for 1988 for the United
States and 1990 for Switzerland. "CAD/CAE" denotes computer aided design/
engineering: design and testing of products. "CAD/CAM" denotes computer
aided design/manufacture: design and control of machines. "NC/CNC" denotes
numerical control machines or computer numerical control in manufacture.
"LAN Tec" denotes local area networks used for exchange of information within
design and engineering departments. "LAN Fac" denotes local area networks
used for exchange of information on the shop floor.

adoption of domestic clothes washers over the period 1920–90 with the
very rapid adoption of video cassette recorders from 1980 to 1990. The
introduction and growth of the Internet across many countries has been
studied by many analysts, including Mowery and Simcoe (2002). Their
analysis suggests that the rate of Internet usage by country is negatively
correlated with price, while also being positively correlated with average income levels, two standard results from demand analysis. From its
initial development in the early 1970s to the beginning of the 1990s,
the growth of Internet use was modest but it has exploded since, with
an estimated rise in the number of Internet hosts (domain names) from
2.2 million in 1994 to 570 million by 2008 (source: the Internet Systems
Consortium (www.isc.org)). Table 7.2 shows the large variation in the
proportion of the population using the Internet, with the lowest rates
being seen in the poorest regions of the world. Even so, these modest
rates of Internet penetration amount to high shares of world usage in
some of the more populous poorer regions (for example, compare Asia
with South America). In addition, the fastest rates of growth are observed
in those countries with the lowest rates of usage. The Internet is both a
personal consumer product and a technology for business. Mowery and
Simcoe (pp. 259–60) state that:

> For all its novelty, the development and diffusion of the Internet
> closely resembles those of other "general purpose technologies," such
> as … electric power. … Like all … major innovations, the Internet under-
> went a prolonged period of "gestation" that dates back more than thirty

Table 7.2. Internet usage by region in 2008.

	Internet penetration (percentage of population)	Share of world usage (%)	Growth in usage 2000–2008 (%)
Africa	5.3	3.5	1,031
Asia	15.3	39.5	406
Europe	48.1	26.3	266
Middle East	21.3	2.9	1,177
North America	73.6	17.0	130
South America	24.1	9.5	669
Oceania and Australia	59.5	1.4	165
World Total	21.9	100	306

Source. All figures for June 2008 are from the Internet World Statistics Web site (www.internetworldstats.com/stats.htm).

years.... Both uncertainty over applications and the prolonged period of incremental improvement and refinement are hallmarks of virtually all major innovations.

We noted above that the introduction of new techniques imposes costs on firms. Canepa and Stoneman (2005) explore the role of financial constraints within the firm on the introduction of new process technology. They comment that the literature on diffusion has largely ignored this factor, despite its prominence in the seminal early work on the subject by Mansfield (1968). Their analysis of the introduction of computer numerically controlled machinery in the U.K. metalworking and engineering industries shows that such financial constraints are clearly binding on firms that are near breakeven point, but are not a constraint for more profitable firms. This makes it harder to design public policy to ease the transition to new technology, as this policy would need to be able to separate firms that are temporarily cash constrained from persistently inefficient firms that do not merit public support.

In a broad study of the diffusion of computer use across countries, Caselli and Coleman (2001) have shown that a wide range of country characteristics are positively associated with the level of computer imports per worker. They use this statistic as a proxy for the level of computer investment per worker, as this measure reflects the whole supply of computers in the majority of the countries studied (without domestic computer industries), and it also includes imports of key components for the few countries that undertake any computer assembly. The key factors that enhance computer adoption are having a high fraction of the workforce that has at least completed primary education and showing patterns of trade openness oriented toward the OECD countries. Other positive factors are the existence of good property rights protection, high rates of investment per worker, and a low agricultural share of GDP. Further discussion of these issues can be found in chapter 9.

7.4 Spillovers and Social Returns to Innovation

The first part of this chapter discussed the process of diffusion. It should be clear that for an innovation to have wide impact on society it is important for diffusion to occur. Our discussion made clear that the diffusion process can take considerable time and there are potential pitfalls. These issues are important in understanding how society *benefits* from innovation. Since there may also be social costs of innovation, our real interest is in the net social benefits, which are known as the *social returns* to innovation. This section analyzes this issue in detail.

The social return to an innovation is defined as the aggregate net benefit to society from the innovation. This includes increased profits to the innovator but also includes any net benefits to consumers or other firms.[9] Conceptually this includes all benefits both now and into the future, although our discussion will not analyze this distinction. Some of the issues relating to social returns were introduced in chapter 5, where we analyzed innovative firms and markets. Chapter 5 discussed how innovators reduce the profits of other firms (business stealing) and box 5.1 also discussed knowledge spillover effects. A knowledge spillover effect is a form of positive *externality*. An externality occurs when the actions of one agent (e.g., the innovator) affect either consumers or firms and there is no market transaction. The most important positive externality in this context is when the knowledge generated by the innovator influences another firm's R&D, or decisions relating to innovation, and there is no license or other payment involved.[10]

---

[9] Here "firms" refers to any organizations that are involved in "production" in the widest sense (i.e., it includes nonprofit organizations and state-owned enterprises).

[10] The definition of externality used here is the standard one used in microeconomics and in welfare economics. The classic examples are when a factory pollutes a river and causes fish stocks to fall (a negative externality), or the fact that a beekeeper has a beneficial effect by the bees pollinating an orchard (a positive externality). In the R&D and innovation literature some confusion occurs since a positive knowledge externality is also called a "knowledge spillover" or "R&D spillover." The definition of externalities does not include, for example, an innovation lowering the price of an intermediary input, which then lowers the price of a consumer good. This is an indirect effect and occurs via the price system (see Mishan 1971; Bohanon 1985). It is sometimes called a pecuniary externality, but here we consider this as an indirect effect on consumer surplus. Note that it is possible that the innovator may increase the profits of some firms in other industries (e.g., it lowers the price of an intermediary input). Again, since there is a market transaction underlying this effect this is not an externality.

There are many routes by which the effects of innovation flow out from the innovator. The potential winners and losers are diverse and this makes identifying the full social returns difficult. This section explores the evidence of benefits accruing to three main groups: consumers, competing firms, and firms in other sectors.

Final Consumers

Innovation leads to lower prices for customers and/or to better quality and more variety of products for the same price, all of which increase their consumer surplus or welfare. When consumers buy the new innovation such effects are easier to identify; however, some innovations have knock-on effects for consumers in other markets. Tracking such effects is difficult and can require specific case studies.

Competing Firms in the Industry

Competing firms may benefit from knowledge spillovers, acquiring information from those researching in similar fields. They may pay fees to license new technology that is subject to a patent, copyright, or design right, but they will still be making extra profits as otherwise they would not adopt the new technology. Externalities also arise when competitors learn from the innovations of others and this improves their own rate of innovation.

Firms in Other Industries

Downstream users of the outputs of innovating firms in other sectors of the economy will benefit from reduced input costs and/or from greater variety and better quality of inputs. Such user firms are often able to develop new products and processes in their own sector as a result of new input technology, leading to increased market share and higher profitability. New technology may also be licensed to firms in other industries.

Benefits to Final Consumers

The basic route by which innovation can influence consumers was discussed in chapter 1. Figure 1.2 illustrated how a fall in price from a process innovation generates greater consumer surplus. Similarly, new and improved products generate consumer surplus by enlarging choice. The use of such diagrams is useful when the innovation relates to a final good that is sold direct to consumers. In some cases, for example computers, the product is sold to both consumers and firms. Firms then use the computers to improve their products or services, or reduce their prices, which again benefits consumers. Tracking all the potential impacts on consumers is a difficult, if not impossible, task. In any of these approaches there is a serious problem in measuring the true impact of innovation. This is an issue already mentioned in chapter 3, but the next section extends this discussion.

Evidence of Falling Real Prices of Innovative Products

As the prices of innovative products are expected to fall through time relative to other goods and services, there will generally be an understatement of the extent of the price fall when the average product quality is rising and there is no adjustment for this quality change. For complex products that are continually evolving in many dimensions and characteristics, it is not enough to collect data on observed market prices per unit sold. We need to seek information about changing quality and to calculate prices that are adjusted for the average quality of products being sold—known as *hedonic price indices*, as discussed in box 3.2.[11] At any given time we expect to pay more for better-quality goods and services as extra quality commands a higher price. Suppose that we record market prices in a period of rising general prices and, on average, any given product is of better quality in period 2 than in period 1 due to innovation. If we interpret all of the price increase as inflation, we are neglecting to count the rise in quality as a rise in real output. We are overstating the rise in price of items that have improved in quality unless we adjust for this quality change. Table 7.3 contains estimates of these biases for the Canadian and U.S. consumer price indices (plus some other measurement biases arising from consumer tactics to avoid goods with rising real prices, the substitution effect, and to avoid higher-priced outlets by switching to cheaper distributors). For the United States the estimate is that the rate of inflation is overstated and output growth is understated, by around half of one per cent per annum due to the introduction of new goods and better-quality products; for Canada the figure is one third of one per cent. These are significant amounts in relation to average annual

---

[11] Examples can be found in Shepler (2004) for camcorders and in Thompson (2004) for VCRs, where both products had falling prices during the period studied, but where also the quality-adjusted prices differed from recorded prices. For camcorders, the average quality of product purchased was rising, as this was still a developing product, so the quality-adjusted price fell faster than the recorded average price. For VCRs, which were a more mature product, the average quality of product purchased was falling, as the tail-end purchasers in this market bought simpler varieties of machines than average. Here the hedonic price of VCRs was falling less rapidly than it appeared once the quality adjustment was made, indicating that the measurement biases in prices are not always in the direction of overestimating the price level.

Table 7.3. Estimates of measurement biases in the consumer price index.

Type of bias	Canada	U.S.
Commodity substitution	0.2	0.4
Outlet substitution	0.1	0.1
Rising quality (including introduction of new goods)	0.3	0.6
Total bias in price index (differences due to rounding)	0.5	1.1

Sources. Column 1 for Canada from Crawford (1993);
column 2 for the United States from Boskin et al. (1996).

output growth rates per capita of two to three per cent and they show the extent to which the benefits of innovation, as revealed in national growth statistics, are likely to be understated.

Benefits to Competing Firms in the Industry

Although innovation gives the firm some market advantage, we have argued that this does not always imply a contraction in market share for rivals; rather there are "two faces of R&D" with respect to the way in which other firms may be affected by any given firm's success. There is the contrast between business, or market, stealing, where the innovating firm gains an advantage and steals customers from other firms, and knowledge spillover effects, when a breakthrough by a firm triggers greater technological opportunity and provides information on which other firms can build. One possibility of knowledge, or technology, spillovers arises from the fact that, as part of a patent application, the inventor must make public the detailed technical information about the invention, including his claims of novelty. Thus, even as firms compete for the private benefits of market leadership from innovation and IPRs, they are generating social benefits in their industry.

Even where an innovation is not made public and is protected by trade secrets there are ways in which other firms can contrive to learn about innovative products and technology. By purchasing a product and stripping it down or subjecting it to chemical analysis, a process called "reverse engineering," the components can often be identified. If the knowledge base is tacit and embodied in the people employed in the innovating firm, then another way to acquire the knowledge is to persuade these workers to move across by offering them more lucrative salaries. Hiring other firms' designers and engineers who have tacit knowledge brings gains to the new employer.

Some evidence of how firms learn about each other's innovations is given by Patel and Pavitt (1995), who surveyed more than 600 industrial R&D directors in the United States, asking them to rank various means of learning about their competitors' product innovations. What this study revealed is that, while firms do learn through licensing others' technology and by reading information in patent documents, these are not the highest-ranked means of learning. Doing independent R&D and reverse engineering are by far the top two methods, while third-ranked is poaching key workers from innovating firms. This supports the idea of the "two faces of R&D," with the first face being the basic investment in innovation and the second face being the need to do R&D to be able to absorb knowledge from other firms.[12] The idea of building absorptive capacity is crucial in many areas, including allowing poorer countries to catch up with richer countries (see chapter 9, especially section 9.4). It also gives credence to the idea that tacit knowledge makes skilled workers important.

Intersectoral Diffusion and Spillovers

The diffusion of innovation and the spread of cost reductions and product improvements are not confined to the sector of invention. Economists also need to be able to track the positive spillovers between R&D-intensive firms in one sector and firms in other sectors. These can arise through:

(1) the sale of innovative products,

(2) the direct transfer of technological know-how.

Interindustry linkages via purchases of intermediate products are an important source of diffusion of the benefits of innovative products. Although measured R&D and patents are concentrated in a few manufacturing sectors, the benefits spread widely through cost reduction and new product creation in other sectors. Scherer (1984, chapter 3) gives the illustration of a new turbojet engine. R&D is performed in the aircraft-engine industry and this results in a better engine, but the productivity effects show up in the airline services sector in lower energy consumption (which is cost-saving for airlines) and in quieter and more reliable flights (which is product quality enhancing for final consumers). The interindustry transmission of goods and services has conventionally been modeled using the Leontief input–output model of the economy, which can be used to highlight linkages between sectors, for example manufacturing and services. The model traces intermediate and capital

---

[12] Given this evidence of the learning face of R&D, we should be less concerned about duplication of research effort from firms all of which are doing research in a given area, because it is necessary for both leading innovators and their imitators to be engaged in independent R&D.

goods purchases made by firms, identifying flows within and between sectors. Every firm in each sector of the economy uses some outputs of other firms, some of which are in other sectors, in the production of its own output.

The Leontief model can be adapted to track the origins and flows of innovation around the economy. The basic idea is that firms in some sectors do more R&D than others and these firms embody their innovations in their production techniques and in their output. These sectors can be denoted as *innovation producer* sectors (historically this was a characteristic of several key sectors of manufacturing). Other sectors then buy and use the new or improved intermediate products to improve their own techniques and to upgrade the quality of their final products. These sectors can be denoted as *innovation user* sectors (historically these were services and utilities).

An early analysis by Scherer (1984) using U.S. data for the mid 1970s attempted a complete mapping of the use made of particular patents taken out by firms. He found that about one in four inventions were for process innovations within the sector, while three quarters related to new products for the innovating firm and were thus sold more widely. Also, only one in four inventions were potentially saleable to final consumers, while half of all inventions were embodied in intermediate and capital goods (see Scherer 1984, p. 36). Thus at the level of individual firms the distinction between process and product innovations is a meaningful one and product innovation dominates. However, in industry and economy terms it seems likely that process innovation dominates, as the innovative products sold as semifinished goods and services, or as capital goods, become inputs for other firms and can greatly affect the techniques used in the production processes of the buying sectors.

Tracing Spillovers Using an Input–Output Model

To trace innovation flows around the U.S. economy, Scherer (1984) first calculated each firm's average R&D expenditure per patent. He then decided whether each patent would be fairly general or narrowly specific in its application. If specific, he then identified up to three main user industries and allocated the implied benefit of the R&D to only these industries. If judged to be general, he allocated the implied benefit of R&D in proportion to interindustry purchases. His findings for selected industries are shown in table 7.4. As expected, this exercise showed strong innovation producers within manufacturing, illustrated here by those with the highest origin/use ratios for R&D, namely computers, radio and telecommunications equipment, motor vehicles, and scientific

Table 7.4. R&D origin and use in the United States ($m, 1974).

R&D producer sectors	R&D origin	R&D use	Ratio origin/use
Computers and office equipment	1,153	132	8.7
Scientific instruments	1,036	147	7.0
Radio and communications	1,228	186	6.6
Pharmaceuticals and agricultural chemicals	744	141	5.3
Motor vehicles	1,518	308	4.9

R&D user sectors	R&D origin	R&D use	Ratio use/origin
Construction and services	266	2,118	8.0
Trade and finance	40	1,138	28.5
Transport and utilities	47	2,001	42.6

Source. Authors' calculations using data extracted
from Scherer (1984, table 3.2, pp. 40–49).

instruments. The main innovation users of the time were in the services sector, illustrated here by those with the highest use/origin ratios for their innovation, namely finance, insurance and real estate, transport services and public utilities, and construction and other services.

In a later study of the U.K. economy Greenhalgh and Gregory (2000) used input–output data for three dates in the period 1979–90 to trace changing flows of R&D embodied in products. Their model assumes that R&D conducted in any sector is proportionately reflected in the flows of that output between sectors. This implies that R&D improves product quality equally for all buyers, regardless of which sector they are part of and whether they are firms or households. Their model and data cover all sectors of the economy and are more in keeping with a dynamic open economy (see box 7.2 for details). Openness to trade leads to some "leakage" of R&D spillovers via exports (but there were no data available on any balancing amount of imported R&D content). The authors calculated the full impacts of the multiple rounds of input uses within the economic system.

Box 7.2. Using an input–output model to calculate the R&D intensity of sectors and trace interindustry transmission of R&D.
The standard input–output model for a closed economy is

$$X = W + Y, \tag{7.2}$$

where X is the vector of gross outputs by sector, W is the vector of supply to intermediate uses, and Y is the vector of final output uses by sector.

The extended model views the destination of gross output to investment as another form of intermediate input:

$$X = W + (K + F), \tag{7.3}$$

where K is the vector of investments and F is the vector of final consumption by sector.

Setting A to be the matrix of intermediate inputs per unit of gross output, so that $W = AX$, the simple model yields

$$X = (I - A)^{-1}Y, \tag{7.4}$$

where I is the identity matrix.

Setting J to be the incremental capital requirement per unit of gross output, so that $K = JX$, the extended model yields

$$X = (I - A - J)^{-1}F. \tag{7.5}$$

The open economy extension of the model is developed by apportioning shares of supply between domestic and foreign suppliers. Since not all of A or J is produced domestically,

$$X = (I - hA - kJ)^{-1}(fF + E), \tag{7.6}$$

where h and k are respectively the matrices of the home shares in A and J, with hA and kJ formed as element-by-element products. Final demand is also divided between fF, the vector of domestic supply going to final consumption, and E, the vector of domestic supply going to exports.

Now we can explore the interindustry transmission of domestic R&D using this model.

The direct R&D intensity of each sector is $r = (R/X)$, where R is the vector of R&D undertaken by sector. Following the input–output model in (7.6), the direct plus indirect R&D intensity reflected in each item supplied from a sector is ρ, where

$$\rho = r(I - hA - kJ)^{-1}. \tag{7.7}$$

This says that the total R&D intensity of any product compounds the R&D from its own sector and the R&D embodied in inputs used by the sector, whether from the same or other sectors. In the empirical analysis we are able to partition ρ.

By looking backward along the supply chain, and partitioning the A and J matrices, we track how much of this comes from within sector and how much is embodied in inputs from other sectors. The ρ coefficients can be converted back to volume flows using final consumption as weights to give figures such as those in table 7.5. It is also possible to

Table 7.5. R&D origin and use in the United Kingdom (£m, 1990).

R&D producer sectors	R&D origin	R&D use	Ratio origin/use
Chemicals	1,121	102	11.0
Electrical equipment	929	100	9.3
Transport equipment	824	129	6.4

R&D user sectors	R&D origin	R&D use	Ratio use/origin
Business services	227	251	1.1
Transport/communications	75	202	2.7
Personal and public services	10	473	47.3

Source. Selected figures from table 3.9 of Greenhalgh and Gregory (2000).

calculate a breakdown by looking forward along the supply chain to see how much each sector transmits R&D to other sectors (see Greenhalgh and Gregory 2000).

Selected evidence from Greenhalgh and Gregory (2000), reproduced in table 7.5, shows similar results to those of Scherer. For the United Kingdom in 1990 strong originating sectors were chemicals, electrical equipment, and transport equipment. Strong user sectors in services include personal and public services, but there were also net users within manufacturing, such as the food and drink sector. It is notable that, even by the year 1990, the United Kingdom's business services sector was already on the point of moving from being an innovation user sector to an innovation producer sector, as its R&D had by then increased significantly.

Greenhalgh and Gregory also conducted further analysis of the onward transmission of R&D by tracing the destinations of the sales of output going forward from the supplying sector; this method gives more weight to suppliers of goods and services that are widely used in the economy, and thus act as onward transmitters of other sectors' R&D. Whereas the flows of R&D embodied in business services output remained about 50:50 between its own R&D and that embodied in bought-in inputs over the period from 1979 to 1990, the proportion of total R&D transmitted forward into other sectors, compared with that staying within the sector, increased rapidly from 40% to 70%. This was due to the strong growth in intersectoral demand for business services output by all other sectors of the economy, which has made this an increasingly important transmission sector for R&D. Symbiosis between manufacturing and services thus allows both sides to act as partners in innovation and growth.

This experience of the United Kingdom during the 1980s was in no sense atypical. Recent analysis on Europe by Kox and Rubalcaba (2007) highlighted the steady growth of business services and the increasing interactions between these knowledge-intensive activities, including software, and all other sectors. They identify three forms of positive spillovers to these customer sectors: besides original innovations and the speeding up of knowledge diffusion, there is the reduction of human capital indivisibilities. This third feature arises because by providing knowledge and skill-intensive services, business services allow firms to outsource a range of activities that were previously done in-house, but with considerable diseconomies of scale. Firms today do not need to employ directly a range of experts within the firm as they can easily access these skills on a part-time basis from specialist business services suppliers. Here we see nondepletable knowledge being exploited to provide a profitable division of labor between suppliers of customized knowledge-intensive services and the knowledge users.

7.5 Empirical Studies of Social Returns

The input–output model gives a broad-brush view of where innovations arise and where they are used. There are a variety of other methods to try and find out more precisely what are the social returns to innovations, including case studies, surveys, and econometric analysis. This section focuses on econometric analysis of knowledge spillovers, as the methodologies used require more explanation. This said, the next section reviews the basic ideas behind case study approaches.

Case Studies of Social Returns to Innovation

Case studies collate information on the various benefits and costs of innovations, including social costs and benefits. Mansfield et al. (1977) provide an important early example of this approach for seventeen innovations—ranging from new construction materials to washing-up liquid—in the United States in the 1950s and 1960s. They use the economic concepts of demand, supply, profit, and consumer surplus (as in chapter 1), but they also look at the R&D effort of all firms (i.e., including those that were working toward similar innovations but failed). The use of consumer surplus in the markets related to the innovation is their main criterion for the assessment of social value. However, in one case, they also make an adjustment for the expected environmental cost of an innovation (this is the effect of "stain remover" on water suppliers). Their method finds a net benefit (NB) for each year that the innovation existed (to 1973) and they then calculated the social rate of return (r) using

$$\text{NB}_t + \frac{\text{NB}_{t+1}}{1+r} + \frac{\text{NB}_{t+2}}{(1+r)^2} + \cdots + \frac{\text{NB}_{t+n}}{(1+r)^n} = 0. \qquad (7.8)$$

Their results show social rates of return varying between zero and 307%, which highlights the fact that social rates of return are likely to vary substantially.

Econometric Studies of Spillovers

The social gains from spillovers of knowledge can also be estimated using econometric analysis. Using these techniques we can analyze both interfirm spillovers within a given industry and spillovers across industrial sectors within the wider economy. This approach is based on the premise that the level of productivity achieved in any single firm or sector increases with the level of technological knowledge that it can access. The empirical methodology is to extend the econometric models of firm performance discussed in chapter 5 for assessing the value of firms' R&D (and in chapter 6 for identifying the gains due to intellectual property).

One approach is to use industry-level output as the dependent variable and relate this to industry-level R&D. In principle this should link the R&D activity of *all* firms in the industry to the output effects of *all* firms, hence the net effect of any knowledge spillovers or business-stealing effects between firms will be included. An example of this approach can be found in Wolff and Nadiri (1993), who use two-digit U.S. industry data (from 1947 to 1977) and find that the social rate of return is 27% in manufacturing.[13] Another approach is to use firm-level productivity (or market value) and include an additional variable that proxies the *relevant* external R&D (to the firm) taking place in the industry and in other related sectors. How could one construct such a proxy for relevant R&D done by other firms? A simple method is to use the total R&D of other firms in the industry. Jaffe (1986) suggested a more sophisticated approach by using patent data. Each firm's patents gave the firm a "technology space," hence one could derive a "technological distance" between two firms that patented. Firms that were close in technology space were more likely to have knowledge spillovers, hence patent data were used to construct the relevant external R&D for each firm.

---

[13] In fact, their paper also looks at knowledge spillovers between two-digit industries (i.e., reflecting the input–output analysis discussed above).

Griliches (1995) collates a number of studies examining the impact of R&D conducted within firms and external R&D to compare private returns to R&D with the value of R&D spillovers. While many authors concentrate on industry, this paper also contains a summary of some early studies relating to U.S. agriculture. For this sector the main routes for spillovers include both public R&D investment and private R&D by firms in the agrochemicals sector, although Griliches focuses on the first of these routes. Agricultural producers have benefited from public R&D investment to breed new varieties of plants that are resistant to diseases or pests, to test new techniques for cultivation, and to engage in new methods of feeding and rearing poultry and livestock. High rates of return to public R&D are demonstrated by many studies of agricultural productivity ranging over forty years from the late 1950s to the 1990s. Considering both the industrial and agricultural studies, Griliches (1995, p. 72) concludes that "R&D spillovers are present, their magnitude may be quite large and social rates of return remain significantly above private rates."

Identifying Spillovers and Business Stealing Effects

McGahan and Silverman (2006) have explored the interactions between rival firms acquiring patents.[14] They distinguish between firms that currently compete in the same industry, as well as exploring the impact of relevant patents acquired by "outside inventors." Outside inventors are not currently active in the same market but they may be in the future.[15] In the study, positive spillover effects dominate negative business-stealing effects in the patent competition between rivals in the same industry. However, if highly cited patents are acquired by a firm or inventor outside the sector, then business stealing dominates. This suggests that firms are better able to respond to important innovation by rivals with which it may share absorptive capacity, but is consistent with the ability of new entrants to exploit radical innovation to unseat successful incumbents. Nevertheless, when complementary assets are introduced the picture changes dramatically. The effect of highly cited patents by outsiders is now dominated by positive spillover effects, suggesting that those incumbent firms with complementary assets are well-situated to

---

[14] Their database builds on that of Hall et al. (2005) for U.S. stock market listed companies, by including observations for nonmanufacturing firms and covering a longer time period.

[15] They also distinguish between industrial sectors according to the Teece (1986) framework, whereby the presence of complementary assets can affect the degree to which a firm can appropriate the returns from its own and others innovations.

bargain with outside innovators, enabling them to license innovations on favorable terms.

Bloom et al. (2007) use a large panel of data on U.S. firms, observed annually from 1980 to 2001, to explore the two countervailing effects—business stealing and knowledge spillovers—of R&D between firms. These authors develop a theoretical model in which an additional testable feature is that R&D done by the firm's product market rivals increases the value of their own R&D (because their knowledge stocks are strategic complements). The empirical methodology hinges on being able to construct measures of the extent to which firms are using similar technology, potentially leading to knowledge or technology spillovers, and the degree of product market competition between firms, hence suggesting business-stealing effects. Bloom et al. describe these dimensions of firm activity as the *technology space* and the *product market space*. They calculate how close or distant firms are in technology space by making detailed comparisons of their patterns of patenting activity across the many technology classes in which patents can be registered (as in Jaffe 1986). Their depiction of product market closeness between any two firms is calculated using the shares of each firm's sales in categories of the Standard Industrial Classification of final goods and services. Bloom et al. then estimate the effects of other firms' R&D operating through these two channels on the market value of the firm, its productivity performance, its rate of patenting, and its level of R&D expenditure. Table 7.6 summarizes the theoretical predictions of their model and compares these with their empirical findings, which substantially support their hypotheses.

To investigate the role for public policy, Bloom et al. present the simulation of an arbitrary increase in R&D spending as a shock to their model (which represents an "interactive" R&D system). They show that the increased R&D generates both positive technology spillovers and negative product business stealing, but that social returns still exceed private returns, thus justifying the need for public subsidy to R&D. They then explore some alternative patterns of public subsidy, which can be neutrally directed to all firms, slanted toward larger firms, or toward small and medium-sized firms. This further simulation analysis suggests that, compared with a neutral policy, there is a bigger rise in R&D and output when a given value of subsidy is directed toward larger firms than if that same subsidy was directed toward SMEs. This is because larger firms are more closely linked to other firms in technology space and so any expansion in their levels of R&D induced by subsidy gives rise to greater positive spillovers.

Table 7.6. Technological spillovers with strategic complementarity of R&D.

Spillover effect (on given firm)	Spillover cause (other firm's activity)	Theoretical sign of spillover effect from model	Sign and statistical significance of empirical estimate
Firm's market value	R&D in same technology field	Positive	Positive (significant)
	R&D in same product field	Negative	Negative (significant)
Firm's productivity	R&D in same technology field	Positive	Positive (significant)
	R&D in same product field	Zero	No effect
Firm's rate of patenting	R&D in same technology field	Positive	Positive (significant)
	R&D in same product field	Zero or positive	Positive (weakly significant)
Firm's R&D expenditure	R&D in same technology field	Ambiguous	No effect
	R&D in same product field	Positive	Positive (weakly significant)

Source. Adapted from table 7 of Bloom et al. (2007).

Spillovers and Trademark Activity

Greenhalgh and Rogers (2007) investigate interactions between U.K. firms to determine if there are spillovers from trademark activity of the type detected by the studies of patents and R&D in U.S. firms. Trademark activity, which is closely connected with new product launch, might be expected to be dominated by business-stealing effects rather than knowledge spillovers. These authors find that, in the short run, higher trademark activity by rivals in the industry reduces the firm's value of output, presumably by putting downward pressure on prices and profit margins through the business-stealing effect. However, in their analysis of subsequent productivity growth and of current stock market values, which incorporate the expectations of future performance, the results are that positive spillovers negate the business-stealing effects. Overall, therefore, they find a net positive impact of rivals' trademarks on the firm's productivity and of rival's patents on the firm's market value. This suggests a wider view of positive spillovers than simply knowledge transfers, as competition through innovation exerts pressure on firms to achieve better productivity and profits.

7.6   Spatial Dimensions of Spillovers

The spatial distribution of spillovers matters for two reasons. First, there is the question of whether and how fast countries or regions will experience convergence in macroeconomic growth, as discussed below in chapters 8 and 9. Second, there is a related issue concerning whether it makes sense to subsidize R&D in the home country to try to maintain relative advantage over trade competitors or wait for spillovers to accrue from other countries' R&D.

If technology diffuses rapidly and completely to all regions and across all economies with all firms moving swiftly to best-practice technology, this will cause more rapid growth in follower countries than in leaders, resulting in a reduced cross-country inequality of income. By contrast, if there is limited diffusion of technology, with the consequent clustering of high-technology supply and methods of production in a limited number of locations, then there will be persistence of competitive advantage in these richer innovative areas so that differences of income per capita will not be eroded. These issues extend into whether policy should encourage clustering of R&D activity within countries or regions.

The effectiveness of public policy in encouraging innovation is also affected by the degree of spatial spillovers. If interregional spillovers are high but international spillovers are low, the government can confidently subsidize R&D activity with the expectation that spillovers will assist productivity and growth in its own territory. However, if international spillovers are rapid, then the social benefits of public subsidy will diffuse everywhere and, although they are not diminished by this fact, there is now an incentive problem for governments. They may decide to operate as free riders on the R&D and technology advances in other countries.

Keller (2002) has investigated the importance of distance from key centers of R&D in a study of twelve manufacturing industries observed from 1970 to 1995. His sample of fourteen countries includes the so-called G5 countries—France, Germany, Japan, the United Kingdom, and the United States—which together undertook more than 90% of world R&D during the period studied. The effects of their expenditure on the total factor productivity of industries in the remaining nine countries is modeled with respect to domestic and foreign R&D, where the effect of foreign R&D has the potential to be moderated by the distance between their capital cities. His findings are that the positive effect of foreign R&D on productivity does considerably diminish with distance. There are also higher benefits to location adjacent to one of the G5 countries than elsewhere at a similar distance. It is also shown that speaking a common language facilitates diffusion. This picture is not static though, as over time the intercountry flows of technology have increased, consistent with improving international communications.

Nevertheless, despite all the improvements to communication, knowledge flows still occur more rapidly via some channels than others. Maurseth and Verspagen (1999) have examined the interrelationships between patents in Europe, as documented by patent citations, to explore further the extent to which knowledge spillovers are geographically localized. This technique was pioneered by Jaffe et al. (1993) for the analysis of patenting across U.S. states and cities. What is being explored in both studies is the extent to which the earlier patents cited in new patent applications are geographically diffused or are clustered in the areas local to the patentee. For both Europe and the United States these studies show that the system of innovation cannot be considered as global. For the United States the finding is that, even when compared with a "control frequency" that reflects the preexisting concentration of related research activity, U.S. patent citations are more likely to be domestic and more likely to come from the same state and city. For Europe the conclusion is similar:

> The European system of innovation, as far as the role of knowledge spillovers is concerned, is characterized as one with polarization between several centers, rather than a single system without barriers for knowledge flows.
>
> Maurseth and Verspagen (1999, p. 168)

7.7 Conclusions

Society receives the full benefits of innovation only when new products and processes are widely diffused through the economy. Models of diffusion demonstrate that interaction between potential customers is important for learning about new techniques and goods, but also potential adopters differ in terms of the costs and benefits for them of adoption. The agent considering adopting new technology needs information about what is available but also faces an economic decision about whether the benefits exceed the costs. This chapter discussed two models—the epidemic and economic models—of diffusion that allow insight into the mechanisms at work. The chapter also reviewed empirical evidence concerning the rate of diffusion. The evidence illustrated that the process of reaching market saturation is slow and often incomplete. This is demonstrated by reference both to older manufacturing technologies and to the more recent building blocks of the information and communications technology age, such as the use of computers. The chapter also discussed the issue of lock-in and network effects in the diffusion of innovations. The famous case of the QWERTY keyboard design suggests that it is possible for an inferior innovation to become dominant due to lock-in and network effects. These issues are just as relevant today, as many new technological innovations have aspects to them that can create lock-in or network effects. Policy is left in a difficult position in such cases since there is great uncertainty surrounding which innovation may be best.[16]

The chapter also reviewed the empirical analysis on assessing the social returns to innovations. For consumer goods, the more widely an innovation is used (i.e., diffused), the greater the likely benefits from higher consumer surplus. The social returns are reduced by "business stealing" from rival firms that produce substitute products, but some rivals may also gain from knowledge spillovers. If the innovation is an input to other industries, the number of firms and consumers potentially affected by the innovation increases. Firms using the innovation may gain via increased profits, although they may also reduce prices for consumers (creating higher consumer surplus). The innovation may also create knowledge spillovers to firms in other industries. Mapping out and attaching a value to the diverse effects is time consuming and difficult. A general feature of the evidence is high variability of social returns. Input–output studies are able to identify significant differences between sectors in their roles as innovation producers and innovation users but, of course, both these types contribute to the diffusion of returns to final consumers.

While the social returns to innovation are of interest, policy makers are often most interested in externalities. The key externality is the possibility of knowledge spillovers between firms. Empirical analysis indicates that these knowledge spillovers are substantial and this implies that policies to encourage innovation and R&D are justified. The chapter highlighted how knowledge spillovers are influenced by the level of absorptive capacity of the receiving firm and, in particular, how conducting R&D can increase a firm's absorptive capacity. This represents the "two faces" of R&D. There is also evidence that spatial proximity is still important in allowing knowledge spillovers.

---

[16] One recent example concerns interactive television technology. There are various different competing standards (innovations) and it is not clear which one is superior. There are lock-in and network effects due to economies of scale in production and distribution. The EU decided to help subsidize one format (MHP) in Italy, which has subsequently been criticized (Matteucci 2008).

Keywords

Epidemic and economic models of diffusion.

Network and lock-in effects.

Social returns to innovation.

Consumer surplus, business stealing, and knowledge spillovers.

Positive externalities.

Input–output analysis.

Spatial aspects to spillovers.

Questions for Discussion

(1) Why is diffusion generally a slow process?

(2) Are there cases when the epidemic model is better than the economic model?

(3) What factors speed up or slow down the adoption of new technology by industry?

(4) Should policy be concerned about "lock-in" or "network effects"?

(5) What lessons can be learnt from input–output analysis of R&D and innovation?

(6) Choose an innovation you are familiar with and outline the potential customers and firms affected by it. How would you attempt to quantify these effects?

(7) Define (a) knowledge spillovers and (b) business stealing. How could one test the relative importance of each?

(8) What are hedonic price indices? Are they important?

(9) What lessons should policy makers learn from the economics of diffusion?

References

Bloom, N., M. Shankerman, and J. Van Reenen. 2007. Identifying technology spillovers and product market rivalry. NBER Working Paper 13060.

Bohanon, C. 1985. Externalities: a note on avoiding confusion. *Journal of Economic Education* 16(4):305–7.

Boskin, M. J., E. R. Dulberger, and Z. Griliches. 1996. *Toward a More Accurate Measure of the Cost of Living.* Final report to the Senate Finance Committee by the Advisory Committee to Study the Consumer Price Index. Diane Publishing.

Canepa, A., and P. Stoneman. 2003. The diffusion of new process technologies: international comparisons. Working Paper 03-15, United Nations University Institute for New Technologies.

——. 2005. Financing constraints in the inter-firm diffusion of new process technologies. *Journal of Technology Transfer* 30(1/2):159–69.

Caselli, F., and W. J. Coleman. 2001. Cross-country technology diffusion: the case of computers. *American Economic Review* 91(2):328–35.

Crawford, A. 1993. Measuring biases in the Canadian CPI: a summary of evidence. *Bank of Canada Review*, Summer.

David, P. 1985. Clio and the economics of QWERTY. *American Economic Review* 75(2):332–37.

Gold, B., W. S. Peirce, and G. Rosegger. 1970. Diffusion of major technological innovations in U.S. iron and steel manufacturing. *Journal of Industrial Economics* 18(3):218–41.

Greenhalgh, C., and M. Gregory. 2000. Labour productivity and product quality: their growth and inter-industry transmission. In *Productivity, Innovation and Economic Performance* (ed. R. Barrell, G. Mason, and M. O'Mahoney). Cambridge University Press.

Greenhalgh, C., and M. Rogers. 2007. Trade marks and performance in services and manufacturing firms: evidence of Schumpeterian competition through innovation. Working Paper 300, University of Oxford, Department of Economics (revised version, January 2007).

Griliches, Z. 1995. R&D and productivity: econometric results and measurement errors. In *Handbook of the Economics of Innovation and Technical Change* (ed. P. Stoneman). Oxford: Basil Blackwell.

Hall, B. 2004. Innovation and diffusion. In *The Oxford Handbook of Innovation* (ed. J. Fagerberg, D. Mowery, and R. R. Nelson). Oxford University Press.

Hall, B., A. Jaffe, and M. Trajtenberg. 2005. Market value and patent citations. *Rand Journal of Economics* 36:16–38.

Jaffe, A. 1986. Technological opportunity and spillovers of R&D: evidence from firms' patents, profits and market value. *American Economic Review* 76(5): 984–1,001.

Jaffe, A., M. Trajtenberg, and R. Henderson. 1993. Geographical localisation of knowledge spillovers as evidenced by patent citations. *Quarterly Journal of Economics* 108(3):577–98.

Karshenas, M., and P. Stoneman. 1992. A flexible model of technological diffusion incorporating economic factors with an application to the spread of colour television ownership in the UK. *Journal of Forecasting* 11:577–601.

Katz, M., and C. Shapiro. 1994. Systems competition and network effects. *Journal of Economic Perspectives* 8(2):93–115.

Keller, W. 2002. Geographic localisation of international technology diffusion. *American Economic Review* 92(1):120–42.

Klemperer, P. 1995. Competition when consumers have switching costs: an overview with applications to industrial economics, macroeconomics and international trade. *Review of Economic Studies* 62:519–39.

Kox, H., and L. Rubalcaba. 2007. Business services and the changing structure of European economic growth. Memoranda 183, CPB Netherlands Bureau for Economic Policy Analysis, The Hague.

Liebowitz, S., and S. Margolis. 1990. The fable of the keys. *Journal of Law and Economics* 33:1–26.

Mansfield, E. 1968. *Industrial Research and Technological Innovation.* New York: W. W. Norton.

Mansfield, E., J. Rapoport, A. Romeo, S. Wagner, and G. Beardsley. 1977. Social and private rates of return from industrial innovations. *Quarterly Journal of Economics* 91(2):221–40.

Matteucci, N. 2008. IPRs and interoperability in the EU digital TV market: economics and policy issues. Paper presented at the EPIP conference, Berne, October 2008.

Maurseth, P. B., and B. Verspagen. 1999. Europe: one or several systems of innovation? An analysis based on patent citations. In *The Economic Challenge for Europe: Adapting to Innovation Based Growth* (ed. J. Fagerberg, P. Guerrieri, and B. Verspagen). Cheltenham, U.K.: Edward Elgar.

McGahan, A. M., and B. S. Silverman. 2006. Profiting from technological innovation by others: the effect of competitor patenting on firm value. *Research Policy* 35(8):1,222–42.

Mishan, E. 1971. The post-war literature on externalities: an interpretative essay. *Journal of Economic Literature* 9(1):1–28.

Mowery, D., and T. Simcoe. 2002. The Internet. In *Technological Innovation and Economic Performance* (ed. B. Steil, D. Victor, and R. R. Nelson). Princeton University Press.

Park, S. 2004. Quantitative analysis of network externalities in competing technologies: the VCR case. *Review of Economics and Statistics* 86(4):937–45.

Patel, P., and K. Pavitt. 1995. Patterns of technological activity: their measurement and interpretation. In *Handbook of the Economics of Innovation and Technological Change* (ed. P. Stoneman). Oxford: Basil Blackwell.

Rogers, E. M. 1995. *Diffusion of Innovations.* New York: Free Press.

Scherer, F. M. 1984. *Innovation and Growth: Schumpeterian Perspectives.* Cambridge, MA: MIT Press.

Shepler, N. 2004. Developing a hedonic regression model for camcorders in the U.S. CPI. Report, Bureau of Labor Statistics (available at www.bls.gov/cpi/cpicamco.htm).

Stoneman, P. 2002. *The Economics of Technological Diffusion.* Oxford: Basil Blackwell.

Teece, D. J. 1986. Profiting from technological innovation. *Research Policy* 15(6):285–305.

Thompson, W. 2004. Developing a hedonic regression model for VCRs in the U.S. CPI. Report, Bureau of Labor Statistics (available at www.bls.gov/cpi/cpivcrp.htm).

Varian, H., J. Farrell, and C. Shapiro. 2004. *The Economics of Information Technology.* Cambridge University Press.

Wolff, E., and M. Nadiri. 1993. Spillover effects, linkage structure and R&D. *Structural Change and Economic Dynamics* 2(2):315–31.

Young, H. P. 2007. Innovation diffusion in heterogeneous populations. Discussion Paper 303, University of Oxford, Department of Economics.

Zettelmeyer, F., and P. Stoneman. 1993. Testing alternative models of new product diffusion. *Economics of Innovation and New Technology* 2:283–308.

Part III

The Macroeconomics of Innovation

8

Models of Economic Growth

8.1 Introduction

Parts I and II of this book focused on the microeconomic issues surrounding innovation, intellectual property, and economic growth. This chapter explains how macroeconomists have modeled the process of economic growth. Economic growth is defined as a situation where GDP per capita increases over time. The objective of this chapter is twofold. First, it aims to provide a short yet rigorous overview of the growth models used by macroeconomists to think about growth in a closed economy. These will, in turn, become useful in thinking about open economies in chapter 9. Second, the chapter aims to highlight the links between these macroeconomic models and the microeconomic concepts from parts I and II. At the outset, we should make clear that innovation is central to economic growth. Microeconomists define an innovation as something that increases "value" to an enterprise, perhaps by raising sales or lowering costs (see chapter 1). At the economy level, GDP measures the aggregate value created by all enterprises (see section 3.5). Hence, innovation at the firm level will be an important driver of GDP growth.

Section 8.2 describes the neoclassical model of economic growth, which is also called the Solow–Swan model. This model assumes there is a positive relationship between the capital and labor employed in an economy and the value or "output" (GDP) produced by that economy. The growth-generating process in the model is the way savings are invested, which leads to an increase in the capital stock, and thereby economic growth. New technology can also raise output, but the model assumes that the growth rate of technology is determined outside the model. Given this basic framework the model analyzes the implications of different rates of saving, population growth, depreciation, and technology growth. The major implication of this model is that long-run economic growth cannot be supported by capital investment alone. Only when there is a positive rate of growth of technology can increases in

GDP per capita be sustained. As will be discussed, the term "growth of technology" in this macroeconomic model has a large overlap with the term "innovation" used by microeconomists.

Section 8.3 discusses a set of models that try to capture the driving forces of long-run growth within the model. These are called endogenous growth models and analyze in detail the creation of knowledge, technology, and human capital, which are all viewed as important factors in economic growth. These models look at the incentives to invest in these factors and whether the market system may provide suboptimal incentives. In these more recent models, the close links to innovation and IPRs are often explicitly acknowledged. Finally, in section 8.4 we discuss some alternative theories that provide a broader, historical view of the process of economic growth.

The United States is estimated to produce about fifty-eight times as much in 1990 as it did in 1870 (Maddison 2001). This sustained economic growth means that in 1990 the United States had an average GDP per capita of $23,214, representing an almost tenfold increase since 1870. In contrast, African countries are estimated to have had an average GDP per capita of $1,385 in 1990: a threefold increase since 1870. Rapid increases in GDP per capita can lead to rapid increases in standards of living.[1] Increases in GDP are also, to some extent, the driving force of changes in social and political conditions within a country, and also the international standing of a country. The sustained economic growth in the United States over the last century has caused it to become the world's superpower (the Soviet Union never managed to equal the United States's sustained growth). The rapid rates of economic growth in China and India over recent decades are dramatically changing their international political power, as well as transforming living standards for many people (see table 3.5).

There is huge interest in understanding the driving force of economic growth. The models presented below are the key models that modern economists use in framing discussions about economic growth. All the models in this chapter are closed-economy models, which means that they do not consider how international factors may affect growth. How economic growth and innovation are determined in a global world is considered in the next chapter.

---

[1] "Standard of living" refers to a wider definition of human wellbeing. Although GDP per capita is an important aspect of wellbeing, societies are clearly interested in health, inequality, education, pollution, sustainability, freedom, and many other issues. This chapter leaves aside these important issues and focuses solely on economic growth.

8.2 The Neoclassical Growth Model

This section discusses one of the key models that modern economists use to think about the process of economic growth.[2] Since this model is based on concepts that are best understood using equations, this section uses more mathematics than is common in the rest of the book. The mathematics used is backed up with written explanations (and there is also a mathematical appendix to consult). The model is often known as the Solow growth model, but sometimes the Solow–Swan model, or just the neoclassical model.

The neoclassical model is based on an aggregate production function of the form

$$Y = Af(K, L). \tag{8.1}$$

This means that GDP (Y) depends on capital (K), labor (L), and the level of technology (A). Other inputs, such as raw materials or energy, are abstracted by focusing on GDP (or "value added") as the measure of output.[3] A production function, such as the one specified in equation (8.1), is a mathematical way of linking inputs to outputs.[4] The output in this case is GDP and the inputs are the available capital (machines, equipment, computers, buildings, etc.) and the number of workers. Hence, to be precise, we should call K the capital stock and L the size of the employed workforce at a specific time. However, we generally refer to capital, labor, and output without their full descriptions. Note that (8.1) represents the entire economy, hence it aggregates manufacturing, services, agriculture, and utilities activity into single variables. Parts I and II of this book analyzed the innovation and growth process starting with firms; the macroeconomic approach used here starts at the economy level. Both approaches can provide insights, but it is important to remember that neither approach is necessarily better than the other.

To assist in the explanation of the basic model, we will assume a specific functional form for (8.2), namely

$$Y = AK^\alpha L^{1-\alpha}, \quad 0 < \alpha < 1. \tag{8.2}$$

---

[2] Solow (1956) and Swan (1956) simultaneously published papers using this basic model. There was, of course, substantial analysis of economic growth before these models. See Eltis (2000) for a discussion of the classical economists—Smith, Malthus, Marx, and Ricardo. Hahn and Matthews (1964) provide a well-known early survey, while recent comprehensive books that review thinking on economic growth include Rostow (1990) and Ruttan (2001).

[3] Hence neoclassical models do not apply to primary-resource-dominated economies such as OPEC countries. As Lucas (1988) notes, these models were originally created to understand the U.S. economy.

[4] Section A.1 in the mathematical appendix gives a more detailed explanation if you are unfamiliar with such functions.

The assumption that α is between 0 and 1 means that increasing capital or labor on their own will increase output, as would be expected, but they do so at a diminishing rate. In economic jargon, equation (8.2) exhibits diminishing marginal products of capital and labor. Box 8.1 explains the mathematics behind these ideas, but the important thing to remember is that if technology and labor are held constant, then increasing capital will increase GDP by ever smaller amounts. A similar outcome would occur if technology and capital were held constant while labor was increased. Hence, in an economy with fixed technology and capital, increasing the population will generate smaller and smaller GDP gains.[5]

Box 8.1. Diminishing returns and returns to scale.

Equation (8.2) is called a Cobb–Douglas production function after two economists who analyzed such functions. The marginal product of capital is the increase in output when capital is increased by a "small" amount. In calculus we define "small" as an infinitesimally small change (dK), hence we can use dY/dK to refer to the marginal product of capital. Differentiating (8.2) with respect to K we have

$$\frac{dY}{dK} = \alpha A K^{\alpha-1} L^{1-\alpha} = \alpha A \left(\frac{K}{L}\right)^{\alpha-1}.$$

Since $0 < \alpha < 1$ this means that as K increases, and if A and L are held constant, then the marginal product of capital will fall (i.e., K to the power of a minus number will fall as K rises). Clearly, in many situations, A or L may increase. If A increases this will increase the marginal product of capital. If L increases this also raises the marginal product of capital. Note that if K and L are growing at the same rate, and if A is a constant, then the marginal product of capital will be constant. The far right-hand term in the above equation makes this clear by expressing the marginal product of capital in terms of the capital to labor ratio.

The production function shown in (8.2) exhibits "constant returns to scale." This means that if the labor and capital inputs are "scaled up," the output will be scaled up by the same amount. To see this, suppose all inputs were doubled. The new output level (Y_{new}) is now

$$Y_{new} = A(2K)^{\alpha}(2L)^{1-\alpha} = A2^{\alpha}2^{1-\alpha}K^{\alpha}L^{1-\alpha}$$
$$= A2^{\alpha+1-\alpha}K^{\alpha}L^{1-\alpha} = 2AK^{\alpha}L^{1-\alpha},$$

---

[5] This is, in effect, a specific example of the "law of diminishing returns" or the "law of increasing opportunity cost." Thomas Malthus (1798) was concerned that increasing population, when land and capital remained in fixed supply, would result in falling living standards (GDP per capita). As history has shown, if capital—and the level of technology—can increase, then living standards can continue to rise. The neoclassical model can, therefore, be thought of as a theoretical investigation of Malthus's concerns.

hence the new output level is just double the old output level. It is possible for the production function to exhibit increasing returns to scale (also called "economies of scale"). This means that doubling capital and labor will more than double output. Similarly, firms can be subject to decreasing returns to scale (diseconomies of scale). In economic theory, constant returns to scale is a convenient assumption since it implies that firms do not have an incentive to become very large. This then allows industries to have more than one firm and hence there is competition between firms.

Note that the level of technology in (8.2) is *assumed* to simply "scale up" or "scale down" all inputs. For example, if the level of technology doubled, then output would also double, even if capital and labor inputs were the same. The neoclassical model assumes that the level of technology is exogenous, in other words, the model does not attempt to describe how it changes. Although this may sound extreme, fifty years ago when Solow and Swan developed their models there was more support for the idea that technology was generated by sole inventors, or in university laboratories, and that this evolved in a way exogenous to the economic system.

Parts I and II of this book explained how the process of innovation depends on complex interactions between firms, universities, and government. How is innovation related to technology—the A term—in the neoclassical model? Although the original models do not address this question directly, the basic answer is that "innovation" is the driving force of any increase in technology as defined in this model. An increase in technology (A) boosts value added for given inputs at the economy level; similarly, a process or product innovation generally leads to an increase in value added, both at the firm level and also more widely as diffusion occurs. Thus, the technology term in the neoclassical model provides a direct link to the analysis in parts I and II of this book.

In order to explain the neoclassical model, we will for now consider A as a constant positive number (although how other macroeconomists have modeled the determination of A will be discussed in detail later in this chapter). Also it is useful to rewrite equation (8.2) in so-called intensive form with output per worker (y) on the left-hand side

$$y = \frac{Y}{L} = \frac{AK^\alpha L^{1-\alpha}}{L} = \frac{AK^\alpha}{L^\alpha} = Ak^\alpha, \tag{8.3}$$

where k is capital per worker; hence this equation simply states that output per worker depends on the level of technology and capital per worker (raised to the power α). Figure 8.1 plots the relationship between

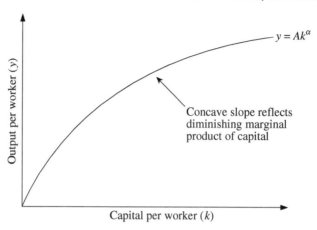

Figure 8.1. The neoclassical production function.

output per worker and capital per worker captured by equation (8.3) for a constant level of technology (A). The slope of the curve is the marginal product of capital and, as can be seen, the concave shape indicates that the marginal product is declining as capital per worker is accumulated.

The production function is one critical component of the neoclassical model. The other is the *accumulation* equation. In any growth model the accumulation equation describes how inputs accumulate and, therefore, how output changes through time. The neoclassical model assumes that only the capital stock can increase through accumulation. The model assumes that gross investment in capital comes from saving a constant proportion of output (s, where $0 < s < 1$). Some of this gross investment is needed to replace worn-out machines, buildings, and the like, which is called depreciation. The model assumes that a constant proportion (δ) of the existing capital stock depreciates in each period. The net change in capital stock—or the rate of accumulation—is therefore given by gross investment less depreciation. Gross investment is assumed to equal total savings ($I = S$); recall that this is a closed-economy model, and that total savings is s times Y. Hence we can write

$$\text{Change in capital stock} = \frac{dK}{dt} = sY - \delta K. \qquad (8.4)$$

Equation (8.4) also uses the notation dK/dt to denote "change in" or "accumulation of" the capital stock. Note that if capital is to accumulate, savings must be greater than depreciation. If, for some reason, depreciation is greater than gross investment, then there will be de-accumulation and the capital stock will fall.

What are the assumptions surrounding labor input? Does this factor also get accumulated? In the neoclassical model the answer is "no," in the sense that there is not an equation describing how this happens. However, the model does include a fixed (exogenous) rate of growth in the labor force, which is decided outside the model. Let n be the growth rate of the labor force, which allows the possibility that n could be zero (i.e., a constant number of workers).

The accumulation equation (8.4) and the production function (8.3) embody the core assumptions of the neoclassical model. In order to understand what they imply about economic growth we need to manipulate the equations mathematically.

Let us start by rewriting the accumulation equation in per-worker terms, since our objective is to understand growth in output per worker. Dividing each side of (8.4) by L gives

$$\frac{dK}{dt} \bigg/ L = \frac{sY}{L} - \frac{\delta K}{L} = sy - \delta k. \tag{8.5}$$

The left-hand side of this equation is unfamiliar and we need to think about what it means. Ideally, we would like the left-hand side to be accumulation of capital *per worker*, not the accumulation of capital stock divided by L. It turns out that to rewrite (8.5) in this form requires some manipulation (see section A.5 in the mathematical appendix), but the answer is

$$\frac{dk}{dt} = sy - (\delta + n)k. \tag{8.6}$$

Let us consider equation (8.6) carefully. The equation states that the change in capital per worker equals savings per worker less a "depreciation and dilution" term. Note that if the growth of labor is zero ($n = 0$), then the equation looks similar to (8.4). Equation (8.4) simply states that the change in capital stock equals gross investment less depreciation. Hence, one can think of equation (8.6) as a close descendant of (8.4), but expressed in per-worker terms. However, if labor is growing ($n > 0$) then the far right-hand term in (8.6) is now depreciation plus labor growth (n). Why should this be? Equation (8.6) says the growth in capital per worker equals gross investment per worker less the investment needed *both* for depreciation and to equip new workers. A growing labor force will require investment just to maintain the same capital per worker even if machines never wear out (i.e., even if depreciation is zero, $\delta = 0$), hence the presence of n in equation (8.6). This need for such investment is often called the "dilution" effect, hence the $(\delta + n)k$ is called depreciation–dilution.

Now that we have the per-worker production function (8.3) and the per-worker accumulation equation (8.6), we are in a position to solve the model. This can be done mathematically, but it is easier to solve it

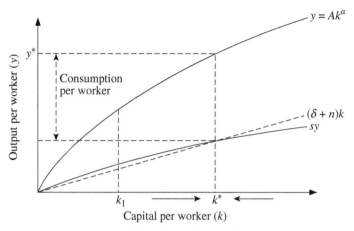

Figure 8.2. Equilibrium in the neoclassical model.

graphically. To do this we need to plot sy and $(\delta+n)k$ on a graph. Since the savings ratio (s), the depreciation ratio (δ), and population growth (n) are constant, it is straightforward to plot each of these terms as shown in figure 8.2.

Suppose the economy starts off at a low level of capital per worker (k_1). The figure shows that the investment per worker curve (sy) is above the $(\delta+n)k$ line, causing capital accumulation, which causes output to increase (look at equation (8.6)). However, at some point the sy and $(\delta+n)k$ lines will cross and the level of capital per worker will become fixed: all gross investment will be spent on depreciation and dilution. When capital per worker is constant, so will be the level of output per worker, and growth in output per worker will cease. This situation is indicated on the diagram by k^*, which is known as the equilibrium, or "steady-state," level of capital per worker. The model suggests that economies will converge to this level. If they start at a point below k^*, there will be growth and accumulation until k^* is reached. Alternatively, if for some reason the economy starts at a point above k^*, there will be negative growth and de-accumulation. The arrows below the horizontal axis indicate the movement of the capital to labor ratio (a longer discussion of this is in section A.5 in the mathematical appendix).

Figure 8.2 encapsulates the basic outcome of the neoclassical model: the economy converges to a steady-state level of capital and output per worker. The diagram indicates the level of consumption per worker associated with this steady-state, or equilibrium, level. This is less than output per worker because some of it is always needed for investment in order to replace worn-out machines and equip new workers (assuming $n > 0$). Note that the further an economy is below the steady-state level the faster its growth rate of output per worker will be. (This is shown graphically by the larger gap between the investment and depreciation-dilution lines relative to the level of k.)

What other insights can we gain from the neoclassical model? The generic way to explore models is to vary key parameters one at a time and investigate the results.

Changes in the Savings Ratio (s)

The easiest way to understand the broad implications of changing the savings ratio is to redraw figure 8.2 with two different savings ratios, s_1 and s_2 (with $s_1 < s_2$), along with their corresponding gross investment curves. This is shown in figure 8.3. Suppose the economy was initially at equilibrium at y_1 and then a new policy increases the savings ratio to s_2. This shifts up the gross investment line, meaning that gross investment is greater than depreciation-dilution, hence the capital stock per worker starts to rise. This rise causes an increase in output per worker. This period of growth continues until a new equilibrium is reached at y_2. From a policy perspective—and, of course, assuming that the neoclassical model is valid—this indicates that increased saving is good for growth in the short to medium term. However, it is important to note that increasing GDP per worker does not always mean that consumption per worker increases. This may sound strange, but remember that consumption per worker is represented by the distance between the gross investment (savings) line and the output per worker line (the top line). In figure 8.3 it appears that this distance is smaller at y_2 than it is at y_1. More generally, it is true that *each* different equilibrium level of capital per worker will have a different level of consumption per worker. In fact, there will be one level of capital per worker that has the maximal level of consumption per worker. To highlight this fact, economists have coined the term "the golden rule" to mean the parameter values that yield the maximal consumption per worker. Box 8.2 discusses this in more detail.

Readers may ask why the savings ratio is exogenous to the model? Surely it is more realistic to allow consumers to choose their rate of savings based on their preferences? The answer is "yes" and the model can be augmented to include a basic model of savings behavior. In the model, consumers are assumed to be rational and forward looking. Consumers balance the rate of return on savings, which equals the marginal product of capital (the only investment available), against their intrinsic rate of time preference. While allowing consumers to choose their rate of savings adds realism to the model, the overall conclusion of the model is the same: the economy converges to a steady-state level of output per capita.

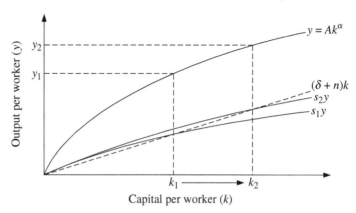

Figure 8.3.   Changing the savings ratio.

The basic reason for this is the assumption of the diminishing marginal product of capital. Graphically this is represented by the "concavity" of the production function. If an economy is faced with such diminishing returns, capital accumulation will eventually cease whatever the saving behavior of the economy.

Box 8.2. The golden rule.

As indicated by figure 8.3, different values of the savings ratio will cause different equilibrium levels of output per worker and, therefore, consumption per worker. What value of the savings ratio would maximize consumption per worker? Graphically, the answer is when the distance between the y curve and the $(\delta + n)k$ line is at a maximum. The $(\delta + n)k$ line is crucial since any equilibrium is always somewhere along this line (i.e., at an intersection between the gross investment line and this line). Thus, given a value of $(\delta + n)$ one can work out the optimal level of the savings rate.

To prove this result more formally, write down the optimization problem as

$$\max_{k} c = y - sy.$$

We know in equilibrium that $sy = (\delta + n)k$, so we can substitute this into the above giving

$$\max_{k} c = y - sy = y - (\delta + n)k,$$

hence differentiating with respect to k gives

$$\frac{dc}{dk} = \frac{dy}{dk} - (\delta + n).$$

The maximal value will be where $dc/dk = 0$, hence where the marginal product of capital equals the sum of depreciation plus population growth. In terms of the diagram, this is where the slope of the production frontier equals the slope of the depreciation–dilution line.

The Role of Population Growth

The implications of different levels of population growth can be investigated in the same way as different savings rates. If one redraws the diagram with a higher population growth rate (i.e., a larger n), one can see that the depreciation–dilution line pivots upward. This, in turn, causes the equilibrium level of output per worker to be lower. The basic implication is that countries with higher levels of population growth will have lower output per worker in *equilibrium*. However, if one compares two countries with different rates of population growth, the exact output levels and growth rates depend on all the other parameters in the model.

Introducing Technology Growth into the Neoclassical Model

So far we have assumed that the level of technology (A) has been constant, which is not the case in most economies. As discussed above, innovation will increase value added for given input levels, a process which the neoclassical model captures by increasing the technology level. As equation (8.3) suggests, when technology increases, output per worker will grow, even if capital per worker is constant. Figure 8.4 indicates how changing technology from level A_0 to A_1 to A_2 affects the steady-state level of k. We assume that the economy is initially at steady state at k_0. As the technology level increases, the production frontier shifts upward, which will also shift up the gross investment curve (this is shown in figure 8.4 but not labeled). The shifting gross investment curve will therefore intercept the static depreciation–dilution line in the positions shown by ❶, ❶, and ❷. This, in turn, means that the "equilibrium" level of k increases from k_0 to k_1 to k_2; and, of course, output per worker increases from y_0 to y_1 to y_2.

While figure 8.4 makes it clear that increasing the level of technology will increase GDP per worker, it is worthwhile thinking about the mechanisms at work. The economy is initially at equilibrium at k_0. An increase in technology will directly cause output to rise (see equation (8.3)), but it will also increase the marginal product of capital (see box 8.1). The gross investment line is now above the depreciation–dilution line, causing further capital accumulation. Output per worker increases due to

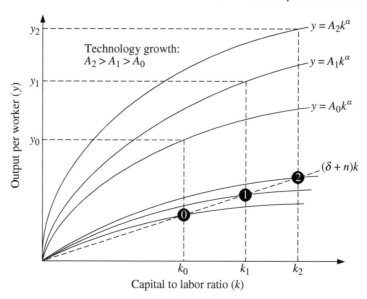

Figure 8.4. Increasing levels of technology.

both a direct technology effect and also a capital accumulation effect. The increase in technology was the driving force for these changes, but capital accumulation was important in obtaining the full benefits. We can relate this back to figure 1.1, which considered the stages of innovation. Stages 1–3 concerned R&D, with stage 4 requiring investment and commercialization. The "technology" in the neoclassical model refers to the outcome of stages 1–3. The "investment" in the neoclassical model includes stages 4 and 5, since the model is looking at the entire economy, hence it assumes that the technology becomes fully diffused among all firms.

With some more mathematics we can calculate the rate of economic growth associated with a rate of technology growth of, say, 2%. If the economy is initially at steady state, then a 2% growth in technology converts directly into a 2% growth in output per worker. This, therefore, dramatically reverses the conclusion of the previous sections (which found that output per worker converged to a constant level and economic growth ceased). The neoclassical model can predict long-run growth in output per worker as long as there is growth in technology. A drawback of the model is, however, that the growth of technology is exogenous to the model. It might be argued that exogenous technology growth is a reasonable assumption for less developed countries or newly industrializing countries, since these countries may be able to learn technology from overseas. However, for more advanced countries the "exogenous technology" assumption is certainly unrealistic—as argued in parts I and II. It is this problem that the endogenous growth models developed in the 1980s and 1990s set out to solve.[6]

8.3 Endogenous Growth Models

Endogenous, or "new growth," theory is the name given to a range of theoretical models that appeared from the mid 1980s onward. All the models yield the result that growth in output per worker could be positive in the long run by internalizing the growth of technology, or human capital accumulation, into the model. Their aim is to capture the essential driving forces of the permanent rates of economic growth that many countries experience. The models also aim to explore the policy issues surrounding economic growth.

The *AK* Model

A simple way to illustrate an endogenous growth model, and to reinforce understanding of the neoclassical model, is to use the *AK* model. The production function in this model is

$$Y = AK. \tag{8.7}$$

This is a simplified version of (8.1), with output Y and technology A. Here, however, we must interpret K as a composite measure of both physical capital and labor, since there is no direct labor input in (8.7). The important characteristic of this production function is that the marginal product of capital is constant (and equal to A).[7] In other words, we have assumed that there are no diminishing returns to capital. The model then uses an accumulation equation very similar to equation (8.4), which we do not specify here.

---

[6] The original authors did realize this shortcoming. Swan (1956, p. 338), for example, states that:

> To this anti-accumulation [of capital], pro-technology line of argument there are at least two possible answers. First, the rate of technical progress may not be independent of the rate of accumulation, or … accumulation may give rise to external economies, so that the true social yield of capital is greater than … private experience. Second, the rate of growth of labor may not be independent of the rate of accumulation.

[7] How to calculate the marginal product of capital was covered in box 8.1. For readers without calculus, the marginal product refers to how output changes as capital changes. In (8.7) it is easy to see that a unit change in composite capital K will always lead to the same change in output (i.e., A), hence the "marginal product" of capital is constant.

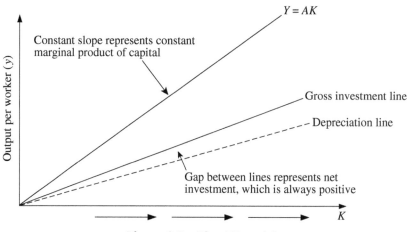

Figure 8.5. The *AK* model.

The fact that there are no diminishing returns to capital will, in turn, mean that long-run growth in output per worker can be positive. Figure 8.5 illustrates the basic logic behind this result. Unlike all the neoclassical diagrams above, figure 8.5 shows a production function that is a straight line, which reflects the constant marginal product of capital assumption. Below this production function, the figure also shows straight lines for gross investment and depreciation. These assume that the savings ratio and the depreciation rate are constant. If the gross investment line is above the depreciation line, capital accumulation will occur and there will be long-run growth in output per worker.

The *AK* model above is a very simple endogenous growth model. Its weakness is in defining a composite capital input (*K*) without any real justification for this. We have also not shown why gross investment (and savings) would be constant (although endogenizing saving is relatively straightforward and does not change the basic implications of the model). However, it is useful in that it highlights the role of the marginal product of capital in maintaining the accumulation of capital. All endogenous growth models make assumptions that allow a long-run incentive to accumulate one of the inputs into the production function. The parallel concept in microeconomics is: why should the incentive to innovate always be present? Many microeconomic studies assume that incentives are always there, but there are countries where little innovation occurs. The closed-economy models do not allow the possibility of using innovations from abroad, or importing technology in the neoclassical model.

The *AK* model also highlights a number of points that are common with many more complex endogenous growth models. One is that changes in the parameters of the model can have a permanent (long-run) effect on economic growth. For example, if the savings ratio is increased, the gross investment line pivots upward, and the rate of growth will increase permanently. This contrasts with the neoclassical model, as in that model any changes in the parameters of the model cause only short-run effects to growth rates.

Knowledge Externality Models

In 1986 Paul Romer published a paper entitled "Increasing returns and long run growth," which provided a model that yielded positive, long-run growth rates without assuming exogenous technical change. Many people consider this paper as starting endogenous growth theory. In it Romer used the word knowledge to define what we have called "technology"—or the letter A—up to this point. This may seem an unnecessary complication, but the term knowledge draws attention to the public good aspect of technology (see chapter 1). At the center of the model is the idea that when one firm generates new knowledge (to use in its production technology), some of this new knowledge can be helpful to other firms. Assuming that there is no payment associated with the transfer of knowledge, this is called a knowledge spillover, or a knowledge externality.

The central idea in Romer's paper is that while individual firms face diminishing returns to investing in knowledge, at the economy level the returns to knowledge can be increasing. Thus, individual firms experience diminishing returns to the factor of accumulation, which in turn means they can be modeled as competitive (since their production functions exhibit constant, not increasing, returns to scale). Economic growth, on the other hand, responds to the economy-level rate of return to knowledge, which is constant. This also means that there are increasing returns to scale at the economy level. Romer's model is therefore attempting to provide a consistent macroeconomic story for how the incentives to innovate for the firm are supported by the spillovers from other firms.

Since Romer's paper is technical, we will illustrate the core ideas using a simplified model. It turns out that these core ideas are contained in an earlier seminal paper by Arrow (1962a) (see Solow (1997) for a recent discussion of this paper). These papers assume that the stock of knowledge (A) is a function of the entire capital stock (K) of the economy. Let us be specific and say that

$$A = K^{\phi}, \quad \text{where } \phi > 0. \tag{8.8}$$

Consider now the standard Cobb–Douglas production function, with capital K and labor L:

$$Y = AK^{\alpha}L^{1-\alpha}, \quad \text{where } 0 < \alpha < 1. \tag{8.9}$$

As before, this can be viewed as an aggregate production function that simply replicates the production function faced by individual firms. However, we have now assumed that the knowledge available in the economy reflects the economy level of capital, hence we can substitute K^{ϕ} for A:

$$Y = AK^{\alpha}L^{1-\alpha} = K^{\phi}K^{\alpha}L^{1-\alpha} = K^{\phi+\alpha}L^{1-\alpha}. \tag{8.10}$$

Hence the model is asserting that aggregate output is governed by equation (8.10), even though the firms within the economy act as if they face (8.9). Note that if $\alpha + \phi$ equals 1, the economy-level marginal product of capital will be constant, implying that the incentive to accumulate capital is always present. Romer's model assumes that $\alpha + \phi$ equals 1, and this allows the economy to have a long-run positive rate of growth. As illustrated by the AK model, as long as the incentive to accumulate is always present, then long-run growth can occur. Readers may ask whether it is reasonable to assume that $\alpha + \phi$ equals exactly 1, and what would happen if $\alpha + \phi$ was above or below 1? In the case where $\alpha + \phi$ was greater than 1, the growth rate predicted by the model would accelerate—something that history shows does not happen for extended periods of time.[8] In the case where $\alpha + \phi$ was less than 1, the growth rate would converge to 0, just as in the neoclassical model. Thus, Romer's model is often criticized for having such a "knife-edge" property (see Solow 1994).

Central to the Arrow and Romer models is the fact that knowledge spillovers (i.e., positive externalities) occur between firms, hence the economy-level production function is different from the firm-level production function. This basic result turns out to have very important implications. The model suggests that:

(1) the competitive growth rate is below the socially optimal growth rate (due to the presence of knowledge externalities);

(2) shocks and policies may have permanent effects on a country's growth rate;

(3) large countries may grow faster (a scale effect).

---

[8] However, the definition of "extended" is not well-defined. For example, estimates indicate that GDP growth in Britain increased from 1.1% in 1700–1750 to a maximum of 2.9% in 1830—an eight-decade slow increase in growth (Crafts et al. 1989).

Let us consider the first of these implications: that the "competitive growth rate" is below the "socially optimal growth rate." The competitive growth rate is the rate of economic growth that the model produces if "government" does not intervene in any way in the economy.[9] It is worth stressing that a major achievement of the Romer model was to create a model that could have a positive long-run rate of growth driven solely by the decisions of firms and consumers (i.e., a "competitive growth rate"). As an example, suppose the competitive growth rate is 2% per annum. The inclusion of knowledge spillovers in the model means that, from the point of view of society, a higher growth rate is preferable (say, 2.5%). Thus, the presence of knowledge externalities in the model is crucial to both explaining the existence of long-run growth and also explaining why competitive markets may invest too little and cause growth rates to be lower than optimal.

The second implication—that shocks and policies can have permanent growth effects—is straightforward to see if they have effects on key parameters of the model (e.g., ϕ). This contrasts with the neoclassical model where shocks or policies would have short-run growth effects and only long-run level effects (i.e., the economy would converge to a new steady-state level of GDP per capita). The third implication—that there are scale effects—is considered later.

Human Capital Models

Another important set of endogenous growth models has placed *human capital* at the center of the growth process. The term human capital is defined as all the knowledge, education, training, and experience that is embodied in workers. Many economists feel happier with talking about human capital, rather than technology or knowledge, since it emphasizes the fact that there is always a human element to production technology.[10]

Lucas (1988) presented the first endogenous growth model highlighting human capital, although again there was an older paper that mapped out many of the basic ideas (Uzawa 1965).[11] Lucas defines human capital

---

[9] Clearly, the model is a simplified version of the real world, hence there is no inclusion of health, defense, education, or other standard government activities, hence we use the word "government" in a rather abstract way.

[10] In our view, all these various terms capture different elements of a complex process. The idea of disembodied knowledge can be useful at times, but often this knowledge is embodied in new forms of capital equipment and, of course, it is ultimately the human capital of workers that allows "disembodied" and "embodied" knowledge to be productive.

[11] Lucas, in fact, presented two models with human capital. In the text we focus on the model that highlights the main aspects of human capital as an engine of growth.

as the skill embodied in workers. The number of workers in the economy is N and each one has a human capital level of h (he assumes equal distribution of human capital). Let us assume that the number of workers in the economy is constant (i.e., population growth is zero, but old workers are replaced with new workers). Lucas assumes that the economy-wide stock of human capital can be used either to produce output (a proportion u) or to accumulate new human capital (a proportion $1 - u$). The production of output (Y) is given by

$$Y = AK^\alpha (uhN)^{1-\alpha} h_a^y, \quad \text{where } 0 < \alpha < 1 \text{ and } y \geqslant 0. \qquad (8.11)$$

Lucas assumed that technology (A) was constant. Note the presence in equation (8.11) of the term h_a^y. The variable h_a is defined as the "average human capital level" and is included to allow for an external effect of human capital (i.e., a positive externality). The idea is that as the average human capital of workers increases this does not just affect output through a direct, internal effect to firms, but there is an external effect that can also influence firms.[12] This external effect is not critical to the model producing long-run growth, but its presence does give rise to an additional market failure. Lucas assumes that human capital accumulation is given by

$$\frac{dh}{dt} = h(1 - u) \quad \text{or} \quad \frac{dh}{dt} \Big/ h = 1 - u. \qquad (8.12)$$

Equation (8.12) means that, as long as there is a constant fraction of human capital devoted to accumulation ($1 - u$), human capital can grow at a constant rate. Since individual workers will die at some point, there is an issue over how, if at all, human capital can be passed between generations. Lucas argues that as long as some human capital is passed between generations, perhaps within a family unit, the formulation in (8.12) can hold.[13] Hence, a constant growth rate of human capital accumulation occurs if $(1 - u)$ is constant. Lucas shows that such an allocation is possible in a competitive economy hence human capital accumulation can yield long-run economic growth. To see this note that as human capital grows, the effect is simply to scale up the input from workers (N in this model). This will increase output directly and also raise the marginal

---

[12] It is not strictly necessary to include h_a, since the model is defined in terms of the average human capital level (h), but Lucas wanted to draw attention to the possibility of an externality. For example, it could be that higher average skills allow workers to communicate better and that this has economy-wide, not intrafirm, effects.

[13] Lucas claims that as long as the human capital of each new generation is proportional to old workers, then (8.12) can hold. He notes that "human capital accumulation is a social activity, involving groups of people in a way that has no counterpart in the accumulation of physical capital" (Lucas 1988, p. 19).

product of capital. This means that output growth is continuous, while the number of workers (and the population) is constant, hence output per worker is growing at the same rate as human capital.

The Lucas model also has a "knife-edge" property, in a similar way to the knowledge-based models. In this case the human capital accumulation equation (8.12) must be precisely of that form. If this were not the case, then the growth rate of human capital would slowly fall or accelerate. In fact, all endogenous growth models tend to have such specific assumptions in order to obtain a steady, permanent rate of economic growth. As a reaction to this, Jones (1995) formulated a semiendogenous growth model, which relies on some exogenous level of population growth to generate a steady, permanent rate of economic growth. This model is discussed in the next section.

R&D and Creative Destruction Models

A further set of endogenous growth models focuses attention on firms as the generators of new technology and knowledge through R&D. These models also highlight the fact that firms are subject to competitive forces, which can destroy profits from existing products. These issues are familiar from part I of this book, which discussed how microeconomists view the process of innovation. The contribution of endogenous growth models based on such ideas is in how they try to model the economy-level implications of such forces.

There are a number of papers that started this modeling approach, including the key contributions by Romer (1990), Grossman and Helpman (1991), and Aghion and Howitt (1992). Here we will sketch an outline of the important aspects of these models in a way that links to the above discussion.[14] Although the models have a production function and a capital accumulation equation, the key driving force of economic growth is an R&D-based accumulation equation such as

$$\frac{dA}{dt} = \beta l_R A, \quad \text{where } \beta > 0. \tag{8.13}$$

This equation links the change in knowledge, or technology, to the labor allocated to the research sector (l_R) and the existing level of technology (A). If we divide both sides of equation (8.13) by A, we see that the growth

---

[14] The models do, in fact, contain some important differences in approach. The text concentrates on some of the key intuitive results. A common feature of these models is that they specify firm-level equations to capture decision making with respect to innovation. Each firm is assumed to be forward looking, rational, and profit maximizing. However, the models differ as to the nature of the innovation, as well as the assumptions made about the nature of competition.

rate of technology equals a positive constant multiplied by l_R. Hence, as long as there is a constant allocation of labor to the research center, then technology can grow at a constant rate. A constant growth rate of technology can generate a constant long-run rate of economic growth (as the basic neoclassical model demonstrates). While this may sound straightforward, the contribution of the model is to explore why firms would allocate labor to R&D in a competitive economy.

As discussed in parts I and II, a firm in a competitive economy realizes that if it can innovate, which the model views as generating some new knowledge, it has the opportunity to increase its profits. Some models assume the new knowledge will lead to a new product (product variety models) or a better version of an existing product (product quality, or ladder, models). Alternatively, the new knowledge could reduce the costs of production. These issues depend on the effectiveness of R&D. Importantly, the models assume that a firm's current R&D effectiveness depends on the economy-level R&D efforts in the past. This embeds the idea of R&D spillovers into the model. In some cases these spillovers may be small, leading to low R&D effectiveness and the possibility that innovation and growth will peter out. On the other hand, it could be that R&D effectiveness constantly increases, perhaps causing explosive growth. Acting as a moderator in this process is the role of competition. To understand this, consider a firm that launches a new successful product and manages to make a higher level of profits. These profits tend to attract new entrants that compete away these profits. Competitive pressure from future rivals is higher when R&D effectiveness is also high; whereas if R&D effectiveness is low, then so is the likelihood of competition from new entrants.

The creative-destruction models have to make various assumptions about the nature of competition. Some models assume that once a new product is invented the firm obtains a patent of infinite length. However, this cannot stop competitors inventing similar products that steadily reduce the profits from this market. Other models assume that firms leapfrog each other in terms of new versions of a set of products, with the latest product taking the entire market. Overall, therefore, the models make a range of assumptions about the effectiveness of R&D, the nature of property rights, demand conditions, and the process of competition. In particular, they assume that entry into R&D is free and that this drives down rates of return to a competitive level that reflects risk involved.[15]

---

[15] See chapter 5 for empirical evidence that suggests that this may not be true and that returns to R&D are often high.

The real interest in such models is in the potential insight they give into market failures. There are three key market failures highlighted by the models. The first is due to the presence of positive externalities, or spillovers, in the process of R&D or knowledge generation. The models assume that one firm's R&D investment can benefit, or spillover to, other firms. Such spillovers occur despite any attempts to protect the knowledge by the creating firm.[16] The presence of such spillovers implies that the competitive growth rate is below the socially optimal rate, hence providing a theoretical justification for intervention. In the context of R&D-based models, the specific intervention is a subsidy to R&D so as to increase firms' investment in R&D. Chapter 11 discusses R&D incentives and other policy options.

While the role of spillovers is often stressed in discussions about such models, it is important to stress that there are two other potential market failures in such models. The second is the appropriability effect, also called the consumer-surplus effect. This occurs since the profit-seeking firm acts like a monopolist, considering only their own profits and neglecting any increase in consumer surplus (which means general welfare accruing to consumers). This has already been discussed in box 5.1, but we recap and relate to the endogenous growth literature in box 8.3. The presence of the appropriability effect suggests that too little R&D is being done. The third effect is the business-stealing effect, also called the creative-destruction effect. This exists since each profit-seeking firm does not take into account the loss of profits to other firms through its new innovation. To see this, consider a situation where a new product from firm A starts making a profit of, say, £1 million per week, but that this new product reduces firm B's profits by £0.8 million. The net gain to society (in terms of profits) is £0.2 million, whereas firm A based all its private investment decisions on the basis of the £1 million. The business-stealing effect means that investment in R&D can be too high from society's point of view.

The presence of the three possible market failures—two suggesting R&D is too low, but one suggesting R&D is too high—means that the overall net outcome depends on the exact assumptions of the model. In general, the models stress that the presence of externalities, or spillovers, will dominate; meaning the competitive market will underinvest in R&D and innovation, hence the possibility of policy intervention. However, it must be stressed that the models are too general and stylized for any robust conclusions on this issue.

---

[16] The nature of spillovers, and specifically the inability of firms to prevent or get paid for them, are key assumptions of the model.

Box 8.3. R&D endogenous growth models and the microeconomics of new entry.

Box 5.1 discussed the microeconomics behind the idea of new entry of products. It was stressed that there are three possible effects, summarized again below.

Effect	Description	Outcome
Business-stealing effect	New firms ignore loss of profits by incumbents	Too many products
Appropriability effect	Firms cannot appropriate all consumer surplus	Too few products
Spillover effect	New products demonstrate knowledge to other firms	Too few products

In the endogenous growth literature, models often use the ideas of (horizontal) product variety and (vertical) product quality (also called product ladder models). Grossman and Helpman (1991) provide a good introduction to these models. In these growth models each firm is assumed to produce a single product, which is protected by an infinite patent. The firms have undertaken R&D in order to discover the new product, and entry into R&D is assumed to be competitive (i.e., reducing private returns to a competitive level). Depending on the specific assumptions of these models, this R&D-driven expansion of products can drive a positive rate of long-run growth.

Does this competitive system produce the optimal rate of economic growth? As above, in such a model there are three possible factors at work: business stealing, appropriability, and spillovers. In most R&D-based endogenous growth models the functional forms they use assume that the business-stealing and appropriability effects exactly offset each other, hence the presence of spillovers (R&D externalities) from new products implies that the socially optimal rate of growth is higher than the private growth rate (see Grossman and Helpman 1991, pp. 72, 106). Hence, despite their complexity, endogenous growth models—just like any other economic model—are dependent on their assumptions.

Competition and Growth

The previous section introduced the role of competitive conditions into the analysis. Here we recap on some of our discussion in chapter 5 and link it to economic growth models. It is helpful to think of two different aspects of competition: competition in the innovation process (dynamic competition) and competition in product markets (static competition).

Dynamic competition means that two or more firms are competing to produce a new innovation that will alter the nature of profits in that industry. As a simple example, suppose a monopolist produces a product and enjoys the associated monopoly profits. New research can discover a new product that will totally replace the old version, destroying the old monopoly but creating a new one. The endogenous growth models assume that the incumbent monopolist and potential entrants are equally good at R&D. They also show that the incumbent monopolist will have *lower* incentives to do R&D. The reason for this is that the incentive to do R&D is determined by the incremental change in profits for a firm, not simply the post-innovation profits. In this case the incumbent monopolist is already earning profits and hence takes the difference between the old and new profits as the incentive. New entrants consider the entire new profits as the incentive. Although these assumptions are extreme in that competition in the product market is unchanging (i.e., it is always a monopoly), it does highlight the role of competition in innovation. Without such competition incumbent firms face low incentives to innovate and, as a result, we would expect lower economic growth.[17]

However, competition in the R&D process need not always be beneficial. Suppose there are economies of scale in R&D at the firm level and an industry currently has, say, ten firms competing against each other in both R&D and in their product market. Reducing the number of firms in the industry may raise R&D per firm and lead to more innovations (since we assume that innovations are proportional to R&D per firm, not total R&D in the industry). Whether this case is realistic does depend on whether there are, in fact, economics of scale at the firm level.[18] This example also shows a link to product market competition, since it is changes in product market competition that will affect the number of firms in the industry.

Let us now consider innovation under static product market competition (PMC). In the early R&D and creative-destruction endogenous growth models the incentive to innovate was proportional to the profits from innovation. If the level of PMC was increased, the immediate effect

---

[17] Chapter 5 provides a fuller discussion of these issues. The low incentives facing the incumbent monopolist are due to the "replacement effect," after Arrow (1962b). It relies on R&D efficiency being the same for incumbent and entrant firms, as well as the new product totally replacing the old.

[18] Perreto (1999) provides a growth model related to this case.

was to lower profits and hence the incentive to innovate. This reduction in innovation in turn caused lower rates of economic growth. This "high-competition, low-growth" result was considered unappealing by economists, since there is a widely held view that "high" levels of competition are good for an economy. There is also some empirical support for such a view (see chapter 5). As a result, economists started to build more sophisticated models. Perhaps the most appealing of these to nonspecialists were those that introduce the possibility that firms may be inefficient to some extent. This could be due to an agency effect, whereby it is difficult to get managers to work as hard as shareholders would like. More generally, there is an extensive literature (mostly outside economics) in which firms are assumed to have some "slack" or "inefficiency." This inefficiency can be reduced as PMC is increased, allowing the possibility that firms will be forced to increase innovativeness.

Other models have introduced more realism to the process of PMC within industries (e.g., Aghion et al. 2001). Let us define *neck and neck* PMC as where all firms in an industry produce similar products. It is possible for a firm to *escape from competition,* at least for a while, if it makes an innovation. The innovation will yield higher profits, hence there is an incentive to escape from competition. However, recall that the incentive to innovate depends on the incremental change in profits: in this case the difference between escape from competition and neck and neck profits. It is possible that this difference may increase with PMC, even though the absolute level of both these types of profits may be lower under more intense PMC. Introducing the idea of firms trying to "escape" from intense PMC by innovating appears to have some real-world relevance, but it is clear that if one firm can constantly innovate away from its competitors, then the market structure would change to that of a monopoly. Given this, the endogenous models tend to include assumptions about the rate of imitation to ensure that firms never lose the threat of neck and neck competition. Overall, the effect of PMC on innovation and growth depends on a range of factors including how incentives change, the ease of imitation and the extent of spillovers.

Scale Effects and Policy Issues

One of the important debates that arises from the endogenous growth models concerns *scale effects.* The Romer R&D model predicted that the larger the size of the economy the higher the rate of economic growth. The basic reason for this can be seen from looking at (8.13). This equation implies that the rate of growth of technology $((dA/dt)/A)$ is directly proportional to researchers employed (l_R) in the R&D sector. An economy with a larger population and workforce would be expected to have more researchers in the R&D sector, hence technology growth would be faster, and so would economic growth. Such scale effects are present in many endogenous growth models. The underlying rationale is that the knowledge generated by one firm can affect all the other firms in the economy, hence the more firms there are the greater the extent of spillovers. Another way of discussing this issue is to say that knowledge is a nonrival, or public, good, hence all firms can benefit from its production. These are all ideas familiar from parts I and II, but endogenous growth models indicate the macroeconomic implications of them.

Some endogenous growth models also suggest that there can be a link between market size and the incentives to innovate. The basic idea is that large economies, such as the United States or the United Kingdom, provide a large potential market for an innovation, which will raise incentives for R&D. Such a link will depend on the nature of competition, but it is possible that scale effects can stem from market size. The presence of scale effects has important implications for policy. In the Romer model, increasing economic growth could be achieved by increasing the number of researchers, possibly by using an R&D subsidy. However, some authors have argued that the presence of scale effects is unrealistic and have developed models that do not contain such effects.[19] Empirical analysis that compares the growth rates of large and small economies has tended to find little evidence of scale effects.[20] It is clear that testing for scale effects is difficult in a world of international trade, finance, and knowledge flows. Equally, the assumption that knowledge is a public good and that all firms can benefit is restrictive. This is highlighted by part I of this book, and the microeconomic work on innovation, but is not something widely recognized in the endogenous growth models. From a policy perspective, scale effects do increase interest in the ideas of networks of innovators.

8.4 Evolutionary and Other Models

The endogenous growth models above are based on rational, profit-seeking firms who make optimal decisions about whether to innovate and invest. There are several other models that do not start with these

---

[19] Jones (1995) and Young (1998) are, perhaps, the best known. Jones (1999) contains a review of "scale effects" in endogenous growth models.

[20] Backus et al. (1992) find some evidence for manufacturing, but little at the economy level. Kremer (1993) looks at economic growth from one million years B.C. and suggests that scale effects are, in fact, important.

assumptions and consider economic growth as a more evolutionary and less optimized process. Perhaps the most famous of these was developed by Nelson and Winter (1982) in a book entitled *An Evolutionary Theory of Economic Growth*. Here they criticize the concept of a production function, which implies that firms know all potential methods of production. Instead they argue that firms explore production possibilities, through learning and by imitating others, leading to an evolutionary process of growth. These ideas have given rise to a literature exploring evolutionary concepts in economic growth (e.g., Engelmann 1994). An alternative way to view the growth process is given by Weitzman (1996). He asks whether the innovation process is really one of new combinations of existing ideas—he calls this *hybridizing growth theory* after the idea of creating new plant varieties. A key insight is that if innovation follows this combinatorial process, then the idea of diminishing returns is unlikely. There are so many potential new combinations of old ideas that there will always be new innovation opportunities. Related to this idea is that some innovations are so important that they spawn a huge range of new opportunities. Recently these have been labeled *general purpose technologies* and examples include electricity, automobiles, electronics, and the Internet (Helpman 1998).

This chapter has had little space to comment on some of the historical issues in economic growth, such as why the industrial revolution started in Britain, how population growth interacts with GDP growth, and whether countries can be trapped in low-growth equilibrium (Crafts 1996). Galor (2005) takes a broader, historical view of economic growth, asserting that it is important that growth theories are consistent with the main characteristics of economic growth through time. The *unified growth theory* that Galor develops pays close attention to historical developments, in contrast to the solely theoretical approach of neoclassical and endogenous growth models. A related approach is to consider the experiences of many countries over the post-World War period. A recent example of this has been the Commission on Growth and Development led by Michael Spence. El-Erian and Spence (2008), in a paper entitled "Growth strategies and dynamics: insights from country experiences," summarize the findings with a list of seven "ingredients" that are important in achieving economic growth:

(1) Using a market system of price signals, incentives, decentralization, and property rights.

(2) A government commitment to sustaining the growth process and to act in the interests of citizens.

(3) Effective governance and leadership policies.

(4) Competent macroeconomic management to secure stable inflation and investment, including foreign investment.

(5) High levels of saving and investment, including public infrastructure, education, and health.

(6) Resource mobility, especially labor mobility.

(7) Leveraging the global economy to accelerate growth.

These seven ingredients have taken us beyond the main focus of this chapter. Some of them also touch on international issues, which are the focus of the next chapter. They do, however, serve to remind us that economic growth is a complex process and that simple models can only help in providing a framework for analysis (see Easterly 2001; Rogers 2003).

8.5 Conclusions

This chapter has reviewed the key models that macroeconomists use to understand the process of economic growth, which we define as growth in GDP per capita. In broad terms, these models use two key relationships to analyze the process of economic growth: the production function and the accumulation function. The production function encapsulates the link between inputs—such as capital (both physical and human), labor, and technology—and the output (or GDP) of the economy. The accumulation equation describes how inputs can be accumulated through a process of investment, whether in capital or technology. Since investment is funded from savings, which is a share of final output (GDP), the two functions work together to produce growth as long as the incentive to invest is always present.

The neoclassical, or Solow–Swan, model looked only at the incentives to accumulate physical capital. Assuming a standard production function with a fixed level of technology, the model predicts that the economy converges to a steady-state level of capital per worker and economic growth stops. However, if technology grows, then it is possible to have a positive rate of economic growth. In the model, "technology" is effectively a parameter that represents innovation as defined in parts I and II of this book. The view that changes in technology, or innovation, drive economic growth may sound obvious, but the contribution of the model is to show clearly why this is the case. Importantly, the result does *not* show that investment in capital is unimportant: it is the combination of new technology and investment that creates economic growth, even though new technology may initiate the process. This result links directly to figure 1.1. In this diagram, stages 1–3 represented research and development, while stages 4 and 5 required investment in capacity for production.

The drawback of the neoclassical model is that the growth of technology is exogenous to the model. This led to the endogenous growth models, where the name reflects their attempt to endogenize the source of long-run growth. Many of these models analyze the process by which technology, also called knowledge, is accumulated. They also incorporated the idea that technology or knowledge generation could lead to spillover benefits to other firms. The presence of these spillovers adds realism to the models and also suggests that the free market may produce a suboptimal growth rate. This issue of market failure is familiar from chapter 1. Some endogenous growth models focus attention on human capital, again allowing for the possibility of externality effects that can lead to market failure. Other models highlight the role of firm-level investment in R&D and innovation, which shows a clear parallel with parts I and II of this book. Finally, some models investigate the role of competition in the growth process. These models find that the effect of increased competition depends on the nature of the market, the innovation process, and the characteristics of the firm. Finally, in section 8.4, we briefly reviewed some other approaches. Evolutionary growth models relax the strong assumptions made by endogenous growth models about optimizing agents. Weitzman's hybridizing growth theory casts some doubt on the neoclassical and endogenous models' fixation on the diminishing returns to capital. Comparative and historical appraisals of economic growth remind us of the complexity of factors involved, with the idea that growth required multiple ingredients, although there is no unique recipe.

All the models in this chapter have looked at growth from the perspective of a single economy, leaving the issues of international trade, finance, and knowledge flows aside. In today's increasingly interconnected world this appears to be a major omission. The next chapter discusses how these models change in an international setting and, more generally, analyzes innovation in the global economy.

Keywords

The neoclassical or Solow–Swan growth model.

The accumulation equation.

Convergence to steady state.

The golden rule.

The AK model and constant marginal returns to capital.

Endogenous growth models.

Growth and level effects of policies and shocks.

Scale effects.

Questions for Discussion

(1) What is the importance of diminishing marginal returns in the neo-classical model? How do other models deal with the possibility of diminishing returns?

(2) Explain the effect of (i) an increase in the savings ratio, (ii) a rise in population growth, and (iii) an increase in exogenous technology growth in the neoclassical model.

(3) What is the golden rule? Can you think of any countries that have broken the golden rule?

(4) What is the "knife-edge" property of endogenous growth models?

(5) Is more competition good for economic growth?

(6) Do scale effects mean that China's growth rate will always be high?

References

Aghion, P., and P. Howitt. 1992. A model of growth through creative destruction. *Econometrica* 60(2):323–51.

Aghion, P., C. Harris, P. Howitt, and J. Vickers. 2001. Competition, imitation and growth with step-by-step innovation. *Review of Economic Studies* 68(3): 467–92.

Arrow, K. 1962a. The economic consequences of learning by doing. *Review of Economic Studies* 29(80):155–73.

———. 1962b. Economic welfare and the allocation of resources for invention. In *The Rate and Direction of Inventive Activity* (ed. R. Nelson). Princeton University Press.

Backus, D. K., P. J. Kehoe, and T. J. Kehoe. 1992. In search of scale effects in trade and growth. *Journal of Economic Theory* 58(2):377–409.

Crafts, N. 1996. The first industrial revolution: a guided tour for growth economists. *American Economic Review* 86(2):197–201.

Crafts, N., S. Leybourne, and T. Mills. 1989. Trends and cycles in British industrial production 1700–1913. *Journal of the Royal Statistical Society* 152(1): 43–60.

Easterly, W. 2001. *The Elusive Quest for Growth: Economists' Adventures and Misadventures in the Tropics*. Boston, MA: MIT Press.

El-Erian, M., and M. Spence. 2008. Growth strategies and dynamics. *World Economics: The Journal of Current Economic Analysis and Policy* 9(1):57–96.

Eltis, W. 2000. *The Classical Theory of Economic Growth*. Basingstoke, U.K.: Palgrave.

Engelmann, F. 1994. A Schumpeterian model of endogenous innovation and growth. *Journal of Evolutionary Economics* 4(3):227–41.

Galor, O. 2005. From stagnation to growth: unified growth theory. In *Handbook of Economic Growth* (ed. P. Aghion and S. Durlauf). Amsterdam: North-Holland.

Grossman, G., and E. Helpman. 1991. *Innovation and Growth in the Global Economy.* Cambridge, MA: MIT Press.

Hahn, F., and R. Matthews. 1964. The theory of economic growth: a survey. *Economic Journal* 74:825–50.

Helpman, E. 1998. *General Purpose Technologies and Economic Growth.* Cambridge, MA: MIT Press.

Jones, C. 1995. R&D based models of economic growth. *Journal of Political Economy* 103(4):759–84.

——. 1999. Growth: with or without scale effects? *American Economic Review* 89(2):139–44.

Kremer, M. 1993. Population growth and technological change: one million B.C. to 1990. *Quarterly Journal of Economics* 108:681–716.

Lucas, R. E. 1988. On the mechanics of economic development. *Journal of Monetary Economics* 22:3–42.

Maddison, A. 2001. *The World Economy: A Millennial Perspective.* Paris: OECD.

Malthus, T. 1798. *An Essay on the Principle of Population.* Published anonymously. (Reprinted by Penguin (London) in 1970.)

Nelson, R., and S. Winter. 1982. *An Evolutionary Theory of Economic Growth.* Cambridge, MA: Harvard University Press.

Perreto, P. 1999. Cost reduction, entry, and the interdependence of market structure and economic growth. *Journal of Monetary Economics* 43:173–95.

Rogers, M. 2003. A survey of economic growth. *Economic Record* 79:112–36.

Romer, P. 1986. Increasing returns and long run growth. *Journal of Political Economy* 94(2):1,002–38.

——. 1990. Endogenous technological change. *Journal of Political Economy* 98(5):71–102.

Rostow, W. 1990. *Theorists of Economic Growth from David Hume to the Present.* Oxford University Press.

Ruttan, V. W. 2001. *Technology, Growth, and Development: An Induced Innovation Perspective.* Oxford University Press.

Solow, R. 1956. A contribution to the theory of economic growth. *Quarterly Journal of Economics* 70:65–94.

——. 1994. Perspectives on growth theory. *Journal of Economic Perspectives* 8(1):45–54.

——. 1997. *Learning from "Learning by Doing": Lessons for Economic Growth. Kenneth J. Arrow Lectures.* Stanford University Press.

Swan, T. 1956. Economic growth and capital accumulation. *Economic Record* 32:344–61.

Uzawa, H. 1965. Optimum technical change in an aggregative model of economic growth. *International Economic Review* 6(1):18–31.

Weitzman, M. 1996. Hybridizing growth theory. *American Economic Review* 86(2):207–12.

Young, A. 1998. Growth without scale effects. *Journal of Political Economy* 106(1):41–63.

9

Innovation and Globalization

9.1 What Is Globalization?

This chapter discusses how our understanding of innovation and growth changes as an economy becomes integrated with the world economy. We define *globalization* as "the increased interdependence of economies across the world." This definition covers a wide range of economic activities, such as trade, technology, finance, and migration. Transnational corporations (TNCs) have played an important role in globalization by increasingly breaking up their activities between countries (Friedman 2005). Globalization also alters the opportunities and threats facing smaller companies. The rise of the Internet and the falling cost of communications mean that all firms, whether small or large, can now more easily gain access to overseas economies. This could enable them to export their products, source inputs from overseas suppliers, or outsource some of their activities.

A major aspect of globalization is the increasing share of international trade as a proportion of world GDP. In 1970, the ratio of world imports to GDP was around 13%; by 1990 this had grown to 20% and by 2005 to 28%. Some of this increase is due to more trade between richer and poorer countries, but the highest growth has occurred in trade between rich countries. Rich countries increased their exports and imports of the same categories of products: a phenomenon known as intraindustry trade. For example, 80% of OECD trade takes place between OECD countries, and in many rich countries around 80% of manufacturing trade is intraindustry.[1] As will be discussed, traditional trade theories do not give strong rationales for this rise in intraindustry trade; in contrast, trade theories built around product innovation do provide some support.

History has also shown that high growth is often associated with rapid growth in exports. As an example, China's recent rapid GDP growth has

---

[1] The statistics in this paragraph are taken from Dean and Sebastia-Barriel (2004). They ask why trade has grown faster than world output and suggest that this has been driven by increased productivity in the tradable goods sector and reductions in tariffs.

been accompanied by rapidly increasing exports to G5 economies (for example, between 2000 and 2005 Chinese exports increased at a rate of around 25% per year, much more than GDP growth). This pattern of rapid export and GDP growth was experienced by Japan in the 1960s, 1970s, and 1980s, as well as by the so-called Asian Tigers (Hong Kong, Singapore, Taiwan, and South Korea). A key question that arises in these cases is causality. Did rapid GDP growth lead to rapid export growth or did exports pull up GDP growth? Or could it be that other factors—such as innovation—were behind the growth of both exports and GDP? The answers to these questions, and the link between globalization and innovation, are still debated and researched.

Another key aspect of globalization concerns international financial flows. Such flows can be divided into two separate types. First, some financial flows are called foreign direct investment (FDI), which means that the inward flow goes directly toward investment in factories, machines, and businesses. Second, there is portfolio investment, which means that the international inward investment is (principally) in shares and bonds. FDI has an important link to economic growth since it is intended to create new productive capacity and, in many cases, this capacity is for exporting. It is less clear how portfolio flows—the purchase of bonds or shares—might affect growth and exports, but it could raise domestic business investment.[2] However, this prompts us to consider another important distinction of FDI: in many cases the finance comes bundled with knowledge of how to produce. Hence it may be the knowledge and technology that accompanies FDI that provides important benefits to the domestic economy.

This leads us to perhaps the most important aspect of globalization: the flow of knowledge relating to new technology. Our discussion about FDI indicates that such flows are not automatic or easy. Learning new technology from overseas may take considerable effort and investment. It may require buying foreign machines and equipment, forming alliances with overseas companies, or enticing a TNC to undertake FDI in its economy. One of the difficulties of learning new technology is that of acquiring *tacit knowledge*; this is knowledge that cannot be written down or codified hence it must be learned by demonstration, discussion, and trial and error. In contrast, some technology can simply be learned by reading books, articles, or patents, although this

---

[2] The difficulty here is in knowing the ultimate impact of a portfolio investment. As a crude example, foreign investment in shares could channel money directly to a company for business investment, or to buy technology; alternatively, the company could use the money to buy overseas property.

may require foreign-language skills and appropriate scientific or technical skills. International migration can also assist in the flow of knowledge and technology, although there is a concern that many able people migrate from the poorer to richer countries (the so-called brain drain). The impact of IPRs on the ability of technology to flow between countries is also a critical issue.

Finally, as an economy opens up to globalization the competitive pressure on domestic firms tends to increase. This can be due to greater openness to imports or from increased TNC production in the country. The impact of competition on innovation and growth has been discussed in chapters 5, 6 and 8. To recap, there is still a debate over how the intensity of competition influences innovation. Some argue that there is an inverted U shape, with either too much or too little competition reducing innovation rates. Given this, the process of globalization could have different impacts on different countries depending on their initial level of competition.

This short discussion gives an indication of how far-reaching, and complex, the issue of globalization can be. In order to structure our discussion we look at four major aspects of globalization: namely trade, technology, finance, and intellectual property. Section 9.2 provides an overview of world trade and this is followed by a discussion of trade, growth, and innovation in section 9.3. Section 9.4 considers technology flows and, specifically, models of technological catch-up. Section 9.5 considers international financial flows and the controversial issue of capital market liberalization. Section 9.6 focuses on the role of intellectual property in a global world.

9.2 World Trade in Historical Perspective

Before looking at theoretical models and specific evidence on innovation and globalization it is worthwhile taking the long view of world trade. The origins of international trade date back at least to the start of the Silk Road (around 7000 B.C.). Animals, pottery, silk, and precious metals were exchanged along the Silk Road, which stretched from the Mediterranean through to China. From the seventeenth century, Britain, along with a few other European countries, increasingly engaged in international trade. In 1870 the world trade to GDP ratio was around 5%. This increased to 8% by 1914, but then fell back to 1870 levels in the 1930s. This decline was associated with the Great Depression in the United States and increased protectionism by many countries. During the 1930s many countries viewed imports as "taking away jobs from domestic workers," hence the use of tariffs. The problem with this argument is that imports are equal to exports at a world level, hence reducing your imports will ultimately create a reduction in your exports. It was only post-1950 that the world trade to GDP ratio grew rapidly, reaching around 18% by 2000 (figures are from Maddison (2001)). This growth is associated with the new institutions such as the GATT (the forerunner of the WTO), the IMF, and the World Bank, whose remit was to ensure freer trade, greater macroeconomic stability, and investment in poorer countries.[3]

9.3 Theories of Trade and Growth

Economists' most basic, and oldest, theory of international trade is the *theory of comparative advantage.* This states that when countries engage in trade, each country will specialize in the good(s) in which it has a relative, or comparative, advantage.[4] There are a number of models that explain trade in this way, but they differ concerning the key sources of comparative advantage. For Ricardo there were geographical differences between countries, such as climate or mineral deposits, and these led to persistent differences in productivity in the production of tradeable goods and services. For Heckscher and Ohlin, and also for Samuelson, whose theories are collectively known as the HOS model, the source of comparative advantage is not productivity, but rather the country's factor endowments (such as labor and capital) and the differential need for these factors to produce different products. In the HOS model of trade all countries are assumed to have access to identical production technology (see also section 10.4).

In either of these frameworks, as each country undergoes the process of specialization when opening to trade, there will be growth in combined GDP, but once specialization is complete growth will stop. This is because the models are static: there is no dynamic or growth element to these models. Nevertheless, we can draw a parallel with the basic neoclassical growth model of chapter 8. In that model growth in GDP per capita stops since the marginal product of capital falls as capital stock increased. The marginal product of capital represents the return

---

[3] GATT stands for the General Agreement on Tariffs and Trade; WTO stands for the World Trade Organization; and IMF stands for the International Monetary Fund.

[4] David Ricardo (1772–1823), who is credited with the theory of comparative advantage, used the example of Portugal and England, which both produced wine and cloth. Portugal had a comparative advantage in wine and England in cloth. Increased trade meant that both countries specialized.

on investment; hence, ultimately, no investors wanted to invest in additional capital per worker.[5] This was the situation for a closed economy. What happens if the economy is now opened to trade? The intuition is that the marginal products on the goods the economy exports will not fall so quickly, creating further growth opportunities.

A more complete way of thinking about this is to note that the marginal product of capital (or return on investment) has both a price component (how much you can sell output for) and an efficiency of capital component (how much output a unit of capital produces). In an economy, as the output of a good is increased we would normally expect both the price to fall and the efficiency of capital to fall, hence the marginal product of capital falls for both reasons. (In chapter 8 we did not consider the price component since the model only had one good.) When a small country opens to trade the price of its exports are set on world markets and, as a rough approximation, we can assume that the world price is independent of the level of exports. Hence, as the small country increases export production there is no price effect that causes the marginal product of capital to fall. This means that the return on investment can stay high for much longer, sustaining the high investment and rapid GDP increases. The so-called East Asian Miracle is often presented as an example of this situation. Through the 1960s, 1970s, and 1980s Hong Kong, Singapore, South Korea, and Taiwan experienced high rates of export and economic growth.[6] More recently, China has experienced very rapid export and economic growth, although it is no longer considered a small economy.[7]

More generally, when we look at fast-growing economies, we see that the goods they produce change substantially through time. Sustaining rapid growth in trade and the associated economic growth requires that countries shift their so-called *product space* into higher-value goods (Hidalgo et al. 2007). This is not to say that the above ideas on the marginal product of capital are wrong, only that these are a partial view of a dynamic situation. The dynamic situation includes changes in technology and design, along with an evolution of cost advantages across different locations. To understand this it is worthwhile to look at

---

[5] To be clear, there is investment in order to replace worn-out capital and maintain a constant capital to worker ratio.

[6] Ventura (1997) provides a theoretical treatment of these issues. The World Bank (1993) provided a major review of these, and other, Asian economies in the 1965–90 period. They stressed that such economies need to get a range of fundamentals correct in order to experience high rates of economic growth.

[7] For example, in 2000 China's exports to GDP ratio was 23%, but this had grown to 37% by 2005. Imports into China have also risen, from 21% in 2000 to 32% in 2005, hence China's current account surplus was approximately 5% of GDP. (These data are from the World Bank Web site.)

another group of trade theories collectively known as *technology theories of trade* or sometimes *product cycle* theories. In these models the underlying determinants of comparative advantage include knowledge and innovation.

An early theory of how and why different countries have varying product spaces was put forward by Raymond Vernon (1966). Vernon's theory considered every product to progress through three stages of development: *new product, maturing product,* and *standardized product.* Each economy has a different income level and tastes; hence domestic entrepreneurs are best at understanding which new products might be successful. This, Vernon suggested, supports the idea that many new products start production in high-income countries (he focused particularly on the United States).[8] In addition, a new product tends to undergo changes and adaptations in its early years and good communications with customers, suppliers, and even competitors are vital during this time. For these reasons, new product development tends to be based in the host economy. As the product matures, firms pay more attention to the benefits of moving production abroad. Such benefits include reducing transport costs and the unit production cost (by accessing cheaper labor or other factors of production). Ultimately, if and when the product has become fully standardized, the incentive to relocate production abroad, and import the product from overseas, becomes large.

Posner (1961) also provided some insight into the rapid rise in trade between advanced countries and, in particular, into the huge growth in intraindustry trade between advanced countries. Each country has a large demand for variety in consumer products, but with economies of scale it is not efficient for each country to produce all the varieties, so there is specialization in brands by country followed by trade in similar products. This again moves away from the HOS model, which assumes constant returns to scale in production.

The basic insights from the Vernon and Posner models of product development and its links to trade have been embedded in formal, mathematical models of trade and growth. Paul Krugman—who was awarded the 2008 Nobel prize in economics—published a paper in 1979 that combined economies of scale, and consumer preferences for diversity, into a trade model (see Krugman 1979). Subsequent models often simplify the world into North and South, where North represents high-income countries and South developing countries. The North is assumed to have an

---

[8] In discussing new product innovation, Vernon stressed the idea that knowledge is not sufficient for production and that there is specific know-how, or tacit knowledge, which is much more difficult to learn.

advantage in innovation and introduces a constant stream of new products or processes. The South has lower labor costs and produces some maturing and standardized products (using Vernon's language). Young (1991) contains an influential model of this kind. Young assumes that growth is an outcome of technological change and links this directly to *learning by doing*. The rate of learning by doing in an industry— and hence industry growth—depends on the size of the entire industry (hence he assumes there are knowledge spillovers within industries). When countries open to trade the model assumes specialization takes place. The South tends to switch resources from maturing products to standardized products, while the North tends to switch more resources into new product innovation. It is assumed that the new and maturing products have an inherently higher growth potential, hence the South ends up specializing in low-growth industries. The overall result is that the North tends to grow faster and the South slower. Such a result means *divergence* of GDP per capita. Despite the fact that divergence implies that the South is disadvantaged, the model shows that the South is still better off than in autarky (i.e., the South's GDP per capita grows faster under free trade).[9] Nevertheless, these types of trade and innovation models suggest that the North can do better from globalization.

An important assumption in Young's model is that knowledge spillovers are confined within the region. It is assumed that these knowledge spillovers augment the process of learning by doing. To be explicit, suppose that the North refers to the United States and consider the example of the aerospace industry. The model asserts that the rate of learning by doing in the U.S. aerospace industry depends on its size and also spillovers from other industries in the United States. These assumptions are roughly in line with the results of empirical research. The assumption of domestic knowledge spillovers is very important in driving Young's results. To carry on the example of the U.S. aerospace industry, Young assumes that the South cannot start an aerospace industry until learning by doing in that industry has fallen to a certain level (i.e., it is becoming a maturing product). If there were international knowledge spillovers, then this situation would be less likely: Southern firms may be able to compete in producing advanced products. The next section focuses on this issue.

---

[9] Young stresses, however, that the dynamics of the model are complex and, for instance, it is possible under certain conditions for the South to catch up: "if the initial difference between the two economies is small enough and the [South] population is large enough, the [South] can draw back the [North] and overtake it" (Young 1991, p. 395). The population size matters since this drives demand and thereby industry size, which is critical due to learning by doing.

9.4   International Knowledge and Technology Flows: Theory and Evidence

In any analysis of globalization perhaps the most critical aspect is if, and how, it affects the flow of knowledge and technology across countries. As countries trade they integrate their economies and move toward new patterns of production. Young's model above indicates that this can push developing countries into lower growth—as they specialize in producing goods that experience little or no technical progress. The way developing countries can avoid such a situation is to learn the technologies in higher-income economies and "leapfrog" up the product space. The basic idea of "technological catch-up" goes back a long way, but Gerschenkron (1962) and Abramovitz (1986) are often credited with seminal discussions.[10] In simple models, the amount of knowledge and technology that a follower country can learn from abroad depends on two factors. First, there is the size of the gap, or technological distance, between the follower and the leading country. Second, the absorptive capacity of the follower country, defined as the country's ability to find, learn, and implement new technology, affects the rate of catching-up. Follower countries that have high absorptive capacity and a sizable gap can experience rapid economic growth for a period of time. Box 9.1 contains a simple model of technological catch-up. This shows that ultimately the growth rate of the follower country will converge on the leading country's growth rate. This said, the formal model shows that even when growth rates converge the follower country will still have lower GDP per capita (i.e., there is no convergence in the level of GDP per capita).

The flow of technology between countries is also influenced by the IPR system. This is discussed in more detail in section 9.6 and chapter 12, but here we can flag some major issues. We concentrate on patents in the first instance; perfectly enforceable, worldwide patent protection for innovators in, say, the United States could prevent any technology transfer for the life of the patent.[11] After this the technology would become freely available. Hence, a perfectly enforceable patent system (with no licensing)—and assuming all technology could be directly learnt from the patent document—would introduce a fixed lag in technology transfer (or international diffusion). Given that much technology is tacit this scenario is unlikely. The existence of tacit knowledge suggests that technology

---

[10] Rogers (2003a) contains a full discussion of the origins of this idea.

[11] By "perfectly enforceable" we mean that there is no possibility of illegal use or copying (which is unrealistic). In addition, the statement rules out licensing the patents to others (which is also unrealistic).

transfer could take much longer and require countries to devote substantial resources (the idea of developing absorptive capacity). If patent protection is imperfect, this would allow technology transfer before the end of the patent as long as obstacles to the transfer were overcome.

Box 9.1. A simple catch-up model.

A starting point for formal analysis is the work of Nelson and Phelps (1966). (See Rogers (2003a, chapter 4) for a full discussion.) Let A be the technology level in the follower country, let T be the technology level in the lead country, and let $\phi(\cdot)$ be the absorptive capacity of the follower. As discussed in the main text, $\phi(\cdot)$ will depend on a range of factors. The growth rate of technology in the follower country is $((dA/dt)/A)$ and we assume it depends on

$$\frac{dA}{dt} \bigg/ A = \phi(\cdot) \left[\frac{T - A}{A} \right]. \tag{9.1}$$

Note that technology can only grow in the follower country by technology transfer (an assumption that can be altered).

Assume that T, the technology level in the leader country, grows at an exogenous constant rate g.[12] This system of differential equations (i.e., equation (9.1) and $dT/dt = gT$) can be solved to show that in the long run the growth of A must equal g (see section A.7 in the mathematical appendix). Intuitively, unless the growth rate of A equals the growth rate of T, the right-hand side of (9.1) must be changing, which in turn means the growth rate of A must be changing. Again looking at (9.1), we can see that if $A = T$, growth of A must be zero. Equally, as A tends to zero its growth rate will tend to infinity. This implies that there is an equilibrium value for $(T - A)/A$ where the growth rate of A equals g. This means we can set the left-hand side of (9.1) to g and rearrange to find that the equilibrium gap is $A/T = \phi/(\phi + g)$. Figure 9.1 illustrates this result.

The model predicts that countries which start with a technology ratio (A/T) below the long-run equilibrium level will experience rapid growth (relative to g). Conversely, countries which start with a technology ratio above $\phi/(\phi + g)$ will experience growth rates lower than g. Note that in equilibrium the level of technology of a follower country is below the level of the leader country. The equilibrium ratio will change if either

---

[12] For information, most empirical work assumes that the value of g is 0.02. This comes from observing that the average growth rate of GDP per capita in the United States over the last 100 years is around 2%. This means that there is an assumption that technology growth equals GDP per capita growth over the long run. This is the assumption in the steady state of the Solow growth model and in many endogenous growth models (see chapter 8).

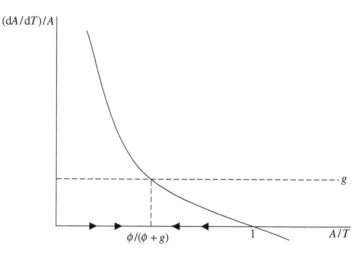

Figure 9.1. A technology catch-up model.

$\phi(\cdot)$ or g changes. For example, if a country was in equilibrium with a low value for A/T, an increase in $\phi(\cdot)$ (absorptive capacity) would lead to a short-run rise in growth rates as the economy adjusts to a new higher value of A/T.

The functional form of (9.1) is essentially arbitrary. In general, any functional form that satisfies the condition that knowledge growth is zero when the technology gap is zero could be considered. An alternative functional form would be

$$\frac{\mathrm{d}A}{\mathrm{d}t} \Big/ A = \phi(\cdot) \ln\left[\frac{T}{A}\right]. \tag{9.2}$$

The use of $\ln(T/A)$ is common in empirical growth work (see Dowrick and Rogers 2002).

A drawback of the catch-up model discussed above is that the empirical work on economic growth shows that many poor countries do not grow rapidly (which is an implication of the model). To add more realism to the model there are three possibilities: (i) redefine the technology gap in terms of an "appropriate technology gap"; (ii) assume the poorest countries have zero absorptive capacity; or (iii) introduce a model where there are fixed costs of learning technology from abroad.

The first possibility involves arguing that the poorest countries are so far behind that little of the technology in the lead country is directly useful. For example, aerospace and microprocessor technology is not directly relevant to poor agrarian economies. A difficulty with this argument is that, in reality, there are a range of countries between follower and leader all with different technology levels. The second argument—that some countries have zero absorptive capacity—is a reasonable description of some countries in some time periods. When China closed its borders to the rest of the world in the fifteenth century it stopped being able to learn from abroad. This was not a problem at the time—as China was a leader in technology—but by the nineteenth century China had fallen significantly behind the United States, the United Kingdom, and other countries.[13] More recently, countries isolated from the world (e.g., North Korea, Myanmar) might be thought of as having near-zero absorptive capacity. However, the third argument concerning the fixed costs of absorbing technology is most realistic. Consider a firm in a poor country that might like to learn about some new technology used overseas. It needs to invest a fixed amount in finding out about the new technology, perhaps by traveling overseas or buying machinery or hiring skilled workers. The fixed costs of these activities can reduce or prevent entirely the process of learning new technology; in terms of the model in box 9.1 they can cause $\phi(\cdot)$ to equal 0. A more formal model of this is contained in Rogers (2003a).

How much evidence is there that technology gaps are a key reason for the differences in GDP per capita across countries? A key problem in answering this question is how to measure "technology" at an economy level. As discussed in section 3.4, some researchers calculate country-level total factor productivity (TFP) and claim that this proxies "technology." Analysis of TFP and GDP per capita across many countries suggests that TFP accounts for a large proportion of the differences in GDP per capita (e.g., Hall and Jones 1999). However, as section 3.4 noted, the use of TFP is controversial and it is really a "residual" from a crude attempt to decompose GDP. Comin et al. (2006) argue that it is possible to measure technology more directly by looking at the intensity of its use across countries. For example, computers per capita and electricity consumption per capita can be calculated across countries and compared with the lead country (the United States). Since Spain's use of computers per capita in 2002 was the same as the United States's in 1989, it can be said that there was a thirteen-year "technology" lag. Comin et al. (2006) calculate ten different technology indicators and find that technology lags and GDP per capita lags are highly correlated. Technology gap models do seem to have a place in understanding growth.

A long-standing debate in the development economics literature has been the issue of protecting so-called *infant industries*. The basic idea

---

[13] Mokyr (1990, chapter 9) contains a full discussion of the stagnation of Chinese technology from 1400 onward; as might be expected, there are many other factors at work and no consensus on the ultimate reasons.

is that an industry and the firms within it require time to grow before they can successfully compete in international markets.[14] Its relevance here is that if poorer countries want to produce new products it may be difficult to jump to a position of international competitiveness. Should the government support these firms and industries? This is a controversial issue and economists differ widely in their attitudes. While it is clear that firms often need time and investment to develop competitiveness, it is less clear how much, if at all, the government should fund learning and investment. If private capital markets are working efficiently there may be no need for government support, as firms are generally thought better at identifying opportunities. However, there is considerable evidence that capital markets are not efficient, especially in poorer countries.[15]

Box 9.2. Technological catch-up viewed as a firm-level process.

This chapter discusses the process of technological catch-up largely in macro terms. In practice, firms are central to the process. Firms in poorer countries must have the incentives and resources to learn and absorb new technology. In most cases they must also seek out new markets, whether in the domestic economy or abroad, to which to sell the improved or new products that they produce. The difficulty in doing these things is why many people refer to the catching-up process as one of innovation. Hobday (2000) refers to such firms as "latecomers" and specifies two challenges they face. The first is one of technology. Latecomer firms lack important technology and are distanced from regions of R&D and innovation. They may also have relatively weak university and government research expertise in their domestic economy together with a lack of skilled labor. Learning and building technological capability is the latecomer's first challenge (see also Lall 1992). The second challenge concerns distance from consumers and markets. In many cases, selling to overseas markets represents a way of jump-starting their sales (the

---

[14] The infant industries argument has a long and controversial history. For example, in the nineteenth century German manufacturing firms argued it to allow them to compete against British firms. A review of the issues is contained in Slaughter (2003) and a detailed discussion of firms in developing countries is in Tybout (2000). In short, the infant industry argument has three main problems: (i) firms can have major difficulties learning the technology required so they never become efficient; (ii) even if firms become efficient they may lobby for continued protection; and (iii) even if firms become efficient the overall (opportunity) cost of the support may outweigh the benefits.

[15] A major contribution to these issues has been made by Hernando de Soto (2000). De Soto gives many examples of how capital markets fail. For example, if land titles are not defined, their owners cannot use these as collateral for loans.

domestic economy may have too low income to provide such a boost), but penetrating overseas markets involves learning about transport, tariffs, distribution, marketing, advertising, and customer expectations. By definition, overseas markets are likely to be far away, have a foreign language and different business culture. The combination of the technological and market-based challenges means that latecomer firms face severe barriers. How do they overcome these?

We will consider the example of Samsung Electronics, now a large transnational corporation in electronics with $100 billion worth of sales in 2007. South Korea's electronics exports increased from $2 billion in 1980 to $20 billion in 1991 and Samsung was one of a few Korean firms that drove this increase (the information here comes, principally, from Hobday (2000) and Kim (1997)). Samsung Electronics was started in 1969 as a joint venture with Sanyo of Japan and 106 employees were sent to Japan for training (this indicates the need to learn tacit knowledge). At the time, the Samsung Group was a large diversified conglomerate with considerable market power and resources. The Korean economy had a number of large firms, called "chaebols," which had close relationships with the government. Samsung undertook other joint ventures, and licensing agreements, with foreign companies in order to learn technologies related to electronic components and televisions. In the 1970s, Samsung decided to diversify into microwaves and video cassette recorders (VCRs) but were unable to find foreign partners. Instead, they decided to reverse engineer. In 1976 they started a project to reverse engineer a Panasonic microwave and build a prototype, completing the project in 1978. They did the same for VCRs starting in 1979. For Samsung Electronics, the process of acquiring the technological and production skills to manufacture and export electronic goods took many years and various different strategies. Their internal technological capability grew over the period with the aid of investment (helped by being part of a large company), but there was also help from the government. For example, in 1968 the government introduced the Electronics Industry Promotion Law and was, throughout the period, building university and research capability.

The history of Samsung Electronics gives an indication of the difficulties facing latecomer firms. There are many cases of firms that did not start, or could not make progress in, developing—although these tend not to be focused on by authors. There is still considerable controversy surrounding how, and if, governments should stimulate or support latecomer firms. Most would agree that any support should be focused

Table 9.1. Private capital flows into emerging
markets and developing countries.

	1996–98	1999–2001	2002	2003	2004	2005	2006
Total private capital flows (net)	167	75.7	90.1	168.3	239.4	271.1	220.9
Private FDI (net)	142.2	177.8	154.7	164.4	191.5	262.7	258.3
Private portfolio flows (net)	61.7	−1.1	−91.3	−11.7	21.1	23.3	−111.9
Bank loans, deposits, etc. (net)	−36.7	−101.1	26.0	14.5	25.1	−17.0	73.6

Source. IMF: World Economic Outlook.

Note. All figures quoted above are in billions of dollars.

and have time limits, to ensure that latecomer firms have maximum
incentives.

9.5 International Financial Flows

As discussed earlier it is useful to distinguish between two main forms of
private capital flows: foreign direct investment (FDI) and portfolio investment. The key difference between them is that FDI normally comes as
a package of investment, technology, and management and represents
a long-term investment; whereas portfolio investment is simply a purchase of shares or bonds.[16] Table 9.1 shows the net private capital flows
into emerging markets and developing countries over the last decade (as
defined by the IMF) together with a breakdown of these flows into FDI,
portfolio, and loans. There was a net inflow in each year, primarily driven
by FDI, but one can see variations across time and the components of
overall private capital flows.[17]

Table 9.1 shows flows into emerging markets and developing countries only, but there are also substantial flows between richer countries.

---

[16] FDI requires the investment to have a "lasting interest in the entity" (IMF 2007).
Clearly, this may be difficult to judge. FDI can include acquisitions, mergers, retained
profits (of a foreign affiliate or subsidiary), and intracompany loans (UNCTAD 2007).
Official, or public, flows of capital can also be important, especially for some poorer
countries, but we do not focus on this here.

[17] For information, out of the $220.9 billion in 2006, around 46% went to Asian countries
and 30% to central and eastern European countries—only 9% went to African countries.

For example, in 2006 around two thirds of total world FDI was into developed countries, with the United States the largest recipient.[18] The U.S. inflows were driven by massive mergers and acquisitions by European and Japanese TNCs. The rise in investment flows between developed countries parallels the rise in trade between such countries.

Foreign Direct Investment

The net benefit of FDI on the receiving economy has been a hotly debated topic for many decades. The possible effects of inward FDI include a direct positive impact on GDP, increased tax revenues, increased exports, increased competition on domestic firms, technology spillovers to domestic firms, and forward and backward linkages to domestic firms (which may, in turn, improve their productivity). Economic models of inward FDI tend to focus on only a subset of these possible effects (e.g., Markusen and Venables (1999), who focus on linkages). Empirical studies try to assess the average impact of FDI on an economy (e.g., its impact on subsequent economic growth or the balance of payments). Empirics indicate, as might be expected, that the impact of FDI on country growth varies according to other characteristics of the economy—such as level of education or trade openness—but there is now a general presumption that FDI can have a net benefit.[19] It is, of course, possible to conduct more detailed social cost–benefit analysis of specific FDI projects. Such studies face a range of problems and, of course, deliberately do not attempt to generalize.[20] Many of these studies focus on the effects of FDI on developing countries as this is where positive benefits would be hoped for. The investment trends of the last two decades make this issue critical as UNCTAD estimate that the inward FDI stock in developing countries is now one third of GDP (up from 10% in 1980).

Here we have focused on the effects of FDI on the receiving economy, but it is important to remember that the levels of FDI are driven by factors in the originating economy and, in particular, the activities of TNCs.

---

[18] The proportion of world FDI flows accounted for by developed countries has averaged 72% over the 1970–2006 period, with a high of 90% in 1974 and a low of 56% in 2004 (these are the authors' own calculations based on UNCTAD (2007) FDI data).

[19] In an empirical study of sixty-nine developing countries Borensztein et al. (1998) find that FDI can raise growth rates through technology flows, although this only occurs above a threshold level of human capital. Nair-Reichert and Weinhold (2001) find that more FDI may raise a country's growth rate, especially if trade openness is high. We should note that trade openness is negatively correlated with a range of other characteristics, such as corruption levels and state intervention in the economy, so that it is always difficult to pinpoint relationships.

[20] Helleiner (1989, p. 1,457 especially) provides a discussion and notes that the majority of such studies tend to find positive net benefits of FDI, although a substantial minority do not.

Helpman et al. (2004) outline a model and present empirics for the U.S. economy. They note that TNC sales have increased even faster than world trade in the last two decades. U.S. firms can serve foreign markets by either exporting, licensing firms in the foreign economy, or using FDI to set up domestic production plants. The higher fixed costs, but lower variable costs, of FDI assumed by their model implies that only the most efficient firms use FDI, something that has support from their empirical analysis.

Portfolio Investment

The role of portfolio investment in economic growth and innovation is, perhaps, even more controversial than FDI. The ease with which money can flow into and out of the economy, as investors buy and sell shares (equities), bonds, land, and other assets, is often discussed under *capital mobility* or *capital market liberalization*. Perfect capital mobility implies that money can freely flow into and out of an economy, for example, due to a change in domestic interest rates or a change in expectations about the value of the stock market. Table 9.1 shows that net private inflows into emerging and developing countries fell from an average of $167 billion in 1996–98 to $76 billion in 1999–2001, a fall associated with the Asian Crisis (see below). All of this fall was due to outflows of portfolio investment, bank loans, and deposits. In the last three decades the G7 economies have pursued capital market liberalization.[21] Controversially, the World Bank and IMF have also pressured many developing countries to pursue liberalization as well.[22]

The basic argument for capital market liberalization is that it allows investors to pursue the best returns, whether these are in the United States or China or any other country. The competition for international funds should improve financial markets everywhere and also allow diversification of investors' portfolios. These forces, in theory, should maximize investment returns and thereby societal wellbeing. This should

---

[21] A short history of capital mobility among leading economies is that in the late nineteenth century more and more countries adhered to the "gold standard" (meaning that currencies were pegged to the value of gold and hence investments of money or gold across borders was largely open). After World War I many countries gave up the gold standard and international capital mobility was reduced. The Depression of the 1930s reduced both trade and capital flows substantially. After World War II the IMF and World Bank, along with the U.S. dollar becoming the world currency, raised international capital mobility.

[22] The World Bank, IMF, and other Washington-based organizations pursued a number of related policies in the 1980s and 1990s that became known as the "Washington Consensus." Williamson (2000) reviews the term he coined and how it has impacted on poverty and growth.

raise economic growth but it also implies that the most innovative firms and countries will benefit the most.

The main argument against capital market liberalization is that it may increase the instability of the financial and economic system. Sudden inflows or outflows of capital can destabilize the banking sector and can cause exchange rates and interest rates to move dramatically. Stiglitz (2000) provides an overview of these aspects and concludes that unfettered capital market liberalization is likely to harm growth. He discusses the large losses in GDP incurred during the Asian Crisis in the late 1990s, a crisis which it is often felt was exacerbated by the absence of short-term capital controls in some Asian countries. In contrast, China and India were two countries with capital controls and these countries were much less affected by the Asian Crisis. Table 9.1 shows that net private capital inflow dropped substantially in the 1999–2001 period and did not recover until 2003. Note also that this fall was driven not by FDI changes, but by changes to portfolio flows and deposits.

The debate over the impact of capital market liberalism on developing and emerging markets is not settled. It is clear that the choice will depend on the economy's characteristics and the international environment. In terms of the latter, global foreign exchange (FX) market turnover has increased from around $880 billion in 1992 to $3.2 trillion in 2007 (Heath et al. 2007). This said, the ratio of FX turnover to total trade has only increased slightly (from 22% to 24%), while the ratio of FX turnover to total trade plus capital flows has decreased slightly.

International Venture Capital

Venture capital (VC) represents a subcategory of FDI that is of vital importance. Venture capitalists seek out new and innovative firms and aim to both invest and supply expertise in order to increase their chances of success. This means that VC is often seen as a critical component in a dynamic and entrepreneurial economy. In fact, the amount of VC is used as an indicator of the innovativeness in an economy. VC investors supply capital to startup firms that are pursuing high-risk strategies, often in high-tech industries (around 60% of OECD VC is estimated to go to high-tech firms (OECD 2005a)). VC investments can be divided into three categories: seed capital (the initial capital to investigate a business idea), start-up capital (product development and marketing), and expansion capital. The world's largest VC market is in the United States, with around US$26 billion invested in 2006 (National Venture Capital

Association 2008).[23] The United States is also the primary international source of VC, although much of this tends to be concentrated in flows to the United Kingdom and Israel. In the United Kingdom, 70% of VC comes from abroad (OECD 2005a). Other countries, such as Norway and Japan, have very low levels of VC from abroad. The lack of globalization of VC reflects the complexity and expertise involved. Investors need to evaluate and monitor firms closely and they also need in-depth knowledge, both of the system of taxation in the country where they are investing and of the workings of international financial markets, in order to allow them to pursue optimal exit strategies when necessary.

9.6   International Aspects of IPRs

Historically each country selected the type of IPR system that it desired and tended to ignore the rights of foreign inventors and creators. In the late nineteenth century this started to change as various international treaties established the principle of "national treatment of foreigners."[24] National treatment means that foreigners are allowed to have the same IPRs as domestic residents. This meant that countries could choose both their national system and whether to join the international conventions. For example, the United States did not join the Berne Convention until 1989. Allowing countries the flexibility to choose their IPR systems sounds like a good idea, but it can lead to some countries engaging in free riding. As discussed in chapter 1, knowledge has the characteristics of a pure public good, hence there is an incentive to let other countries generate it and then to free ride. This incentive to free ride creates a situation where countries would choose less IPR protection than a world government that was attempting to maximize world welfare. Box 9.3 discusses these issues in more detail.

Box 9.3. Choice of patent system in a two-country model.

Let us consider there to be two countries, A and B. Invention is possible in both countries and we assume that the inventor receives a patent of duration T_A or T_B. Given this situation, what type of IPR system would each country choose? In this simple model the only two choices involved

---

[23] As a percentage of GDP the United States spends around 0.36% on VC. The only OECD country that was higher was Iceland (0.5%), although this may have been overtaken by the events of 2008. These figures are for 2000–2003 and are drawn from OECD (2005a).

[24] The 1883 Paris Convention started this process for patents and other industrial property; in 1886 the Berne Convention started the process for copyright.

are length of patent protection and how to treat foreigners. A formal model of this situation is contained in Scotchmer (2004), but here we focus on the key intuition.

A first observation is that each country appears to have an incentive not to allow foreigners IPRs, since in doing so they will simply generate a flow of profits to residents in the other country. An extreme case of this is when, for example, country B has no domestic inventors. Having an IPR system in country B will simply allow inventors from A to charge monopoly prices and make profits. In such a situation country B would like to free ride. The prevention of this is the rationale of the international treaties to create "national treatment" mentioned above.

If we now assume that there is national treatment, what lengths of protection will each country select? As before, an extreme case is when country B has no domestic inventors. This implies that $T_B = 0$ (an outcome the same as if there was no national treatment). More realistically, each country would want to set $T_i > 0$ ($i = A, B$) to encourage domestic inventors. The discussion of optimal patent length in section 2.7 and in box 2.1 might be thought to cover this case, but in an international context this is not the case. As one country increases T it offers more incentive to both domestic and foreign inventors and, of course, foreign inventors extract a flow of profits.

Suppose country A attempts to maximize domestic welfare by choosing a duration of protection. A key issue to recognize here is that country A does not consider the welfare of country B. Country A realizes that if it increases T_A, then the outflow of profits to foreign innovations will increase. Thus it recognizes that innovation in B will increase, and that more patents will be taken out in its own country, but it does not include the profits or welfare associated with these in country B. The fact that neither country considers the welfare of the other will cause the final choices of T_A and T_B to be inefficient from a global point of view. A global government would want protection to be longer in both countries, but the countries acting individually will always choose lower levels of protection.

The main results of the formal analysis of international IPRs are as follows (remembering that "national treatment" means giving the same IPR rights to foreigners).

- Without any international treaties to enforce "national treatment," each country has an incentive to free ride on other countries' innovations by not granting IPRs to foreigners.

- With "national treatment" each country will select length of protection to maximize their own welfare. Both countries will choose a globally inefficient outcome, with patent protection too short (i.e., $T_i < T^*$), since they do not give any weight to welfare improvements in the other country.

These results imply that there is an argument for international harmonization of length of protection. In 1996 the TRIPS agreement started this process for many countries.[25] Signing up to TRIPS also became necessary for membership of the WTO. The TRIPS agreement specifies minimum lengths of patent protection (and other IPRs) for all countries: twenty years in the case of patents. This does not prevent individual countries granting more protection, but it does limit the possibility of free riding. Despite the above comments, the TRIPS agreement is highly controversial and many developing countries view it as a way in which intellectual property producing countries (e.g., the United States) can extract profits from poor countries.[26] We return to a discussion of TRIPS in chapter 12. This is an issue not directly covered by the model in box 9.3, since it involves the *distribution* of welfare across countries (i.e., the globally efficient outcome simply looks at maximizing total welfare and not at how this was shared among countries). The intuition of this case can be seen if we consider country B to have no inventors, hence it has no interest in having patent protection to encourage domestic invention. Imposition of a twenty-year patent as mandated by TRIPS will raise prices in country B and extract a flow of profits. Nevertheless, it could be argued that TRIPS will increase the number of inventions in country A (since the incentive to an inventor in country A will now be profits in both A and B). Can this increased invention outweigh the obvious direct losses to country B?

Helpman (1993) tries to answer just this question. In order to do so it is important to consider trade links between the two countries, something that the above model discussion has not. In addition, he makes the assumption that off-patent products can be produced in country B (as it is assumed that country B has lower wage costs). Adding trade and different wage costs considerably complicates the model. For example, if country A produces more and more new goods, then its terms of trade will fall making it worse off. The basic answer from Helpman's model is that country B will not benefit from stronger IPRs. Country A can benefit, especially if it can use FDI to locate some production in low-wage country B, but even this depends on the exact parameters of the model.

---

[25] Although TRIPS came into force on January 1, 1996, developing countries were given various extensions of time to achieve compliance (see Watal 1998).

[26] The origins of TRIPS are reviewed in Drahos and Braithwaite (2002), which includes a discussion of the role of U.S. companies' lobbying power.

9.7 Conclusions

Globalization—defined as the increasing interdependence of economic activity—has many elements and this chapter has focused on trade, technology, and finance. The rapid growth of trade and financial flows has important links to economic growth in some countries. The association between rapid export growth and GDP growth in such countries as Japan, South Korea, and, more recently, China is an important feature of high-growth economies. The export–growth nexus is complex and we should draw attention to two issues. First, export success relies on access to overseas markets. Historically, a country's access to the U.S. market was critical and this meant political relationships were important (both Japan and South Korea enjoyed good relations with the United States). Second, the direction of causality is not clear. Does export success drive economic growth? Or does rapid economic growth drive exports? Or, indeed, are there other factors that drive both exports and growth? Technology may well be such a factor. Technology, in this context, essentially means the ability of domestic firms to innovate by using techniques and ideas from overseas.[27]

How do domestic firms in developing countries learn new technology? This chapter has summarized the answer to this difficult question by introducing the idea of absorptive capacity. This represents the capacity of the country to access, learn, and implement new ideas from abroad. Some of these ideas may require adaptation to local conditions. The process of absorbing new ideas into an economy is underpinned by a range of general and specialist factors, including the strength of business, educational, and scientific links with advanced countries. Building up absorptive capacity, therefore, requires time and investment.

International financial flows are also a critical aspect of globalization. FDI can bring a bundle of capital, know-how, and access to overseas markets directly into an economy. For this reason FDI can be a powerful force in raising the level of economic growth and trade. The outcome of FDI is not always positive, as sometimes the projects selected, and the commitment made, are not conducive. FDI also has effects on domestic firms, such as through direct competition or from buying inputs, which can have positive or negative effects. Portfolio investment has an even more contentious role. In theory, open capital markets should increase the efficiency of investment, leading to higher returns and growth. In practice,

---

[27] Paul Romer (1992, 1993) has written about these issues in terms of "idea gaps." Countries first need to generate ideas—which includes those relating to technology, innovation, marketing, management, etc.—before they can pursue investment and export opportunities. He cites the example of Mauritius, where migrants brought new ideas that then laid the foundation for investment.

there are concerns that open capital markets may lead to rapid inflows and outflows which can destabilize the economy by introducing volatility into exchange and interest rates. Such macroeconomic instability can, in turn, reduce investment and growth.

The chapter also highlighted that the effects of globalization are likely to vary across countries. Poorer countries, high-growth countries, and developed countries are all likely to experience different effects. Poor, low-growth economies by definition have low rates of innovation and absorptive capacity, hence are less likely to gain from potential technology flows. The TRIPS agreement may antagonize this situation (see also chapter 12). Such countries may struggle to develop export markets and imports may impose high and destructive rates of competition on domestic firms.[28] In contrast, high-growth economies have conducive domestic factors that allow innovation and investment (e.g., good education, low corruption, well-defined property rights, functioning banking systems). Their higher absorptive capacity, and the increased potential for exports and FDI created by the globalization process, act to reinforce their success.

The arguments in the previous paragraph suggest that globalization may be polarizing the performance of countries: the poor countries may be getting poorer, while some emerging markets experience high growth rates. The empirical evidence for such a process is mixed. If one looks at evidence going back to 1870—which incorporates the period of globalization up to 1914 and the post-1945 period—there is some evidence that suggests that polarization has occurred.[29] However, analyses over the post-1960 period, over a wide range of countries, are ambiguous about whether inequality between countries is getting worse. Furthermore, the strong growth performance of China and India in the last fifteen years—if one takes account of their large populations—indicates that worldwide average GDP per capita is becoming more equal (Milanovic 2007).

This chapter also took a first look at international aspects of IPRs (section 9.6). The main message is that individual countries have an incentive to "free ride" on the intellectual property created by other countries. The idea of national treatment—giving the same IPRs to foreigners—is intended to prevent such free riding. The first international treaties

---

[28] The poorest countries may also rely on agricultural exports that often face trade barriers. The fact that the United States, Europe, and Japan subsidize and protect their agriculture, sometimes to the detriment of poorer countries, has been studied by Stiglitz and Charlton (2005).

[29] Pritchett (1997), in a paper entitled "Divergence, big time," analyzes countries' growth experiences from 1870 to 1990. He finds that the gap between rich and poor countries has risen fivefold.

to foster national treatment date from the late nineteenth century and TRIPS can be seen as an extension of these. Despite this, the distributional aspects of TRIPS are very contentious—an issue we return to in chapter 12.

This chapter has not focused on the impact of globalization on high-income economies. Many of the key elements of globalization—trade, FDI, and TRIPS—have been driven by the large TNCs that are based in developed economies. This suggests that the profits and shareholders of TNCs benefit. In addition, various theoretical models suggest that high-income economies should benefit; there is also no empirical evidence to suggest that their growth rates have fallen. However, there are concerns that increased world trade and off-shoring have led to many jobs being lost in developed countries. Clearly, the growth of exports from poorer countries implies that some types of jobs in richer countries will be lost, but the expectation is that new jobs will be created as the economy shifts its structure to new products. The complex relationships between employment, technology, and trade are the subject of the next chapter.

Keywords

Transnational corporations (TNCs).

The theory of comparative advantage.

Exports and diminishing returns to capital.

Trade and product development models.

Technological catch-up and absorptive capacity.

FDI and portfolio investment.

National treatment and free riding.

Questions for Discussion

(1) What theories of trade are best able to explain the rapid rise in world trade to GDP ratio since 1950?

(2) Do exports *cause* economic growth?

(3) Which model is best for understanding technological catch-up by poorer countries?

(4) "International financial flows can only hinder economic growth." Discuss.

(5) What conceptual factors are involved in international IPR agreements?

(6) Under what circumstances might the TRIPS agreement damage welfare in poorer countries?

References

Abramovitz, M. 1986. Catching up, forging ahead, and falling behind. *Journal of Economic History* 46(2):385–406.

Borensztein, E., J. De-Gregorio, and J. W. Lee. 1998. How does foreign direct investment affect economic growth? *Journal of International Economics* 45(1): 115–35.

Comin, D., B. Hobijn, and E. Rovito. 2006. World technology usage lags. NBER Working Paper 12677.

Dean, M., and M. Sebastia-Barriel. 2004. Why has world trade grown faster than world output? *Bank of England Quarterly Bulletin* 3:310–20.

de Soto, H. 2000. *The Mystery of Capital: Why Capitalism Triumphs in the West but Fails Everywhere Else.* Oxford University Press.

Dowrick, S., and M. Rogers. 2002. Classical and technological convergence: beyond the Solow–Swan model. *Oxford Economic Papers* 54(3):369–85.

Drahos, P., and J. Braithwaite. 2002. *Information Feudalism: Who Owns the Knowledge Economy?* London: Earthscan.

Friedman, T. 2005. *The World Is Flat: A Brief History of the Globalized World in the 21st Century.* London: Penguin.

Gerschenkron, A. 1962. *Economic Backwardness in Historical Perspective.* Cambridge, MA: Harvard University Press.

Hall, R., and C. Jones. 1999. Why do some countries produce so much more output per worker than others? *Quarterly Journal of Economics* 114:83–116.

Heath, A., C. Upper, P. Gallardo, P. Mesny, and C. Mallo. 2007. *Triennial Central Bank Survey: Foreign Exchange and Derivatives Market Activity in 2007* (available at www.bis.org/publ/rpfxf07t.pdf?noframes=1). Basel: Bank for International Settlements.

Helleiner, G. 1989. Transnational corporations and direct foreign investment. In *Handbook of Development Economics* (ed. H. Chenery and T. Srinivasan). Amsterdam: North-Holland.

Helpman, E. 1993. Innovation, imitation and intellectual property rights. *Econometrica* 30:27–47.

Helpman, E., M. Melitz, and S. Yeaple. 2004. Export versus FDI with heterogeneous firms. *American Economic Review* 94(1):300–316.

Hidalgo, C., B. Klinger, A. Barabasi, and R. Hausman. 2007. The product space conditions for the development of nations. *Science* 317:482–87.

Hobday, M. 2000. East Asian latecomer firms: learning the technology of electronics. *World Development* 23(7):1,171–93.

IMF. 2007. *Balance of Payments.* IMF Manual (available at www.imf.org/external/np/sta/bop/BOPman.pdf).

Kim, Y. 1997. Technological capabilities and Samsung electronics: international production network in Asia. BRIE Working Paper 106.

Krugman, P. 1979. Increasing returns, monopolistic competition, and international trade. *Journal of International Economics* 9:469–79.

Lall, S. 1992. Technological capabilities and industrialization. *World Development* 20(2):165–86.

Maddison, A. 2001. *The World Economy: A Millennial Perspective.* Paris: OECD.

Markusen, J. R., and A. J. Venables. 1999. Foreign direct investment as a catalyst for industrial development. *European Economic Review* 43(2):335–56.

Milanovic, B. 2007. *Worlds Apart: Measuring International and Global Inequality.* Princeton University Press.

Mokyr, J. 1990. *The Lever of Riches: Technological Creativity and Economic Progress.* Oxford University Press.

Nair-Reichert, U., and D. Weinhold. 2001. Causality tests for cross-country panels: a new look at FDI and economic growth in developing countries. *Oxford Bulletin of Economics and Statistics* 63(2):153–71.

National Venture Capital Association. 2008. Industry statistics. Web resource (available at www.nvca.org/ffax.html).

Nelson, R., and E. Phelps. 1966. Investment in humans, technological diffusion, and economic growth. *American Economic Review* 56:69–75.

OECD. 2005a. *Science, Technology and Industry Scoreboard.* Paris: OECD.

Posner, M. 1961. International trade and technical change. *Oxford Economic Papers* 13:323–41.

Pritchett, L. 1997. Divergence, big time. *Journal of Economic Perspectives* 11(3): 3–17.

Rogers, M. 2003a. *Knowledge, Technological Catch-up and Economic Growth.* Cheltenham, U.K.: Edward Elgar.

Romer, P. 1992. Two strategies for economic development: using ideas and producing ideas. In *World Bank Annual Conference on Development Economics, Washington, DC*, pp. 63–91. (Also published in 1998 in *The Strategic Management of Intellectual Property* (ed. D. A. Klein), pp. 211–38. Butterworth-Heinemann.)

——. 1993. Idea gaps and objects gaps. *Journal of Monetary Economics* 32:543–73.

Scotchmer, S. 2004. *Innovation and Incentives.* Cambridge, MA: MIT Press.

Slaughter, M. 2003. Infant-industry protection and trade liberalization in developing countries. Report submitted to USAID by Nathan Associates (available at www.nathaninc.com).

Stiglitz, J., and A. Charlton. 2005. *Fair Trade for All: How Trade Can Promote Development.* Oxford University Press.

Tybout, J. R. 2000. Manufacturing firms in developing countries: how well do they do, and why? *Journal of Economic Literature* 38(1):11–44.

UNCTAD. 2007. *World Investment Report.* New York/Geneva: United Nations.

Ventura, J. 1997. Growth and interdependence. *Quarterly Journal of Economics* 112(1):57–84.

Vernon, R. 1966. The product cycle hypothesis in a new international environment. *Quarterly Journal of Economics* 80:255–67.

Watal, J. 1998. The TRIPS agreement and developing countries: strong, weak or balanced protection? *Journal of World Intellectual Property* 1:281–307.

Williamson, J. 2000. What should the World Bank think about the Washington consensus? *World Bank Research Observer* 15(2):251–64.

World Bank. 1993. *The East Asian Miracle: Economic Growth and Public Policy.* Oxford University Press.

Young, A. 1991. Learning by doing and the dynamic effects of international trade. *Quarterly Journal of Economics* 106:369–405.

10
Technology, Wages, and Jobs

10.1 Introduction

This chapter focuses on the consequences of innovation for the labor market, by investigating how innovation and the diffusion of new technology affect the level of employment, wages, and the occupational structure. The chapter also explores the interaction between labor market institutions, specifically workers' unions, and the rate of R&D spending, as well as examining union influence on the sharing of the profits from innovation. The first half of this chapter sets out the microeconomics of labor markets, exploring the role of new technology and product innovation at the firm and industry level. We also review some empirical microeconomic evidence to see whether it supports the predictions of the economic theory.

Over the long term, innovation is seen as fundamental to the growth of output, which in turn sustains the demand for workers. The latter half of the chapter returns to the interactions between innovation, international trade, and economic growth, but with a focus on how these forces determine the composition of the job market as well as their impact on the wage differentials between skilled and unskilled workers. In the modern era of the *knowledge economy*, where, in advanced countries, the majority of workers are employed in service activities, the predominant view is that high-skilled workers are complementary to high-technology capital and knowledge stocks, while those with lower skills are substitutes for capital. The term *skill-biased technological change* has been coined to describe this phenomenon. It implies that high-skilled workers will benefit from new technology, while low-skilled workers will suffer a loss of demand leading to lower wages and higher unemployment.

10.2 Microeconomic Models of Innovation and Labor Markets

Innovation and Employment

As discussed in chapter 1, a process innovation causes a lowering of costs, with the possibility of increased demand and, thus, output expansion, leading to more jobs. Equally, a product innovation makes the firm's output more attractive to its potential customers, also expanding its market share and employment. When innovation reduces the real cost of production this must be welfare enhancing for all workers as consumers. So why is it that for many centuries there has been an enduring negative perception about innovation and jobs? There is a view that the introduction of new technology, particularly in the form of better capital equipment, causes job losses for workers. What is the basis for this opposing view on the relationship between innovation and jobs, which often dominates debates?

Those who oppose the introduction of new technology in the workplace are frequently termed *Luddites*. This name refers to a workers' movement in the early nineteenth century in England, Luddism, whose adherents strove to smash the new equipment being introduced into the British textile industry in protest against the loss of craft jobs. Their complaint was about the destruction of skilled jobs through the introduction of looms that could be operated by cheaper unskilled labor, leading to a lowering of wages.[1] However, the label of Luddite has been used since then to describe anyone opposed to the introduction of new technology in the workplace for whatever reason. In modern neoclassical economics the term *Luddite fallacy* has been coined to describe the misconception that, with increased productivity, employers would continue to produce a constant output with fewer workers, rather than expanding their output from a given workforce.[2] But is this too generous an interpretation by economists keen to see the workings of the market driven by the profit motive as universally beneficial?

The Luddite view may still have relevance for some groups of workers when we look at the demand for labor at the level of the firm or the industrial sector. New production technology frequently eliminates some types of jobs even as it creates others. While on balance, and at the macroeconomic level, innovation may be expected to have a net positive effect on the overall demand for labor, some workers will be disadvantaged by new production techniques and by new patterns of demand for products. But which jobs are reduced in number, and which jobs are expanded, depends on the particular technology or the range of new products being introduced. The key issue for any worker is whether or not their skills are being made redundant, for example by new machinery that offers a cheaper substitute for their skilled work, or

---

[1] For a sympathetic treatment of this movement in its historical context see Thompson (1968).
[2] The Luddite fallacy is discussed in Easterly (2001).

whether their skills are enhanced and demanded in greater volume, as they are complementary to the new technical machinery or production methods.

In economic models of employers' demand for labor, this demand is expected to be subject to pressures to minimize the cost of producing any given amount of output.[3] Input factors will be combined with the aim of yielding the highest possible return; clearly, this will not be achieved if too much of one expensive input is used when a cheaper substitute, or combination of inputs, can be used. But, of course, how expensive any worker or piece of capital is judged to be turns on the productivity in use of this input factor—for example, a highly skilled worker costs more in salary but produces more than an untrained worker. So for all factors there is a need to consider both costs and productivity. Ultimately, the level of input use is determined where the marginal addition to revenue from that factor's output (termed the *marginal revenue productivity*) is equated to the price of the last unit employed (termed its *marginal factor cost*).

The introduction of new techniques of production can change the relationships that underlie the marginal productivity of factor inputs. Economic literature has explored concepts of both *neutral* technological change (which affects the productivity of factors in a similar way) and *factor-biased* technical change, which differentially affects the productivity of capital and labor. Also, the market structure within which goods or services are supplied with the new technology can affect the speed with which any cost savings in production are transferred forward into price cuts for the consumer. This influences the demand for the final product and this feeds back into the derived demand for factor inputs, including labor. In box 10.1 some precise definitions are given and an example is followed through to show the effect on demand for workers of a change in process technology that makes labor more efficient.

While there can be differently specified models, what such mathematical models generally show is that there are indeed opposing influences of new technology on employment. As any factor becomes more efficient, less of it would be needed for the current level of production using the current combination of inputs. Yet this factor has effectively become cheaper precisely due to the rise in its efficiency, so more of it will be used in combination with other inputs wherever factor substitution is possible, as this is the way to minimize costs. This substitution effect increases relative demand for the more efficient factor, partly

---

[3] For extensive treatments of economic models of demand for labor see Hamermesh (1993) or Bosworth et al. (1996, chapter 10).

countering the negative effect of increased efficiency. Furthermore, the output of goods and services on which the workers are employed has become cheaper to produce, so if some of these gains are passed through and the output price falls, then demand for the product expands causing a rise in the number of jobs. The net size of all these effects will differ from one industry to another, so it becomes an empirical question whether employment in a given occupation and sector rises or falls when the technology alters.

Box 10.1. The impact of process innovation on employment.

The production of value added using capital and labor is described by many authors using a function that displays a constant elasticity of substitution (CES) between the two factor inputs. (For reference, the Cobb–Douglas production function in equation (8.2) has a constant elasticity of substitution of 1.) The following description draws on Van Reenen (1997).

To model the introduction of new technology that improves the efficiency of factors in production there are three ways of representing the changes:

T represents Hicks-neutral technical change; this is equally productivity enhancing for both factors leaving the ratio of the factor marginal products unchanged; hence the K/L ratio remains constant for any given prices of the two factors.

A represents Harrod-neutral technical change; here the new technology augments the productivity of labor but leaves the ratio of Y/K constant.

B represents Solow-neutral technical change; the new technology augments the productivity of capital but leaves the ratio of Y/L constant.

With these dynamic elements inserted, the CES production function then has the form:

$$Y = T[(AL)^{(\sigma-1)/\sigma} + (BK)^{(\sigma-1)/\sigma}]^{\sigma/(\sigma-1)}, \qquad (10.1)$$

where Y is value added, L is the number of workers, K is capital stock, and σ is the constant elasticity of substitution. (Note that σ shows how far capital and labor are substitutes for one another in production.)

We can focus on technological improvement that makes labor more productive relative to capital. This derivation sets $T = 1$ and $B = 1$, so there is no other technological change taking place apart from the labor-augmenting A type. Then it can be shown that the demand for workers is given by

$$\ln L = \ln Y - \sigma \ln(W/P) + (\sigma - 1) \ln A. \qquad (10.2)$$

The method also assumes that the marginal productivity of labor is set equal to the real wage (W/P), consistent with cost-minimizing choice of inputs. From this, Van Reenen shows that the elasticity of demand for labor with respect to new technology, η_{LA}, can be expressed as

$$\eta_{LA} = \eta_P \theta + (\sigma - 1), \tag{10.3}$$

where η_P is the price elasticity of demand for the product, θ is the elasticity of marginal supply cost with respect to the technology improvement, and the assumption is made that the product is supplied competitively where price equals marginal cost.

The first term of (10.3), which is called the "output expansion effect," will be larger when the cost of the product falls significantly and this is passed on to customers, who then react to the lower price by buying significantly more of the commodity. Whether η_{LA} is positive or negative overall then depends on the values of these elasticities together with that of the substitution elasticity σ.

What this means in empirical terms is that, following a labor-enhancing technological change, there will be a rise in demand for labor provided that labor and capital are close substitutes (i.e., the elasticity of factor substitution is greater than unity) or, if σ is less than 1, it is sufficiently close to 1 that the output expansion effect makes up the gap. If the product market is not competitive, the firm may choose not to pass on any cost reduction from the new technology to consumers and in this case the output expansion effect falls to zero.

Innovation and Wages

Innovation and technological change can affect wages by various means. First, there is an issue of how wages within the innovating firm may be changed if some "rent sharing" of the excess profits occurs. As we have shown in earlier chapters, firms obtain monopoly power through patents and support their market position with trademarks that identify their unique brands. This leads to excess profits that cannot be easily competed away by other firms in the short run. So when innovation leads to excess profits in a formerly competitive firm, does this result in higher wages in that firm? We might argue that the firm has no reason to share the gains from its R&D investment with the workers, as it needs this financial reward for its efforts. However, Van Reenen (1996) sets out a number of reasons why negotiations over pay determination between an employer and a union would be likely to result in sharing of these gains. Workers who are given a fair share will be more likely to work efficiently for fear of losing a job that is paying a premium and they are less likely to oppose changes in work practices arising from innovation.[4]

The second route by which technology affects wages within the firm can be viewed as being due to *increased productivity* for those with complementary skills. We noted above that the level of employment was determined by the comparison of marginal revenue productivity to wage costs. This equation also works in reverse for the determination of rates of pay. If an employer wants to retain a worker whose productivity has risen, then they must pay the worker's marginal value or else risk another employer bidding the worker away from the firm. As an example of these issues, there has been particular interest over the last quarter of a century in changes in work patterns arising from the introduction of computers into workplaces. The question that has been asked is: do computers make people more productive? If so, has this led to a rise in wages for those working with computers as compared with other workers? This is an issue we return to below.

Labor Unions and Innovation

Another interrelationship that has been examined is the role of labor unions in affecting the rate of innovation itself. Historically, many industrial relations analysts took a rather negative view of union activity, seeing their emphasis on raising wages as being likely to reduce the retained profits available for investment. This leads to the hypothesis that the presence of unions lowers the rate of investment and particularly reduces the willingness to engage in risky investment, such as R&D.[5]

From the other side there is the issue of whether unions will welcome or resist changes in work practices and employment arising from innovation. Union members may fear the job-destroying effects of innovation and be less confident about the positive gains. The economic theory of union resistance to labor-saving innovation is set out in an article subtitled "When are unions Luddites?" by Dowrick and Spencer (1994). These authors analyze the effect of various alternative structures of industrial relations interacting with the structure of the market for final products. The case of highly competitive product markets is contrasted with the situation of competition between a few large firms for market share, which economists term an oligopoly and is generally less price competitive. Unions can be organized at the level of a craft occupation, at the

---

[4] The idea that workers are more efficient if they are paid more is known as "efficiency wage theory."

[5] For a summary of research into unions and productivity and a survey of the evidence, see Metcalf (2003) and Hirsch (2007).

level of the single production location, termed enterprise unionism, or at the level of the industry. The different structures of bargaining interacting with alternative product markets will lead to different outcomes. These authors use economic theory to predict that opposition to the introduction of new technology is more likely with either an industry or craft-based union organization facing an oligopoly as its product market structure. It is less likely when there is enterprise unionism and the industry is highly competitive, as in this case the workers are effectively competing with other unions for shares in industrial employment.

In another mainly theoretical study of unions and innovation, Ulph and Ulph (1989) explore the impact of both the bargaining strength of the union and the coverage of the bargaining process, focusing particularly on whether the union can bargain about when a new process technology is to be introduced. They distinguish the decision to undertake R&D from the decision to introduce a new process when a discovery has been made. The study demonstrates that increased union strength does not always imply a reduction in the likelihood that the firm will successfully innovate. However, if the union has the power to delay the introduction of innovations, then the model predicts a reduction in the success rate of R&D.

A more positive view of unions stresses the likelihood that they might improve the firm's productivity. This view was originally propounded by Freeman and Medoff (1979, 1984), who argued that the level of job satisfaction could rise with union activity, as unions give a collective voice to the grievances of workers, leading to bargained solutions and hence fewer quits and better productivity. As a consequence of lower turnover, firms will find it profitable to invest more in training their workers, as they face a smaller probability of their workers leaving before the value of this investment can be realized. Given that skills may be complementary with conducting R&D and with adopting best-practice, high-technology production methods, this suggests a more positive influence of unions on R&D, innovation, and diffusion. This view struck a new chord in the industrial relations literature: in Freeman and Medoff's work and in much subsequent analysis it stands alongside the traditional idea of unions using their bargaining power to raise wages and reduce profits, leading to the paradox that unions can be good for workers and beneficial for economic performance, but not always good for the company's bottom line.

The idea of human capital being complementary to R&D has been formalized in a model of a growing economy by Redding (1996), using the endogenous growth approach that was discussed above in chapter 8. He argues that R&D and skills both generate positive externalities and that investments in human capital and in physical and knowledge capital are *strategic complements*. This means that the more of one type of capital exists, the greater the incentive to invest in the others. We shall explore these ideas further below in our examination of the detailed theory and evidence concerning skill-biased technological change. For the moment we note that to the extent that unions enhance their employer's returns to vocational training leading to increased investment in skills, this may also create a force in favor of investment in R&D and/or the rapid adoption of new technology.

10.3 Innovation and Labor Markets: Evidence from Firms

Employment Studies

Our first task is to examine whether the evidence shows that innovation creates more jobs. The most comprehensive study of innovation and employment using firm-level data is by Harrison et al. (2008). These authors use data from the Community Innovation Survey (CIS) for four European countries to examine the impact of both product and process innovation on the growth rates of employment in manufacturing and services firms. As noted above in chapter 3, innovation in the CIS is defined very broadly and includes the introduction of products and processes that are new to the market, which we define as innovation, as well as the adoption of these items by later imitators or licensees, which we prefer to define as diffusion of innovation. The firms studied for each country are large samples of those employing ten or more employees, excluding new entrants and firms affected by mergers or demergers. The average rates of employment growth vary but are strongly positive in all four countries for both sectors, although higher job growth is observed in services than in manufacturing. In the CIS database, firms report the proportion of their sales attributable to newly introduced products, as well as reporting their process and product innovations during the year. This permits the authors to eliminate ongoing trends in labor productivity in existing products and to distinguish the effects of innovation, as well as being able to identify the separate impacts of process and product innovations. Table 10.1 gives a summary of these estimates.

What is striking about these results is the consistency across countries and sectors in the relative size and the signs of the product and process innovation effects. In each country, and for each sector, there is a strongly positive contribution to employment arising from product innovation. In contrast, the effects of firm-specific process innovation in existing products are very small—barely different from zero. This

Table 10.1.   Employment effects of innovation
in firms over the period 1998–2000.

	France	Germany	Spain	U.K.
Manufacturing employment growth	8.3	5.9	14.2	6.7
Process innovation	−0.1	−0.6	0.3	−0.4
Product innovation	5.5	8.0	7.4	4.8
Services employment growth	15.5	10.2	25.9	16.1
Process innovation	−0.1	0.1	0.0	0.2
Product innovation	8.0	7.6	6.5	5.4

Source. Harrison et al. (2008, table 5).

Notes. All figures are percentage rates of employment growth over the two-year period 1998–2000. "Process innovation" here reflects the effect on employment of the introduction of new technology in the production of existing or "old" products. "Product innovation" reflects the *net* employment effect after allowing for any substitution of new products for old products. The other elements contributing to the firm's overall employment growth (details not shown) are the industry productivity trend and growth of output of old products. For all four countries and for both sectors, excepting German manufacturing, the effects of positive output growth in old products exceeded trend labor-saving productivity, leading to net job growth outside of innovation.

shows that the output expansion effects, made possible by the cost savings from improved efficiency, as shown in box 10.1, offset the labor-saving aspects of new technology. The underlying trends in productivity growth common to all firms in the industry were quite strongly labor saving, but this effect was counterbalanced by output growth arising from buoyant demand in the late 1990s. Alongside these changes, product innovation consistently contributed between 2.5% and 4.0% per annum to employment growth in both manufacturing and services.

Although this evidence from Harrison et al. (2008) reflects a short time period of two years, it certainly supports the ideas coming from the economic analysis of innovation, namely that product innovations will increase employment, whereas process innovations are subject to the two opposing forces and thus may not show a strong movement in either direction.[6] It seems that the Luddites were misguided about the overall impact of new technology on employment but were right to fear job losses in particular occupations. As yet we have still to examine the issue of which jobs were in decline and which increasing, an issue we return to below using more aggregated evidence. For the moment we continue

---

[6] Some earlier studies are available for longer panels of firm data, but generally these are not able to distinguish clearly between process and product innovations: see Van Reenen (1997) and Greenhalgh et al. (2001). These studies also find that the net effect of innovation is positive for employment in U.K. manufacturing.

our exploration of firm-level evidence to look for movement in wages and the impact of unions.

Innovation and Wages in Firms

First, we consider whether there is supporting evidence for the proposition that innovative rents (excess profits) are shared with workers. Two studies of British firms claim to have found support for this practice. The first study, by Van Reenen (1996), explores a sample of just under 600 publicly quoted companies observed from 1976 to 1982, three quarters of which were innovators in this period. The innovations monitored in this study were drawn from a specialized sample relating to the first commercialization of a major breakthrough and hence this excludes elements of the diffusion of innovation. In the raw data, the average wages in innovative firms were 12% higher than in noninnovating firms. The econometric model that was used measures rents in alternative ways, both relating to short-term profits and also to long-term expected profits, as revealed in the stock market valuation of the company. Other determinants of rents include market structure, reflecting domestic competition, and import penetration, mirroring foreign competition. The hypothesis is that wages will be influenced positively by both union presence and by rents. The findings show that the innovation variable is an important determinant of rents and the rent variable is a significant determinant of higher wages, with around 20–30% of an increase in rents being awarded to workers.

In a later study of a sample of 1,000 U.K. production firms from 1986 to 1995, Greenhalgh and Longland (2001) monitored the innovative activity of firms using both patent and trademark activity as well as R&D intensity. Again the focus was on whether the rents from innovation were shared. Their study found that trademark applications and R&D were associated with higher wages than the industry average, but patents were not. This is consistent with the view that patents may be taken out well before a new product launch and with varying lags involved, whereas trademarks are more consistently applied for close to the commercial introduction of the innovation. Also, trademarks are largely related to product innovations by firms, whereas patents relate to a mixture of product and process innovations, for which the benefits for workers are more ambiguous. The authors acknowledge that the positive impact on wages of R&D may be, in part, due to the need to hire further skilled workers, whose wages are above the industry average, but the findings for trademarks are consistent with the rent-sharing hypothesis. Of course, the above studies confirm the idea that workers tax innovation, but it does not automatically follow that firms do not receive an adequate return to R&D as this also depends on the productivity of their workers (which can increase due to improved motivation when they are better rewarded).

We now move to evidence for our second route for increases in wages due to innovation: is there increased productivity of workers using new technology? An early investigation of the role of computers in changing the wage structure was that by Krueger (1993), who analyzed the wages of U.S. workers in the 1980s, which was a period of widening dispersion of earnings with rising skill differentials. Krueger found that workers who used computers in their work earned 10–15% more than those who did not. He also inferred from his statistical analysis that the increasing use of computers during the 1980s explained between one third and one half of the rise in returns to education. His findings tend to support the view that computers and educational skills are complementary, leading to higher returns for these workers.

However, as Entorf and Kramarz (1997) note in their study of French wages, Krueger was unable to distinguish unambiguously between two interpretations of the "computer effect": the first is that those who work with computers are a selected group, who are more able than others; the second is that the existence of the new technology *increases* the productivity of a worker with given skills. To make this distinction requires detailed evidence about individual pay before and after the introduction of the computer-based technology. Evidence for French workers observed during the 1980s, and again in the early 1990s, supports the view that those selected for work with computers are the more able individuals.[7] Once this is allowed for, the average wage differential between workers of given ability, working with and without computers, is much smaller than the estimates of Krueger for the United States. These selected workers gained small wage increases with the duration of their experience with computers, so working with this type of technology only gradually enhanced their productivity. This suggests a very modest impact of this technology on productivity, but reinforces the idea of skills being complementary with technology, even if the precise nature of these skills is hard to observe outside the firm. Entorf and Kramarz (1998) make further inferences, as they are able to differentiate between workers in various occupations. They find that the higher is the skill and occupational status of the worker, the less is their use of modern technology compensated, as essentially it is part of the definition of the job of managers, engineers, and technicians.

---

[7] For analysis of the mid 1980s see Entorf and Kramarz (1997, 1998). For similar evidence from the 1990s see Entorf et al. (1999).

Labor Unions and R&D

What evidence exists that the rent-seeking activity of labor unions acts as a tax on the returns to investment in long-lived capital and intangible assets generated by R&D? In an early empirical study, Hirsch (1991) analyzed data for around 500 publicly listed manufacturing firms in the United States, comparing unionized with nonunion companies while controlling for many industry and firm characteristics. He estimates that the average unionized firm has 13% lower capital investment and 15% lower R&D expenditure than a similar nonunion firm. These overall reductions come from the sum of a direct effect of unions taxing returns and an indirect effect that having lower profits leads to higher financing costs (as firms have access to fewer internally generated funds and have to borrow or raise capital from the stock market). In his later survey, Hirsch (2007) confirms that many subsequent studies of either Canadian or U.S. firms have found similar reductions in investment.

However, these findings are not universal. In a study of U.K. firms, Menezes-Filho et al. (1998) demonstrate that it would be wrong to infer that British unions are the cause of similarly low rates of investment. While it is true that in the raw data, unionized firms have lower rates of R&D, it is also the case that unionized companies are mostly located in older declining industries, while new firms in high-technology sectors are less often unionized. Once the characteristics of the firm are controlled for in the estimation, the effect of a union presence on R&D drops to become statistically insignificant from zero. The authors present a direct comparison of their estimates with the same empirical specification applied to Hirsch's data for the United States, confirming that results for the two countries differ. They offer an explanation of the difference based on British and American industrial relations systems, arguing that U.S. unions have traditionally placed a higher emphasis on increasing wages rather than on trying to protect jobs, which has been of greater concern in the United Kingdom. This difference is revealed by larger union wage differentials in the United States than in most other OECD countries.[8]

What of the idea that unions help the firm to enhance its skill base and that, as skills are complementary with R&D, this might increase the rate of innovation? There are two links in this chain. The first is, do unions enhance skill formation? Booth et al. (2003) have shown strong evidence that the presence of trade unions increases vocational training and the returns to such training for male workers in Britain. The second link is, do extra skills increase R&D? This is taken up by Nickell and Nicolitsas

---

[8] For evidence on union relative wages see Blanchflower and Bryson (2002).

(2000), who explore the links between human capital, physical capital investment, and innovation in British manufacturing firms from 1976 to 1994. They test whether a shortage of skills at the industry level can lead to a reduction in investments and R&D expenditure in firms and they find that an increase in the number of firms reporting skill shortages in the industry is associated with a temporary reduction in R&D, so there is a postponement of investment in innovation. This evidence confirms the idea that human capital (skills) is a strategic complement to knowledge capital.

Our examination of the literature has revealed some contrasting effects of unions. There is some U.S. evidence that they inhibit R&D investment by taxing the returns to innovation. In contrast, there is European evidence that they encourage innovation with their positive contribution to training and skills. In some countries such as the United Kingdom, where union strength has weakened dramatically in the last quarter of a century, these factors are now less important than previously. In other countries like France where, despite low rates of union membership, the coverage of collective bargaining agreements is very high, these are still forces to be reckoned with.

10.4   Macroeconomic and Trade Models of Innovation and Labor Markets

Let us now analyze the broader picture of the impact of innovation on aggregate employment and wages. As we have shown above, there can simultaneously be job losses in some occupations and increased demand for other workers with more relevant skills as a result of the introduction of new products and new processes. These changing demands can lead to imbalances of supply and demand for workers in various occupational labor markets. Because workers cannot immediately retrain and transfer into the areas of expanding work, these imbalances are likely to have an impact on relative wages and unemployment rates. These effects are likely to persist into the medium term, until the relative supply can adjust to the new demand patterns.

Where supply exceeds demand, as happens for those whose skills have become redundant, there is downward pressure on wages and a rising rate of unemployment. Where supply fails to match increased demand, as happens for those whose skills complement the new technology, and for skilled workers in sectors experiencing a rapid demand expansion for innovative new products, wages will rise as firms compete to acquire the necessary skills. The next section reviews recent evidence on these issues.

The Changing Fortunes of the Skilled and the Unskilled

We shall begin with the facts about employment and wages that need to be explained. These facts are documented by many authors, including Machin (2001) and Machin and Van Reenen (1998), and we draw on their research in table 10.2. This shows that over a twenty-year period starting around 1980 there is strong evidence that the demand for skilled workers has outpaced any increase in supply in the United States and in the United Kingdom. Other studies such as Nickell and Bell (1995) demonstrate similar phenomena for many advanced industrial countries.[9] The proportion of skilled workers in employment has risen sharply, yet simultaneously their relative wages have also risen strongly, not fallen as would be predicted if a rising supply of highly educated workers had outstripped the demand for this type of worker. The rapid rise in the wage differential in the United States was particularly striking, having begun from a lower level than that seen in the United Kingdom in 1980, when the United Kingdom's supply of graduates was very limited. The skilled wage differential in each of the two countries reached around 65% by 2000.

What explanations have been suggested for the changes shown in table 10.2? There are three main suggestions:

(1) skill-biased technological change;

(2) factor endowments, specialization, and globalization;

(3) changes in the composition of final demand.

The following sections consider each of these in turn.

Skill-Biased Technological Change

The hypothesis favored by Machin (2001), and by several other authors cited in his review, such as Berman et al. (1994), is that skill-biased technological change (SBTC) is the underlying cause of changes in relative employment and wages. The SBTC theory rests on the idea introduced in the first half of the chapter when looking at innovation in firms that some

---

[9] Note that in Machin's (2001) study, "skill" is proxied by education, but it is well-known that graduates enter the higher-skilled professions and gain more vocational training than other workers. In an earlier study of ten OECD countries using a lower skill threshold, Nickell and Bell (1995) also identify the falling relative demand for the unskilled as a significant contributory factor in their rising unemployment and falling relative wage rates during the 1970s and 1980s.

Table 10.2. Relative employment and relative wages in the
United States and the United Kingdom, 1980–2000.

	Share of graduates in total employment (%)		Relative wages of graduates to nongraduates	
	U.S.	U.K.	U.S.	U.K.
1980	19.3	5.0	1.36	1.48
1990	23.8	10.2	1.55	1.60
2000	27.5	17.2	1.66	1.64

Sources. Data extracted from table 1 of Machin (2001, p. 756). U.S. data are drawn
from the Current Population Survey; U.K. data are drawn from the Labour Force
Survey and the General Household Survey.

Notes. Employment data relate to people aged 16–64 in work and earning, whether
full or part time. Relative wages relate to full-time workers in both countries and
reflect hourly wages for the United States but weekly wages for the United Kingdom;
estimates of wage premiums were derived by Machin using regressions to control
for age and gender of workers.

types of jobs will be destroyed but for others demand will be increased.
At the firm level, new technologies are introduced that are complementary with knowledge skills and individual ability, thus increasing the relative demand for skilled workers. This phenomenon of strategic complementarity of skills and technology is most likely to occur in high-growth
services sectors, such as business and personal financial services, but it
also impinges on manufacturing firms, where there is a rise in demand
for workers who can design innovative products or supervise sophisticated production technology. We could characterize this as a world
in which the productivity of skilled workers is rising faster than that of
unskilled workers. A formal representation of the impact of such a model
on workers' relative wages was outlined in Katz and Murphy (1992) and
this is described briefly in box 10.2.

**Box 10.2. Skill-biased technological change and the relative wages of
skilled and unskilled workers.**

We contrast here two models of relative wages compared by Hornstein
et al. (2005). The first model is drawn from Katz and Murphy (1992)
and it posits factor-specific productivity. Skilled and unskilled labor are
deemed to be substitutes in production to some degree, but they also
have different productivities. Here σ_{su} is defined as the elasticity of substitution of the two types of labor in production. The real wages of skilled

and unskilled labor are w_s and w_u. In this model, which assumes competitive labor markets and firms choosing inputs to minimize costs, the relative wage equation that can be derived is

$$\ln\left(\frac{w_s}{w_u}\right) = \left[\frac{\sigma_{su}-1}{\sigma_{su}}\right]\ln\left(\frac{A_s}{A_u}\right) - \left[\frac{1}{\sigma_{su}}\right]\ln\left(\frac{l_s}{l_u}\right). \tag{10.4}$$

The relative wage of skilled to unskilled labor is driven by two ratios. The first is the difference in productivity growth of each type of labor, denoted by A_s/A_u, and the second is the relative supply of each type of labor, denoted by l_s/l_u. The exact nature and driving forces of the rise in the relative productivity of skilled workers are not specified.

What equation (10.4) predicts is that, if the productivity of skilled labor rises faster than that of unskilled labor, the wage ratio for skilled workers will increase. In contrast, if the supply of skilled labor rises faster than that of unskilled, then the wage ratio will decrease. The higher is the degree of substitutability (i.e., the value of σ_{su}), the larger is the positive effect of rising relative productivity on wages and the smaller is the negative effect of rising relative supply. From empirical analysis, Katz and Murphy estimate σ_{su} to be 1.4. However, to fit the empirical trends in wages and supply in the United States, Hornstein et al. comment that the relative productivity of skilled labor would have had to have grown by 11% per year, which they deem unlikely.

The second model outlined by Hornstein et al. comes from Krusell et al. (2000). As well as different factor-specific productivities, there are also different elasticities of substitution between capital equipment (k_e) and the two types of labor. The elasticity of substitution between unskilled labor and equipment is here denoted as $\sigma_{ue} = 1/(1 - \phi)$, while that for skilled labor and equipment is $\sigma_{se} = 1/(1 - \rho)$. The maintained hypothesis is that unskilled labor is more easily substitutable with equipment than is skilled labor, so $\sigma_{ue} > \sigma_{se}$. The derived relative wage equation is now

$$\ln\left(\frac{w_s}{w_u}\right) = \left[\frac{\sigma_{ue}-1}{\sigma_{ue}}\right]\ln\left(\frac{A_s}{A_u}\right) - \left[\frac{1}{\sigma_{ue}}\right]\ln\left(\frac{l_s}{l_u}\right) + \frac{\lambda(\phi-\rho)}{\rho}\left(\frac{k_e}{l_s}\right)^\rho. \tag{10.5}$$

The important feature of equation (10.5) is that there is an additional effect driving demand for skilled labor due to its complementarity with equipment. The relative wage will now rise as long as there is an increase in the ratio of equipment to skilled labor, even if the first two terms were to remain constant. From the Krusell et al. (2000) estimates of $\phi = 0.4$ and $\rho = -0.5$, the elasticities of substitution are, respectively, $\sigma_{ue} = 1.67$ and $\sigma_{se} = 0.67$, showing support for the hypothesis that the unskilled are most easily substituted for capital when the price of capital falls.

These authors demonstrate that their model fits the U.S. experience of changing relative wages from the 1960s to the 1990s very well.

At the same time, the invention of "clever" machines increases the productivity of capital, making it profitable to increase capital intensity. There is strong evidence to support the view that capital equipment has become cheaper to produce over time with a recent acceleration in this process occurring. Hornstein et al. (2005) provide evidence that the productivity of the equipment (investment goods) sector in the United States was running at an annual rate of 1.6% from 1947 until 1975, accelerating to average 3.6% per year in the last quarter of the twentieth century, and rising to almost 5% per year in the 1990s, which led to a sharp fall in the relative price of investment goods.

Cheaper and better equipment gives rise to the opportunity for firms to raise their capital intensity. In services, the rise in capital intensity was characterized by adding a computer to almost every desktop. The corollary is that the service-sector worker must have the capability to work with this new equipment. Within manufacturing production capital–labor substitution occurs, replacing the jobs of those who previously undertook repetitive manual tasks requiring craft skills (e.g., by using robots and other automated production techniques instead). Those whose manual skills are made redundant may either retrain or join the ranks of the unskilled looking for jobs. A formal statement of a model in which the higher skilled are complementary to capital equipment, while the low skilled are substitutes, is given in Krusell et al. (2000) and summarized in Hornstein et al. (2005) (see box 10.2).

To demonstrate the impact of computers on the relative demand for skilled workers, Autor et al. (1998) examined the rising wage share of college graduates in the wage bills of U.S. industries. This share was positively correlated with the stock of computing equipment per worker in both manufacturing and nonmanufacturing, after controlling for other capital stock usage. For manufacturing, this correlation was still present when the R&D ratio to sales was also included. They conclude that

> skill-biased technological and organizational changes that accompanied the computer revolution appear to have contributed to faster growth in relative skill demand ... starting in the 1970s.
>
> Autor et al. (1998, p. 1,203)

In a later study also using U.S. data, Autor et al. (2003) explore the impact of computerization at the level of job tasks. They show that computer capital substitutes for workers whose jobs, or parts of jobs, comprise routine tasks that are conducted following explicit rules, whether in manual or office work. At the same time, computer capital complements workers involved in nonroutine problem solving and complex communications tasks. The authors estimate that these task shifts explain 60% of the change in relative demand for college-educated labor observed in the 1970s and 1980s.

Factor Endowments, Specialization, and Globalization

If the type of goods and services produced in advanced economies for export to world markets has changed, in a direction that requires the use of more skilled workers, this could also have caused the observed pattern of increased relative demand for skills. This does not mean that SBTC is unimportant, only that there may be other forces at work.

As discussed in chapter 9, one of the striking features of international trade and growth over the last thirty years has been the transformation of several Asian economies from relatively closed economies into highly open trading economies contributing a significant share of world trade in manufactures. This process began with the "Asian tigers" (Hong Kong, Singapore, South Korea, and Taiwan) and has continued with the more recent rapid growth in trade with China and India. While the first four countries have relatively small populations, China and India together constitute 37% of the world population in 2008, many of whom are low-paid unskilled workers. What does economic theory predict will be the effect on advanced industrial countries of the entry into world trade of countries with such large endowments of unskilled labor?

A starting point is the Heckscher–Ohlin and Samuelson (HOS) model of trade in which comparative advantage is determined by factor endowments. The original model assumed two factors of production (capital and labor) and two countries. For our purposes here, we can assume that the two (immobile) factors of production are skilled and unskilled labor, while the two "countries" are the developed and developing countries. The developed countries have a higher proportion of skilled workers than the developing countries, but the wages of both types of workers are higher in the developed countries. In autarky, both countries make products that are intensive in the use of each factor, but when trade begins each country will specialize according to their comparative advantage, which is based on their dominant factor endowments. With trade, the low-wage developing country supplies goods that are intensive in unskilled labor to the high-wage advanced country, and the employment and wages of the less skilled workers in the developed world will fall. An important and influential book by Wood (1994) made this argument almost before the impact of China and India had begun to be felt; his argument is summarized on the first page of his book:

> Expansion of trade has linked the labor markets of developed countries (the North) more closely with those of developing countries (the South). This greater economic intimacy has had large benefits, raising average living standards in the North, and accelerating development in the South. But it has hurt unskilled workers in the North, reducing their wages and pushing them out of jobs.

This prediction of the static HOS model produces a once and for all shift in factor rewards following the opening of trade with low-wage countries. Chapter 9 also discussed a dynamic view of comparative advantage based on innovation. This view holds that new technology and innovative products are seen as driving the pattern of exports from the high-income countries, while there is a continual transfer of knowledge to developing countries about techniques of production and designs of more standardized goods. In this "product cycle" there is again continued pressure on the less skilled jobs of those working for high wages in the rich countries. This type of employment is eroded as multinational firms seek higher profits by sourcing the less complex stages of the production supply chain in low-wage countries.

So, for those with low skills or redundant skills in the rich countries, the fall in demand for their services will lead to fewer jobs, but does this translate into lower wages or higher unemployment? This will depend on institutional features of labor markets, such as the existence of minimum wages, or the strength of unions, or other institutions such as systems of vocational training. For example, Card and DiNardo (2002) have argued that a major factor contributing to the widening wage dispersion in the United States during the 1980s was the fall in the real value of the federal minimum wage. They argue that, for the United States, too much reliance has been placed on the SBTC hypothesis and particularly on the idea that skill complementarity with computer-related technology was an important feature. What they do not discuss in detail is why, when the minimum wage fell, such a large proportion of workers were dragged down to this lower level of wages.

How far wages fall, or unemployment rises, following technology or trade shifts in demand depends on how easily people switch occupation; this, in turn, is a function of whether they have general labor market skills or have only sector-specific skills. It also depends on whether some of these workers can move into supplying nontraded goods and services, such as restaurant meals, haircuts, or taxi services; hence the size of the nontraded sector matters for maintaining the employment and wages of those displaced by trade and technology.

Skills Bias in the Derived Demand for Labor

A third possible source of unequal shifts in demand for skilled and unskilled labor is that of the changing composition of demand for final products. Economists classify products according to how their demand rises as incomes rise. Goods and services are termed *luxuries* when their demand is income elastic (i.e., demand rises more than proportionately to income), or are labeled as *necessities* when their demand is inelastic (demand rises less than proportionately to income). There is also a category of goods that are termed *inferior* in that, as incomes rise, their consumption actually falls (e.g., cheaper, unbranded products). It seems reasonable to expect that high-technology innovative products will be luxuries rather than necessities and that older vintage standardized versions of products will be inferior goods. Then, as economic growth raises average living standards through rising incomes per capita, the share of skill-intensive high-technology goods and services will increase as a proportion of total consumer purchases.

In summary, there are three hypotheses, each leading to the prediction that the demand for skills will rise relative to the demand for less skilled workers:

Skill-biased technological change. This emphasizes the idea of process innovation being biased toward the use of more skilled workers, as they are complementary with complex capital inputs in production and with sophisticated marketing and distribution systems.

Factor endowments, specialization, and globalization. Greater specialization in international trade has occurred, partly based on the comparative advantage of advanced countries, with their relatively high endowment of skills compared with developing countries that are highly endowed with unskilled workers. Alongside this, there is the idea of innovation constantly releasing new products in the richer world and feeding a dynamic version of comparative advantage based on new process technology and product innovation.

Skills bias in the derived demand for labor. This assumes that innovative products are more appealing as incomes rise, hence there is a displacement of the inferior substitutes produced by less skilled labor.

All three hypotheses rest on innovation and new technology as a driving force for what is on offer to producers in their choice of techniques or to

Table 10.3. Three causes of skill bias in demand
for labor in the United Kingdom 1979–90.

	Final demand	Net exports	Technological change	Total change in employment
High skill	28.2	−4.1	4.6	28.8
Intermediate skill	21.1	−4.8	−16.2	0.1
Low skill	17.9	−5.7	−27.1	−14.9
Total change	22.0	−4.8	−13.7	3.5

Source. Gregory et al. (2001, table 2).

Notes. Employment is calculated as full-time equivalent jobs. All figures are percentage changes from 1979 to 1990.

The methodology employed by Gregory et al. combines an input–output model of the economy with a factor content of production and trade approach. The figures presented here thus represent the derived demand for labor generated by the changes in final demand, goods entering trade, or changes in technology, looking back through the entire supply chain including the labor content of intermediate goods used as inputs.

Skill class was defined by the U.K. Standard Occupational Classification, which is defined hierarchically on entry qualifications, skills, and experience. High-skill occupations were those in managerial, professional, and technical jobs. Intermediate-skill jobs included clerical and secretarial, crafts, protective and personal services, and sales representatives. Low-skill jobs included machine operatives and other occupations.

consumers in their choice of goods and services. Is it possible to assess empirically the relative importance of each of these forces?

One study that has done so is Gregory et al. (2001). This uses an input–output model of an open economy to trace the contributions to employment change of each of these three contributory factors. Table 10.3 summarizes the results for the whole economy for three levels of skill, but these computations are aggregated from a study of changes in the employment of nine occupational groups employed in fifteen sectors covering primary, manufacturing, and services sectors. What is striking about these results for the United Kingdom in the 1980s is that all three forces of SBTC, globalization, and demand are shown to be skill-biased. Net job creation was positive, but the employment of high-skilled managers and professional and technical personnel rose by nearly 30%, while 15% of low-skilled employment disappeared.

Looking at the relative impact of the three causal factors shows there are large differences in the degree of skill bias contributed by each factor. Changes in production technology (SBTC) caused the most dramatic differences in demand by skill, generating a small net rise in demand for high-skill workers (4.6%) but a very large loss of jobs for the low skilled

(−27.1%). Rising final demand created jobs at all levels, but there was faster growth in the derived demand for high skills (28.2%) than for low skills (17.9%). The net effect of the changing composition of exports and imports over this period of the 1980s is shown to have made a rather modest contribution to skill bias, but of course these data predate the recent rapid expansion of trade with China and India. There is also the issue of whether competition from international trade generates some of the pressure to adopt labor-saving technology in the production of import competing products. As Gregory et al. (2001) note, this decomposition of employment attributes changes to their proximate cause, but makes no allowance for the likely interactions and feedbacks between trade, technology, and demand.

Nevertheless, the advantage of input–output analysis is that it can reveal all of the changing patterns in the supply chain.[10] What is notable about the generation of growth in employment in recent decades is the strong effect of growth in services, both "business services" (finance, insurance, real estate) and "nonbusiness services" (retail and wholesale trade, hotels and catering, transport and communications, personal and public services). As individual incomes rose there was a rise in the demand for recreational activity associated with shopping, local tourism, and meals taken away from home. Nonbusiness services also became more highly represented in the intermediate inputs used in the production of other goods, reflecting for example the rise in promotional events for advertising and increased business travel. At the same time, specialized business services were being demanded by all sectors of the economy to a far greater degree as intermediate inputs into the production process. These services were increasingly skill intensive as their customers, whether individual consumers or other businesses, demanded ever more sophisticated services supplied by highly trained workers. New information technology, based on the development of computers, mobile phones, and eventually the Internet, permitted these skilled workers to supply individually tailored service products.

10.5 Conclusions

In our exploration of the relationships between innovation, new technology, employment, and wages we have been forced to confront the painful truth publicized by the protests of the Luddites two centuries ago. As well as creating jobs for some types of workers, new technology

---

[10] For details of the contributions of different sectors to job generation see Greenhalgh and Gregory (2000).

destroys jobs for others. In many sectors of activity, process innovations have involved the substitution of machines for workers and some types of skills are thereby made redundant. Examples vary from tasks involved in car assembly, such as the welding of body parts now done by robots, to aspects of banking, such as the withdrawal of cash from automated teller machines.

Nevertheless, the main message of the economics of innovation is that lower production costs, greater variety, and higher quality of products will all help firms to survive and sell more in the marketplace. The derived demand for workers need not fall in total, but it will change drastically in its composition. In innovating firms, workers will be demanded in different proportions to undertake a range of service activities, involving the advertising, marketing, and delivery of their wider range of goods and services to customers. At the same time workers are needed for the design and development of novel products and equipment, and for the ongoing maintenance of the new automated machinery set up to do the tasks of the now-redundant production workers. These compositional changes are seen in the changing sectoral balance of employment, as firms have outsourced many of their service needs to specialist firms rather than continuing to supply them in-house.

The key feature of labor demand in rich countries for the last three decades has been that skilled workers have been increasingly in demand relative to the unskilled. This has arisen from a combination of several factors all working in the same direction, and all, in some way, are linked with technology. Skill bias in the workplace has come about with the development of computer-assisted production technologies and this is a feature of both manufacturing and many types of services. International trade has expanded and evolved, resulting in greater specialization in production between rich countries and the newly developing countries. Growth of average GDP per capita, due to rising productivity per worker, has led to even higher growth of discretionary spending on luxuries. This category includes many high-technology products that are skill intensive in their production, as they embody more science and technology than mature products and thus also require skilled labor in their production, distribution, and servicing. The changes in the relative demand for workers of different skill types, and in particular the loss of manufacturing jobs and the rise in service-sector jobs, have led to stresses and strains in systems of education and vocational training.

Where supply has not matched the new structure of demand then, in countries with flexible wages such as the United States and the United Kingdom, this skill bias has led to a rise in the relative wage for the skilled. In many European countries with more institutional constraints on movement in wages, the shift in relative demand has increased the unemployment rate of the unskilled relative to the skilled. Either way this translates into a problem for the less skilled. There can be a way out if a significant share of workers with few or redundant skills can retrain to join one of the occupational groups that are now in increasing demand. The evidence of increasing relative wages and differential unemployment rates suggests that few advanced countries have achieved a sufficiently rapid upgrading of their workforces to match the increase in demand for skills.

Keywords

Luddites.

Factor-biased technological change.

Rent sharing.

Unions and innovation.

Wages and employment effects of technological change.

Skill-biased technological change.

The Heckscher–Ohlin and Samuelson (HOS) trade model.

Questions for Discussion

(1) Can the "Luddite view" be justified?

(2) Why does it matter whether or not technical change is factor-biased?

(3) Why is the impact of innovation on wages and employment difficult to determine?

(4) Do unions help or hinder (a) innovation, (b) the adoption of new processes, and (c) exports?

(5) Discuss the trends in the relative wages of skilled to unskilled workers in your country.

(6) What forces might affect relative wages in (a) developed economies and (b) developing countries?

References

Autor, D., L. Katz, and A. Krueger. 1998. Computing inequality: have computers changed the labor market? *Quarterly Journal of Economics* 113:1,169–214.

Autor, D., F. Levy, and R. Murnane. 2003. The skill content of recent technological change: an empirical exploration. *Quarterly Journal of Economics* 118(4): 1,279–333.

Berman, E., J. Bound, and Z. Griliches. 1994. Changes in the demand for skilled labour within US manufacturing: evidence from the annual survey of manufactures. *Quarterly Journal of Economics* 109:367–97.

Blanchflower, D., and A. Bryson. 2002. Changes over time in union relative wage effects in the UK and the US revisited. NBER Working Paper 9395.

Booth, A., M. Francesconi, and G. Zoega. 2003. Unions, work-related training, and wages: evidence for British men. *Industrial and Labor Relations Review* 57(1):68–91.

Bosworth, D., P. Dawkins, and T. Stromback. 1996. *The Economics of the Labour Market*. Harlow, U.K.: Addison-Wesley Longman.

Card, D., and J. DiNardo. 2002. Skill-biased technological change and rising wage inequality: some problems and puzzles. *Journal of Labor Economics* 20(4):733–83.

Dowrick, S., and B. Spencer. 1994. Union attitudes to labor-saving new technology: when are unions Luddites? *Journal of Labor Economics* 12(2):316–44.

Easterly, W. 2001. *The Elusive Quest For Growth: Economists' Adventures and Misadventures in the Tropics*. Cambridge, MA: MIT Press.

Entorf, H., and F. Kramarz. 1997. Does unmeasured ability explain the higher wages of new technology workers? *European Economic Review* 41(4):1,489–510.

——. 1998. The impact of new technologies on wages: lessons from matching panels on employees and on their firms. *Economics of Innovation and New Technology* 5(2–4):165–98.

Entorf, H., M. Gollac, and F. Kramarz. 1999. New technologies, wages and worker selection. *Journal of Labor Economics* 17(3):464–91.

Freeman, R., and J. Medoff. 1979. The two faces of unionism. *Public Interest* 57(Fall):69–93.

——. 1984. *What Do Unions Do?*. New York: Basic Books.

Greenhalgh, C., and M. Gregory. 2000. Labour productivity and product quality: their growth and inter-industry transmission in the UK 1979–90. In *Productivity, Innovation and Economic Performance* (ed. R. Barrell, G. Mason, and M. O'Mahoney). National Institute of Economic and Social Research/Cambridge University Press.

Greenhalgh, C., and M. Longland. 2001. Intellectual property in UK firms: creating intangible assets and distributing the benefits via wages and jobs. *Oxford Bulletin of Economics and Statistics* 63:671–96 (Special Issue: The Labour Market Consequences of Technical and Structural Change).

Greenhalgh, C., M. Longland, and D. Bosworth. 2001. Technological activity and employment in a panel of UK firms. *Scottish Journal of Political Economy* 48(3):260–82.

Gregory, M., B. Zissimos, and C. Greenhalgh. 2001. Jobs for the skilled: how technology, trade and domestic demand changed the structure of UK employment. *Oxford Economic Papers* 53(1):20–46.

Hamermesh, D. 1993. *Labour Demand*. Princeton University Press.

Harrison, R., J. Jaumendreu, J. Mairesse, and B. Peters. 2008. Does innovation stimulate employment? A firm-level analysis using comparable micro-data from four European countries. NBER Working Paper 14216.

Hirsch, B. T. 1991. *Labour Unions and the Economic Performance of U.S. Firms*. Kalamazoo, MI: Upjohn Institute for Employment Research.

Hirsch, B. T. 2007. What do unions do for economic performance? In *What Do Unions Do? A Twenty-Year Perspective* (ed. J. T. Bennett and B. E. Kaufman). Piscataway, NJ: Transaction Publishers.

Hornstein, A., P. Krusell, and G. L. Violante. 2005. The effects of technical change on labor market inequalities. In *Handbook of Economic Growth* (ed. P. Aghion and S. Durlauf), volume 1B. Amsterdam: North-Holland/Elsevier.

Katz, L., and K. Murphy. 1992. Changes in relative wages, 1963–87: supply and demand factors. *Quarterly Journal of Economics* 107:35–78.

Krueger, A. 1993. How computers have changed the wage structure: evidence from micro-data 1984–1989. *Quarterly Journal of Economics* 108(1):75–98.

Krusell, P., L. Ohanian, J.-V. Rios-Rull, and G. L. Violante. 2000. Capital skill complementarity and inequality: a macroeconomic analysis. *Econometrica* 68: 1,029–53.

Machin, S. 2001. The changing nature of labour demand in the new economy and skill-biased technical change. *Oxford Bulletin of Economics and Statistics* 63:753–76 (Special Issue: The Labour Market Consequences of Technical and Structural Change).

Machin, S., and J. Van Reenen. 1998. Technology and changes in skill structure: evidence from seven OECD countries. *Quarterly Journal of Economics* 113: 1,215–44.

Menezes-Filho, N., D. Ulph, and J. Van Reenen. 1998. R&D and unionism: comparative evidence from British companies and establishments. *Industrial and Labor Relations Review* 52(1):45–63.

Metcalf, D. 2003. Unions and productivity, financial performance and investment: international evidence. In *International Handbook of Trade Unions* (ed. J. T. Addison and C. Schnabel). Cheltenham, U.K.: Edward Elgar.

Nickell, S., and B. Bell. 1995. The collapse in demand for the unskilled and unemployment across the OECD. *Oxford Review of Economic Policy* 11(1): 40–62.

Nickell, S., and D. Nicolitsas. 2000. Human capital, investment and innovation: what are the connections? In *Productivity, Innovation and Economic Performance* (ed. R. Barrell, G. Mason, and M. O'Mahoney). National Institute of Economic and Social Research/Cambridge University Press.

Redding, S. 1996. The low-skill, low-quality trap: strategic complementarities between human capital and R&D. *Economic Journal* 106:458–70.

Thompson, E. P. 1968. *The Making of the English Working Class*. London: V. Gollancz.

Ulph, A., and D. Ulph. 1989. Labour markets and innovation. *Journal of the Japanese and International Economies* 3:403–23.

Van Reenen, J. 1996. The creation and capture of rents: wages and innovation in a panel of UK companies. *Quarterly Journal of Economics* 111(1):195–226.

———. 1997. Employment and technological innovation: evidence from UK manufacturing firms. *Journal of Labor Economics* 15(2):255–84.

Wood, A. 1994. *North–South Trade Employment and Inequality*. Oxford: Clarendon.

Part IV

Economic Policy

11

Microeconomic Policies to Promote Firm-Level Innovation

11.1 Introduction

This chapter discusses microeconomic policy with respect to promoting firm-level innovation. The focus is on two main areas: intellectual property rights (IPRs) and R&D. These are normally considered to be the front line of policy relating to innovation. Policies surrounding IPRs are, in short, controversial. It has been said that if the patent system did not exist it would be very difficult to justify creating it.[1] This statement sums up the lack of understanding about the overall effects of the patent system and other forms of IPRs. Nevertheless, policy makers must attempt to unravel some of the issues at stake and how these relate to the wider objective of promoting innovation. R&D policy is also a hotly debated topic. More and more OECD countries are introducing R&D tax subsidies, in effect creating competition between countries in offering the best location for R&D. There has also been a long history of R&D grants and the financing of basic research. This chapter reviews the evidence surrounding policies that aim to encourage R&D expenditure by firms. These two main topics—IPRs and R&D—take up most of the space in this chapter. However, section 11.4 provides a brief overview of some other relevant policy areas that influence innovation: universities, SME policy, competition policy, standards, and procurement.

11.2 Is the Intellectual Property System Working?

This is a difficult question to answer and one that elicits very different opinions from different people. In this section we provide an overview of the debates and issues concerning each of the main types of intellectual property.

---

[1] See Hall (2007), who attributes this statement to Penrose (1951).

A reasonable place to start our discussion is with the debate over the performance of the U.S. patent system. Between 1965 and 1985 the number of patents granted each year in the United States hovered between a minimum of 52,412 (in 1979) and a maximum of 81,790 (in 1971). Since then the numbers have risen, reaching 182,901 in 2008.[2] The rapid growth has occurred across a range of major industries, including biotechnology and electronics, but has also been fueled by the new patents allowable for software and business methods. There are two main questions that are relevant here:

(a) What caused this strong growth and, specifically, did policy play a role?

(b) Is the rapid growth in patenting conducive to innovation and productivity growth?

What Caused the Strong Growth in U.S. Patents?

The question of what caused the rapid growth is central. It could be that the growth in patents simply reflected increasing levels of innovation and R&D. Such a view is extreme and implies that the patent system has no *effect* on the incentives to do R&D and innovate. Most commentators, however, point to a series of policy and legal changes that, taken together, caused major changes to the U.S. patent system; and they suggest that it was these changes that underpinned the rapid growth in patenting. Starting in the early 1980s the United States Supreme Court gradually extended patent protection to cover new areas such as biotechnology, software, business methods, and scientific research methods (see Hall 2007). Universities have also become much more active in patenting since the Bayh–Dole Act in 1980.[3] In 1982 the United States created a Court of Appeals for the Federal Circuit to handle cases of patent infringement and validity. The result was a strengthening of patent holders' rights.[4] In 1984 the Drug Price Competition and Patent Restoration Act allowed an extra five years of patent protection when companies had spent time gaining approval for the patented drug. In the early 1990s the

---

[2] The United States Patent and Trademark Office (www.uspto.gov/web/offices/ac/ido/oeip/taf/reports.htm). The text focuses on the U.S. case, but the number of patents has also increased at the European Patent Office, tripling between 1985 and 2005 (see Hall (2007) and see figure 3.1 for other countries).

[3] The Bayh–Dole Act allowed universities to apply directly for patents (and then license these) for scientific advances that arose from federally funded research projects. See the discussion in section 4.5.

[4] Over the period 1982–90 around 90% of patents that had been found to be valid and infringed were upheld on appeal, compared with 62% over the period 1953–78 (Gallini 2002, p. 134).

USPTO was made a "profit center" and, it is argued, this made it keen to process more patents and reduce the costs of examining. In 1994 the United States increased the term of protection for patents from seventeen years to twenty years in adherence to the TRIPS minimum standard. At the same time, developments in information technology have allowed faster and better searches, hence lowering the costs of using the patent system.

Did this series of policy and legal changes drive the growth in U.S. patenting? Kortum and Lerner (1998) analyzed the situation up to 1995. First, they note that excluding biotechnology and software patents still leaves 90% of the increase unexplained. Second, they argue that the "friendly court" hypothesis (i.e., that the new Court of Appeals was friendly toward patentees) should have also encouraged an increase in foreign patenting in the United States. They argue that this did not occur, at least when they consider French, German, and British patenting in the United States.[5] Eliminating these two possibilities causes them to stress a "technological opportunities" explanation: greater opportunities combined, perhaps, with better management of research and intellectual property were major factors. Hall and Ziedonis (2001), however, find that for the semiconductor industry at least, the "friendly court" hypothesis receives support.[6] More recent work, summarized in the books by Jaffe and Lerner (2004) and Bessen and Meurer (2008) (discussed below), also argues strongly that the rapid growth in patents has been policy led.

Is the Rapid Growth in U.S. Patenting Conducive to Innovation and Growth?

Given that there is some evidence that the patent explosion was policy related, and did not simply reflect technological or research-related changes in the economy, we move to question (b). Asking whether the increase in patenting was conducive to innovation and growth may appear an odd question, but this question has attracted considerable debate in the United States.[7] While there is some research into this

---

[5] The U.S. patent and trademark data referenced above shows that from the 1960s onward the share of foreign patenting in the United States has risen steadily from around 20% to 50%. This suggests some caution in accepting Kortum and Lerner's argument.

[6] Hall (2005) shows that the structural break in the growth of U.S. patenting occurred in 1984 and that this was driven by computer, electrical, electronic, mechanical, and communications related patents.

[7] One result of the debate was the United States Patent Reform Act of 2007, which attempted to improve the working of the patent system. The House of Representatives passed the act in September 2007 but the Senate did not. A new Patent Reform Act 2009 has just been introduced in March 2009 for consideration by both the Senate and the House of Representatives. At the time of writing this has not yet been approved.

(difficult) question, there is no consensus. Here we summarize the key issues and trade-offs involved.

Chapter 3 stated that a major indicator of innovation is R&D expenditure and table 3.2 showed that the ratio of R&D to GDP in the United States was 2.76% in 2003. Over the period 1986–2006, R&D intensity in the United States remained roughly stable, with a dip around 1994. Hence, there is no immediate indication that the surge in patenting was associated with increased R&D effort. Table 3.4 also showed that the growth rate of U.S. GDP per hour worked did increase from 1995 to 2005, an outcome that has attracted much discussion. How much, if any, of this productivity growth was related to the increases in patenting in the 1990s is not known. In fact, the relationship between patenting, innovation, and growth is controversial (an issue we return to in chapter 12, where we look at cross-country evidence).

Even if we have difficulty assessing the link between patenting, innovation, and growth, is there any reason to think that it could be harmful? This is an issue that the book has already discussed, especially in chapter 6, but we recap and extend the discussion here. There are four generic areas of concern:

(1) **Strategic use of patents can reduce competition.** Patents may create barriers to entry and raise the production costs of incumbent or new firms. The use of so-called patent thickets is an example (see sections 6.4 and 6.6).

(2) **Patents can hinder sequential innovation.** Patents held by one firm can increase the costs of other firms' R&D, which then affects the next generation of innovations. This is especially applicable when there is "sequential innovation"—where one innovation builds on previous innovations—but also when innovation requires research methods that are patented.

(3) **The patent system adversely affects smaller firms and start-ups.** Both (1) and (2) above can create problems for smaller firms and start-ups. In addition, the high cost of monitoring, obtaining, and defending patents creates problems (see section 6.5).

(4) **Patent races are inefficient.** Competition to be the first to patent can lead to excessive and inefficient R&D spending (see section 6.2). This is also called the "common pool problem," which means there is excessive competition to win the prize.

These possible detrimental effects of patenting have been discussed in the U.S. case. Jaffe and Lerner (2004) provide an extended discussion and argue that the U.S. patent system reduces innovation. The title of their book, *Innovation and Its Discontents: How Our Broken Patent System is Endangering Innovation and Progress, and What to Do About It*, sums up their opinion. Their book draws attention to three specific failings:

Low patent quality. Too many patents are granted in the United States for obvious and not new inventions. This clogs up the patent system and devalues even the novel and nonobvious patents.[8]

High uncertainty. This is related to the above, but also to the litigation system, which has made some very large awards, as well as to the strategic use of patents by firms.[9]

High costs. This is a problem both for the USPTO and for users of the patent system. The overall cost of the patent system is now several billion dollars per year and there is an "arms race" effect where all companies struggle to keep up.[10]

Bessen and Meurer (2008) also argue that the U.S. patent system is failing. Their approach is to consider the basic question of whether the patent system is beneficial to firms (i.e., they investigate the private values and do not attempt the more difficult assessment of social values). They find that for U.S. chemical and pharmaceutical firms there is a net benefit, but for all other industries and firms there is a net cost (especially since 1994). In short, they argue that the costs associated with litigation, and trying to avoid litigation, are now greater than the benefits. They note, for example, that patent litigation in software is almost twice as likely as the average for all types of patents. More strikingly, around 14% of business method patents end up in litigation in the United States (Bessen and Meurer 2008, p. 191).

The U.S. experience over the last twenty or so years has given some background and insight into the functioning of the patent system. Some authors argue that the U.S. patent system is underperforming, and there is some evidence for this. There is little recent evidence from other

---

[8] Their book lists various apparently trivial patents, such as the "Method for swinging on a swing" and the "Sealed crustless sandwich."

[9] The number of patent cases initiated in the United States has risen from around 1,250 per annum in 1991 to around 2,500 in 2001, with an increasing share of the patent cases ending up at trial before juries (Jaffe and Lerner 2004, pp. 14, 123). One example surrounds the actions of Rambus, a company that designs memory chips. A patent it filed in 1990 was (correctly) used as a basis to collect royalties, but as chip technology evolved Rambus attempted to alter its original application. It attempted to claim royalties by bringing patent infringement suits through the 1990s. In 2001, a judge threw out one of the cases saying that "Rambus knew, or should have known, that its patent infringement suit was baseless, unjustified, and frivolous" (Jaffe and Lerner 2004, pp. 86–72).

[10] One example of this was the popular book *Rembrandts in the Attic*, which encouraged firms to search for options to acquire and exploit new intellectual property (Rivette and Kline 1999).

countries. Branstetter (2004) reviews two studies on Japan—a country that strengthened its patent system in the 1980s and 1990s—and finds no evidence that stronger patent protection improved R&D, although they stress that Japanese firms faced other problems at this time (e.g., low demand growth, failure to diversify R&D). In contrast to the situation in the United States, U.K. patenting activity by large firms has been static or falling, prompting questions about whether U.K. business is underperforming (Rogers et al. 2007).

Policy Options for Patents

Policy makers are interested in ensuring that the patent system achieves the best outcome for the economy and for society. Recent U.S. debates suggest that their patent system is underperforming. There are many changes and adjustments that have been suggested for the United States and, more generally, there are many aspects of the patent system that can be altered. This is the case even if countries have signed up to TRIPS, since this only specifies minimum standards in many areas (such as length of protection) and does not specify all parts of the intellectual property system. Table 11.1 provides a list of some potential policies that can be used, along with some comments on and examples of them.

The Role of Licensing and Technology Markets

A key issue in the debates on the working of the IPR system is the role of licensing. If firms and inventors could find out about relevant patents quickly, and then license them for a reasonable cost, then much of the criticism would dissipate. It is useful to distinguish two basic types of firms that are interested in licensing. First, firms that want the license for production, some of which may be direct competitors to the licensee. Second, innovators who want to license a technology or process to assist in their innovative activity. The fact that today's innovators may rely on previous innovations is sometimes called sequential innovation or cumulative innovation, or, more generally, "standing on the shoulders of others."

Consider a firm that wants to innovate where this requires using others' patented technology. If the complexity and cost of obtaining the necessary licenses, and the risk of being sued if any are missed, are high, then innovation may be stifled. Bessen and Meurer (2008, p. 8) recount that a firm thinking of selling online in the United States potentially has 11,000 patents that they could be infringing. The potential innovator

Table 11.1. Examples of patent policies.

IPR policy	Comments
Patent insurance	There has been widespread interest in encouraging or providing patent insurance for many years. This could alleviate fear of litigation, which may be especially beneficial for SMEs. Reports for the European Commission concluded that there were no examples of successful insurance markets, despite companies reporting a need (CJA Consultants Ltd 2003, 2006). In general, insurance markets are limited when there is a lack of information about risks and an adverse selection problem. The idea of a compulsory insurance scheme, which would avoid adverse selection, is therefore thought to be the only option.
Dispute resolution	Intellectual property offices can offer independent advice on IPR disputes and also offer mediation services (e.g., the U.K. IPO's patent mediation service). The idea is to reduce costs by avoiding litigation.
Lengthening protection	This should encourage more use of IPRs and may increase innovation. The United States increased its patent term from seventeen to twenty years in 1994. It also increased its copyright term by twenty years, to author's life plus seventy years, in 1998. Note that TRIPS only sets minimum lengths of protection for IPRs.
Enforcement	Most concerns surround copyright infringement and trademark infringement (counterfeiting). Authorities can increase resources for detecting and stopping such activities.
Scope and/or breadth	Legislative or legal rulings can alter the scope or breadth of IPRs. Sakakibara and Branstetter (1999) analyzed increase patent scope in Japan in 1988, finding it had little impact on R&D activity.
Nonobviousness or "inventive step"	"Nonobviousness" (U.S. terminology) or "inventive step" (European) is a concept meaning that the patented invention should not be obvious to a person skilled in the relevant art (e.g., it should not be a combination of existing techniques). Altering the criteria for the inventive step for a patent (or the criteria for granting a trademark or design) will alter the number of patents issued and, in turn, will alter a firm's incentives to patent. See Encaoua et al. (2006) for a discussion of this.

may not be a competitor to the patent holders, but their entry into markets is impeded or stopped. If the firm is a potential competitor, then the license holder may try to hold up or prevent entry (although such actions may violate antitrust legislation: see sections 6.4 and 11.4). Patents may also impede basic research activities if certain research tools that involve patenting and licenses are expensive.[11] On the other hand, technology

---

[11] Walsh et al. (2003) consider patenting and licensing changes in biomedical innovation and conclude that "drug discovery has not been substantially impeded by these changes" (p. 285).

Table 11.1. Continued.

IPR policy	Comments
Opposition or reexamination system	The EPO has an opposition system for patents, while the USPTO has a reexamination system. Both systems offer the possibility of a "second stage" check on patent quality. Graham et al. (2002) find that the EPO system is thirty times more likely to be used than the U.S. system. Altering the mechanisms of such systems will alter patent quality but also present strategic opportunities to firms.
Cost of obtaining and maintaining IPRs	The application and renewal fees for patents and trademarks will have an impact on the numbers of applications and the stock of IPRs. Traditionally, most intellectual property offices have used low application fees to encourage applications. The rapid increase in applications in many offices has led to an interest in analyzing how fees should be optimally set (e.g., Gans et al. 2004; Baudry and Dumont 2006).
Utility models	TRIPS allows countries the option of having a "utility model," which is best described as a cross between a patent and a design (see section 2.5). These can be introduced as a way of helping smaller and new firms. IP Australia (2005) suggests that the Australian "innovation patent" has met its objective of encouraging SMEs to use the IPR system.
Education and outreach activities	Inform firms, especially SMEs, of the possible benefits of IPRs. IP Genesis at the French Industrial Property Office offers a free intellectual property audit to SMEs who are not using the intellectual property system, especially the patent system.

Notes. This table focuses on patents, but section 11.2 below discusses some specific copyright and trademark policies.

markets have the potential to improve R&D efficiency by allowing firms to specialize. Both Arora and Fosfuri (2000) for the chemical industry and Hall and Ziedonis (2001) for semiconductors find that licensing allows specialization and vertical disintegration to occur.

These two opposite effects—reducing innovation due to patent complexity and increasing R&D effectiveness due to specialization—imply that the overall effect of the patent system depends on the functioning of markets for technology. Hence, the problem for policy makers is that, for example, strengthening the patent system might have an adverse effect if the markets for technology are not well developed. Where there is a lack of information about patentees and licenses, together with high transaction and high legal costs, strengthening patents would make things worse. Hence, as might be expected, patent policy is entwined with innovation policy more broadly defined and, ultimately, with the concept of "national systems of innovation" discussed in chapter 4.

IP Offices: Delays and Opposition

The rapid growth in patent applications to the USPTO in recent years has put strain on the patent system and, in particular, the examination process. The patent examiners' main duty is to evaluate applications for novelty and nonobviousness. A major part of this is searching the *prior art*—the stock of all knowledge relating to the patent application whether in prior patents, publications, books, theses, or the like. Rapid increases in applications, combined with increased length and complexity of patent applications, mean that this task becomes more and more difficult unless the resources devoted to the examination process keep pace.[12] For example, the USPTO saw an increase of 73% in the backlog of patent applications between 2002 and 2007, and forecasts suggest it will be unable to recruit sufficient examiners to reduce this backlog. One response to the backlogs, and a way of improving the examinations system in general, is to try new methods of assessing prior art.[13] The rise in trademark applications has generated much less concern, at least in academic and policy forums. Part of this is due to the fact that trademark applications do not require examination for novelty and nonobviousness and are generally short documents. Furthermore, at least some of the monitoring process is placed on others through the opposition process.

Is Copyright Working?

The first copyright law in the United States in 1790 provided for an initial term of fourteen years plus a renewal of equal length.[14] The United States revised copyright in 1831 (to twenty-eight years plus fourteen years renewal), 1909 (renewal to twenty-eight years), 1962 (renewal to forty-seven years), 1976 (to life of author plus fifty years), and 1998 (life plus seventy years). Other countries have had similar patterns of slowly

---

[12] One way of assessing the increasing complexity is to count the average number of claims made in each patent. Guellec and van Pottelsberghe (2007, chapter 7) note that claims per European patent doubled between 1980 and 2005; Hall (2007) refers to evidence that Japanese patent claims tripled between 1990 and 2003. The length of patent applications has also increased, with some now having thousands of pages. Comparing the EPO and USPTO in 2004, Guellec and van Pottelsberghe (2007, chapter 7) find that applications per examiner are twice as high at the USPTO.

[13] For example, the USPTO and the U.K. Intellectual Property Office have trialed a "Peer to Patent" system where practitioners and researchers can suggest relevant prior art (*Economist*, September 8, 2007, pp. 25–26).

[14] This reflected the situation in England, which dated from the earlier Statute of Anne in 1710.

increasing copyright protection.[15] Currently, members of the World Trade Organization must adhere to TRIPS, which specifies a minimum copyright term of life of the author plus seventy years. It is also worth noting that, in many OECD countries, industries that rely on copyright account for an expanding share of GDP.[16]

The increasing length of protection for copyright is one of the broad areas of controversy for policy. In comparison with the twenty years for patents, copyright protection looks overly long. It is important to remember that copyright protects the *expression* of ideas and not the ideas themselves—a distinction that is not applicable for inventions. This implies that copyright offers only very narrow protection, whereas patents can be considered wider in coverage. Even so, the long and increasing length of protection for copyright is contentious. From an economic perspective, policy should balance out the incentives (of an extra year of protection) against the loss in consumer welfare and any impact on subsequent creators of copyright.[17] The latter can be important since most creators draw inspiration from, and often reuse (or remix), generic ideas. In contrast, extending copyright from, say, 100 to 101 years provides very little additional economic incentive.[18] In general, this economic approach to copyright term extension has been ignored. This is, perhaps, shown most clearly by the fact that the U.S. 1998 extension was applied to existing creative works (most of which were created many years ago) so the legislation was essentially retroactive. Obviously, there is no possibility of an incentive effect since the work has already been created (Akerlof et al. 2002). Instead, the decisions to lengthen copyright have often relied on arguments about fairness, pension income, and supporting companies.[19]

---

[15] See the discussion above in section 2.6. The length of copyright varies according to the type of work (e.g., music, film, books) and also whether it was created as a "work for hire" (e.g., when a film company employs a writer but copyright is retained by the company).

[16] It is estimated that such industries now account for 6% of U.S. GDP and 7.3% of U.K. GDP (WIPO 2005; HM Treasury 2006).

[17] See Corrigan and Rogers (2005) for a detailed explanation of the economics of copyright.

[18] The economic incentive is based on the present value of the additional profit made in year 101. The present value of $1 in year 101 is calculated using the formula $1/(1+r)^{101}$, where r is the discount rate, which equals $0.007 when $r = 0.05$ (or 5%): see section A.2 in the mathematical appendix. There is also the issue that such long periods are outside most people's planning horizon.

[19] For example, the 2008 EU Directive on extending copyright protection to performers and sound recordings to ninety-five years (from fifty years) stresses that this will allow performers a source of pension income and give companies additional profits to allow them to invest and "adapt to the rapidly changing business environment" (Press Release IP/08/1156, EU, Brussels).

The issue of supporting companies and creators in the creative industries is directly related to the issue of copyright infringement, which is often referred to as *piracy*. Piracy has long been a problem—Charles Dickens campaigned against U.S. book publishers immediately copying his books in the nineteenth century—although recent technological advances in copying technology (photocopiers, computers, the Internet, file-sharing software) have increased its scope. Nevertheless, the issue is not just that of how many copies are made, but rather the question at issue for policy is whether the incentives to creators and authors are in fact reduced by piracy. This hinges on whether the production and sale of originals is reduced (as pirate copies are substitutes for originals) or remains the same (when pirate copies are complementary, reaching a new audience).[20] The policy response to infringement should perhaps be to improve enforcement rather than increase the length of copyright protection, and there are attempts to do this. One of the difficult issues authorities face is that infringement has an international aspect; hence cooperation between countries is required (see chapter 12).

The increasing importance of copyright in advanced economies, combined with the lengthening protection and calls for greater enforcement, is behind a movement calling for a *reduction* in copyright protection. Lessig (2002, 2004) and Boyle (2003) are two prominent proponents of the idea that copyright in particular, and IPRs in general, are increasingly stifling creativity and innovation. Again, the phrase "tragedy of the anti-commons" is used to describe the situation where too many aspects of the societal knowledge base are held as IPRs and that this is stifling the creation of new knowledge.[21] Despite the arguments for this, as well as many supporting anecdotes, it is difficult to find empirical evidence for the overall effects of copyright on the economy. As Corrigan and Rogers (2005) and others have pointed out, there is a strong need for further empirical analysis of these issues.

With increasing copyright coverage, new creators and users need to be aware of whether they are infringing and also understand and pursue the possibility of obtaining licenses. For copyright this is hampered by the lack of a compulsory register of all copyright—something that is expressly prohibited by the Berne Convention (see section 2.6). Given this situation, the difficulty in finding copyright owners can be severe and the name "orphan work" is given to the many cases where ownership cannot

---

[20] Note that, despite the possibility of copying music, many customers do buy copies of songs (e.g., from iTunes). The reasons for this include convenience and a sense of fairness.

[21] For example, proponents point out that no one will be able to do to Disney what Disney did to the Brothers Grimm or to Victor Hugo.

be traced. Varian (2006) provides a summary and an economic analysis, indicating that there is a market failure since neither the owner of the copyright nor the potential user will have sufficient incentive to search for each other. This means that policy has a role in encouraging owners to use a copyright registry and ensuring that the legislation surrounding infringement is fair to both parties. Failure to minimize the costs associated with this process will have an impact on creative activity.[22]

A final set of policy-related issues can be illustrated by considering the Google Library Project and the Google Publisher Project. Since 2005 Google Library has scanned and indexed millions of books from major libraries around the world. For books that are out of copyright, the full text of the book is available. For books that are in copyright the service only allows access to small portions of text. Why is it that Google can scan books in copyright and provide this service? They argue that this is allowable under the "fair use" clause in U.S. copyright law (called "fair dealing" in the United Kingdom). This allows small portions of, say, a book to be used for education, reporting, research, or parody. The Google Publisher Project scans in recently published books with the permission of the publisher, indexes them, and allows people to view a few pages. The publishers have an interest in this since it allows "sampling," which may generate more sales of the books. Both of these examples indicate how low-cost search methods, combined with legal frameworks that generate incentives for the creation of databases, have the potential to improve social welfare.

Do We Really Need Patents and Copyright?

Boldrin and Levine (2002) believe that the optimal length of a patent, or copyright, may be zero. This reflects a much older and ongoing concern surrounding the need for IPRs. In the mid-nineteenth century the "Patent Controversy" in Europe criticized the patent system as reducing economic efficiency and it was thought unnecessary to create incentives to innovate in this way. The debate caused the Dutch to abolish their patent system in 1869 and delayed the introduction of patent systems in Germany (1877) and Switzerland (1888) (see Guellec and van Pottelsberghe 2007).

In their recent analysis Boldrin and Levine (2002) make a distinction between the *right of first sale* when an item is placed on the market and the *downstream licensing* of intellectual property arising from continued

---

[22] The United States is currently considering the Orphan Works Act (www.copyright. gov/orphan/). In the United Kingdom, Gowers (HM Treasury 2006) also drew attention to the need for a registry of copyright.

protection under intellectual property law. In their view, ownership of the first is necessary but the second is not. They argue that there is sufficient profit available to innovators from the advantages of being the first to bring their innovative product to market without the need for continued protection (which is what causes much of the distortion leading to welfare losses).

Their model relies on innovators gaining substantial revenue from the first sale of the product. In many fields of scientific invention this seems unrealistic, for example in pharmaceuticals, where the crucial inventions can precede the bringing to market of the product by up to a decade, or even more, due to the high level of product testing required in this field. Conceptually, the point of first sale in this case is the sale of the knowledge of the chemical structure or production method to a firm that would produce the drug, but even this knowledge may leak out during testing.

More generally, there is the inherent difficulty of establishing the value of a knowledge-based invention without revealing its properties, and once the knowledge is revealed nobody will bid anything if there is no IPR protection. Further criticism of the Boldrin and Levine thesis is given in Encaoua et al. (2006), but these authors also remind us that firms have always had the option of protecting their inventions by secrecy and choosing not to patent. When IPRs are weak the firm can choose to rely on trade secrecy law and the slow process of discovery through reverse engineering, thus avoiding the need to disclose its findings via a patent. Chapter 6 shows that trade secrecy is, in fact, rated more highly than patents as a means of appropriability (see figure 6.1).

Another example of this debate appears in copyright literature concerning the first sale of music or books, where the buyer is paying for the right to copy and sell the song. The original analysis of this idea, which looked at the sale of journals to libraries and their right to copy them, was by Liebowitz (1985). In the case of selling journals in libraries one can see how the price set for a journal could be high since subsequent copying has a well-defined value and is controlled. In contrast, with today's technology, selling music over the Internet allows anyone to copy and distribute, making the possibility of the first sale generating large revenues quite small.

Further strong arguments against the standard view—that IPRs are justified by market failure in knowledge generation—are advanced by Dosi et al. (2006). They make three criticisms: first, that markets are not just devices for allocating resources but are dynamic instruments (albeit imperfect ones) for the production and testing of "novelty"; second, that markets are embedded and depend on a whole ensemble of nonmarket institutions, such as the public science community; and third, that there is a misleading identification of knowledge with information, which neglects the processes generating useful knowledge and includes much that is tacit. As Nelson (2006) warns, there is not always a sharp division between the interests of firms and the interests of the public in the design of IPRs. He quotes examples where producers in sectors as varied as pharmaceuticals and software can have a preference for an IPR system that does not block progress by imposing too high a cost on the use of others' technology.

Are Trademarks Useful?

The basic argument for having trademarks is that they help to solve potential information asymmetries between sellers and buyers. A firm can use a trademark to signal that a product or service is of a certain, consistent quality. This reduces the search costs for customers and can potentially benefit both firm and consumer. Chapters 2 and 6 also noted that this basic role is linked to innovation. Without trademarks— or some legislation relating to unfair competition—competitors could imitate products or services using the same name, logo, and packaging, which would rapidly remove the incentive for investment in quality improvements. A formal registration system for trademarks is intended to reduce inadvertent imitation, as well as discourage deliberate imitation (counterfeiting), as the registry can be searched and, if necessary, provides clarity in legal cases.[23] Note also that the existence of trademarks generates incentives for firms to *maintain* the quality of products, since any deviation from this (e.g., product recalls, health or safety fears) leads consumers to make an immediate, direct link to the firm. In addition, the existence of trademarks plays a part in allowing greater flexibility in the way production is organized. An example of this is franchising in the food and drink industry. The upstream firm (the franchisor) specializes in marketing and innovation, while downstream firms (franchisees) specialize in supplying the food and drink.[24]

---

[23] All major economies have laws relating to "unfair competition" and most have common-law trademark protection for unregistered trademarks. Unfair competition (also called "palming off" in the United States and "passing off" in the United Kingdom) covers cases where a competitor, deliberately or not, misrepresents themselves as another. Potentially this covers a wider set of circumstances than trademark infringement, such as using similar advertising campaigns or marketing methods. This means that both unfair competition and trademark infringement are often involved in legal disputes (Jacob et al. 2004).

[24] Useful overviews of the economic role of trademarks can be found in Landes and Posner (2003) and Economides (1998).

A first question is: why have trademark registrations increased so much in some countries in recent years (see figure 3.2)? There are a number of possible reasons, including increased innovation, a rise in information asymmetry, the expansion in the types of trademarks allowable (e.g., colors, smells, music, shapes), shifts in economic activity toward more intensively trademarking sectors, and, finally, the possibility of a change in management "fashion" creating a rush to register existing marks. Separating out the factors involved is not straightforward. Trademarks are used extensively in the service sector, and there has been a shift in economic activity toward services, but some studies have found that the manufacturing sector is more trademark intensive (Greenhalgh and Rogers 2008). As discussed above, there has been an increase in patent activity alongside the growth in trademarks, but it is difficult to prove that this has been the result of increased innovation. Analysis of the causes of the growth in trademarks is limited and there is little more we can say; the only two studies (known to us) that analyze trademark growth (both in Australia) conclude that many of the above factors appear to be at work (Loundes and Rogers 2003; Jensen and Webster 2004).

The next set of questions concerns whether the rapid growth in trademarking has been beneficial or harmful for society. Chapter 6 made clear that there is evidence that trademarks improve the private performance of firms. This is an important result, but ideally we would like to know more. For example, it could be that trademarking helps large incumbent firms but acts as a barrier to entry to new firms or disadvantages smaller firms. Trademarks could act in this way for a number of reasons. First, trademarks support a strategy of brand differentiation, which has been claimed to reduce the ability of new firms to enter a market.[25] The idea is that an incumbent firm can break the market down into many different submarkets, meaning that entrants have difficulty in gaining market share. Second, incumbent firms can attempt to trademark all the best marks that could be used in the market—a strategy known as "banking" trademarks—something that is generally not allowed, but which we discuss further below. Third, an incumbent can oppose a new entrant's trademark applications to try and alter their strategy (see table 6.3). All of these strategies could also be used against current competitors, not just entrants to the market. Is there any evidence that such activities do occur?

The extent to which all trademarks support brand differentiation and, in turn, how important this is across industries in the economy is not

---

[25] The original study was that by Schmalensee (1978) on the breakfast cereal market.

known.[26] More is known about the issue of "banking" trademarks. Under U.S. trademark law, a trademark is only issued if there is "intent to use" within six months, hence the possibility of banking unused trademarks to prevent competitors using them is illegal. In Japan, trademarks unused after three years are supposed to be canceled. However, a survey in 1996 found that 32% of Japanese registered trademarks had never been used, leading to a tightening of the system (Landes and Posner 2003, p. 180). A European Community trademark must be used within five years of registration otherwise it is revoked. Overall, therefore, especially in Europe there is some limited scope for "banking," but it is clear that the legal system recognizes this and aims to prevent it. The issue of "banking" is clearly illustrated by the "cybersquatters" of the 1990s. Cybersquatters registered large numbers of Internet domain names intending to charge firms for them at a later date. The U.S. Anticybersquatting Consumer Protection Act in 1999 prohibited such behavior.

A further issue concerns the opposition system. At some stage in a trademark application a public notice (publication) is issued so that oppositions can be made.[27] For Community trademarks a three-month period is given for opposition and, for the period 1996–2004, 17% of all trademark publications received oppositions.[28] Von Graevenitz (2008) finds that some companies gain reputations for an aggressive defense of their trademark portfolios, but it is not clear exactly how this affects their performance, let alone the wider issues of entry and competition. It does, however, appear to be the case that firms use the opposition process strategically, not just to stop competitors' trademarks but also to influence the nature and scope of their trademarks (see chapter 6).

There is also a wider set of issues concerning brands and persuasive advertising that discussions about the role of trademarks sometimes touch upon. In summary, some argue that high levels of advertising can cause a welfare loss to society since companies exploit consumers using sophisticated advertising and marketing techniques. In many countries the possibility of this is recognized: for example, advertising of cigarettes and alcohol is regulated. Equally, there are normally standards governing the accuracy and nature of advertising. A full discussion of these issues

---

[26] In recent years, industrial organization has increasingly studied individual industries, rather than attempting to assess broad relationships that apply across industries.

[27] In the United Kingdom a trademark publication is issued about three months after application and then three months are allowed for oppositions to be made. In the United States the opposition period is thirty days.

[28] Von Graevenitz (2008) states that the equivalent figure for U.S. trademarks is around 6%. Rules and legislation on the importance of the opposition system vary across countries.

is outside the scope of this book but, in any event, the link to trademark activity is fairly weak.

11.3 Incentive Systems for Encouraging Firm-Level R&D

Chapter 5 discussed research showing that the private returns to R&D are often found to be "high" (i.e., above the typical hurdle rate for investment projects). Why then would governments decide to offer tax incentives for firms to undertake R&D? The answer is that (as indicated in figure 1.6) the social returns to R&D are thought to be in excess of private returns, hence governments want to encourage more private R&D as it is beneficial to aggregate innovation and growth.[29] There are a number of ways to stimulate private R&D, including tax incentives, direct subsidies and grants, and encouraging joint ventures. This section provides an overview of the issues and arguments surrounding these methods.

R&D Tax Incentives

R&D tax incentives are relatively common in OECD countries. OECD (2002) indicates that eighteen OECD countries use some form of R&D tax incentives—these include the United States, France, Japan, and the United Kingdom. The two main types of R&D tax incentives are "level" and "incremental."[30] A "level" or "volume" scheme provides the tax relief on the total amount of R&D (although there may be upper limits). An "incremental" system gives the tax relief on *increases* in R&D over a base figure. The base figure can be calculated in various ways, such as average R&D expenditure over the last three years, but its central objective is to increase R&D spending. A "level" R&D tax incentive is more straightforward to implement, but does give tax relief on R&D that would have been conducted anyway. An "incremental" scheme avoids this problem but— depending on exactly how the base figure is calculated and updated—can create some quite complex, and even negative, incentives for firms (see Bloom et al. 2001). As an indication of this, if the base figure is simply last year's R&D, a firm should realize that increasing R&D now will reduce tax relief in the future (since base year spending will rise). These

---

[29] Chapter 5 briefly discussed the empirical evidence on social returns. Nadiri (1993, abstract) states that "the evidence points to sizable R&D spillover effects both at the firm and industry levels; the social rates of return of R&D often vary from 20% to over 100% in various industries."

[30] To be completely accurate, tax incentives can also be either "tax credits," which is when a percentage of R&D can be deducted from payable income tax, or "tax allowances," which is when a multiple of actual R&D is deducted from taxable income.

issues mean that many countries opt for a "level" system or, possibly, a combination of both.

In 2000, the United Kingdom substantially altered its policy with regard to tax incentives by introducing a tax credit for SMEs. This allowed SMEs to deduct 150% of qualifying R&D from taxable profits. In addition, if the SME did not make profits, it could "surrender" its R&D losses for a cash payment of 24% of their value. This example indicates how tax relief can be targeted at certain firms, as well as how schemes can be linked to providing finance. The R&D tax relief was extended to large firms in 2002 (but at the rate of 125%). In contrast, the United States introduced an incremental tax credit in 1981, using a base figure from the past three years.[31] A major reason for its introduction was a fear that the United States was falling behind other countries, in particular Japan, in terms of R&D and innovation.[32] Was the U.S. 1981 R&D tax credit successful in raising business R&D? Hall (1992) provides a detailed assessment of what is, in fact, a difficult question to answer.[33] She finds that the tax credit stimulated around $2 billion extra in R&D each year for a loss of tax revenue of around $1 billion each year.

In general, evidence on the effectiveness of R&D tax incentives from different OECD countries suggests that they do increase R&D. Hall and Van Reenen (2000) review the evidence in detail and find that a rough guide is that a $1 increase in R&D occurs for every $1 of tax relief. While it is useful to have knowledge about the cost of increasing R&D, ideally one would like more detail about the societal benefits of the increased R&D. The estimates of the social rate of return to R&D suggest it is high. Nevertheless, more specific information on the tax-based increases would be useful. For example, Tassey (2007) finds that the level of *basic research* by industry has been relatively stable in the United States since the early 1980s—and it was this basic research that the U.S. 1981 tax credit aimed to increase (i.e., the increases in R&D in the United States came primarily from increases in the development phase of research). Since some

---

[31] The U.S. Economic Recovery Tax Act of 1981 refers to a "Research and Experimentation" (R&E) tax credit, and not R&D, but the term R&D is more common. The use of experimentation was intended to emphasize significant advances in technology, rather than incremental improvements. The conditions used to define "qualifying expenditures" reflected this intention (Tassey 2007).

[32] As chapter 3 indicated, the U.S. economy's performance in terms of growth in GDP per hour worked did subsequently improve, although the main improvement was in the late 1990s (see table 3.4).

[33] The difficulty arises from a number of issues: ideally one should model firms' decision making, but this requires a range of assumptions; other aspects of the tax system in the United States were changing during the 1980s; and there is always a concern that firms are simply relabeling existing activities as R&D.

studies find that basic research has the highest social value, this implies a more critical evaluation of the U.S. tax credits.

Another important issue relates to the responsiveness of *real* R&D spending to tax incentives. A good way to understand this issue is to assume that scientists and engineers do all R&D and that there are no capital or other input costs (e.g., laboratories or chemicals). Furthermore, scientists and engineers require long periods of education and training in the university system. Hence, the short-run response of firms to a tax credit is constrained by a fixed (or very inelastic) supply of scientists and engineers, and therefore real R&D effort cannot change. However, it is likely that some firms will try to hire extra researchers and this would start to increase the wages of researchers. Ultimately, this wage pressure may cause nominal R&D to rise, although the real R&D effort would be the same (i.e., the same number of researchers are employed). Clearly, such a situation is extreme: researchers could be enticed from abroad or from retirement; new capital could be purchased; etc. However, these issues indicate that measuring real R&D spending is important.[34] Equally, it also points to the fact that policies need to be coordinated (as discussed in chapter 4).

Direct R&D Grants and Other Schemes

Many countries also operate direct R&D grant schemes whereby firms can apply for grants or joint ventures are funded. OECD (2007) reports that such grants are becoming less important as a share of business R&D (down from 11% of total business R&D in 1995 to 7% in 2005). It can, however, be important in funding specific firms (e.g., for SMEs, as in the United Kingdom's SMART program) or technologies (e.g., the United States's Advanced Technology Program) or in encouraging joint research ventures (e.g., the United Kingdom's LINK scheme).[35]

Evaluating the impact of R&D grant programs requires some thought. Jaffe (2002) draws attention to the problems of "selectivity" and "crowding out." Selectivity occurs since the government agency is, of course, trying to select the best R&D projects or the best firms to fund; hence, any ex post evaluation has a biased sample of good projects and firms with no comparable group. This makes it difficult to isolate the impact of the grant scheme itself. Crowding out refers to the idea that the grant may simply replace private R&D spending since the good project would

---

[34] Goolsbee (1998), in an analysis of U.S. R&D, suggests that accounting for the wage increases of scientists and engineers suggests that R&D tax policy is between 30% and 50% less effective than previously thought.

[35] OECD (2006) contains a review of such schemes in ten countries.

have been funded anyhow.[36] This said, where there are financing difficulties for R&D, the award of a government grant will raise R&D and may,
in fact, "crowd in" other R&D (since banks or venture capital firms may
free ride on the government's evaluation process).

Other Incentives for Innovation: Prizes, Awards, and Patent Buyouts

In 1714 the British government offered a substantial prize for anyone
that came up with a method of determining a ship's longitude. The
inability to do this caused acute problems for navigation, and hence for
Britain's military and trading situation. John Harrison finally won the
prize in 1773 after he spent decades working on the project. Throughout history many other prizes have been offered, such as Napoleon's
food preservation prize in 1795 and the 1895 *Chicago Times–Herald*
prize for a motor vehicle that could travel fifty-four miles. Even today
there is a range of prizes on offer, including the U.S. Project Bioshield
(for countermeasures against bioterrorism), the Grainger Challenges (a
filtration system for well water in developing countries), and the Virgin
Earth Challenge (to remove greenhouse gases (Krohmal 2007)). In each of
these cases a well-defined objective and criteria are specified ex ante (i.e.,
ahead of the innovation). A closely related incentive scheme is to offer
an award for contributions in a particular area, where the award does
not specify an amount. For example, after World War II the U.S. Patent
Compensation Board was established to provide awards for innovations
in atomic energy, where patents were not allowed for security reasons
(i.e., the disclosure of information in patents would allow foreign countries to learn about the innovation). The advantage of such awards is that
they provide incentives for diverse innovations; the disadvantage is that
the innovators do not know the amount of the award that they might
receive.

   The limited use of prizes and awards is an indicator of one of the fundamental issues at stake: innovators come up with contributions in many
different areas, some of which have not even been considered ex ante.
This situation is one of asymmetric information, where the innovator
knows more than the prize giver. In fact, if there was no asymmetric
information, then public authorities (or the gainers from innovations)
could either pay for the R&D directly or give a prize for the equivalent
amount and obtain the innovation.

---

[36] Jaffe (2002) discusses the standard econometric methods that can help in these situations. He also mentions the possibility of incorporating the government agency's initial
rankings of projects into econometric analysis.

A related idea comes from Kremer (1998). He argues that the government could buy out patents after they have been granted and, importantly, that one should use an auction to determine a baseline private value of the patent.[37] Let us recap on the issues. Patents are used to provide an incentive for invention. It is not possible for governments to fund specific inventions because of asymmetric information (although general R&D subsidies can be used: see the next section). However, as chapter 2 discussed, once a patent is granted this creates a monopoly, which distorts the market by restricting the use of the new invention. Yet, at the same time, the profits from the monopoly do not fully reflect the social benefit, so the patent does not provide the socially optimal incentive. Kremer's solution is to (a) auction the patent to find private value, (b) pay the inventor a markup over this private value (to reflect its social value), and then (c) allow the invention to be freely used by all (speeding up diffusion and social benefits). In theory, this is a rather neat solution to the problem of providing incentives and maximizing benefits.[38] In practice, there are concerns over whether auctions would return fair values in all cases, and over the resources needed to fund and operate such a scheme (see Abramowicz 2001). Nevertheless, this sort of mechanism might be well suited to encouraging research into vaccines for diseases prevalent in developing countries (Glennerster and Kremer 2001).

11.4 Other Innovation Policies

This section provides a brief overview of some of the other policy areas that have an effect on innovation. As indicated in chapter 4, there are many factors involved and our aim here is only to offer some brief comments and references. The brevity is not to be taken as an indication that these policy areas are less important.

Policy toward Universities

Chapter 4 provided an overview of how universities contribute to the national system of innovation. Here we draw attention to a number of

---

[37] This idea, in fact, has a long history. The most famous example is probably the purchase by the French government in 1839 of the patent for the Daguerreotype process, which was the first process to allow photographic images to be created.

[38] The necessary incentive to create can in some areas be less than the full social value; for example, authors and composers may only require small grants to produce works of high social value when distributed at social cost.

policy-related issues. First, the way in which universities treat intellectual property is thought to be important. We mentioned the 1980 Bayh–Dole Act, which opened the way for U.S. universities to become more active in patenting and licensing, and many European countries have followed this lead. An important part of this process has been the establishment of technology transfer offices (TTOs).[39] The possible benefits of these changes include improved research focus and incentives for faculty, additional revenues to the universities, and wider diffusion (since previously, research results could have been lost in academic journals). Possible drawbacks of these changes include a shift of focus away from fundamental, "blue sky" research and less diffusion (since charging for licenses will limit uptake). A review of the evidence relating to these questions is presented in chapter 4.

A second, related, aspect is universities' involvement in entrepreneurship and spin-off firms. Again, chapter 4 has outlined the main issues at stake. Whereas university patenting (and licensing) has clear potential drawbacks, involvement in spin-off activity is less controversial, although it is possible that universities oversubsidize such activities and academics may divert their energies from research. There has been considerable study into how such spin-offs should be organized (e.g., the optimal shares of equity between scientist, faculty, and university; involvement of external entrepreneurs; financing) and Siegel et al. (2007) suggest that an important role for policy is to spread best practice. The third key role for universities is the education and, at times, training of future entrepreneurs, engineers, scientists, and production workers. Many governments spend large amounts on undergraduate teaching, although private contributions from students are also common, and there is a hope that this will supply the necessary workforce skills in the future. In some subjects—such as mathematics, chemistry, and engineering—there are regularly reports, often from industry associations, of shortages. Understanding and monitoring the human capital requirements needed for future innovation are important tasks for policy, as market signals (i.e., wages) may have slow and imperfect effects.

SMEs, High-tech Start-ups, and Entrepreneurship

There are a plethora of government policies designed to assist smaller firms. The main areas of activity can be classified as follows:

---

[39] In the United States, the number of TTOs increased from 600 in 1980 to 3,278 in 2005. Annual licensing revenue generated by U.S. universities rose from $160 million in 1991 to $1.4 billion in 2005 (Siegel et al. 2007).

Enterprise culture. Policies are intended to inform people, especially school and university students, of the opportunities of becoming an entrepreneur or working for smaller firms. For example, the United Kingdom conducts an "enterprise week" with a wide range of events, something that has led to the first "global enterprise week" (in 2008), with forty countries taking part.

Knowledge and skills. Programs that provide free, or subsidized, advice to smaller firms are common, including specialist courses on, for example, "how to use intellectual property" or "how to secure financing." The U.K. government operates a voucher scheme allowing firms to purchase consultancy or training. Policies may also encourage networking between firms and mentoring.

Access to finance. Loan guarantee schemes, grants, encouraging equity markets, and venture capital may all be part of a government's strategy to help smaller firms or start-ups. R&D tax credits are one aspect of this.

Regulation. All firms are subject to a host of regulations relating to accounting, tax compliance, environment, law, employment, and workplace. There is a concern that the burden of regulation can fall more heavily on smaller firms, hence various policies aim to monitor and streamline regulations.

Section 4.6 discussed the United States's Small Business Innovation Research (SBIR) Program, which started in 1982 and is regarded as successful (Lerner 1999). In general, the effectiveness of policies varies substantially and, in many cases, an assessment of effectiveness is difficult due to poor design or lack of follow-up (OECD 2008).

Competition Policy

The possible tension between competition (antitrust) policy and intellectual property is clear. Competition policy seeks to encourage and maintain competitive markets, which implies multiple firms none of which have substantial market power. An intellectual property system sets out to award a property right for an invention or innovation that can lead to market power. From a legal perspective this tension is resolved by various exemptions in competition law for intellectual property and R&D. These exemptions reflect the fact that both competition and intellectual property policy do, in fact, have the same ultimate objective: to raise societal welfare by promoting the supply of new and existing products and services at low prices (see Audretsch et al. 2001; Encaoua and Hollander

2002). A recent United States Supreme Court ruling stated that "[to] safeguard the incentive to innovate, the possession of monopoly power will not be found unlawful unless it is accompanied by an element of anticompetitive conduct."[40] This implies that antitrust policies should not interfere with IPRs stemming from innovation, but, as might be expected, there is often considerable argument as to what is the exact source of the monopoly power. One area of policy, which concerns both competition authorities and intellectual property policy makers, is that of the setting of industry standards for such areas as measurement, performance, safety, testing, and interoperability. The issue of who sets industry standards remains very pertinent to the efficient operation of business in a changing technological environment, as well as having many overlaps with competition policy.

Industry Standard Setting

In many industries standard setting is done by voluntary negotiation, involving the creation of private-sector standard-setting organizations (SSOs), many of which have a long history. Schmalensee (2008) cites the example of the Institute of Electrical and Electronics Engineers Standards Association (IEEE-SA), which has evolved from activities begun in 1896 and by 2001 had 866 standards and more than 450 working groups examining a further 526 projects.

Schmalensee asks whether competition authorities need to be concerned that these organizations may not work in the public interest, as generally the authorities do not approve of collaboration between competitors. He argues that the competition authorities may in fact welcome their activity, as achieving a more homogeneous product increases the need to compete on price, which enhances competition. Why, though, do SSOs behave well? For large firms, with broad patent portfolios, mutual forbearance can avoid engaging in costly infringement litigation. The consensus to charge each other low royalties holds, as any bad behavior by one firm in one period can be punished in the future, as the same firms repeatedly interact over time.

In his extensive policy review, Schmalensee goes on to explore whether there is any basis for preferring those who work their patents (i.e., integrated firms that both innovate and manufacture) over those who are innovation specialists and who engage in acquiring and licensing patents without production (the so-called patent trolls discussed in chapter 6). In his view, strategic behavior affects the royalty setting by both groups

---

[40] This was from the *Verizon Communications Inc. v. Law Offices of Curtis v. Trinko* case in 2004.

and there is no argument to defend a policy that favors one or the other. There remains an inherent difficulty with the fragmented ownership of intellectual property required for an industry standard that can involve hundreds of patents owned by many firms. This fragmentation gives rise to uncertainty about the royalty rates that will need to be paid after the standard is agreed. Conventions to be encouraged include the policies adopted by many SSOs of requiring participants to disclose in advance any patents likely to be involved in the effective operation of any given standard and to commit to "fair, reasonable, and nondiscriminatory" (FRAND) royalties before the standard is set. However, the tension for policy remains, in that permitting any more specific prior communications about royalties could encourage collusive behavior by patent holders.

Standard Setting for Networks

This is an important issue affecting the spatial diffusion of knowledge in the technology of communications, where the issue of network externalities from compatible systems is a key feature of the ability to communicate. The historian of science and innovation Paul David has been persistent in voicing the need to consider issues of international standards to ensure compatibility for interfaces in communications systems and to facilitate interoperability (see, for example, David 1995; David and Steinmueller 1996). He has noted that digital information and communication technologies carry enormous potential, not only for enlarging spatial boundaries and thus facilitating the diffusion of innovation, but also for extending product service markets due to the bundling of previously distinct products. David and Steinmueller envision a global information infrastructure that includes not only voice telephony but also data networking and multimedia content delivery. The necessary infrastructure differs radically from the traditional model of national post telegraph and telecommunications systems. It also sits uneasily with the natural tendency of producers to use innovation to create differentiated products, not compatible with those of rivals.

Since these papers were written there has been a dramatic improvement in the ability to transmit packages of information across the world, for example using mobile phones, where some operators have been willing to recognize each others' systems for the benefit of travelers. Gruber and Verboven (2001) use a database of 140 countries to explore the effect of government policies on the developing global mobile telecommunications market. They find that regulatory delay in issuing first licenses held back convergence, while setting a single technological standard accelerated the diffusion of earlier analogue technology. In regard to more recent digital technology their results are less well-defined and they conclude that it remains to be seen "whether the advantages from systems competition in the digital era ... are outweighed by the network and scale advantages from a single standard" (p. 1,211). In recent years the world has experienced huge growth in the ability to engage in video telephony and to demand television services via the Internet, all of which have required expansion of bandwidth as well as compatible standards. The fear now is focused less on compatibility and more on capacity: see, for example, the article by Cugnini (2008), who questions whether there is sufficient bandwidth to accommodate peaks due to webcasts by popular media figures like Oprah Winfrey.

Government Procurement Policy

As a large purchaser of goods and services, the government can influence business activity in terms of both the quantity and the quality of supply. Purchasing contracts can be targeted not only on the delivery of a variety of inputs to the provision of government services but also on the development of innovative products. For example, in decisions about purchasing computers and database storage systems a government agency can commission new features of hardware and software. U.K. government policy aspirations in this regard are summarized in a briefing by NESTA (2007) that highlights two main routes by which government procurement can assist innovation. First, government can create a market for innovative products and processes through its large scale of purchasing and by setting new performance standards, such as commissioning public buildings with zero carbon emissions. Second, government can support innovative SMEs by acting as "early users" of new products (i.e., by being early adopters, in the language of chapter 7). By providing feedback on the products, along with revenues, these purchases can help smaller suppliers to refine and improve their products for eventual supply to a wider market.

In an extensive review for the European Commission, Edler et al. (2005) report on nine case studies of procurements involving innovative technology in six European countries. (These authors also document the underlying procurement structure and policy in nineteen countries including the United States and Australia.) From their case studies they identify several pitfalls and key factors influencing the success of what can be a risky undertaking. The pitfalls include confusion of direct purchasing cost with overall cost, and inadequate technical expertise in the commissioning department. Avoiding the first involves a life cycle assessment of any project, with monitoring of all direct and indirect costs and benefits over the whole procurement cycle. Solutions to the problem of technical competence and risk management include the development of intelligent customers within the government, which requires high-level academic training, as well as experience, for civil servants.

11.5 Conclusions

This chapter has discussed policies to promote innovation at the firm level with a focus on IPRs and R&D. There is an ongoing debate surrounding whether IPRs help or hinder innovation. The long history of this debate—begun in earnest in the nineteenth century—gives an indication of our limited understanding of the issues. As has been said, if we did not have an IPR system it would be difficult to justify creating one; equally, now that we have one it is difficult to provide evidence that it is not working. These issues have become hotly debated due to the rapid rise in patenting, especially in the United States but also in other countries. Two recent books on the U.S. situation argue strongly that the U.S. patent system has been acting to reduce innovation. Despite this, there is still a wide range of opinions on what reform is needed.[41]

The controversy over the working of the IPR system prompts two questions. First, can the system be altered to improve outcomes? We have outlined a range of policy options, and we should also make clear that many options are available even under the regulations imposed by TRIPS (see chapter 12). Examples include policies that improve the efficiency of dispute resolution, renewal fee schedules, and "utility models." The sections on trademarks and copyright also argue that the specific details and operation of each IPR can have important effects on overall outcomes. In many cases, the policy options have been known about for many years, but what is often lacking is empirical evidence on their effectiveness.

Second, if the IPR system is not performing, what other incentive mechanisms could be used? The main alternative is seen to be R&D subsidies, and increasingly these are routed through the tax system as R&D tax credits. The majority of OECD countries now have some form of R&D tax incentive scheme. The empirical evidence suggests that, on average, these are effective at increasing R&D expenditure. However, there are a number of potential pitfalls. One is that the real R&D effort should be

---

[41] For example, in respect of the United States Patent Reform Act of 2009, Wikipedia lists four organizations that are in favor and fourteen against the act, including in the opponents many business groups (see http://en.wikipedia.org/Patent_Reform_Act_of_2009).

measured, rather than relying on nominal R&D expenditures. The basic idea here is that the number of skilled scientists and engineers in an economy may be in fixed supply, so that increasing real R&D effort in the short term is not possible. A second is that, even though R&D expenditures have increased, there is a concern that the composition of R&D may be changing. If the tax incentives simply encourage more "D" (i.e., development), possibly due to firms slightly altering internal accounting systems, then the social benefits of R&D tax incentives may be lower than expected. Despite these concerns, there is widespread agreement that R&D tax incentives are effective and important policies in promoting innovation.

It should also be clear that IPR and R&D policies are only parts of a more complex system. As an example, we discussed the role of licensing and technology markets. If these are working well, allowing firms to locate and negotiate with intellectual property holders at reasonable cost, then this improves the efficiency of the IPR system. New technology and policies may be able to improve the working of these markets. Finally, section 11.4 provided a brief discussion of some other areas for policy. As chapter 4 made clear, there really is a "national system of innovation" and policy makers must be aware of the interactions across this system.

Keywords

U.S. patent debate.

Licensing and markets for technology.

Copyright extension.

Rewards and patent buyouts.

R&D tax incentives.

Questions for Discussion

(1) Why has patenting increased so much in recent years? Will this trend continue?

(2) What policies might improve the working of the (a) patent, (b) copyright, and (c) trademark systems?

(3) Should patents be replaced by a system of rewards and prizes?

(4) Why are "markets for technology" important?

(5) How would you evaluate the effectiveness of an R&D tax incentive scheme?

(6) Are direct R&D grants a better policy than either R&D tax incentives or patents?

(7) Would the money spent on R&D tax credits be better spent on educating scientists?

References

Abramowicz, M. 2001. Perfecting patent prizes. Working Paper 01-29, George Mason University, Land and Economics.

Akerlof, G., K. Arrow, T. Bresnahan, J. Buchanan, R. Coase, L. Cohen, M. Friedman, J. Green, R. Hahn, T. Hazlett, C. Hemphill, R. Litan, R. Noll, R. Schmalensee, S. Shavell, H. Varian, and R. Zeckhauser. 2002. The Copyright Term Extension Act of 1998: an economic analysis. Amici brief filed in the case of Eldred v. Ashcroft, 20 May.

Arora, A., and A. Fosfuri. 2000. The market for technology in the chemical industry: causes and consequences. *Revue d'Economie Industrielle* 92:317-34.

Audretsch, D. B., W. J. Baumol, and A. E. Burke. 2001. Competition policy in dynamic markets. *International Journal of Industrial Organization* 19(5):613-34.

Baudry, M., and B. Dumont. 2006. Patent renewals as options: improving the mechanism for weeding out lousy patents. *Review of Industrial Organization* 28:41-62.

Bessen, J., and M. Meurer. 2008. *Patent Failure.* Princeton University Press.

Bloom, N., R. Griffith, and A. Klemm. 2001. Issues in the design and implementation of an R&D tax credit for UK firms. Briefing Note 15, Institute of Fiscal Studies.

Boldrin, M., and D. Levine. 2002. The case against intellectual property. *American Economic Review* 92(2):209-12.

Boyle, J. 2003. The second enclosure movement and the construction of the public domain. *Law and Contemporary Problems* 66:33-74.

Branstetter, L. 2004. Do stronger patents induce more local innovation? *Journal of International Economic Law* 7(2):359-70.

CJA Consultants Ltd. 2003. *Patent Litigation Report: A Study for the European Commission on Possible Insurance Schemes against Patent Litigation Risks.* Report for the European Commission.

——. 2006. *Patent Litigation Insurance: A Study for the European Commission on the Feasibility of Possible Insurance Schemes against Patent Litigation Risks.* Final Report to the European Commission.

Corrigan, R., and M. Rogers. 2005. The economics of copyright. *World Economics: The Journal of Current Economic Analysis and Policy* 6(3):53-174.

Cugnini, A. 2008. Did Oprah crash the Internet? *Display Daily*, March 10, 2008. Insight Media online (available at http://displaydaily.com/2008/03/10/did-oprah-crash-the-internet).

David, P. A. 1995. Standardization policies for network technologies: the flux between freedom and order revisited. In *The Political Economy of Standards in Natural and Technological Environments* (ed. R. Hawkins, R. Mansell, and J. Skea), pp. 15-35. Cheltenham, U.K.: Edward Elgar.

David, P. A., and W. E. Steinmueller. 1996. Standards, trade and competition in the emerging global information infrastructure environment. *Telecommunications Policy* 20(10):817–30

Dosi, G., L. Marengo, and C. Pasquali. 2006. How much should society fuel the greed of innovators? On the relations between appropriability, opportunities and rates of innovation. *Research Policy* 35(8):1,110–21.

Economides, N. 1998. Trademarks. In *New Palgrave Dictionary of Economics and the Law* (ed. P. Newman). New York: Palgrave.

Edler, J., L. Hommen, J. Rigby, and L. Tsipouri. 2005. *Innovation and Public Procurement: Review of Issues at Stake.* Study for the European Commission (coordinated by the Fraunhofer Institute).

Encaoua, D., and A. Hollander. 2002. Competition policy and innovation. *Oxford Review of Economic Policy* 18(1):63–79.

Encaoua, D., D. Guellec, and C. Martinez. 2006. Patent systems for encouraging innovation: lessons from economic analysis. *Research Policy* 35:1,423–40.

Gallini, N. 2002. The economics of patents: lessons from recent U.S. patent reform. *Journal of Economic Perspectives* 16(2):131–54.

Gans, J., S. King, and R. Lampe. 2004. Patent renewal fees and self-funding patent offices. *Topics in Theoretical Economics* 4(1), Article 6, p. 1,147.

Glennerster, R., and M. Kremer. 2001. A better way to spur medical research and development. *Regulation* 23(2):34–39.

Goolsbee, A. 1998. Does government R&D policy mainly benefit scientists and engineers? *American Economic Review* 88(2):298–302.

Graham, S., B. Hall, D. Harhoff, and D. Mowery. 2002. Post-issue patent "quality control": a comparative study of U.S. patent re-examinations and European patent oppositions. NBER Working Paper 8807.

Greenhalgh, C., and M. Rogers. 2008. Intellectual property activity by service sector and manufacturing firms in the United Kingdom, 1996–2000. In *The Evolution of Business Knowledge* (ed. H. Scarbrough). Oxford University Press.

Gruber, H., and F. Verboven. 2001. The evolution of markets under entry and standards regulation—the case of global mobile telecommunications. *International Journal of Industrial Organization* 19:1,189–212.

Guellec, D., and B. van Pottelsberghe. 2007. *The Economics of the European Patent System.* Oxford University Press.

Hall, B. 1992. R&D tax policy during the eighties: success or failure? NBER Working Paper 4240.

——. 2005. Exploring the patent explosion. *Journal of Technology Transfer* 30(1/2):35–48.

——. 2007. Patents and patent policy. *Oxford Review of Economic Policy* 23(4): 568–87.

Hall, B., and J. Van Reenen. 2000. How effective are fiscal incentives for R&D? A review of the evidence. *Research Policy* 29:449–69.

Hall, B., and R. Ziedonis. 2001. The effects of strengthening patent rights on firms engaged in cumulative innovation: insights from the semiconductor industry. In *Entrepreneurial Inputs and Outcomes: New Studies of Entrepreneurship in the United States* (ed. G. Libecap). Advances in the Study of Entrepreneurship, Innovation, and Economic Growth, volume 13. Amsterdam: Elsevier Science.

HM Treasury. 2006. *Gowers Review of Intellectual Property.* London: Her Majesty's Stationery Office.

IP Australia. 2005. Review of the innovation patent. Issues Paper, September 2005 (www.ipaustralia.gov.au/pdfs/news/InnovationPatentReviewr.pdf).

Jacob, R., D. Alexander, and L. Lane. 2004. *A Guidebook to Intellectual Property Law.* London: Sweet and Maxwell.

Jaffe, A. 2002. Building programme evaluation into the design of public research support programmes. *Oxford Review of Economic Policy* 18(1):22–34.

Jaffe, A., and J. Lerner. 2004. *Innovation and Its Discontents: How Our Broken Patent System is Endangering Innovation and Progress, and What to Do About It.* Princeton University Press.

Jensen, P., and E. Webster. 2004. Recent patterns of trade marking activity in Australia. *Australian Intellectual Property Journal* 15(2):112–16.

Kortum, S., and J. Lerner. 1998. Stronger protection of technological revolution: what is behind the recent surge in patenting? *Carnegie-Rochester Conference Series on Public Policy* 48:247–304.

Kremer, M. 1998. Patent buyouts: a mechanism for encouraging innovation. *Quarterly Journal of Economics* 113(4):1,137–67.

Krohmal, B. 2007. Prominent innovation prizes and reward programs. Research Note 1, Knowledge Ecology International.

Landes, W., and R. Posner. 2003. *The Economic Structure of Intellectual Property Law.* Boston, MA: Belknap/Harvard.

Lerner, J. 1999. The government as venture capitalist: the long-run impact of the SBIR program. *Journal of Business* 72(3):285–318.

Lessig, L. 2002. *The Future of Ideas: The Fate of the Commons in a Connected World.* New York: Random House.

——. 2004. *Free Culture: How Big Media Uses Technology and the Law to Lock Down Culture and Control Creativity.* London: Penguin Press.

Liebowitz, S. 1985. Copying and indirect appropriability: photocopying of journals. *Journal of Political Economy* 93(5):945–47.

Loundes, J., and M. Rogers. 2003. The rise of trade marking in Australia in the 1990s. Working Paper 8/03, Melbourne Institute of Applied Economic and Social Research.

Nadiri, M. 1993. Innovations and technological spillovers. NBER Working Paper 4423.

Nelson, R. R. 2006. Reflections of David Teece's "Profiting from technological innovation...". *Research Policy* 35(8):1,107–09.

NESTA. 2007. Driving innovation through public procurement. UK Government, National Endowment for Science Technology and the Arts Policy and Research Unit, Policy Briefing, February.

OECD. 2002. *Tax Incentives for Research and Development: Trends and Issues.* Paris: Science Technology and Industry, OECD (available at www.oecd.org/dataoecd/12/27/2498389.pdf).

——. 2006. *Government R&D Funding and Company Behaviour: Measuring Behavioural Additionality.* Paris: OECD.

——. 2008. *OECD Framework for the Evaluation of SME and Entrepreneurship Policies and Programmes.* Paris: OECD.

Penrose, E. 1951. *The Economics of the International Patent System.* Baltimore, MD: Johns Hopkins University Press.

Rivette, K., and D. Kline. 1999. *Rembrandts in the Attic.* Cambridge, MA: Harvard Business School Press.

Rogers, M., C. Helmers, and C. Greenhalgh. 2007. An analysis of the characteristics of small and medium enterprises that use intellectual property. Report for UK Intellectual Property Office (available at http://users.ox.ac.uk/~manc0346/research.html).

Sakakibara, M., and L. Branstetter. 1999. Do stronger patents induce more innovation? Evidence from the 1988 patent law reforms. NBER Working Paper 7066.

Schmalensee, R. 1978. Entry deterrence in the ready-to-eat breakfast cereal industry. *Bell Journal of Economics* 9:305–27.

——. 2008. Standard setting, innovation specialists and competition policy. MIT Working Paper (available at http://ssrn.com/abstract=1219784).

Siegel, D., R. Veugelers, and M. Wright. 2007. Technology transfer offices and commercialization of university of intellectual property: performance and policy implications. *Oxford Review of Economic Policy* 23(4):640–60.

Tassey, G. 2007. Tax incentives for innovation: time to restructure the R&E tax credit. *Journal of Technology Transfer* 32:605–15.

Varian, H. 2006. Copyright term extension and orphan works. *Industrial and Corporate Change* 15(6):965–80.

von Graevenitz, G. 2008. Which reputations does a brand owner need? Evidence from trade mark opposition. Discussion Paper 215, Governance and the Efficiency of Economic Systems (GESY), LMU München.

WIPO. 2005. *WIPO Magazine*, May/June (www.wipo.int).

Walsh, J. P., A. Arora, and W. M. Cohen. 2003. Effects of research tool patenting and licensing on biomedical innovation. In *Patents in the Knowledge-Based Economy* (ed. W. M. Cohen and S. A. Merrill), pp. 285–340. Washington, DC: National Academies Press.

12

Macroeconomic Issues and Policy

12.1 Introduction

The issues of IPRs, innovation, and growth are clearly not solely national issues. Chapter 9 discussed how innovation is related to globalization. This chapter deepens this discussion in a number of areas and stresses the policy issues. One of the most important and controversial aspects of globalization is TRIPS, which is short for the Agreement on Trade-Related Aspects of Intellectual Property Rights. The legal and economic issues involved in TRIPS are complex and are still not fully understood. This chapter reviews these issues with a specific focus on the economic aspects of the debate. A major conclusion is that TRIPS affects economies in different ways. Since a few rich countries generate and own most of the world's IPRs, it was expected that the introduction of TRIPS would increase net royalty payments to these rich countries. Less expected was the fact that even among the other countries there can be different effects depending on their income level and other characteristics.

Before the discussion of TRIPS, section 12.2 asks what macroeconomic evidence there is that strong IPRs are conducive to economic growth. There is a range of economic studies that attempt to test whether countries with strong IPRs experience higher economic growth. This is a difficult question to answer, not least because economists do not have reliable models of economic growth (see chapter 8). The results of the research indicate that strong IPRs can, at times, have positive associations with economic growth.[1] In particular, in order to benefit from strong IPRs a country needs to have a range of other, conducive factors. A further indication from historical studies is that the strength of IPRs may affect the *nature* of innovation in a country rather than the *level* of innovation. This result reflects the microeconomic evidence that firms can rely on trade secrecy at times and on IPRs at others. Section 12.3

---

[1] The word "associations" is used here since statistical analysis can only indicate, but not prove, causality.

considers TRIPS in detail, including how TRIPS is related to trade, foreign direct investment, and technology transfer.

Section 12.4 takes a closer look at the issues of *exhaustion* and *parallel imports*. Exhaustion is the legal idea that once a product with intellectual property protection has been sold, these IPRs are exhausted, so it can be resold without the permission of the owner of the intellectual property. This can also apply in an international context since, for example, selling a patented product in the United States may mean that it can be "parallel imported" into Europe, even if the producer does not approve of the importation and sale by the new distributor. These are questions about how much power an IPR holder should have over their product(s) and, in effect, over the functioning of the free market. Section 12.5 looks at piracy, the name associated with mass copyright infringement, and counterfeit, the infringement of trademark. Both issues have a strong international dimension.

One of the interesting aspects of globalization is that it appears to be relocating R&D across more countries. The large transnational corporations (TNCs) now aim to conduct their R&D in whichever country provides the best value for money. Section 12.6 reviews the evidence on such reallocations. Finally, section 12.7 discusses the role of skilled human capital migration in innovation and diffusion.

12.2   Macroeconomic Evidence on IPRs and Economic Growth

Previous chapters have demonstrated that economic growth comes from innovation and diffusion. The national system of innovation (NIS) and, within this, the central role of R&D are critical in generating economic growth. The role of R&D is confirmed by firm-, industry-, and economy-level empirical studies that show a positive link between R&D intensity and performance. Even so, the evidence we have cited so far about the precise role of IPRs in macroeconomic performance is more tenuous. A positive role for IPRs is confirmed by firm-level empirical studies, although there is debate about the overall impact of IPRs at the industry and economy levels. There is also a concern that IPRs may be beneficial for only some economies. In view of this, there is interest in analyzing the association between IPRs and economic growth at the economy level. Conceptually, any findings represent the *net* aggregate effects of IPRs on economic activity. Clearly, a critical aspect will be the ability to control for the large number of other possible determinants of economic growth (see section 8.4). This is a major problem when trying to gain insight from IPR and economic growth analysis, as economists are not confident of understanding all the determinants of economic growth. In empirical studies this has led to the use of a vast range of variables to try and model economic growth (Rogers 2003; Sala-i-Martin 1997). With this caveat in mind, various studies have tried to assess the association between IPRs and economic growth.

An illustrative study is that by Park and Ginarte (1997). They use an index of IPRs (see below) in a cross-country regression analysis of the growth in GDP per worker for sixty developing and developed countries (over the period 1960–90). The Park and Ginarte paper uses a complex modeling structure. In short, they simultaneously model the growth of GDP per worker, the investment to GDP ratio, and the R&D to GDP ratio as a system of equations.[2] Their results suggest that IPRs have no direct impact on the growth rate, although stronger IPRs do appear to have a positive effect on capital investment and R&D in developed countries. Thus IPRs have an indirect role by encouraging two processes that lead to invention, innovation, and diffusion.

Figure 12.1 gives an indication of why modeling the link between IPRs and economic growth is so complex. The left-hand side encapsulates the role of IPRs, which includes how many are used, their duration, and their enforcement. IPRs have an impact on a range of so-called proximate factors, such as investment, trade, FDI, and R&D. These are shown in the central column under "Proximate factors." There is feedback among these factors: for example, increasing levels of trade may encourage domestic firms to apply for more patents. The proximate factors then have an impact on economic growth, although the exact magnitudes and time lags may be complex. The last column also includes other dimensions of development such as health, inequality, and education. As we discuss below, there are cases when IPRs may directly affect these, with the main example being developing country access to medicines that are covered by patents. The complexity of these relationships in the last column was also stressed in chapters 8 and 9, which looked at various theoretical models.

There are a number of other studies of IPRs that have used cross-country data sets over the last thirty or forty years.[3] The main result from these is that it is difficult to find a consistent, positive association between the strength of IPRs and economic growth. One of the reasons for this could be that the indices of IPRs are a poor proxy for

---

[2] Econometrically this approach involves writing down an equation for each of the three dependent variables and then using an estimator known as a "seemingly unrelated regression" estimator.

[3] See Chen and Puttitanun (2005) and Falvey et al. (2006) for recent empirical work and reviews of previous studies.

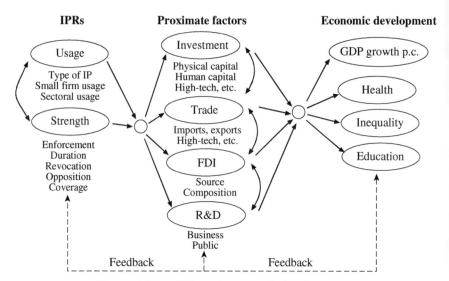

Figure 12.1. IPRs and economic development.

the actual effects of intellectual property. The Park and Ginarte (1997) index is the average of five different dimensions of patent protection: coverage, membership of international patent agreements, provisions for loss of protection, enforcement, and duration. The first four dimensions are assessed using three criteria; for example, patent coverage is assessed by considering whether (a) a "utility model" is available in the country (see section 2.5), (b) pharmaceutical products are covered, and (c) chemical products are covered. If a criterion is met, a value of "1" is recorded, and then these unit values are summed to find the overall mark for that dimension. The construction of this index gives an indication of the multifaceted nature of patent protection, but it only assesses the prevailing laws and not, for example, the strength of enforcement. This means that the index will have considerable "measurement error," which will, in turn, make finding any relationship between the index and economic growth difficult.[4]

There are two further difficulties in understanding the relationship between IPRs and economic growth. The first concerns causality. It is likely that the higher GDP per capita (caused by high economic growth) will *cause* the increasing use and enforcement of intellectual property. Lerner (2002), in a study of patent laws over 150 years, finds

---

[4] An updated version of the index is contained in Park (2008). Rapp and Rozek (1990) and Ostergard (2000) produce alternative IPR indices, with Ostergard's also considering trademarks and copyright.

that wealthier countries do have more patent protection.[5] The second concerns the likelihood that any effect of IPRs on economic growth will depend on other factors, such as the level of education, R&D, and international trade. In fact, many researchers have looked for variation in the impact of IPRs according to the level of GDP per capita. For example, Falvey et al. (2006) find that low-income countries gain from stronger IPRs, as do high-income countries. However, their analysis, based on seventy-nine countries over the period 1975–94, finds that middle-income countries do not benefit from stronger IPRs. Why should the effects of IPRs vary? They argue that in middle-income countries there are two offsetting effects: a positive effect via increased FDI and trade, and a negative effect due to the inability to imitate and use knowledge. In contrast, low-income countries gain from increased FDI and trade since they are not (yet) active in imitation. The possibility that the impact of IPRs differs across groups of countries has also been studied in the context of TRIPS (see the next section).

Another way of gaining insight into the IPR and economic growth nexus is to look at historical data. Moser (2005) does this by looking at innovations present in two world fairs in the nineteenth century (London in 1851 and Philadelphia in 1876). Some of these innovations were patented and some were not, which was partly a result of the fact that not all countries had patent laws at that time. The findings suggest that patent protection is not critical to innovation but it does have a strong effect on the distribution of innovative activity. In countries without patent protection, innovation tended to concentrate in industries where secrecy was effective. Textiles, food processing, and watch making were examples; and countries such as Switzerland, which had no patents, concentrated on these industries. In contrast, in the United States, which had relatively low-cost and effective patent protection, innovation was concentrated in machinery. The Netherlands abolished its patent laws in 1869 and this led, according to Moser, to a substantial increase in innovations in the area of food processing, where secrecy was important.

The broad-based studies of IPRs and economic performance find some evidence that IPRs can be beneficial in some situations. However, as might be expected given the complexity of issues, any impact of IPRs is dependent on a range of other factors, including the GDP per capita of the country concerned. These findings imply that it might be best to allow countries to choose their own IPR system. This viewpoint is argued strongly by authors such as Chang (2002) and Wade (2003). Specifically,

---

[5] He also finds that democratic countries are more likely to have better patent protection and that the legal traditions of the country have an impact.

they point out that when the current rich countries were developing they often had weaker IPRs, especially for foreign nationals. A phrase used to summarize this viewpoint is that the rich countries are "pulling up the ladder behind them." Given these points, any move to harmonize IPRs across countries will be controversial and it is to this we now turn.

12.3   Trade-Related Aspects of Intellectual Property (TRIPS)

TRIPS is one of the most contentious international agreements, with many commentators feeling that it disadvantages developing countries. Some related issues have already been discussed in section 9.6, when we reviewed theoretical models. In this section we will cover the issues more fully. As noted in chapter 9, in 1996 the TRIPS agreement started the process of harmonizing intellectual property protection across countries.[6] In particular, signing up to TRIPS also became necessary for membership of the WTO. TRIPS specifies minimum lengths of intellectual property protection for all countries (twenty years in the case of patents).[7] The most direct effect of a strengthening of IPRs should be to increase the flow of royalties to intellectual property producing countries. IMF data show that the country with the largest surplus is the United States, with $28 billion in 2003.[8] However, there is likely to be a range of indirect effects that could easily outweigh such royalty payments. We start our discussion by looking at whether TRIPS will have different impacts on different countries.

Differential Impacts of TRIPS

A good place to begin is with some research that ranks countries according to whether or not they are likely to benefit from the introduction of TRIPS. Lall and Albaladejo (2002) examine the potential significance of IPRs by classifying countries according to the likely impact of enhanced protection of intellectual property. The classification is based on technological activity and other related characteristics for a sample of eighty-seven developed, developing, and transitional countries with significant industrial sectors between 1985 and 1998. To understand the results, we will review some very simple theory analyzing the potential effect of TRIPS on various measures of economic performance.

---

[6] Although TRIPS came into force on January 1, 1996, many developing countries were given until 2000 or even later to implement all its aspects fully.

[7] See Drahos and Braithwaite (2002) for background on the creation of TRIPS.

[8] This surplus refers to estimates of "net royalty and license transfers." The U.S. figure in 1992 was $15.7 billion. In 2003, the United Kingdom had a surplus of $2.5 billion and France had a surplus of $1.5 billion, which was just above Japan's surplus. Most other countries have deficits, including Germany and China. All of these figures are from IMF (2004); see also McCalman (2001).

With respect to trade volume, there are two conflicting forces that can be expected to operate when international intellectual property protection becomes stronger. TRIPS may be expected to increase market power for innovating firms, which will increase price and hence reduce trade volumes. However, strong IPRs are also likely to increase the size of the market for the product, leading to an elimination of local imitation and thus increasing export volumes. Strong IPRs are also expected to have conflicting effects in terms of FDI. Weak IPRs may induce firms to undertake FDI, so that the control of proprietary information is maintained through local production. On the other hand, strong IPRs may be seen as a prerequisite for doing business in the local economy.

Lall and Albaladejo divide the eighty-seven countries into four groups using, inter alia, measures of R&D, U.S. patents per capita, exports per capita, and the share of medium- and high-technology products in manufactured exports. The classification results in a "high-technology effort group" comprising Japan, the United States, many of the countries of Northern Europe, Switzerland, New Zealand, and newly industrializing countries such as Hong Kong, Singapore, Korea, and Taiwan. The moderate-technology group is comprised of Greece, Spain, and Portugal, Eastern Europe, South Africa, Mexico, and parts of Latin America. The low-technology effort group consists of North Africa, parts of the Middle East, parts of Latin America, and much of Asia, including China and India. The negligible-technology group is represented by parts of the Middle East and sub-Saharan Africa.

Lall and Albaladejo (2002) argue, as one would expect, that the high-technology group will gain the most from stronger IPRs, for the reasons noted above. The moderate group are expected to gain, but will still face costs because of adjustment to existing IPR regimes. The low-technology group is expected to face clear and significant costs, but possible long-term benefits if the local economy is, or becomes, receptive to foreign multinational corporations. The poorest countries fare the worst in Lall and Albaladejo's calculations. Countries in this group face short-term and long-term costs due to higher prices for protected products and technologies. This paper may be criticized on the grounds that it quantifies in a somewhat crude way the technological capability of many different countries, but it is useful in highlighting that countries will respond very differently to TRIPS depending on their existing state of development.

TRIPS and Trade

As figure 12.1 indicates, disentangling the effects of TRIPS on trade flows is a difficult task since so many factors are interrelated. However, the empirical evidence suggests that trade flows are positively correlated with strength of IPR protection.[9] An influential study supporting this conclusion is Maskus and Penurbarti (1997), which studied exports from twenty-two OECD countries, of which seventeen were high-income and five were large developing countries. The sample of importers was twenty-five developing countries, of which seventeen were large and eight small. Note that Hong Kong, Singapore, and South Korea were described as large developing countries in this sample. The authors studied data for twenty-eight categories of bilateral flows of manufactured goods using the value of trade at world prices. The findings indicated that stronger patent laws in developing countries have a positive impact on imports, and these effects are present for both large and small importing countries. However, the sizes of the import expansion effects appear to be quite small.[10]

TRIPS and FDI

Turning to FDI, the Commission on IPRs (2002) noted the paucity of studies relating stronger patent protection to changes in foreign investment. Maskus (2000) reviews the literature in this area and concludes that FDI is sensitive to the IPR regime, arguing that the "amounts of possible additional investment as a result of patent reforms could be large." He argues that dynamic benefits arising from knowledge spillovers could overcome losses in terms of trade for those countries that suffer in the short to medium term in a transition to stricter IPR requirements. But since the empirical specifications do not model dynamics explicitly, there is little firm basis for this argument. There may be a slightly stronger case that middle-income countries could gain some benefit in terms of technology transfer from FDI.[11] As the Commission on IPRs (2002) noted, this is probably due to strong IPRs facilitating access to sophisticated and protected technologies, through foreign investment or by licensing.

---

[9] Maskus (2000) identified two problems with the empirical literature in this area. The first is that studies often use aggregate data and models, making it impossible to identify possibly crucial sectoral or cross-sector effects. The second problem is that there are no explicitly dynamic analyses, in spite of the manifest importance of dynamic effects in disseminating useful knowledge and in economic growth more generally.

[10] Increased imports can, in turn, have other effects. Coe et al. (1997) found that productivity is increased because of high-tech imports made by developing economies. The World Bank (2002) found that the largest impacts were found in countries like Brazil and Argentina, which have high imitation capacities.

[11] See work by Lee and Mansfield (1996), Javorcik (2004), and Yang and Maskus (2001).

TRIPS and Technology Transfer

This brings us to the more fundamental question of technology transfer. Technology transfer takes many forms, and any technology transfer that takes place requires complementary absorptive capacity in the domestic economy to be effective. Such absorptive capacity will depend on things such as institutions, levels of education, and innovative and imitative capacity (see also chapter 9). This is a fact often overlooked in empirical and theoretical work, which simply sees IPRs playing a role in technology transfer in the world economy.

What insights do economic theory and evidence give us about IPRs and technology transfer? Theoretical predictions fall at, or between, two extreme positions (Maskus 2000). On the one hand, increased standards of IPR protection raise the costs of unauthorized and uncompensated imitation, and thus stronger rights will impede technology transfer that had previously worked through this channel. On the other hand, strong IPRs may encourage licensing and thereby reduce the cost of imitation. In other words, even after paying a license fee, the overall cost of the technology may be less than undertaking unauthorized imitation. While these two extreme cases usefully summarize the basic issues, in reality the actual outcome will depend on the specific conditions of the technology, and the characteristics of both the developing country and the owner of the technology. For example, there is some evidence that the degree of openness of an economy affects the interaction between technology transfer and patent strength, with more open economies benefiting from effective IPR protection because of greater capacity to innovate (see Braga and Willmore 1991). There is also some rather weak empirical evidence that the licensing of foreign technology increases with stronger patenting laws (see Ferrantino 1993; Yang and Maskus 2001).

Branstetter et al. (2006) have data on U.S. TNCs' activities in sixteen countries in the period 1982–99 and analyze how patenting, royalties, and R&D expenditure vary after patent reform. The countries considered include China, Columbia, Japan, Mexico, and South Korea. They find that after patent reform the subsidiaries of U.S. TNCs increase royalty payments and patenting. More R&D is also spent by the subsidiaries. Branstetter et al. take this as evidence of increased technology transfer within the TNCs themselves. They note, however, that they cannot assess the impact on domestic firms. Park and Lippoldt (2008) do try to capture effects on the domestic economy as a whole. Using a new IPR index for 1990–2005 they find that stronger IPRs tend to be associated with higher imports and FDI. For developing countries they find that stronger patent protection has a positive association with high-tech imports, suggesting that (embodied) technology transfer is raised.

Contentious Aspects of TRIPS

Having remarked above that TRIPS restricts the flexibility of development policy in many countries, it must also be noted that TRIPS does confer a reasonable amount of flexibility in how developing countries decide to introduce new systems of intellectual property protection. The Commission on IPRs (2002) notes that this flexibility gives grounds for both progress and controversy with respect to the implementation of TRIPS in a number of important areas such as pharmaceuticals, education, traditional knowledge, and the patenting of living organisms.

Perhaps the most controversial aspect of TRIPS concerns its effect on pharmaceuticals. While most developing countries have patent laws for pharmaceuticals, few countries enforce these laws.[12] Enforcing TRIPS would cause an increase in the price of medicines for people in the poorest countries of the world (see Watal (1996) for a calculation of static price effects in India), and a number of measures have been considered to improve access and to lower the cost of essential medicines. Perhaps the most prominent among those under discussion has been the option to use compulsory licensing. Compulsory licensing involves the government of a nation conferring a license upon, for example, a drug manufacturer, which would then give it the right to manufacture and sell the patented drug product without obtaining the consent of the patent holder. This could be done if the government deems the price of the drug to be excessively high. A major issue is how countries without pharmaceutical manufacturing capacity can take advantage of compulsory licensing. One way that is being investigated is for countries with similar needs to group together. It is also important to mention that many recent bilateral trade deals, for example between the United States and developing countries, now include an update to TRIPS, such as more stringent rules on when compulsory licensing can be used (Rossi 2006).

Some argue that a better alternative to compulsory licensing is to ensure that pharmaceutical companies supply drugs at low prices to developing countries. One interesting aspect of this debate is that TRIPS is not incompatible with a system of differential charging, so that developing countries could pay less for drugs. This system would obviously require mechanisms to prevent drugs sold in the developing world leaking back to the developed world, such as differential product labeling

---

[12] TRIPS only allows country exceptions to enforcement of intellectual property rights if enforcement is "contrary to its essential security interests."

and clauses restricting reexporting (see also the discussion on parallel imports below).

Another issue of dispute between rich and poor countries concerns the relationship between intellectual property systems and traditional knowledge (e.g., local tribal knowledge about the medicinal nature of plants). Many corporations in the developed world are eager to use or exploit traditional knowledge, but traditional knowledge poses difficult problems for intellectual property. Such knowledge has the characteristics of a collective good and is therefore of uncertain ownership (World Bank 2002). Not only is traditional knowledge of uncertain ownership, but its date of creation is uncertain and its often unwritten form poses unique difficulties for Western-oriented intellectual property systems.

TRIPS does not contain any provisions concerning the definition and regulation of such collective goods. Even so, protection may be obtained for traditional knowledge using the existing IPR system and also through sui generis protection, although there is concern that a single sui generis system may not be flexible enough to accommodate local needs. A key need is to establish means for valuing such knowledge appropriately and for providing payments and other incentives so that such resources are exploited efficiently and fairly. To this end, databases cataloguing traditional knowledge from developing countries are being created, and these catalogues should eventually be included in the search documentation of international patent offices (Commission on IPRs 2002).

A key aspect of TRIPS relates to agriculture, since farming is an important economic activity in many developing countries (World Bank 2002). Under TRIPS, countries are obliged to award patents to agricultural chemicals, some microorganisms, and biotechnological inventions. Plant breeders' rights may also be strengthened under TRIPS. There is also concern that agricultural research relevant to developing countries has decreased in recent years, and that private firms in the West are unlikely to devote an optimal amount of research effort directly connected to the needs of developing countries.

The Enforcement Aspect of TRIPS

One serious obstacle that will impede the full implementation of TRIPS in many developing countries is that they are simply unable to afford the costs associated with erecting and maintaining a modern national IPR system. As *The Economist* noted in 2002, "Putting in a rigorous patent system will not make Angola a hotspot of biotechnology any time soon; a license to drive is of little use without a car." National systems require the use of scarce resources, including financial resources and highly skilled workers, who are often in short supply in developing countries.

Enforcing IPRs also requires extensive, effective, and functioning legal systems that can support public and private claims to intellectual property. Again, developing countries may not consider funding enforcement to be a priority. Finally, in some situations a developing country may wish to pursue a legal claim against the citizens, corporations, or governments of the developed world for IPR infringement. This is costly and requires specialist knowledge. The World Intellectual Property Organization (WIPO) is aware of the various problems that developing countries face and undertakes various assistance schemes.[13]

12.4   Intellectual Property Rights, Exhaustion, and Parallel Imports

Another important international aspect of IPRs relates to the issue of *exhaustion*. Once an intellectual property protected good has been sold, the relevant IPRs are said to be exhausted. As the WIPO states, "unless otherwise specified by law, subsequent acts of resale, rental, lending or other forms of commercial use by third parties can no longer be controlled or opposed by the originating [enterprise]."[14] There is consensus that it is reasonable to apply such laws in the domestic context, hence all countries follow *national exhaustion*. However, there is much more controversy concerning the extent to which an intellectual property protected good becomes exhausted on its sale in international markets (i.e., *international exhaustion*). This is of particular relevance for the issue of *parallel importation*. Parallel importation refers to goods that are produced legally in the home country but which also arrive in foreign countries through channels other than those used by the official distributor. Consequently, such goods are often referred to as "gray goods" (Heath 1999), since there is no contract between the manufacturer and the parallel importer. Hence the issue of international exhaustion revolves around the question: does the intellectual property owner have the right to oppose parallel importation based on the IPRs owned for a particular product by a manufacturer? At present, the WTO and TRIPS allow each country to decide on what type of rules to apply, and there continues to be an active debate on the merits of different

---

[13] The WIPO adopted a development agenda in October 2007 with forty-five recommendations.

[14] See www.wipo.int/sme/en/ip_business/export/international_exhaustion.htm.

rules.[15] The United States practices national exhaustion on patents and copyright, but permits parallel imports of trademarked goods under some conditions. The European Union follows community exhaustion (i.e., within the EU) but generally bans parallel imports, while Japan permits parallel imports unless explicitly excluded in commercial contracts (Grossman and Lai 2008). The differences in rules across countries and IPR types mean that court rulings on parallel imports are closely followed. Heath (1999) reports that courts in Japan and the United Kingdom have "recently confirmed the lawfulness of parallel importation of patented products in the absence of any indication to the contrary." Tancer and Mosseri-Marlio (2004) discuss the differences in opinions in the EU's Court of Justice and the United States Supreme Court in two trademark disputes.

There are conflicting arguments concerning the economic effects of international exhaustion. On the one hand, international exhaustion reduces the returns to innovative activity, and hence should be treated warily by policy makers. On the other hand, international exhaustion may increase competition and lower prices. Szymanski (1999a), noting the lack of empirical work in this area, concludes that the negative effects probably outweigh the positive. The implications for developing countries were discussed in a companion paper (Szymanski 1999b). This paper conducted a welfare analysis of international exhaustion in terms of the effects on domestic high-income consumers and overseas low-income consumers. His results show that the welfare gain or loss is a function of the type of contract made between the owners of intellectual property and their licensees. Prices will equalize across countries if there is competitive arbitrage of the product (i.e., parallel imports occur), which obviously improves the economic welfare of consumers who would otherwise pay high prices and diminishes the welfare of those who would otherwise pay low prices. So although international exhaustion of rights might seem to be advantageous, giving room for arbitrage (parallel imports) and common prices across countries, the downside is that it inhibits price discrimination between rich and poor countries. The lack of price discrimination harms the poor, who pay higher prices when there is a common price, and gives greater welfare (higher consumer surplus) to the rich, who pay less than under discrimination. In contrast, Grossman and Lai (2008) present a model in

---

[15] TRIPS states that "for the purposes of dispute settlement under this Agreement... nothing in this Agreement shall be used to address the issue of exhaustion of intellectual property rights."

which prohibiting parallel imports can reduce the incentives to innovate and conclude that this can, ultimately, reduce welfare in poorer countries.[16]

12.5 Piracy and Counterfeit

Piracy is a word that has become associated with the large-scale infringement of copyright. As discussed in chapter 2, there are some cases when copies of copyrighted work can be made legally (for example, for educational, journalistic, or research activities). However, large-scale infringement based on illegal copying can also occur, especially for music, films, and software. The international aspect of this is that firms in developing countries can engage in piracy of copyrighted products created in the United States or other major economies. The extent of such activities is difficult to assess. The International Federation of the Phonographic Industry, in its Piracy Report 2005, estimates that there were 1.5 billion pirated CD sales in 2004, which, at an estimated $3.05 each, represents $4.6 billion of lost sales.[17] These pirated sales amount to around one half of legitimate sales. Other organizations, often funded by the creative industries themselves, produce estimates of piracy rates and some of these data are used by the United States Trade Representative (USTR). The USTR is tasked with assessing countries' intellectual property protection. Countries that are adjudged ineffective in enforcing IPRs may be investigated and, in turn, trade sanctions may be applied. Hence there can be considerable controversy over piracy estimates and there are relatively few academic studies of their accuracy.[18]

The argument of the richer countries, or more specifically the large music, film, and software companies, is that the actions of poorer countries significantly affect their profits and are, in any case, illegal under TRIPS. In contrast, the poorer countries argue that it is costly to enforce

---

[16] This result—a fall in the worldwide incentive to innovate—reflects the discussion in section 9.6. That section discussed how if countries could choose their own IPR system there would be a tendency to "free ride" on the incentives provided by other countries.

[17] The "pirate" price is estimated to vary across countries: for example, $1.12 in China and $4.81 in Spain. Furthermore, sales are not the same as profits (which are sales less costs). For example, although sales may fall due to illegal use of new technology, costs for the companies may also fall, making the overall effect on profits unclear. In addition, new technology may generate new sales, such as for mobile phone ringtones.

[18] Peitz and Waelbroeck (2004) look at cross-country evidence on CD sales. Png (2008), in a paper entitled "On the reliability of piracy statistics," finds that they have acceptable correlations with other rule of law indices. However, independent assessment of the data appears to be lacking.

copyright and they have many other priorities for expenditure. The rich-country argument, backed up by TRIPS, is tending to dominate and poorer countries are now under increasing pressure to tighten IPR enforcement.

A counterfeit product is one that carries the name, design, and packaging of a trademarked product but is produced by a different firm. As such, counterfeit goods undermine the value of trademarks since consumers can no longer be sure of the origin of their purchases (see section 2.4). From an economic viewpoint, it is useful to think of two categories of counterfeits: deceptive and nondeceptive. Deceptive counterfeit goods are bought by consumers or firms without realizing that they are counterfeits. Deceptive counterfeits can be very dangerous: for example, pharmaceutical drugs or aeroplane or automotive spare parts. In such cases consumers can be directly hurt by the fact that the product does not have the quality or basic characteristics that they rely upon. There is wide agreement that deceptive counterfeits should be eliminated by law enforcement. The other type of counterfeits— nondeceptive—needs more discussion. First, by definition, consumers realize that they are not buying the real product. To take a specific example, consider buying a counterfeit Rolex watch (at a 500th of the price of a real Rolex). The consumer realizes that what they are buying may look a little like a real Rolex, but it would not fool anyone for long and it is also likely to have very low quality. Some economists point out that the counterfeit is simply filling a different price–quality "space" or, put another way, they allow consumers to separate the "status good" aspect from the "quality" aspect of expensive brands (Grossman and Shapiro 1988). From this perspective, the counterfeit simply provides consumers with more choice. However, the firms that produce the real brands may lose sales and object to nondeceptive counterfeits.[19] Bosworth (2006) reviews these various arguments and also makes two important points. First, whereas counterfeiting used to be the preserve of small-scale manufacturing firms, often in developing countries, it has now transformed into a much larger-scale industry often run by organized crime. Second, there are very few data on the extent and nature of such activities, making a full evaluation of the problem impossible.

---

[19] Lost sales might come from people switching to counterfeit goods, although some would argue that a customer for the real branded good is very unlikely to buy a counterfeit. It is possible that the presence of counterfeits may reduce the "status" of the real brand, making it less appealing and thereby reducing sales. This said, some argue that counterfeits may generate more demand for the real brand (i.e., there is a "demonstration" effect at work).

12.6   R&D in the Global Economy

Are R&D Spillovers Global?

At various points in earlier chapters, R&D knowledge spillovers, or externalities, have been discussed. The extreme case is when R&D by one firm produces knowledge that is a public good. Is this public good then available to all firms in the industry, sector, economy, or world? Chapter 9 made clear that costless diffusion of knowledge across countries is unrealistic and introduced the idea of absorptive capacity as a conditioning factor. Empirical studies have investigated the question of whether R&D spillovers are international. Coe and Helpman (1995) analyze twenty-one OECD economics (1970–90) and find that R&D spillovers occur between countries and that greater trade openness increases the strength of such spillovers (they looked for the impact of R&D on total factor productivity). Other studies have extended this work to data sets with more countries and looked at other factors affecting R&D spillovers, such as education levels: see Engelbrecht (1997) on education in OECD countries, Coe et al. (1997) on education in poorer countries, and Guellec and van Pottelsberghe (2004), who include public-sector R&D. These large-scale macro approaches have been complemented by various studies that look at bilateral spillovers. For example, Griffith et al. (2006) suggest that there are substantial R&D spillovers from U.S. manufacturing to U.K. firms and, importantly, it is the U.K. firms that undertake R&D in the United States that appear to benefit the most. This means that in order for U.K. firms to develop absorptive capacity they need to carry out R&D in proximity to U.S. firms. The implication is that policies that solely promote domestic R&D may be counterproductive. Overall, these studies indicate that R&D spillovers, especially between OECD economies, are important but, as expected, absorptive capacity is critical.

The Globalization of the Innovation Process

TRIPS implies that at least some elements of R&D could be done anywhere in the world depending on the availability of the key inputs needed. In addition, the competitive pressure in many industries means that firms, and TNCs in particular, may seek out foreign research talent and lower costs. Modern communications also mean that firms may similarly break up the research process: for example, carrying out repetitive testing of new products and processes in a low-cost country. Equally, the world's time zones can be used to speed up the research process by using all twenty-four hours. How important is the globalization of the innovation process?

A first point to make is that the process is not new in itself—U.S. TNCs located some research facilities in the United Kingdom and Europe in the 1950s and 1960s—however, the speed of globalization appears to have increased substantially in recent years. One study has suggested that U.S. TNCs' share of R&D done overseas increased from 15% in 1995 to 22% in 2001 (Roberts 2001). A UNCTAD (2005) study of the world's largest R&D firms found that on average 28% of R&D was done overseas, although this masked major differences across regions (European firms spend 41% overseas, Japanese firms 15%, and U.S. firms 24%). A second point is that it appears that emerging markets—such as China and India—are becoming part of the process. For example, estimates suggest that R&D carried out by U.S. companies in China grew from $7 million in 1994 to $646 million in 2002 (the equivalent figures for India are $5 million and $80 million (UNCTAD 2005)). Box 12.1 discusses some examples of foreign R&D activity.

Box 12.1. The globalization of R&D to China and India.

In 2004, China had around 700 foreign R&D centers and almost all of these were in three clusters around Beijing, Shanghai, and Guangzhou. This clustering reflects, in part, the location of universities and public research centers: for example, there are 40 universities and 130 research institutes in Beijing. Once a cluster starts to become established, new centers will tend to choose the location because of the benefits to research of having other similar centers close by. The benefits include knowledge spillovers and an active labor market in scientists, engineers, etc. There may also be specialist services, such as intellectual property lawyers or venture capitalists. This means that the growth of research-based clusters tends to be self-reinforcing. IBM first located a research center in Beijing in 1994 and around 60% of the research centers are now in information, communications, and technology. The Chinese company Lenovo—who purchased IBM's PC division in 2005 and is currently the world's third largest PC producer—has research centers in Beijing, including a joint one with Intel (UNCTAD 2005).

Intel has a worldwide network of R&D centers. In China in 2005 it had around 225 researchers, while in Bangalore, India it had around 800, and a further 340 in Russia (UNCTAD 2005). The research cluster around Bangalore, originally centered on IT but now diversified into other areas, is especially notable. Basant and Chandra (2007) discuss the central role of educational and public research institutions in attracting TNCs and domestic firms. Many of these institutions were started decades ago, indicating that research clusters—and the ability to attract

TNCs—require effort over many years. The seven famous Indian Institutes of Technology, the first of which was set up in 1951, are illustrative, although for much of their existence it is said that they supported overseas clusters, such as Silicon Valley, as many of their graduates migrated to the United States (Friedman 2005, p. 105). This type of "brain drain" is an aspect of globalization that can reinforce the geographical location of clusters.

In summary, the process of globalizing R&D expenditure appears to be underway. TNCs are increasingly seeking out opportunities to locate R&D in different economies where there are some forms of comparative advantage. This said, the process is still in its infancy: the ten largest R&D economies still accounted for 86% of total R&D expenditure in 2002 (UNCTAD 2005). Bhide (2008) considers whether the globalization of R&D and innovation will threaten U.S. living standards—a fear that is sometimes raised by journalists and politicians. Bhide argues that this fear is not warranted. In particular, he draws attention to the multidimensional nature of innovation (not all aspects can be done overseas) and the fact that the service sector dominates the U.S. economy (accounting for around 70% of GDP).

12.7   International Migration of Skilled Labor

From the late seventeenth century, other European nations were keen to learn about the new production techniques in metallurgy, textiles, and steam being developed in Britain. A great deal could be learnt from visits, publications (including patents), and reverse engineering, but in many cases the new techniques contained tacit knowledge. As a result, many British skilled workers and engineers were enticed to other European countries. In fact, various (ineffective) laws were in place to try to prevent such outflows from the United Kingdom between 1695 and 1843 (von Tunzelman 1995, p. 161). The importance of skilled labor migration as a mechanism for technology transfer has been widespread throughout history. This is particularly the case when it comes to innovation, since the latest techniques often require tacit knowledge.

A related example of how migration can boost innovation is given by Silicon Valley in the United States. Since the 1960s Silicon Valley has been the world's leading high-tech region, with companies such as Hewlett-Packard, Apple, Cisco, and 3Com having their origins there. While the foundation of Silicon Valley's success lay in the research base provided by universities (especially Stanford University) and research centers such as Xerox's Palo Alto Research Center (PARC), once the high-tech region became established it drew entrepreneurs and skilled workers not just from the United States but from all over the world. In 1990, it is estimated that 30% of the high-technology workforce was foreign born (Saxenian 2002), with this figure growing to 50% by 2000 (*Economist* 2007). The influx of foreign human capital was made possible by U.S. immigration policy, which enabled migration for skilled workers. Since the terrorist attack on September 11, 2001, together with concerns over the offshoring of jobs, U.S. immigration policies have been tightened.[20] Some have argued that this has created skill shortages in places such as Silicon Valley and will harm innovation. It is also valid to ask what effect this type of "brain drain" has on the home countries of those skilled workers. On the negative side, the home country loses (at least temporarily) some highly skilled workers and entrepreneurs. On the positive side, these migrants may start businesses that trade with, and invest in, their home countries. They may also return to their home country after having learnt considerable skills. Some argue that this "circulation" of human capital from poorer countries such as India and China and into innovation clusters such as Silicon Valley is good for both home and host countries (Saxenian 2006).

12.8 Conclusions

The most controversial aspect of international policy with respect to innovation is TRIPS. The creation of a uniform, minimum standard of IPRs across countries represents a major change in policy. Historically, countries had the opportunity to select many aspects of their IPR system to suit their circumstances—this opportunity is now dramatically reduced. The main focus of this chapter was on understanding the potential effects of TRIPS. Estimates suggest that major intellectual property producing countries will, as expected, increase their net royalties on the basis of TRIPS. Net importers of intellectual property related goods, including technology, face increased costs. Apart from these direct effects there is a range of possible indirect effects. The optimists point to the following:

- TRIPS, if accompanied by enforcement, will encourage firms to license technology. An increase in licensing has the potential to speed up the flow of technology into poorer countries and, in turn, generate investment and growth in GDP per capita.

---

[20] The number of H-1B visas, those for highly qualified foreigners, was reduced from 195,000 in 2003 to 65,000 in 2007 (*Economist* 2007).

- Stronger IPRs will also encourage TNCs to increase FDI, and this may also help growth.

- TRIPS, and the development of intellectual property in some emerging markets, will promote innovation and R&D in these countries. It is also an enabling factor in the global allocation of R&D.

This said, some commentators think the above arguments carry little weight. They point out, rightly, that TRIPS forces poorer countries to develop with a set of rules that were not applied to Japan in the 1950s and 1960s, to the United States in the nineteenth century, or to the United Kingdom in the eighteenth century. They argue that licensing, even if it does occur, may not create substantial benefits, and that FDI can damage local economies. Moreover, they argue that large TNCs are exploiting the traditional knowledge of poorer countries. Unfortunately, economists have not been able to accurately assess the merits of these different arguments. The pervasive lack of data is one obstacle, as is the hugely complex nature of economic growth and development. Even without these two obstacles, the impacts of TRIPS are only just being experienced and it will take many years to gather the evidence needed.

This chapter also discussed the globalization of R&D. The evidence suggests that this process has accelerated in recent years, driven to a large extent by R&D activity in China and India. The globalization of R&D should both speed up the world's rate of innovation and also help facilitate technology catch-up for those countries that are part of the process. For the poorest countries, which are not part of the process, the danger is that this will further increase the technology gap. Finally, the international migration of skilled labor has always played a role in driving innovation and also diffusing its benefits. The increasingly international education market along with TNC activities and modern communications suggest that this "circulation" of skilled labor is here to stay.

Keywords

IPRs, proximate factors, and economic development.

Trade-Related Aspects of Intellectual Property (TRIPS).

Winners and losers from TRIPS.

Parallel imports, copyright piracy.

Deceptive and nondeceptive counterfeits.

International R&D spillovers.

Questions for Discussion

(1) Why might strong IPRs hinder economic development?

(2) Classify the potential effects of TRIPS by (a) income level of country and (b) mechanism of effects (e.g., FDI).

(3) What is the difference between deceptive and nondeceptive counterfeit goods? Does the distinction matter for policy?

(4) Conduct some research on the importance of piracy and counterfeit. What is the extent of lost sales to major companies in the United States?

(5) What forces are driving the globalization of R&D? What effects will it have on the countries involved?

(6) Can the "brain drain" of skilled labor from poorer to richer countries ever be a good thing?

References

Basant, R., and P. Chandra. 2007. Role of educational and R&D institutions in city clusters: an exploratory study of Bangalore and Puna regions in India. *World Development* 35(6):1,037–55.

Bhide, A. 2008. *The Venturesome Economy: How Innovation Sustains Prosperity in a More Connected World.* Princeton University Press.

Bosworth, D. 2006. Counterfeiting and piracy: the state of the art. Unpublished paper (available at www.oiprc.ox.ac.uk/EJWP0606.pdf).

Braga, H., and L. Willmore. 1991. Technological imports and technological effort: an analysis of their determinants in Brazilian firms. *Journal of Industrial Economics* 39(4):421–32.

Branstetter, L., R. Fisman, and C. Foley. 2006. Do stronger intellectual property rights increase international technology transfer? Empirical evidence from U.S. firm-level panel data. *Quarterly Journal of Economics* 121(1):321–49.

Chang, H. J. 2002. *Kicking Away the Ladder—Development Strategy in Historical Perspective.* London: Anthem Press.

Chen, Y., and T. Puttitanun. 2005. Intellectual property rights and innovation in developing countries. *Journal of Development Economics* 78(2):474–93.

Coe, D., and E. Helpman. 1995. International R&D spillovers. *European Economic Review* 39:859–87.

Coe, D., E. Helpman, and A. Hoffmeister. 1997. North-south R&D spillovers. *Economic Journal* 107(440):134–49.

Commission on IPRs. 2002. *Integrating Intellectual Property Rights and Development Policy.* CIPR Report (available at www.iprcommission.org/home.html).

Drahos, P., and J. Braithwaite. 2002. *Information Feudalism: Who Owns the Knowledge Economy?* London: Earthscan.

Economist. 2007. Deportation order. *Economist,* April 28, 2007.

Engelbrecht, H. J. 1997. International R&D spillovers, human capital and productivity in OECD economies: an empirical investigation. *European Economic Review* 41(8):1,479–88.

Falvey, R., N. Foster, and D. Greenaway. 2006. Intellectual property rights and innovation in developing countries. *Review of Development Economics* 10(4): 700–719.

Ferrantino, M. 1993. The effect of intellectual property rights on international trade and investment. *Weltwirtschaftliches Archiv* 129(2):300–331.

Friedman, T. 2005. *The World Is Flat: A Brief History of the Globalized World in the 21st Century.* London: Penguin.

Griffith, R., R. Harrison, and J. Van Reenen. 2006. How special is the special relationship? Using the impact of U.S. R&D spillovers on U.K. firms as a test of technology sourcing. *American Economic Review* 96(5):1,869–75.

Grossman, G. M., and E. Lai. 2008. Parallel imports and price controls. *Rand Journal of Economics* 39(2):378–402.

Grossman, G. M., and C. Shapiro. 1988. Foreign counterfeiting of status goods. *Quarterly Journal of Economics* 103(1):79–100.

Guellec, D., and B. van Pottelsberghe. 2004. From R&D to productivity growth: do the institutional settings and the source of funds of R&D matter? *Oxford Bulletin of Economics and Statistics* 66(3):353–78.

Heath, C. 1999. Parallel imports and international trade. Report, World Intellectual Property Organization.

IMF. 2004. *Balance of Payments Statistics.* Washington, DC: IMF.

Javorcik, B. 2004. The composition of foreign direct investment and protection of intellectual property rights: evidence from transition economies. *European Economic Review* 48(1):39–62.

Lall, S., and M. Albaladejo. 2002. Indicators of the relative importance of IPRs in developing countries. Working Paper QEHWPS85, University of Oxford, Queen Elizabeth House.

Lee, J., and E. Mansfield. 1996. Intellectual property protection and US foreign direct investment. *Review of Economics and Statistics* 78(2):181–86.

Lerner, J. 2002. 150 years of patent protection. *American Economic Review* 92(2): 221–25.

Maskus, K. 2000. *Intellectual Property Rights in the Global Economy.* Washington, DC: Institute for International Economics.

Maskus, K., and M. Penurbarti. 1997. Patents and international trade: an empirical study. In *Quiet Pioneering: Robert Stern and his International Economic Legacy* (ed. K. Maskus, P. Hooper, E. Leamer, and J. D. Richardson). Ann Arbor, MI: University of Michigan Press.

McCalman, P. 2001. Reaping what you sow: an empirical analysis of international patent harmonization. *Journal of International Economics* 55(1):161–86.

Moser, P. 2005. How do patent laws influence innovation? Evidence from nineteenth-century world's fairs. *American Economic Review* 95(4):1,214–36.

Ostergard Jr., R. L. 2000. The measurement of intellectual property rights protection. *Journal of International Business Studies* 31(2):349–60.

Park, W. 2008. International patent protection: 1960–2005. *Research Policy* 37: 761–66.

Park, W., and J. Ginarte. 1997. Intellectual property rights and economic growth. *Contemporary Economic Policy* 15:51–61.

Park, W., and D. Lippoldt. 2008. Technology transfer and the economic implications of the strengthening of intellectual property rights in developing countries. Working Paper 62, OECD Trade Policy.

Peitz, M., and P. Waelbroeck. 2004. The effect of internet piracy on CD sales: cross-section evidence. CESifo Working Paper 1122.

Png, I. 2008. On the reliability of software piracy statistics. SSRN article (available at http://ssrn.com/abstract=1099325).

Rapp, R., and R. Rozek. 1990. Benefits and costs of intellectual property protection in developing countries. NERA Working Paper 3.

Roberts, F. 2001. Benchmarking global strategic management of technology. *Research-Technology Management* 44(2):25–36.

Rogers, M. 2003. A survey of economic growth. *Economic Record* 79:112–36.

Rossi, F. 2006. Free trade agreements and TRIPS-plus measures. *International Journal of Intellectual Property Management* 1:150–72.

Sala-i-Martin, X. 1997. I just ran two million regressions. *American Economic Review, Papers and Proceedings* 87(2):178–83.

Saxenian, A. 2002. Silicon Valley's new immigrant high-growth entrepreneurs. *Economic Development Quarterly* 16:20–31.

——. 2006. *The New Argonauts: Regional Advantage in a Global Economy.* Cambridge, MA: Harvard University Press.

Szymanski, S. 1999a. *International Exhaustion of Rights: Review of the Economic Issues.* London: Intellectual Property Institute.

——. 1999b. Some welfare implications of international exhaustion under alternative selling regimes. Manuscript, Imperial College Management School (available at www.ms.ic.ac.uk/stefan/exhaustion.pdf).

Tancer, R. S., and C. Mosseri-Marlio. 2004. Intellectual property rights exhaustion—opposite viewpoints: United States/Europe. *Thunderbird International Business Review* 46(1):85–92.

UNCTAD. 2005. *World Investment Report.* New York/Geneva: United Nations.

von Tunzelman, G. 1995. *Technology and Industrial Progress: The Foundations of Economic Growth.* Cheltenham, U.K.: Edward Elgar.

Wade, R. 2003. What strategies are viable for developing countries today? The WTO and the shrinking of development space. *Review of International Political Economy* 10(4):621–44.

Watal, J. 1996. Introducing product patents in the Indian pharmaceutical sector: implications for prices and welfare. *World Competition* 20(2):5–21.

World Bank. 2002. Intellectual property: balancing incentives with competitive access. *Global Economic Prospects and the Developing Countries, 2002.* Washington, DC: World Bank.

Yang, G., and K. Maskus. 2001. Intellectual property rights, licensing, and innovation in an endogenous product cycle model. *Journal of International Economics* 53(1):169–87.

Mathematical Appendix

A.1 Production Functions

Economists often use mathematical functions in their efforts to understand the world. The main example in this book is the *production function*. The production function is a way of linking, or mapping, the inputs of a production process to the output(s). The production function can be thought of as representing the activities of a firm, although production functions are also used to represent a sector's or a country's activity.

Consider the equation

$$Y = f(K, L), \tag{A.1}$$

where Y stands for output, K stands for capital input, and L stands for labor input. This equation simply means that output depends on capital and labor, or in mathematical jargon that output is a *function* of capital and labor. The function is represented in the above by the $f(\cdot)$ notation. In general, any letter outside the brackets can symbolize a function: for example, $g(\cdot)$ or $h(\cdot)$.

The above function is entirely general. It does not specify the exact nature of the relationships involved. In fact, the exact relationships are often very difficult to ascertain and economists make considerable efforts to estimate them.

It is also common to add A for the level of technology:

$$Y = Af(K, L). \tag{A.2}$$

In (A.2) the A is placed in front of the $f(\cdot)$, indicating that technology can scale up output for given levels of K and L. This is sometimes referred to as Hicks-neutral technology. Alternatively, one could write $f(K, AL)$, so that technology augments labor, or $f(AK, L)$, meaning that technology augments capital.

Let us consider an example. Suppose you have a firm producing ball bearings. The capital inputs are the buildings and machines that the firm uses, labor is the workers, and output is the number of ball bearings produced per year. In many cases the output is measured in monetary terms (e.g., dollars of ball bearings produced per year), which clearly involves setting a price per unit of output. The technology level (A) is more difficult to define, but one can think of it as representing the techniques used, the efficiency of the machines, and the organization of the factory.

A commonly used production function is the Cobb–Douglas production function:

$$Y = AK^\alpha L^\beta, \quad \alpha > 0, \ \beta > 0. \tag{A.3}$$

This is the basis for much theoretical and empirical work, hence there are a number of related issues that should be stressed. First, the exact values of α and β are important since they determine the nature of *economies of scale*. The term economies of scale refers to the relationship between output and inputs. For example, if when both labor and capital are doubled, output also doubles, we say that the production function exhibits constant returns to scale. On the other hand, if doubling inputs more than doubles output, we have increasing returns to scale. As can be demonstrated, either algebraically or using some examples, the relationship between economies of scale and α and β is defined as follows:

$$\alpha + \beta = 1, \quad \text{constant returns to scale,}$$
$$\alpha + \beta > 1, \quad \text{increasing returns to scale,}$$
$$\alpha + \beta < 1, \quad \text{decreasing returns to scale.}$$

The assumption of constant returns to scale is very common since without this assumption it implies that firms would get larger and larger (if $\alpha + \beta > 1$) or smaller and smaller (if $\alpha + \beta < 1$). While economies are certainly dominated by large firms, assuming increasing returns to scale implies that they should be dominated by one large firm in each industry.

A.2   Present Discounted Value

Economists are often interested in calculating the value in today's money of a stream of revenues or costs that extend into the future. The basic issues are illustrated as follows. Consider investing \$1 at an interest rate of r (where 5% interest would mean $r = 0.05$). After a year the value of the investment would be $(1 + r)$, after two years $(1 + r)(1 + r)$, or $(1 + r)^2$, after three years $(1 + r)^3$, and so on. In general, we can say that \$1 invested for T years will yield $(1 + r)^T$.

Now consider the reverse situation: if someone offers to give you \$1 in T years' time, how much would this be worth today. In other words, we are trying to find a value \$$x$ which, when invested at r, will yield \$1 in T years' time. From the above, it is clear that we want to solve for x

in the following equations:

$$1 = x(1+r)^T \quad \text{or} \quad x = \frac{1}{(1+r)^T}. \tag{A.4}$$

In general, if one wants to find the *present discounted value* (PDV) of an amount Z in T years from now, you can use the formula

$$PDV = \frac{Z}{(1+r)^T}. \tag{A.5}$$

Another useful result is the PDV of an infinite series of payments. Suppose you were given a payment A in every year from now until infinity. The PDV of this is

$$PDV = \frac{A}{1+r} + \frac{A}{(1+r)^2} + \frac{A}{(1+r)^3} + \cdots . \tag{A.6}$$

It can be shown that this infinite series has a finite value, namely

$$PDV = \frac{A}{r}. \tag{A.7}$$

A.3 Derivatives

The properties of a function are often described in terms of the derivative(s) of the function. The first derivative of a function that has only one variable (e.g., $y = f(x)$) is simply the slope of the line. In words, the derivative is the change in y for a change in x. This is generally expressed as dy/dx but can be written in a number of ways, including

$$\frac{dy}{dx}, \quad \frac{df}{dx}, \quad \frac{df(x)}{dx}, \quad f'(x), \quad \text{or} \quad f_x.$$

Figure A.2 shows an example of a function that has a positive first derivative. In addition this function can also be called "monotonic," which means that there is always a unique value of y associated with any x.

Being able to calculate the derivative of a specific function is useful. Calculating the derivative is called "differentiation," a full discussion of which can be found in various maths books. Here we will simply state some common rules of differentiation. In the following, c, a, and n are constants.

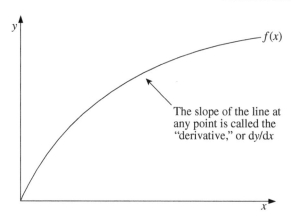

Figure A.2.   A monotonic function.

Function	Derivative rule
$y = x^n$	$\dfrac{dy}{dx} = nx^{n-1}$
$y = ax^n$	$\dfrac{dy}{dx} = nax^{n-1}$
$f(x)g(x)$	$\dfrac{df}{dx}g(x) + \dfrac{dg}{dx}f(x)$ (product rule)
$f(g(x))$	$\dfrac{df}{dg}\dfrac{dg}{dx}$ (chain rule)

When a function depends on two variables, such as the production function in (A.1), we say that it has two *partial derivatives*. In simple terms, finding a partial derivative uses the same rules as above while assuming that the other variable is a constant. Some examples of this are shown in the next section.

A.4   Marginal Products and Diminishing Returns

Taking the Cobb–Douglas production function shown in (A.3), the marginal products of labor $\partial Y/\partial L$ and capital $\partial Y/\partial K$ are given by

$$\frac{\partial Y}{\partial L} = \beta A L^{\beta-1}K^\alpha = \beta\frac{Y}{L} \tag{A.8}$$

and

$$\frac{\partial Y}{\partial K} = \alpha A K^{\alpha-1}L^\beta = \alpha\frac{Y}{K}. \tag{A.9}$$

Assuming that $\alpha + \beta = 1$, and that A and K are constant, $\partial Y / \partial L$ declines as L increases. Similarly, $\partial Y / \partial K$ declines as K increases (with A and L constant). These results reflect the *law of diminishing returns* often discussed in microeconomics textbooks. The declining marginal product of capital is also the reason why the Solow-Swan growth model converges to a steady state in the absence of technical change. Note that if $\alpha + \beta = 1$, the marginal product of capital can be rewritten as

$$\frac{\partial Y}{\partial K} = \alpha A K^{\alpha - 1} L^{\beta} = \alpha A \left(\frac{L}{K}\right)^{\beta}. \tag{A.10}$$

This indicates that as long as the capital-labor ratio is constant then the marginal product of capital will also be constant (assuming A is constant).

A.5 Accumulation Equations and Growth Rates

The expression $\mathrm{d}Y / \mathrm{d}t$ means the change in Y over time; similarly, $\mathrm{d}K / \mathrm{d}t$ means a change in K over time. An equation with $\mathrm{d}Y / \mathrm{d}t$, $\mathrm{d}K / \mathrm{d}t$, etc., in it is known as a differential equation. The mathematics of differential equations are extensive, but generally economists use only a few basic equations and results. These can often be understood with some thought and the use of diagrams.

In chapter 8 we discussed various differential equations, starting with (8.4). The key equation that was analyzed was (8.6) and the text stated that to move from (8.4) to (8.6) required some manipulation. The steps are as follows:

Start with $\dfrac{\mathrm{d}K}{\mathrm{d}t} = sY - \delta K$; dividing by L then yields $\dfrac{\mathrm{d}K}{\mathrm{d}t} \bigg/ L = sy - \delta k$.

Note that $\dfrac{\mathrm{d}k}{\mathrm{d}t} = \dfrac{\mathrm{d}(K/L)}{\mathrm{d}t} = \left[\dfrac{\mathrm{d}K}{\mathrm{d}t}L - \dfrac{\mathrm{d}L}{\mathrm{d}t}K\right] \bigg/ L^2$ (quotient rule).

Simplify to $\dfrac{\mathrm{d}K}{\mathrm{d}t} \bigg/ L - \left(\dfrac{\mathrm{d}L}{\mathrm{d}t} \bigg/ L\right)\dfrac{K}{L}$ or $\dfrac{\mathrm{d}K}{\mathrm{d}t} \bigg/ L - nk$ (since n is labor growth and $K/L = k$).

Hence $\dfrac{\mathrm{d}k}{\mathrm{d}t} + nk = \dfrac{\mathrm{d}K}{\mathrm{d}t} \bigg/ L = sy - \delta k$.

Hence $\dfrac{\mathrm{d}k}{\mathrm{d}t} = sy - (\delta + n)k$.

Let us analyze the above accumulation equation (which is equation (8.6)). In words it says that the change in the capital-labor ratio depends on gross savings per worker (sy) less "depreciation plus population growth" $(\delta + n)$ multiplied by k. Since this model uses the Cobb–Douglas production function, we can rewrite sy as sAk^α.

As in chapter 8, the best way to solve this differential equation is to plot a diagram with y on the vertical axis and k on the horizontal axis. We then plot the sAk^α line and $(\delta + n)k$ on this diagram as in figure 8.2. There are three cases of interest:

$$sAk^\alpha > (\delta + n)k, \quad dk/dt > 0, \quad k \text{ is increasing,}$$
$$sAk^\alpha = (\delta + n)k, \quad dk/dt = 0, \quad k \text{ is constant,}$$
$$sAk^\alpha < (\delta + n)k, \quad dk/dt < 0, \quad k \text{ is decreasing.}$$

Since we are interested in when k stops growing it is clear that the "solution" to the differential equation is found where $sAk^\alpha = (\delta + n)k$.

This example suggests a methodology for solving differential equations. First, rearrange the equation to have the differential on the left-hand side and then see if one can plot the right-hand side's terms on a diagram.

A.6 Logarithms and Production Functions

Economists use natural logarithms regularly in theoretical and applied work. There are two rules that prove useful:

$$\ln(xy) = \ln x + \ln y, \qquad \ln(x^n) = n \ln x. \tag{A.11}$$

Hence, taking logarithms of both sides of (A.3) we find

$$\ln Y = \ln A + \ln K^\alpha + \ln L^\beta = \ln A + \alpha \ln K + \beta \ln L. \tag{A.12}$$

A.7 Differential Equations and a Catch-up Model

Box 9.1 outlined a technological catch-up model. It used the equation

$$\frac{dA}{dt} \Big/ A = \phi(\cdot)\left[\frac{T - A}{A}\right], \tag{A.13}$$

where A represented the level of technology in the follower country and T was the technology level in the lead country. Technology was assumed to grow at a constant rate g in the lead country (i.e., $(dT/dt)/T = g$).

These two equations form a system—in other words they are related, since growth of T has an effect on the technology gap and thereby on growth of A in the follower. The system can be written

$$\frac{dA}{dt} = \phi(\cdot)[T - A], \tag{A.14}$$

$$\frac{dT}{dt} = gT. \tag{A.15}$$

Writing in matrix form we have

$$\begin{bmatrix} \dot{A} \\ \dot{T} \end{bmatrix} = \begin{bmatrix} -\phi & \phi \\ 0 & g \end{bmatrix} \begin{bmatrix} A \\ T \end{bmatrix}, \tag{A.16}$$

where the dot notation is used for time derivatives. The mathematics for solving such a system are covered in advanced maths for economists books (e.g., Lambert 1985) and we do not attempt a full explanation here. However, in short, the eigenvalues for the matrix of coefficients are $-\phi$ and g, which have corresponding eigenvectors $(1, 0)$ and $(\phi/(\phi+g), 1)$, which yield a general solution

$$\begin{bmatrix} A \\ T \end{bmatrix} = b_1 \begin{bmatrix} 1 \\ 0 \end{bmatrix} e^{-\phi t} + b_2 \begin{bmatrix} \phi/(\phi+g) \\ 1 \end{bmatrix} e^{gt}. \tag{A.17}$$

Solving for the constants b_1 and b_2, using the fact that A_0 and T_0 are initial technology levels at time 0, allows the time path for A to be expressed as

$$A = [A_0 - T_0(\phi/(\phi+g))]e^{-\phi t} + T_0(\phi/(\phi+g))e^{gt}. \tag{A.18}$$

Therefore, as $t \to \infty$, the growth of A tends to g. Whether the growth rate of A is falling or rising depends on $A_0 \neq T_0(\phi/(\phi+g))$. If A_0 exactly equals $T_0(\phi/(\phi+g))$, then the growth rates are equal initially. Equally, the ratio $A/T = \phi/(\phi+g)$ represents the long-run steady-state condition.

A.8 Estimating Production Functions

Box 5.3 indicated that researchers may wish to estimate a production function like

$$\ln Y_{it} = \alpha_1 \ln L_{it} + \alpha_2 \ln K_{it} + \beta_1 \ln(\text{R\&D}_{it}^{\text{stock}}) + \beta_2 \ln(\text{Patents}_{it}) + \varepsilon_{it}. \tag{A.19}$$

This equation has added subscripts i and t, where i indicates a firm (or industry) and t indicates a year (or period). The equation has also added an error term, ε_{it}, which reflects the fact that there is "noise" in the data. While one can use simple ordinary least squares to estimate a production function, there are a host of potential problems for which reference to econometric textbooks is required (see, for example, Greene 1993; Johnston and DiNardo 1997; Kennedy 2003). There are also a number of more advanced issues (see Griliches and Mairesse (1995) for an introduction).

The estimation of the marginal returns to R&D is often not covered in the literature. We proceed by taking first differences of (A.19) to give

$$\Delta \ln Y_{it} = \alpha_1 \Delta \ln L_{it} + \alpha_2 \Delta \ln K_{it} + \beta_1 \Delta \ln(\text{R\&D}_{it}^{\text{stock}})$$
$$+ \beta_2 \Delta \ln(\text{Patents}_{it}) + \Delta \varepsilon_{it}, \tag{A.20}$$

where R&D^{stock} is the R&D stock. This equation is now in a growth form (since the first difference of two natural logarithms is approximately equal to the growth rate).

We proceed by rewriting the first difference of the stock of R&D as follows:

$$\Delta \ln(\text{R\&D}_{it}^{\text{stock}}) = \ln(\text{R\&D}_{it}^{\text{stock}}) - \ln(\text{R\&D}_{i,t-1}^{\text{stock}})$$

$$= \ln \left[\frac{\text{R\&D}_{it}^{\text{flow}} + (1 - \delta)\text{R\&D}_{i,t-1}^{\text{stock}}}{\text{R\&D}_{i,t-1}^{\text{stock}}} \right]$$

$$= \ln \left[\frac{\text{R\&D}_{it}^{\text{flow}}}{\text{R\&D}_{i,t-1}^{\text{stock}}} + (1 - \delta) \right] \approx \frac{\text{R\&D}_{it}^{\text{flow}}}{\text{R\&D}_{i,t-1}^{\text{stock}}}, \quad (A.21)$$

where δ is the (assumed) rate of depreciation of R&D.

Hence, under the assumption that δ and $\text{R\&D}_{it}^{\text{flow}}/\text{R\&D}_{i,t-1}^{\text{stock}}$ are close to zero, the $\Delta\text{R\&D}_{it}^{\text{stock}}$ term is approximately $\text{R\&D}_{it}^{\text{flow}}/\text{R\&D}_{i,t-1}^{\text{stock}}$. The parameter β_1 is the elasticity of R&D (i.e., $[dY/d\text{R\&D}_{it}^{\text{stock}}] \times [\text{R\&D}_{it}^{\text{stock}}/Y]$), hence equation (A.20) can be rewritten as

$$\Delta \ln Y_{it} = \alpha_1 \Delta \ln L_{it} + \alpha_2 \Delta \ln K_{it} + \alpha_3 \frac{\text{R\&D}_{it}^{\text{flow}}}{Y_{it}} + \beta_2 \Delta \ln(\text{Patents}_{it}) + \Delta\varepsilon_{it},$$

$$(A.22)$$

where α_3 is now the gross marginal rate of return to R&D. See Kafouros (2004) for a more detailed discussion and a review of R&D productivity studies.

References

Greene, W. 1993. *Econometric Analysis*. New York: Macmillan.

Griliches, Z., and J. Mairesse. 1995. Production functions: the search for identification. NBER Working Paper 5067.

Johnston, J., and J. DiNardo. 1997. *Econometric Methods*, 4th edn. New York: McGraw-Hill.

Kafouros, M. 2004. R&D and productivity growth at the firm level: a survey of the literature. Working Paper 57, Kent Business School.

Kennedy, P. 2003. *A Guide to Econometrics*. Oxford: Basil Blackwell.

Lambert, P. 1985. *Advanced Mathematics for Economists*. Oxford: Basil Blackwell.

Index